FISH COOKBOOK

FISH COOKBOOK

Editor-in-Chief **C.J. Jackson**

Managing Editor Dawn Henderson
Managing Art Editor Marianne Markham
Senior Jackets Creative Nicola Powling
Senior Presentations Creative Caroline de Souza
Senior Production Editor Jennifer Murray
Senior Production Controller Man Fai Lau
Creative Technical Support Sonia Charbonnier

DK INDIA
Senior Editor Chitra Subramanyam
Senior Art Editor Neha Ahuja
Managing Editor Glenda Fernandes
Managing Art Editor Navidita Thapa
DTP Manager Sunil Sharma
Senior DTP Designer Pushpak Tyagi

Pages 314–351 and 354–391 are based on content first
published in *The Cook's Book of Ingredients* in 2010

This edition first published in Great Britain in 2011
by Dorling Kindersley Limited
80 Strand, London WC2R 0RL

Penguin Group (UK)
2 4 6 8 10 9 7 5 3 1
001 – 176400 – May/2011

A CIP catalogue record for this book is available
from the British Library.

ISBN 978-1-4053-5912-2

Printed and bound by L Rex, China

Discover more at
www.dk.com

Contents

Foreword

I have always been completely fascinated by fish and water. A vivid memory as a child is watching the Saturday matinée of the Ernest Hemingway classic *The Old Man and the Sea* and the battle of an old man trying to land a huge marlin: it remains a favourite movie of mine today.

My family lived an almost self-sufficient lifestyle in Kent and I remember preparing seasonal fruit and vegetables in the kitchen with my Mum, as well as cooking meat and fish. Cooked crab was a particular favourite of mine, which my parents – who enjoyed all things fishy – often served us for dinner. Winkles were a weekend treat and enticing the snail out of the shell and dipping it in vinegar is another treasured early memory.

Childhood holidays were spent on the banks of the River Findhorn on the Moray Firth in Scotland, fishing for salmon and trout. I remember the 30lb salmon we sent for smoking and helping with the cleaning and cooking of other catches. My own first catch was a feisty emerald green eel that kicked up a big fuss and nearly had me in the water! I was less enthused by this (lovely looking, I hasten to add) creature – its strong earthy smell stays with me today.

A career based around food was a natural calling. I trained at the London Le Cordon Bleu school and taught on their courses. French cuisine includes many seafood classics and it was there that I really learnt how to appreciate and cook fish. I always wanted to travel and I spent much time in the 1980s and 1990s globetrotting, which opened my eyes to different cuisines and the seafood they use. But it was at Leith's School of Food and Wine in London that I became so focused on all types of seafood.

Today, as Director of Billingsgate Seafood Training School at Billingsgate Market, the UK's largest inland fish market situated in east London, I learn more about fish every day – and it's all here, in this book.

My passion for fish is based on respect. I find it inspirational and humbling that creatures that live in an environment so different from our own offer us fantastic food. With the vast expanse of the ocean, fish really are the best "free-range" meat. But we must never forget our place. Above all else, we must look out for the well being of the ocean and its fish.

So many people tell me they would love to cook fresh fish but are not sure where to start. I'm convinced

this uncertainty stems from the diversity of seafood: if all fish looked like salmon, for example, we'd all be experts at preparing it. Round fish, flat fish, prawns, squid, clams, crab: they all have particular preparation techniques. But they're worth mastering. Nothing is quite so rewarding as sitting down to a fish so fresh you had to scale and gut it yourself, or producing your first perfectly skinned Dover sole.

Many countries have feasted on the fish in their oceans for hundreds of years, so it's no wonder that seafood recipes are true classics, all made with fantastic ingredients. I've included all my favourites: simple treats, like fisherman's pies and fishcakes, suitable for anything you might find at the fish market; sushi, so exquisite and delicate but demanding of the freshest fish; the incomparable fish soups for which so many countries are renowned; and old-fashioned hits like traditional poached salmon and the very best prawn cocktail you'll ever eat. There's a recipe for most fish families and all recipes list alternative fish that work just as well. One important note: it is essential to try to choose responsibly sourced fish where possible – we can all make a difference to the long-term survival of our oceans. If you want to identify something obscure, find the best way to cook a particular fish, or discover sustainable alternatives for over-fished, but well-loved, varieties, turn to the Fish gallery for the perfect "dip-into" resource. It starts with round fish and flat fish before listing the world's seafood.

The fish world is changing and we now face more issues of sustainability and the responsible sourcing of what we eat. But this just offers us new challenges and opportunities: this is the perfect time to discover a new species and also to support your local fishery – if you are lucky enough to live near a harbour.

I hope that this book inspires you to seek out sustainable seafood and eat more of it. The fish in our oceans are a resource we must treasure and we have a responsibility to make sure they are still swimming – in all their variety – for future generations to enjoy.

C.J. Jackson

Sustainable fish – what's the story?

Mention the words "fish" and "sustainability" and many people think of worrying press headlines about dwindling fish stocks. Such articles often correctly highlight the negative issues but rarely praise the positive work that is being done, resulting in an incomplete and sometimes misleading picture.

What went wrong?

World sustainability of all our food sources is a complex and emotive subject, and this is certainly true when it comes to seafood. There are many different views within and without the seafood industry but all agree that some species of fish are under threat, and some near collapse and extinction. Over-fishing is often highlighted as a key culprit, but there are other forces at work here.

Over-fishing occurs when a particular species is removed from the water at such a rate that the stock left behind does not have time to replenish itself. Understanding how quickly each species of fish grows and matures is key to the success of fishing. Orange roughy is a popular species caught around the New Zealand coast. It was extensively fished some decades ago, but only when stocks began to dwindle did it become apparent that the fish took many years to mature. This species is now protected and monitored carefully to allow stocks to replenish. It can be difficult for customers to know which fish they should be avoiding to aid this replenishment – the situation is always changing, and moreover it may be the case that stocks of a fish are relatively healthy in one sea area yet worryingly low in another. What is certain though, is that the current situation, whereby there is only serious demand for a few well-known species, is damaging, and matters would be improved if a greater number of different species were to be targeted. Different methods of fishing also have a direct effect on the ecosystem. With high-impact methods such as trawling (whereby large nets are dragged through the water behind a

Legislation determines what fishing gear can be used, which varieties of fish can be caught, and the size of the catch.

boat), the fisherman will produce a large bycatch of sealife that he does not want. By the time these creatures are returned to the water, they are often dead or dying. Beam trawling is an even more destructive method whereby the nets are attached to metal beams that drag along the seabed, ploughing up large quantities of flora and fauna and causing enormous damage to the ocean environment. Line-fishing is rightly considered a more responsible way to fish, but it should be noted that this somewhat generic term covers a number of methods, some of which also produce a considerable bycatch. Longlining, for example – a technique whereby hundreds of baited hooks hang from a single main line via a series of branch lines – is known to claim the lives of significant numbers of turtles and sea birds, and is less useful than some nets for allowing immature fish to escape.

What is being done?

Now that these problems are well known, there is more legislation in place. Strict fishing quotas have been introduced by many governments to ensure that their coastal waters are

Trawling for prawns scoops up other sealife – choose organically farmed specimens.

"Quotas ensure that coastal waters are fished responsibly"

fished responsibly. These "catch quotas", which detail exactly how many specimens of a particular species can be caught over a fixed period of time, are advised upon by government scientists who have researched the subject in detail.

A minimum landing size helps to control the stock levels of many species: if a fish that measures less than the designated size is caught, it cannot be sold as part of the catch. (Traditionally, it would be returned to the water, but with the odds of survival being negligible, several countries have now banned this practice of "discarding", in order that the bycatch figures can be more closely monitored. Action can then be taken – for example, sea areas can be closed for fishing – if the bycatch levels become excessive.) A minimum landing size can change annually, but the idea is that a fish isn't caught until it has reached sexual maturity and produced the next generation. To avoid catching undersize fish, many countries have strict controls to determine the size of mesh that can be used, the intention being that only mature fish will be held in the nets, while younger fish will be able to escape.

There are various bodies committed to supporting such practices. The Marine Stewardship Council (MSC) is an independent international organization that certifies sustainable fisheries. Anyone believing that they are sourcing fish sustainably can apply to the MSC for certification. Currently, there are over 5,000 MSC-labelled products on sale.

Another international group working to promote sustainability is the Seafood Choices Alliance. This works with people and organizations across the industry, from fishermen to retailers, with the aim of ensuring an environmentally and economically sustainable future.

The rapidly growing fish farming industry is, by definition, a sustainable way to bring fish to market and about 45 per cent

Large-meshed nets prevent immature fish from being trapped, allowing those fish to reproduce and replenish the stock.

"The current situation, whereby there is only serious demand for a few well-known species, is damaging"

Alaskan pollock is one to try – its taste rivals that of cod and it is considerably more abundant worldwide.

Farmed mussels feed on naturally occurring plankton, so are very sustainable.

Responsible farms are monitored closely to ensure their fish are in good health and their cages are clean and secure.

"Fish farming is seen as one of the best ways to take pressure off wild fish stocks in the long term"

of the fish that we now consume is farmed. Commercial fish farming is only a few decades old, but in this relatively short space of time, a number of serious issues have had to be confronted. Chemicals that were used to keep fish healthy were affecting other life forms and damaging the environment, while pollution issues arose from both fish faeces and wastage of excess food. Much of this has been corrected and tighter laws and legislation are now in place.

While it seems that sustainability might almost be taken for granted in a farming operation, issues have arisen further down the food chain. The fish meal pellets that are used as food for farmed fish are made from smaller wild fish, and if these are not sourced sustainably, there could end up being insufficient levels in rivers and oceans to sustain the larger fish that would naturally feed on them in the wild. Finding

solutions to this has proved difficult in some cases, but there are an increasing number of "responsible" farms where they use fish meal that comes labelled as sustainable, or sometimes even farm the food on the same site as the fish. Efforts will continue to be made to improve fish farming practices, as it is seen as one of the best ways to take pressure off wild fish stocks in the long term.

What should I buy?

You, the customer, can have your say by choosing fish that are caught in a responsible way. Fishing methods that are selective, including hand-lined, fishing with large-meshed nets that allow small fish to escape, or, in the case of shellfish, hand-gathered, diver-caught, or any method that catches the seafood alive so that they can be returned easily to the sea if they are too small, are best. Additionally, these methods of fishing generally do little damage to the environment.

There are a number of ways to find out this information. Looking at packaging is one – those large retailers that do source their fish sustainably will often make a feature of it. Meanwhile, any product certified as sustainable by the MSC will feature the organization's logo: a blue oval with a white tick. Although not all sustainable fisheries subscribe to MSC certification, this is a good place to start.

A number of comparable labelling systems exist in different parts of the world. In the UK, the Marine Conservation Society (MCS) charity has a well-known and established "traffic light"

system for showing what is a sustainable choice and what isn't. No system is infallible of course: MCS recommendations often come with caveats about where the fish is from or how it was caught, with the downside that the key information about a product can sometimes be lost before it reaches retailers.

The same information ought also to be available if you are buying your fish from a fishmonger or fish market where the produce does not come pre-packaged. The seller should be able to help you make the best choice (see below). When weighing up the impact your choice of fish will have on the environment, you might also consider the carbon footprint. Unless you live near the coast, it may not be possible to buy local, and you should consider the merits of buying frozen rather than fresh. In many cases, frozen fish will have been transported over land and sea and will have a smaller carbon footprint than fresh fish that may have travelled considerable distances by air. For the best flavour, look out for fish that is labelled as "frozen at sea", which will have been frozen within a few hours of being landed.

Look for farmed fish that have been responsibly farmed, using sustainable fish meal. In addition, there are some particularly good farmed species of fish to look out for, such as tilapia, which can be sustained partly by a vegetarian diet. When it comes to shellfish, rope-grown mussels are also an excellent choice (see page 352).

"Frozen fish may have a smaller carbon footprint, as it is more likely to have travelled by boat and not air-freighted"

Your decisions in the fishmongers or supermarket can make a difference to the varieties of fish that are caught and sold, and what fishing methods are used to land them. If retailers are convinced that people want responsibly sourced fish, and will buy different varieties rather than just the same old few, then that is what they will offer. Enough people voting with their feet and their wallets is the surest way of hastening a future in which all fish is sourced sustainably.

Questions to ask

Talk to your fishmonger. Knowing what questions to ask is imperative for supporting sustainable fishing.
- How and where was the fish caught?
- Is the fish carrying roe (see page 180)?
- Is the fish farmed? If so, where is the farm and what are their policies? Do they use sustainable fish meal, for instance?
- Is the fish certified by any organizations, such as the MSC?

Tilapia feeds partly on vegetation, making it an environmentally friendly choice for farming.

A good fishmonger will know where his fish have come from, and will be able to help you choose responsibly sourced produce.

RECIPES

Salmon recipes

Whole poached and dressed salmon (see page 224)

Salmon jungle curry (see page 154)

Salmon fishcakes (see page 56)

Salmon with mushrooms and pak choi
(see page 196)

**Roasted salmon with Swiss chard
and herb butter** (see page 196)

Salmon en papillote (see page 197)

Oriental cucumber salad with smoked salmon (see page 74)

Rich smoked salmon croustades (see page 34)

Salmon rillettes (see page 37)

Further recipes

- **Marinated salmon** (see page 62)

- **Salmon salad with mint yogurt dressing** (see page 75)

- **Salmon chowder with whisky** (see page 87)

- **Salmon and prawn fish pie** (see page 117)

- **Salmon in puff pastry** (see page 119)

- **Salmon, horseradish, and kale bake** (see page 126)

- **Crisp salmon with coriander pesto** (see page 167)

- **Saltimbocca of salmon** (see page 167)

- **Baked salmon with salsa verde and cucumber** (see page 194)

- **Poached salmon with dill butter** (see page 224)

- **Jerk salmon** (see page 246)

- **Smoked salmon and pancetta crostini** (see page 30)

- **Smoked salmon with mustard and dill dressing** (see page 62)

Salmon coulibiac (see page 119)

Trout recipes

Smoked trout mousse (see page 37)

Smoked trout with beetroot, apple, and dill relish (see page 63)

Smoked trout, fennel, and mascarpone crostini (see page 31)

Steamed trout in lettuce (see page 229)

Trout with orange-mustard glaze (see page 236)

Further recipes

- **Smoked trout with pickled cucumber and minted yogurt** (see page 63)

- **Smoked trout and pancetta salad** (see page 75)

- **Creamy smoked trout soup** (see page 87)

- **Pan-fried trout with almonds** (see page 172)

- **Sautéed trout with hazelnuts** (see page 174)

- **Truite au bleu** (see page 220)

Tuna recipes

Tuna and aubergine yakitori skewers with soy dipping sauce (see page 28)

Griddled tuna steaks with salsa (see page 246)

Marinated sweet and hot tuna steaks (see page 242)

Seared tuna with a black sesame seed crust (see page 170)

Further recipes

- **Tuna carpaccio** (see page 60)
- **Salade Niçoise** (see page 73)
- **Tuna and bean salad** (see page 78)
- **Risotto al tonno** (see page 103)
- **Penne with tuna and roasted onion** (see page 111)
- **Tuna and pasta bake** (see page 127)
- **Seared tuna with cucumber and fennel** (see page 170)

Prawn recipes

Keralan prawn soup (see page 93)

Prawn and courgette balls with caper cream (see page 69)

Spaghetti mare e monti (see page 112)

Tom yum goong (see page 94)

Pan-fried prawns in garlic butter (see page 183)

Barbecued prawn satay (see page 240)

Prawn gumbo (see page 137)

Sesame prawn toasts (see page 35)

Further recipes

- **Dublin Bay prawns with lemon and garlic mayo** (see page 28)
- **Classic prawn cocktail** (see page 55)
- **Prawn spring rolls** (see page 56)
- **Thai fishcakes** (see page 58)
- **Salt and pepper prawns** (see page 69)
- **Prawn, grapefruit, and avocado salad** (see page 77)
- **Vietnamese salad of grilled prawns with papaya** (see page 77)
- **Prawn risotto** (see page 104)
- **Salmon and prawn fish pie** (see page 117)
- **Pad Thai** (see page 144)
- **Sweet and sour prawns** (see page 144)
- **Soba noodles with prawns and avocado** (see page 145)
- **Prawn diabolo** (see page 146)
- **Green curry of prawns with aubergines and basil** (see page 161)
- **Prawn dhansak** (see page 161)
- **Green prawn curry with fresh dill** (see page 162)
- **Prawn balti** (see page 163)
- **Pan-fried prawns, olives, and tomatoes** (see page 178)
- **Prawns with garlic and chilli** (see page 178)
- **Breaded fried prawns** (see page 187)
- **Egg fu yung** (see page 187)
- **Sesame barbecue prawns** (see page 240)
- **Griddled prawns with hot pepper sauce** (see page 242)

Chilli prawns with coriander and lime (see page 67)

Scallop recipes

Pan-fried scallops with chilli, ginger, and an anchovy dressing (see page 179)

Scallops with bacon (see page 65)

Scallop and pesto crostini (see page 31)

Coquilles St Jacques (see page 124)

Steamed scallop curry (see page 160)

Linguine with scallops (see page 112)

Grilled scallops with prosciutto and lime (see page 45)

Scallops skewered with Parma ham
(see page 45)

Scallops with sweet chilli sauce (see page 66)

Further recipes

- Scallop and tobiko sashimi
  (see page 52)

- Creamy scallop bisque (see page 92)

Crab recipes

Crab and mango salad (see page 76)

Dressed crab (see page 70)

Minced crab balls (see page 57)

Pasta with crab and lemon (see page 111)

Crab salad with grapefruit and coriander (see page 76)

Crab croustades (see page 34)

Thai crab cakes (see page 58)

Further recipes

- **Nori maki** (see page 48)

- **Crab stir-fried with curry powder** (see page 146)

- **Stir-fried yellow curried crabs** (see page 147)

- **Chilli crab** (see page 162)

- **Crab and mango curry** (see page 163)

Mussel recipes

Fish soup with fennel (see page 92)

Moules marinières (see page 40)

Spaghetti frutti di mare (see page 108)

Coley and mussel chowder (see page 86)

Laksa lemak (see page 157)

Pineapple curry of mussels (see page 150)

Mussels in ginger and chilli broth (see page 132)

Further recipes

- **Mouclade** (see page 90)
- **Waterzooi** (see page 98)
- **Mussels in fennel broth** (see page 132)
- **Bourride** (see page 223)

Starters and Light Bites

Dublin Bay prawns with lemon and garlic mayo

Excellent summer casual entertaining bites. You'll need 6 wooden skewers.

The fish

Dublin Bay prawns, or tiger prawns, scallops, or monkfish

- **PREP** 30 mins • **COOK** none
- **MAKES** 6 skewers

Ingredients

12 cooked Dublin Bay prawns

2 large mangos, peeled and diced

For the mayonnaise

150ml (5fl oz) mayonnaise

5 tbsp crème fraîche

1 garlic clove, crushed

grated zest of 1 lemon and juice of ½

1 tbsp finely chopped flat-leaf parsley, and sprigs of parsley, to garnish

salt and freshly ground black pepper

lemon or lime wedges, to garnish

1 Peel and devein the prawns (see page 285) and thread on to the skewers with cubes of mango. Arrange on a large platter.

2 Mix together all the ingredients for the mayonnaise and season well to taste. Spoon into a dipping bowl and arrange in the centre of the skewers. Garnish with parsley and arrange the lemon wedges around the outside.

Prepare ahead

Mix everything together for the mayonnaise except the parsley. Cover, and chill for up to 1 day. The garlic flavour will become stronger. Mix in the parsley just before serving.

Variations

Grilled monkfish with melon

Cut 1 medium ripe melon into cubes and thread on to skewers with 350g (12oz) grilled, cubed monkfish.

Lobster and papaya

Replace the Dublin Bay prawns with 350g (12oz) lobster meat, and the mango with cubed papaya.

Griddled scallop and avocado

Griddle 24 scallops (see page 306) and thread on to skewers with 3 large avocados, peeled, stoned, and cubed.

Tuna and aubergine yakitori skewers with soy dipping sauce

Bamboo skewers of fish make an excellent canapé or an informal start to any meal. You'll need 12 wooden skewers, soaked in water for 30 minutes to prevent scorching.

The fish

Tuna, or swordfish, mahi mahi, or monkfish

- **PREP** 40 mins, plus marinating
- **COOK** 2 mins • **MAKES** 12 skewers

Ingredients

1 large aubergine, cut into 1cm (½in) chunks

350g (12oz) tuna steak, cut into 2.5cm (1in) chunks

1 tbsp vegetable oil

shiso leaves, or sprigs of coriander, to garnish

For the marinade

3 tbsp dark soy sauce

1 tsp sesame oil

1 tbsp sugar

1 tsp lemon juice

2 tsp mirin

1 tbsp sake (optional)

salt and freshly ground black pepper

1 Put the aubergine into simmering water. Boil for 2 minutes, drain, and cool.

2 Put the aubergine and tuna into a shallow dish. Mix the marinade ingredients and pour over. Stir, cover, and marinate for 30 minutes.

3 Thread 2 pieces of aubergine on to a skewer, a piece of tuna, and 2 more pieces of aubergine. Bring the marinade to a boil in a saucepan.

4 Preheat a griddle pan until smoking. Brush with the oil and put in the skewers. Cook for 2 minutes, turning once, and basting with the marinade. They will be golden brown and shiny. Put the remaining marinade in a small bowl.

5 Arrange on a platter with the dipping sauce and shiso or coriander leaves, and wash down with Japanese beer or sake.

Variation

Scallop and shiitake yakitori skewers

Use 400g (14oz) shiitake mushrooms instead of aubergine and skip step 1. Use 12 large scallops instead of tuna.

TUNA FLAVOUR PAIRINGS: A great fish with the Japanese flavours of shoyu, sesame, teriyaki, shiso leaf, rice wine vinegar, and wasabi. It's also good with robust Mediterranean ingredients, such as garlic, tomatoes, and olives.

Anchovy and olive bruschetta

These salty canapés are ideal with pre-dinner drinks.

The fish

Anchovies, or smoked mackerel

▪ **PREP** 10 mins ▪ **COOK** 5 mins ▪ **MAKES** 12

Ingredients

12 slices Italian bread, such as ciabatta, about 2cm (¾in) thick

½ garlic clove

extra virgin olive oil

3–4 tbsp bottled tomato sauce, or passata

salt and freshly ground black pepper

115g (4oz) mozzarella cheese, drained, and cut into 12 thin slices

1 tsp dried mixed herbs

6 black olives, pitted and sliced

60g jar or can anchovies in olive oil, drained, and cut in half lengthways

1 Preheat the grill on its highest setting and position the rack 10cm (4in) from the heat. Toast the bread until golden on both sides. Rub 1 side with the cut side of the garlic. Brush the same side of each slice with oil.

2 Spread each bruschetta with 2 tsp tomato sauce and season with salt and pepper. Put a slice of mozzarella on each, sprinkle with herbs and top with olive slices and 2 pieces of anchovy in a criss-cross pattern.

3 Grill the bruschetta for 2–3 minutes, or until the mozzarella has melted and is bubbling. Serve hot with chilled prosecco or cold beer.

Prepare ahead

The bruschetta bases can be made 2 hours in advance. Assemble and grill before serving.

Smoked salmon and pancetta crostini

The crème fraîche here is light and refreshing against the deep-flavoured fish.

The fish

Cold-smoked salmon, or cold-smoked trout

▪ **PREP** 10 mins ▪ **COOK** 10 mins ▪ **MAKES** 12

Ingredients

12 small slices of bread, cut from a baguette or ficelle

5 tbsp olive oil

6 slices of pancetta

200g (7oz) smoked salmon

200ml (7fl oz) crème fraîche

2 tbsp wholegrain mustard

3 tbsp capers, rinsed, drained, and finely chopped

1 tsp grated lemon zest

1 tsp lemon juice

freshly ground black pepper

12 whole chives, snipped into 2.5cm (1in) lengths, to garnish

1 Preheat the oven to 200°C (400°F/Gas 6). Brush each side of the bread with olive oil, place on a baking tray, and bake for 10 minutes, or until crisp. Leave to cool.

2 Preheat the grill on its highest setting. Grill the pancetta until crisp on both sides. Drain on kitchen paper.

3 Cut the smoked salmon into strips about 2cm (¾in) wide.

4 Mix the crème fraîche with the mustard, capers, lemon zest, and lemon juice. Season to taste with pepper.

5 Place the bread slices on a serving plate, divide the crème fraîche mixture between them, and top with smoked salmon, pieces of pancetta, and chives to garnish.

Prepare ahead

The bread slices can be baked up to 2 hours ahead. The crème fraîche mixture can be made 24 hours in advance, covered, and refrigerated. Assemble just before serving.

Scallop and pesto crostini

These canapés also make a stylish first course.

The fish

Scallops, or tiger prawns, monkfish, or cockles

- **PREP** 10 mins ▪ **COOK** 7 mins ▪ **MAKES** 12

Ingredients

12 slices Italian bread, such as ciabatta, about 2cm (¾in) thick

½ garlic clove

3 tbsp olive oil

6 scallops, roe removed

1 tbsp lemon juice

salt and freshly ground black pepper

2 tbsp bottled pesto

2 tbsp tomato purée

12 basil leaves, to garnish

1 Preheat the grill on its highest setting. Toast the bread until golden on both sides. Rub 1 side with the cut side of the garlic. Lightly brush the same side of each slice with oil. Set aside.

2 Heat the remaining oil in a large frying pan over a medium heat. Add the scallops, sprinkle with lemon juice, and season. Fry for 2 minutes each side, until cooked but tender; keep warm.

3 Spread one half of each crostini with pesto and the other half with tomato purée.

4 Halve each scallop horizontally and put 1 half on each crostini. Grind pepper over and garnish each with a basil leaf. Serve at once.

Prepare ahead

The crostini bases can be made 2 hours ahead.

Smoked trout, fennel, and mascarpone crostini

The fennel lifts the taste of the trout into a truly special mouthful.

The fish

Hot-smoked trout, or smoked mackerel or kiln-roasted smoked salmon

- **PREP** 25 mins ▪ **COOK** 15 mins ▪ **SERVES** 4

Ingredients

30g (1oz) flaked almonds

2 tbsp olive oil

4 thick slices crusty sourdough bread

salt and freshly ground black pepper

1 garlic clove

2 hot-smoked trout, about 300g (10oz) each

150g (5½oz) fennel bulb, trimmed, halved, and thinly sliced

120ml (4fl oz) mascarpone cheese

juice of ½ lemon

sprigs of chervil, to garnish

1 lemon, cut into wedges, to serve

1 Preheat the oven to 200°C (400°F/Gas 6). To toast the almonds, spread out over the bottom of a small dry, frying pan. Toast over a medium heat for a few minutes, until golden, stirring frequently to prevent them scorching.

2 Pour the olive oil on to a baking tray, then gently press the bread into the oil on both sides. Season with salt and pepper. Bake in the oven for 12–15 minutes until golden brown. Remove, and lightly rub each slice with the garlic. Set aside on a wire rack to keep crisp.

3 Meanwhile, remove the skin and bones from the trout, and gently remove the flesh in big flakes. Put the trout, fennel, mascarpone, almonds, and lemon juice in a bowl. Season with pepper, and gently mix.

4 Arrange the trout mixture over the crostini, season with more pepper, and garnish with the chervil. Serve immediately, with lemon wedges.

Prepare ahead

Make the crostini bases and toast the almonds 2 hours in advance. Assemble the crostini just before serving.

Fried whitebait

Whitebait are very immature members of the herring and sardine family, so should not be eaten regularly. For a similar, but more sustainable recipe, try the Herbed Pollock Goujons on page 68.

The fish

Whitebait, or any mixed, very small fish

- **PREP** 15 mins **COOK** 20 mins **SERVES** 4

Ingredients

sunflower oil, for deep-frying

50g (1¾oz) plain flour

1 tsp cayenne pepper

1 tsp salt

450g (1lb) whitebait

1 lemon, cut into wedges, to serve

1 Heat the oil to 180°C (350°F) in a large pan or deep-fat fryer (see page 308).

2 Meanwhile, put the flour, cayenne, and salt in a large bowl and mix together.

3 Toss the whitebait in the seasoned flour, making sure they are evenly coated. Tip them into a sieve to shake off the excess flour.

4 Fry the whitebait in batches for 2–3 minutes each, or until they turn lightly golden. (Frying in small batches prevents them clumping together or turning soggy.) Use a slotted spoon to remove them from the oil and drain on kitchen paper. Serve immediately, with lemon wedges and brown bread and butter.

Marinated anchovies

This is a traditional Spanish recipe, usually served as a chilled tapas.

The fish

Anchovies, or sprats

- **PREP** 35 mins, plus marinating
- **COOK** none **SERVES** 4

Ingredients

250g (9oz) fresh anchovies

2 tbsp coarse sea salt

300ml (10fl oz) sherry vinegar

4 tbsp extra virgin olive oil

grated zest of 1–2 lemons, to taste

sprigs of marjoram or thyme

freshly ground black pepper

1 Rub the scales from the anchovies with your fingers, then gut and bone the fish. Wash and pat dry. Lay them in a single layer in a shallow dish, sprinkle with salt, then pour over the vinegar. Cover and refrigerate for 12–18 hours.

2 Drain away the salt and vinegar cure, and pat the fish dry. Arrange on a clean serving dish and sprinkle with the olive oil, lemon zest (add a squeeze of lemon juice, too, if you like), and marjoram. Season with pepper, and serve with crusty bread, providing toothpicks for your guests to use to spear the anchovies.

Prepare ahead

The anchovies must be cured at least 12 hours ahead, so you will only need to drain away the vinegar, and add the dressing to serve.

ANCHOVY FLAVOUR PAIRINGS:

The definite, exquisite taste of anchovies is great with sherry or white wine vinegars, shallots, oregano, sage, thyme, parsley, or fruity olive oil.

Rich smoked salmon croustades

Horseradish gives these bite.

The fish

Smoked salmon, or smoked trout

- **PREP** 10 mins, plus chilling ■ **COOK** 12–14 mins
- **MAKES** 12

Ingredients

120ml (4fl oz) crème fraîche

1 tbsp creamed horseradish

freshly ground black pepper

12 croustade baskets (see Crab croustades, left)

60g (2oz) smoked salmon, sliced

25g (scant 1oz) orange lumpfish caviar

25g (scant 1oz) black lumpfish caviar

1 Mix the crème fraîche and horseradish. Season with pepper, and chill for 30 minutes.

2 Fill each croustade with 1 tsp crème fraîche and horseradish, some smoked salmon, and a little of each type of caviar. Serve within 1 hour.

Prepare ahead

The croustade baskets will keep, in an airtight container, for up to 1 month.

Variation

Salmon and tarragon cream croustades
Mix 120ml (4fl oz) crème fraîche, 150g (5½oz) chopped smoked salmon, 2 tbsp chopped tarragon, 1 tbsp lemon zest, and pepper. Chill for 30 minutes, then spoon into croustades.

Crab croustades

Lightly spiced crab meat with a crispy case. You'll need a 5cm (2in) pastry cutter and a 12-hole mini-muffin tin.

The fish

White crab meat, or lobster or Dublin Bay prawns

- **PREP** 10 mins ■ **COOK** 12–14 mins
- **MAKES** 12

Ingredients

4 large slices white or wholemeal bread

1 tbsp melted butter or olive oil

For the filling

200g (7oz) white crab meat

1cm (½in) fresh root ginger, grated

grated zest and juice of 1 lime

3 tbsp mayonnaise

1 tbsp chopped coriander leaves

2 spring onions, finely chopped

salt and freshly ground black pepper

1 red chilli, deseeded and finely chopped, to garnish

1 Preheat the oven to 180°C (350°F/Gas 4). Remove the crusts from the bread, flatten the slices with a rolling pin, and brush with the butter or oil.

2 Using the pastry cutter, stamp out 3 pieces from each slice of bread. Push the bread, butter-side down, firmly into the muffin tin and bake for 12–14 minutes, or until golden and crisp. Remove from the tin and leave to cool.

3 In a bowl, mix together the crab meat, ginger, lime zest and juice, mayonnaise, coriander, and spring onions, and season with salt and pepper.

4 Divide the mixture between the croustade baskets and sprinkle each with the red chilli. Serve within 1 hour.

Prepare ahead

The croustade baskets will keep, in an airtight container, for up to 1 month. The filling can be made several hours in advance and kept, chilled, until needed. Assemble just before serving.

Anchovy, olive, and basil tarts

Piquant fishy bites, gooey with mozzarella. You'll need a 4-hole muffin tin.

The fish

Anchovy fillets in olive oil

- **PREP** 15 mins, plus chilling
- **COOK** 25–30 mins ▪ **MAKES** 4

Ingredients

oil, for the tin

plain flour, to dust

1 sheet ready-rolled puff pastry (preferably all-butter)

2 eggs

175ml (6fl oz) single cream

2 tbsp freshly grated Parmesan cheese

salt and freshly ground black pepper

4 anchovy fillets in olive oil, drained

4 balls bocconcini (baby mozzarella) cheese, torn

8 kalamata olives, pitted

8 cherry tomatoes, halved

4 fresh basil leaves or small sprigs, plus more to serve

1 Preheat the oven to 200°C (400°F/Gas 6). Lightly brush a 4-hole muffin tin with oil.

2 On a lightly floured work surface, cut the pastry into 4 squares. Use to line the holes in the muffin tin, pushing the pastry gently into the corners. Refrigerate for 1 hour.

3 Combine the eggs, cream, and Parmesan in a bowl, and season. Mix well.

4 Place an anchovy in each of the pastry cases, along with a bocconcini, 2 olives, and 4 cherry tomato halves. Spoon the egg mixture into the cases, and top each with a basil leaf or sprig. Grind over a little pepper.

5 Bake the tarts for 25–30 minutes until golden. Serve warm, garnished with a fresh basil leaf or sprig.

Sesame prawn toasts

A combination of flavours that work surprisingly well together.

The fish

Tiger prawns

▪ **PREP** 25 mins ▪ **COOK** 5 mins ▪ **MAKES** 12

Ingredients

250g (9oz) raw tiger prawns, peeled and roughly chopped (see page 285)

2 spring onions, roughly chopped

1cm (½in) fresh root ginger, grated

1 tsp light soy sauce

½ tsp sugar

½ tsp sesame oil

1 small egg white, lightly beaten

freshly ground black pepper

3 large slices white bread, crusts removed

2 tbsp sesame seeds

vegetable oil, for deep-frying

coriander leaves, to garnish

1 Put the prawns and spring onions in a food processor, and process for a few seconds to make a paste. Transfer to a bowl and stir in the ginger, soy sauce, sugar, sesame oil, and enough egg white to bind. Season with pepper.

2 Cut each slice of bread into 4 triangles and spread thickly with the prawn paste. Sprinkle the sesame seeds evenly over the top.

3 Heat the oil to 180°C (350°F) in a large pan or deep-fat fryer (see page 308). Fry the toasts, in batches, prawn-side down, for 2 minutes. Carefully turn over and fry for another 2 minutes, or until golden brown and crisp.

4 Lift the toasts from the pan with a slotted spoon and drain on kitchen paper. Serve warm, garnished with coriander leaves.

Salt cod and red pepper dip

An unusual, moreish, and piquant appetizer.

The fish

Salt cod, or salt pollock

- **PREP** 25 mins, plus soaking • **COOK** 1 hr
- **SERVES** 12

Ingredients

2 red peppers

2 garlic cloves

1 small red onion, finely chopped

4 tbsp olive oil

salt and freshly ground black pepper

2 tbsp finely chopped Spanish onion

400g can chopped plum tomatoes

500g (1lb 2oz) salt cod, soaked overnight

2 tbsp finely chopped marjoram

2 tbsp finely chopped dill

handful of basil leaves, finely chopped

handful of flat-leaf parsley, finely chopped

juice of 1 lemon

1 Preheat the oven to 200°C (400°F/Gas 6). Slice the tops from the peppers, and remove the seeds and membrane. Put a garlic clove and half the chopped red onion in the cavity of each, and lay them on an baking tray lined with baking parchment. Drizzle with 1 tbsp of the oil, and season. Roast for 1 hour. Set aside.

2 Heat the remaining oil in a heavy frying pan over a low heat. Add the Spanish onion, and sweat for about 5 minutes until soft. Tip in the tomatoes, and cook for 10 minutes. Season.

3 Skin the salt cod, and flake the flesh into chunks. Add to the tomato sauce, and cook gently for a further 10 minutes. Set aside to cool.

4 Put the peppers in a food processor with the tomato mixture. Purée until smooth. Transfer to a serving bowl, and season. Stir in the herbs and lemon juice. Serve with crostini.

Prepare ahead

The salt cod dip can be made – without the herbs – up to 2 days in advance, covered, and refrigerated. The flavours will deepen. Stir in the herbs just before serving.

Smoked mackerel pâté

This always disappears quickly.

The fish

Smoked mackerel, or hot-smoked trout

- **PREP** 5 mins • **COOK** none • **SERVES** 4

Ingredients

3–4 smoked mackerel fillets, skinned

300g (10oz) cream cheese

juice of 1–2 lemons

freshly ground black pepper

1–2 tbsp Greek-style yogurt

4 thin slices brownbread, toasted

1 lemon, cut into wedges

1 Break the mackerel into chunks, and add to a food processor. Whizz until broken up.

2 Spoon in the cream cheese, and whizz again until smooth. Add the lemon juice, a little at a time, to taste. Season with plenty of black pepper, and whizz again.

3 Add the yogurt, and blend again until smooth. Spoon into a serving dish or 4 ramekins. Serve with toasted brown bread and lemon wedges.

Prepare ahead

Make a day ahead, and keep covered in the refrigerator until ready to serve.

Variations

Spicy smoked mackerel pâté
Add a pinch of cayenne pepper.

Light smoked mackerel pâté
Leave out the yogurt to dilute the richness a little, though the pâté will be less creamy.

Salmon rillettes

This pâté from France should have a
fairly rough texture.

The fish

Hot-smoked salmon, or hot-smoked trout

- **PREP** 15 mins ▪ **COOK** none ▪ **SERVES** 4

Ingredients

60g (2oz) butter, softened

250g (9oz) hot-smoked salmon fillets, skinned

4 tbsp Greek-style yogurt

finely grated zest and juice of ½ lemon

2 tbsp snipped chives

50g jar keta caviar

handful of watercress, to garnish

lemon wedges, to garnish

1 Put the butter in a bowl and beat with a
wooden spoon until smooth. Break up the
salmon into small pieces, add to the bowl,
and mash with a fork.

2 Add the yogurt, lemon zest and juice, and
chives, and stir until evenly combined.

3 Spoon on to serving plates – or small
rounds of pumpernickel for canapés – and
top with caviar. Garnish with watercress
sprigs and lemon wedges.

Prepare ahead

The rillettes can be prepared up to 24 hours
in advance, covered, and refrigerated, or frozen
for up to 1 month.

Smoked trout mousse

This dish is lifted with pungent horseradish
and fragrant dill, and lightened with yogurt.
You will need a terrine mould or loaf tin.

The fish

Hot-smoked trout, or smoked mackerel
or hot-smoked salmon

- **PREP** 20–25 mins, plus chilling
- **COOK** none ▪ **SERVES** 8–10

Ingredients

2 hot-smoked trout, in total about
750g (1lb 10oz)

1 tbsp powdered gelatine

vegetable oil, for the mould

2 eggs, hard-boiled and chopped

leaves from a small bunch of dill, chopped

3 small spring onions, finely sliced

120ml (4fl oz) mayonnaise

120ml (4fl oz) plain yogurt

60g (2oz) grated fresh horseradish, or to taste

juice of 1 lemon

salt and freshly ground black pepper

175ml (6fl oz) double cream

bunch of watercress

1 Peel the skin from the trout, then lift the flesh
from the bones and gently flake.

2 Sprinkle the gelatine evenly over 4 tbsp
cold water in a small bowl and let it stand
for 5 minutes, until spongy. Brush a 1.2-litre
(2-pint) terrine mould with oil, or line a loaf tin
with cling film.

3 Put everything except the cream, watercress,
and gelatine in a bowl and stir. Taste; it should
be well seasoned.

4 Whip the cream until soft peaks form. Melt
the gelatine in a small saucepan over a low
heat. Add it to the trout mixture and mix
thoroughly. At once, fold in the cream. Spoon
into the mould and smooth the top. Cover
with a lid, or with cling film, and chill for
3–4 hours, until set.

5 Run a knife around the edges of the mould.
Dip the base in warm water for a few seconds,
then set a plate on top and invert to unmould
the mousse. Serve with sprigs of watercress.

Prepare ahead

The mousse can be made up to 3 days ahead,
covered, and stored in the refrigerator. Return
to room temperature before serving.

Brandade de morue

This dish of creamed salt cod is especially popular in the South of France.

The fish

Salt cod, or salt pollock

- **PREP** 15–20 mins, plus soaking
- **COOK** 15–20 mins ▪ **SERVES** 4

Ingredients

450g (1lb) salt cod

2 garlic cloves, crushed

200ml (7fl oz) olive oil

100ml (3½fl oz) hot milk

2 tbsp chopped flat-leaf parsley

freshly ground black pepper

extra virgin olive oil, to drizzle

triangles of white bread, fried in olive oil, to serve

Mediterranean black olives, to serve

1 Soak the fish in a bowl of cold water for 24 hours, changing the water 3 or 4 times.

2 Drain the cod and place in a large, shallow pan, then cover it with fresh cold water and bring to a gentle simmer. Cook for 10 minutes, then remove the pan from the heat and leave the cod to sit in the water for a further 10 minutes before draining.

3 Remove the skin and bones from the fish, then flake the flesh into a bowl and pound to a paste with the garlic.

4 Put the fish paste in a pan over a gentle heat. Beat in sufficient olive oil and milk, a little at a time, to make a creamy white mixture that holds its shape. Serve hot, sprinkled with parsley, pepper, and extra virgin olive oil, with the bread triangles and olives.

Prepare ahead

The salt cod and garlic paste can be made up to the end of step 3, then covered, and chilled, for up to 1 day before serving. The flavour of the garlic will deepen. Bring the paste back to room temperature before continuing.

Tapenade

A full-flavoured olive and anchovy spread, popular all around the Mediterranean.

The fish

Anchovy fillets in olive oil

- **PREP** 15 mins ▪ **COOK** none ▪ **SERVES** 4–6

Ingredients

2 large garlic cloves

250g (9oz) Mediterranean black olives, pitted

1½ tbsp capers, drained and rinsed

4 anchovy fillets in olive oil, drained

1 tsp thyme leaves

1 tsp chopped rosemary

2 tbsp lemon juice

2 tbsp extra virgin olive oil

1 tsp Dijon mustard

freshly ground black pepper

12 slices baguette, toasted, to serve

1 Place the garlic, olives, capers, anchovies, thyme, and rosemary in a food processor or blender, and process until smooth.

2 Add the lemon juice, extra virgin olive oil, mustard, and black pepper to taste, and blend until a thick paste forms. Transfer to a bowl, cover, and chill until ready to use.

3 Bring to room temperature, and serve with slices of toasted baguette. This is also good to eat with crudités and other Mediterranean appetizers, such as stuffed vine leaves.

Prepare ahead

The tapenade can be made, covered, and chilled for up to 2 days before using. The flavours will deepen. Bring back to room temperature before serving.

SALT COD FLAVOUR PAIRINGS: The strong flavours of salt cod stand up well to garlic, orange, capers, onion, parsley, or even coconut, as they prepare it in the Caribbean.

Taramasalata

"Tarama" is Turkish for the salted fish roe that is traditionally used in this recipe.

The fish

Smoked cod's roe, or salted grey mullet roe

- **PREP** 15 mins, plus chilling • **COOK** none
- **SERVES** 4–6

Ingredients

250g (9oz) piece smoked cod's roe

juice of 1 lemon

60g (2oz) fresh white breadcrumbs, soaked in 3 tbsp cold water

75ml (2½fl oz) extra virgin olive oil

1 small onion, grated, patted dry with kitchen paper

paprika, for sprinkling

1 Split the roe down the centre using a sharp knife and carefully peel away the skin. Place in a blender with the lemon juice and soaked breadcrumbs. Blend well.

2 With the motor running, very slowly add the oil in a thin steady stream until the mixture resembles mayonnaise.

3 Stir in the onion and spoon into a small serving dish. Cover and chill for 30 minutes, then serve sprinkled with paprika.

Prepare ahead

The taramasalata can be prepared up to the end of step 2, covered, and chilled up to 2 days in advance.

SMOKED COD'S ROE FLAVOUR PAIRINGS:

The taste of this exquisite roe should be enjoyed fairly plain; flatter it with plentiful good-quality olive oil, garlic, and lemon juice.

Moules marinières

This classic French recipe – mussels in wine, garlic, and herbs – translates as "in the fisherman's style".

The fish

Mussels, or palourde or hard-shell clams

- **PREP** 15–20 mins • **COOK** 15 mins
- **SERVES** 4

Ingredients

60g (2oz) butter

2 onions, finely chopped

3.6kg (8lb) mussels, prepared (see page 278)

2 garlic cloves, crushed

600ml (1 pint) dry white wine

4 bay leaves

2 sprigs of thyme

salt and freshly ground black pepper

2–4 tbsp chopped flat-leaf parsley

1 Melt the butter in a large, heavy saucepan, add the onions, and fry gently until lightly browned. Add the mussels, garlic, wine, bay leaves, and thyme. Season to taste. Cover, bring to a boil, and cook for 5–6 minutes, or until the mussels have opened, shaking frequently.

2 Remove the mussels with a slotted spoon, discarding any that remain closed. Transfer them to warmed bowls, cover, and keep warm.

3 Strain the liquor into a pan and bring to a boil. Season to taste, add the parsley, pour over the mussels, and serve at once.

Oysters Rockefeller

A traditional lunch dish from New Orleans that also makes an excellent first course.

The fish

Oysters

- **PREP** 20 mins - **COOK** 35 mins - **SERVES** 4

Ingredients

100g (3½oz) baby leaf spinach

24 oysters, in their shells

75g (2½oz) shallots, finely chopped

1 garlic clove, chopped

4 tbsp chopped flat-leaf parsley

115g (4oz) butter

50g (1¾oz) plain flour

2 anchovy fillets in olive oil, drained and finely chopped

pinch of cayenne pepper

salt and freshly ground black pepper

rock salt

3 tbsp Pernod

1 Wilt the spinach in a pan over a medium heat for 5 minutes. Drain well, squeeze to remove excess liquid, and set aside.

2 Discard any open oysters. Shuck the oysters (see page 278), reserve their liquid, then return the oysters to their shells. Separately cover and chill both the oysters and their liquid.

3 Chop the spinach finely and mix with the shallots, garlic, and parsley. Set aside.

4 Melt the butter in a small saucepan over a medium heat. Add the flour, and stir for 2 minutes. Slowly stir in the oyster liquid, until smooth. Stir in the spinach, anchovies, cayenne, and salt and pepper. Cover and simmer for 15 minutes.

5 Preheat the oven to 200°C (400°F/Gas 6). Arrange a thick layer of rock salt in 4 serving dishes, then put them in the oven to warm.

6 Uncover the pan and stir in the Pernod. Taste, and adjust the seasoning. Remove the dishes from the oven, and arrange 6 oysters in their shells on each. Spoon the sauce over and bake for 5–10 minutes, or until the sauce looks set. Serve immediately.

Oysters with shallot and vinegar dressing

European tradition, dating back to the Romans, serves oysters raw on the half shell. Both Pacific and native oysters can be used.

The fish

Oysters, or hard-shell clams or whelks

- **PREP** 10 mins - **COOK** none - **SERVES** 4

Ingredients

24 oysters, in their shells

crushed ice

4 tbsp red wine vinegar

1 large or 2 small shallots, very finely chopped

1 Shuck the oysters (see page 278), taking care not to tip out any of the juices. Arrange the oysters on a traditional oyster plate with ice, or pack 4 serving dishes with lots of crushed ice and place the oysters on top.

2 Mix the vinegar and shallot together and put into a small dish. Place in the centre of the oysters – or the middle of the table – and serve.

Variation

Oysters with lemon and Tabasco

Shuck the oysters as directed and serve on crushed ice, with lemon wedges and Tabasco sauce on the side. Allow your guests to choose their dressing, or to eat the oysters unadorned.

Abalone with oyster sauce

Abalone is expensive and often sold canned as well as fresh. It is particularly popular in China.

The fish
Abalone

- **PREP** 15 mins - **COOK** 10 mins - **SERVES** 4

Ingredients
1 wild or 2 farmed abalone

2 tbsp sunflower or groundnut oil

1 bunch of spring onions, finely sliced

1 tsp finely grated fresh root ginger

2 tbsp oyster sauce

1 tbsp dark soy sauce

pinch of sugar

2 tsp cornflour

1 Shell the abalone, reserving any juices. To clean, hold the main body and let the viscera hang down. Cut off and discard these. Scrub off the black film along the side of the abalone. Cut off and discard the curled edges and the tough, pointed end. Using a mallet, beat the abalone well to flatten and tenderize. Slice thinly.

2 Heat the oil in a large frying pan, tip in the spring onions and ginger, and stir over a low heat for 3–4 minutes. Add the abalone and toss together to heat through.

3 Mix together the oyster sauce, soy sauce, sugar, and 5 tbsp water. Stir in the cornflour and the reserved abalone juices. Add the sauce to the abalone, and stir over a medium heat until it just comes to a boil and the sauce has thickened. Add more water if you would prefer a thinner sauce, and serve.

Prepare ahead

This dish is very quick to make once the abalone has been cleaned, and beaten flat. It can then be covered and refrigerated for up to 1 day. Bring the abalone to room temperature before completing the recipe.

Variation

Canned abalone with oyster sauce
Drain a 340g can abalone, reserving the liquid. Slice the abalone thinly. Proceed as above, adding the reserved abalone liquid at the same time as the cornflour.

Clams in white wine

Versions of this dish can be found throughout the Mediterranean.

The fish
Clams, or mussels

- **PREP** 10 mins, plus soaking - **COOK** 15 mins
- **SERVES** 4–6

Ingredients
1kg (2¼lb) clams, thoroughly washed

2 tbsp olive oil

1 onion, finely diced

2 garlic cloves, finely chopped

2 bay leaves

1 tsp fresh thyme or a pinch of dried thyme

120ml (4fl oz) dry white wine

1 tbsp chopped flat-leaf parsley

1 Soak the clams for 1 hour to clean them. Discard any that are already open, or that have broken shells. Heat the oil in a large, flameproof casserole. Add the onion and garlic and fry, stirring, for 4–5 minutes, or until translucent.

2 Add the clams with the bay leaves and thyme. Stir thoroughly, cover, and allow to steam for 3–4 minutes, or until the clams have opened. Discard any that remain shut.

3 Add the wine and cook for a further 3–4 minutes, shaking the pot a few times to allow the sauce to thicken slightly.

4 Sprinkle with parsley and serve straight from the casserole with crusty bread, to soak up the juices.

Grilled scallops with prosciutto and lime

A delicious, elegant dish.

The fish

King scallops, or monkfish or tiger prawns

■ **PREP** 10 mins ■ **COOK** 5 mins ■ **SERVES** 6

Ingredients

18 king scallops

30g (1oz) butter, melted

2 garlic cloves, chopped

juice of 1 lime, plus lime wedges to serve

handful of chopped herbs, such as basil, parsley, chives, and coriander, plus extra to serve

salt and freshly ground black pepper

3 thin slices prosciutto, cut into strips

1 Trim off and discard the small white muscle from each scallop and divide them between scallop shells, or place in an ovenproof dish. Preheat the grill on its highest setting.

2 Combine the butter, garlic, lime juice, and herbs, and spoon the mixture over the scallops.

3 Season with salt and pepper, and scatter with the prosciutto. Place under the grill and cook for 5 minutes. Serve immediately with wedges of lime and a scattering of fresh herbs, and warm crusty bread to soak up the delicious flavoured butter.

Scallops skewered with Parma ham

Both dainty and meaty, a starter for parties.

The fish

Scallops, or monkfish or prawns

■ **PREP** 10 mins ■ **COOK** 5–8 mins ■ **SERVES** 8

Ingredients

8 scallops, halved

1 tbsp olive oil

juice of 1 lemon

salt and freshly ground black pepper

8 slices Parma ham, halved

1 Preheat the oven to 190°C (375°F/Gas 5). Mix the scallops with the oil and lemon, and season.

2 Wrap each scallop half in Parma ham, then thread on to 8 soaked short wooden skewers.

3 Lay the skewers on a baking sheet, and roast in the oven for 5–8 minutes until the ham starts to crisp. Serve hot with a wild rocket salad.

Variation

Marinated skewered scallops
Omit the ham. Marinate the scallops in the lemon mix for 30 minutes. Cook for 5 minutes.

SUSTAINABILITY CHOICE

Be informed

When choosing fish, one of the key things to be aware of is how they were harvested from the ocean. More often than not, this is by net. Fixed nets are considered the most sustainable because, unlike other types of net, they barely touch the seabed and so cause minimal damage to the fishes' environment. Weights anchor the net and floats provide buoyancy to create a structure similar to a tennis net. A trammel net, a type of fixed net (shown here), has three layers of netting. The mesh size is adapted to target certain species, which minimizes the amount of bycatch.

Cured mackerel nigiri

Keep a bowl of vinegared water to hand to prevent the rice from sticking, but avoid using it too much.

The fish
Mackerel

- **PREP** 20 mins ▪ **COOK** none
- **MAKES** 20 nigiri

Ingredients
⅙ recipe sushi rice (see page 293)

a little wasabi paste

1 mackerel fillet, cured and pinboned (see page 294)

1 Take a small amount of rice in dampened hands, gently moulding it into a rounded lozenge. Spread a little wasabi over the top.

2 Cut the mackerel into strips and lay across the wasabi, gently pressing together.

Prepare ahead
Cure the fish up to 3 hours in advance, cover, and refrigerate. Return to room temperature before assembling the nigiri sushi.

Variations

Salmon nigiri
Cut 175g (6oz) salmon fillet into strips. Shape the rice as above and top with a little wasabi and then the salmon. Cut a thin strip of nori seaweed and use this to wrap around the middle of the salmon. Makes 20.

Prawn nigiri
Shape half of the rice and top with wasabi as above. Butterfly 8 tiger prawns split open from the base (see page 295) and drape neatly across the top of the rice. Makes 8.

Squid nigiri
Shape the rice and top with wasabi as above. Open 10 squid tubes out flat and carefully score, then cut each in half (see page 282). Drape each lozenge with half a squid tube. Makes 20.

Kingfish nigiri
Shape the rice and top with wasabi as above, using 175g (6oz) kingfish fillet (as prepared for mackerel). Makes 20.

Nori maki

You will need a bamboo mat to make these California-style rolls.

The fish
White crab meat, or surimi (ocean sticks)

- **PREP** 5 mins ▪ **COOK** none
- **MAKES** 16 nori maki

Ingredients
splash of rice vinegar

4 sheets nori seaweed, halved

⅙ recipe sushi rice (see page 293)

a little wasabi paste

½ avocado, thinly sliced

115g (4oz) white crab meat, or 4 pieces of surimi (ocean sticks), halved

1 Lay a bamboo mat on a board. Have to hand a bowl of tepid water mixed with the vinegar.

2 Lay a half piece of nori seaweed on the bamboo mat, shiny side down. Using wet hands, take a small handful of rice and spread it on the nori, pressing gently, and leaving a 2.5cm (1in) border at one end. Don't use too much water or the nori will become wet and tough.

3 If using a single ingredient (such as the smoked salmon variation below), use a little more rice to fill the rolls. Make an indentation down the centre of the rice, spread on a little wasabi paste, the avocado, and crab or surimi.

4 Roll up the sushi, pressing on the bamboo mat to help keep the roll even.

5 To cut the roll, use a very sharp, wet knife and do not saw, but pull the knife towards you. Cut the roll in half, then in half again and stand each upright. Wipe the knife between cuts.

6 Arrange the cut sushi on a large tray to serve. Serve with dark soy sauce, pickled sushi ginger, pickled daikon, and wasabi paste.

Variations

Smoked salmon nori maki
Substitute 115g (4oz) smoked salmon for the crab, and use only half the nori sheets.

Tobiko and cucumber nori maki
Use only half the nori sheets, fill with strips of cucumber, skin and seeds removed, and top with tobiko (flying fish roe), or salmon keta caviar.

Tuna nori maki
Use only half the nori sheets, and fill with thinly sliced, fresh, sashimi-grade tuna.

KINGFISH FLAVOUR PAIRINGS: The sweet, rich flesh of kingfish is great with wasabi, or in curries with other Asian spices such as hot chilli, ginger, and sour tamarind.

Tamaki sushi

An excellent, if slightly cheating, way to serve sushi: get your guests to roll their own!

The fish

Tuna, salmon, snapper, lemon sole, surimi (ocean sticks), tobiko (flying fish roe), or salmon keta caviar

- **PREP** 15–20 mins ▪ **COOK** 5 mins
- **MAKES** 12–14 rolls

Ingredients

For the Japanese omelette (optional)

3 eggs

2 egg yolks

1 rounded tsp cornflour, mixed with 2 tsp water

splash of vegetable oil

For the rest of the dish

$1/2$ recipe sushi rice (see page 293)

2 sheets of nori seaweed per person, cut in two

a choice of fillings, such as 1 fillet per person of sashimi-grade tuna, salmon, snapper, or lemon sole, 2–3 surimi (ocean sticks) per person, 1 x 110g jar tobiko (flying fish roe), or salmon keta caviar

a selection of vegetables cut into sticks, such as cucumber, avocado, or green beans and asparagus (both trimmed, and blanched for 2–3 minutes in boiling water)

1 Whisk together the eggs, yolks, and cornflour. Brush a large frying pan with the oil and heat for 1 minute. Pour in enough egg to cover the bottom and cook for a few seconds, or until set. Flip and cook the second side, then slide on to a plate. Cook the remaining mixture. Cut into slices and arrange on a plate.

2 Pile the prepared rice into a bowl and arrange the other ingredients on a large platter.

3 Serve your guests; each person should have a dipping bowl of hand-hot vinegared water. You may need to demonstrate how to assemble the first cornet: hold a piece of nori seaweed in one hand and arrange a little rice across the middle. Make an indentation in the rice and add fillings of your choice. Wrap the ends of the nori seaweed around to form a cornet. It doesn't matter if fillings stick out of the top – this is part of the roll's beauty.

4 Serve with wasabi and Japanese soy sauce for dipping.

Chirashi sushi

This type of sushi requires no rolling and is very easy to make. Serve in individual bowls or on a large platter.

The fish

Tuna, salmon, kingfish, tiger prawns, mackerel, or squid

- **PREP** 15 mins ▪ **COOK** none ▪ **SERVES** 4

Ingredients

$1/2$ recipe sushi rice (see page 293)

Any selection of the following:

shredded daikon

thinly sliced cucumber

1 fillet sashimi-grade tuna, thinly and evenly sliced

1 fillet sashimi-grade salmon, thinly and evenly sliced

1 fillet sashimi-grade kingfish, thinly and evenly sliced

8–12 prepared and cooked tiger prawns (see page 295)

1 cured mackerel fillet, thinly sliced (see page 294)

1 thin squid tube, scored and cut into pieces (see page 282)

1 Pile the sushi rice into a large, shallow serving dish, or four individual bowls.

2 Arrange the vegetables and fish on top and serve with wasabi and Japanese dark soy sauce.

Prepare ahead

Prepare and cook the prawns up to 3 hours in advance, cover, and refrigerate. Return to room temperature before continuing.

SALMON KETA CAVIAR FLAVOUR PAIRINGS: The quite exceptional, rich taste of this bright orange roe is great with sushi rice, or melba toast, chopped hard-boiled egg white, and chopped onion.

Scallop and tobiko sashimi

The essence of sashimi is its simplicity, the beauty of the presentation, and for this recipe, the intense freshness of the scallops.

The fish

Scallops, or monkfish, tuna, or salmon, and tobiko (flying fish roe)

▪ **PREP** 15 mins ▪ **COOK** none ▪ **SERVES** 4

Ingredients

16 scallops, roe removed

2 tbsp tobiko (flying fish roe), green or golden

shiso leaves (perilla), to garnish

Japanese soy sauce, to serve

pickled sushi ginger, to serve

wasabi paste, to serve

1 Cut the scallop meat horizontally into very even 0.5cm (¼in) slices. Arrange, overlapping, on a platter (preferably lacquered). Spoon the tobiko around the edge.

2 Decorate with the shiso leaves and add small bowls containing soy sauce, ginger, and wasabi to serve in the centre.

Variation

Monkfish, tuna, or salmon, and tobiko sashimi
Slice 450g (1lb) sashimi-grade monkfish, tuna, or salmon and use in place of the scallops.

Cured mackerel sashimi with salad

In spring and summer, mackerel has quite a soft texture; curing it firms the flesh.

The fish

Mackerel, or tuna or bonito

▪ **PREP** 30 mins ▪ **COOK** none ▪ **SERVES** 4

Ingredients

2 very fresh mackerel (preferably still with rigor mortis), filleted, cured, and pinboned (see page 294)

60g (2oz) rocket, washed

2 Baby Gem lettuces, washed and torn into strips

large handful of cress, washed

handful of cherry tomatoes, halved

½ small cucumber, peeled and thinly sliced

1 ripe avocado, diced

2 tbsp chopped pickled sushi ginger

Japanese soy sauce, to serve

wasabi paste, to serve

For the dressing

1 tsp runny honey

1 tbsp mirin

1 tbsp rice wine vinegar

1 tsp sesame oil

2 tbsp sunflower oil

1 Slice the mackerel very thinly, and set aside.

2 Put the salad ingredients into a big bowl and toss together. Put the dressing ingredients into a bowl, whisk to blend, then add to the salad, and toss together.

3 Pile the salad on to a large platter and arrange the sliced mackerel on top. Serve with the dark soy sauce and wasabi in small dishes on the side.

Prepare ahead

Cure the fish up to 3 hours in advance, cover, and refrigerate. Return to room temperature before assembling the salad.

TOBIKO FLAVOUR PAIRINGS: This fine-grained, crunchy roe can be dyed black with cuttlefish ink, or green with wasabi, and is great with sashimi, or buckwheat blinis, and soured cream.

Escabeche

A Spanish classic traditionally made with mackerel, bonito, tuna, or sardines, escabeche works well with firm white fish, too.

The fish
Any white fish, such as pollock, tilapia, meagre, snapper, and sea bass

- **PREP** 15–20 mins, plus marinating
- **COOK** 15–20 mins **SERVES** 4

Ingredients
450g (1lb) white fish fillets, pinboned and skinned

1 tbsp flour

sea salt and freshly ground black pepper

4 tbsp olive oil

1 tsp paprika

2 garlic cloves, sliced

1 bay leaf

2 strips of orange zest

½ tsp dried thyme

½ tsp dried oregano

6 peppercorns

150ml (5fl oz) white wine vinegar

200ml (7fl oz) medium white wine

handful of rocket leaves, to serve

3 tomatoes, thickly sliced, to serve

1 red onion, finely sliced, to serve

12 black olives, pitted, to serve

1 Cut the fish into 5–6cm (2–2½in) pieces. Put the flour on a plate and season well. Roll the fish in the seasoned flour and shake off excess.

2 Heat half the oil in a frying pan, add the fish in batches and cook for 2–3 minutes each side, or until golden brown. Lift into a deep dish.

3 Put the remaining oil into the pan, add the paprika and garlic and fry for 1 minute. Add the remaining ingredients with 150ml (5fl oz) water; take care, as the pan will sizzle when the liquid hits. Bring to a boil and simmer for 3–4 minutes. Remove from the heat and cool.

4 Pour the escabeche over the fish and refrigerate for 12 hours, preferably overnight.

5 Lift from the marinade and put on a platter, with rocket, tomatoes, onion, and olives.

Prepare ahead
The escabeche must be made at least 12 hours, preferably 1 day, before you need it.

Classic prawn cocktail

A 1960s prawn cocktail was served with shredded soft lettuce, but the Iceberg leaves used here don't turn limp so quickly.

The fish
Prawns, or tiger prawns, scampi tails, or cockles

- **PREP** 15 mins **COOK** none
- **SERVES** 4 generously

Ingredients
450g (1lb) cooked prawns

150ml (5fl oz) mayonnaise (or mixed crème fraîche and mayonnaise)

4 tbsp tomato chutney

1 tsp tomato purée

2–3 tsp Worcestershire sauce

2–3 tsp creamed horseradish

1 tsp brandy

salt and freshly ground black pepper

splash of Tabasco

lemon juice, to taste

½ small Iceberg lettuce, very finely shredded

½ tsp paprika

thinly sliced brown bread, lightly buttered, to serve

1 Peel and devein all but 8 of the prawns, and discard the shells (see page 285). Set aside.

2 Mix the mayonnaise, chutney, tomato purée, Worcestershire sauce, horseradish, and brandy together. Season and add the Tabasco and lemon juice to taste.

3 Divide the lettuce evenly between 4 large wine glasses, or glass bowls.

4 Mix the prawns into the mayonnaise and pile on top of the lettuce. Dust lightly with paprika. Arrange 2 unpeeled prawns on top of each glass and serve with brown bread and butter.

Variation
Prawn cocktail, Mexican-style
Omit the mayonnaise flavourings above and instead use 1 tbsp sun-dried tomato purée, 1 tbsp chopped coriander, 1 small diced avocado, 2 tbsp sweetcorn kernels, the juice of 1 lime, and Tabasco sauce. Stir in the prawns and serve as above, topped with sprigs of coriander.

POLLOCK FLAVOUR PAIRINGS: The firm, meaty, yet subtly flavoured flesh of pollock works well with tomatoes, chilli, bacon, pancetta, or basil.

Prawn spring rolls

"Spring" rolls are named because they were eaten to celebrate Chinese New Year, or the first day of spring.

The fish
Prawns, or white crab meat

- **PREP** 25 mins ▪ **COOK** 15 mins ▪ **SERVES** 12

Ingredients
225g (8oz) raw prawns, peeled, deveined, and chopped (see page 285)

½ red pepper, deseeded and finely chopped

115g (4oz) mushrooms, chopped

4 spring onions, thinly sliced

115g (4oz) beansprouts

2cm (¾in) fresh root ginger, grated

1 tbsp rice wine vinegar

1 tbsp dark soy sauce

vegetable oil, for shallow frying

225g (8oz) cooked chicken, chopped

1 tbsp cornflour

12 spring roll wrappers

6 Chinese cabbage leaves, halved

sweet chilli sauce, to serve

1 In a bowl, mix together the prawns, red pepper, mushrooms, spring onions, beansprouts, ginger, vinegar, and soy sauce.

2 Heat 2 tbsp oil in a frying pan, add the prawn mixture, and stir-fry for 3 minutes. Set aside to cool, then stir in the chicken.

3 In another small bowl, mix the cornflour with 4 tbsp cold water.

4 Lay a spring roll wrapper on a work surface and top with half a cabbage leaf and 1 tbsp of the prawn mixture. Brush the edges of the wrapper with the cornflour mix and roll up, tucking in the sides and pressing the brushed edges together to seal. Repeat with the remaining wrappers and filling.

5 Shallow-fry the rolls in hot oil until golden brown. Drain on kitchen paper and serve with sweet chilli sauce.

Prepare ahead
Make the prawn filling up to 3 hours in advance (only add the chicken when it is completely cold), cover, and refrigerate. Assemble the rolls just before frying.

Salmon fishcakes

The classic fishcake. Use leftover cooked salmon instead, if you have it.

The fish
Salmon, or trout or haddock

- **PREP** 15 mins ▪ **COOK** 30 mins ▪ **SERVES** 4

Ingredients
900g (2lb) potatoes, peeled and cut into chunks

knob of butter

900g (2lb) salmon fillets, pinboned and skinned

handful of curly parsley, finely chopped

salt and freshly ground black pepper

plain flour, for dusting

vegetable oil, for shallow frying

tartare sauce, to serve

lemon wedges, to serve

1 Boil the potatoes in salted water for about 15 minutes or until soft, drain well, and mash with the butter until smooth. Set aside.

2 Put the salmon in a large frying pan, and cover with water. Poach for 5–8 minutes. Remove. Using your fingers, flake into pieces.

3 Gently mix the fish with the potato. Add the parsley, and season well. Take a small handful of the mixture at a time, roll into balls, then flatten into cakes. Dust each with flour.

4 Heat a little oil in a frying pan over a medium heat. Fry the fishcakes for 5 minutes each side. Serve with tartare sauce and lemon wedges.

Prepare ahead
Make these up to 1 day ahead, cover, and chill. Return to room temperature before frying.

Variation
Maryland crab cakes
Mix the juice from 1 lemon with 1kg (2¼lb) crab, 125g (4½oz) breadcrumbs, chopped parsley and dill, 4 tbsp mayonnaise, 2 beaten eggs, and salt and pepper. Form into 16 cakes. Fry for just 3–4 minutes, and serve with a sweetcorn relish and lemon wedges. Serves 8.

Smoked haddock and herb fishcakes

Crisp fishcakes make a great starter, and the smoky flavours here work well with mustard.

The fish

Smoked haddock, or smoked cod

- **PREP** 10 mins, plus cooling ▪ **COOK** 30 mins
- **SERVES** 6

Ingredients

300g (10oz) smoked haddock fillet, pinboned and skinned

140g (5oz) potatoes, peeled and cut into chunks

salt and freshly ground black pepper

knob of butter

½ tsp Dijon mustard

3 spring onions, finely chopped

grated zest and juice of ½ lemon

30g (1oz) chopped flat-leaf parsley

45g (1½oz) plain flour

1 egg, beaten

85g (3oz) dried breadcrumbs

sunflower oil, for shallow frying

1 Preheat the oven to 190°C (375°F/Gas 5). Place the haddock in an ovenproof dish with 2–3 tbsp water, cover with foil and bake for 15 minutes. Leave to cool, then flake into pieces.

2 Boil the potatoes in salted water for about 15 minutes until soft. Drain well, and mash with the butter until smooth.

3 Place the mashed potato, mustard, spring onions, lemon zest and juice, and parsley in a large bowl, add the smoked haddock and mix well. Season to taste.

4 Divide the mixture into 12 equal portions and shape each portion into rounds. Place the flour in a small dish, the egg in another dish, and the breadcrumbs in a third. Roll each fishcake in the flour, then dip into the egg, and finally coat with breadcrumbs.

5 Shallow fry the fishcakes in a little oil, in batches, for 5–7 minutes, turning once, or until crisp and golden all over. Drain on kitchen paper, and serve hot with a simple salad of rocket and watercress, and tartare sauce or mayonnaise for dipping.

Prepare ahead

You can prepare these up to the end of step 3 several hours in advance. Chill until required.

Minced crab balls

These Thai-style bites are a great alternative to Thai fishcakes (see page 58).

The fish

White crab meat

- **PREP** 10 mins ▪ **COOK** 15 mins ▪ **SERVES** 4

Ingredients

350g (12oz) fresh white crab meat, or canned white crab meat, drained

1 red chilli, deseeded and roughly chopped

2 garlic cloves, roughly chopped

handful of fresh coriander

grated zest and juice of 1 lemon

1 tsp Thai fish sauce

2 eggs, beaten

salt and freshly ground black pepper

125g (4½oz) fresh breadcrumbs

3 tbsp vegetable oil, for shallow frying

dark soy sauce, to serve

sweet chilli sauce, to serve

1 Put the crab, chilli, garlic, coriander, lemon zest and juice, and fish sauce in a food processor. Whizz until a rough paste forms, then add the egg and plenty of salt and pepper. Whizz again.

2 Scoop the mixture up and roll into 2.5cm (1in) balls. Tip the breadcrumbs on to a plate, and roll the crab balls in them until well covered.

3 Heat a little of the oil in a frying pan over a medium heat. Add a few of the balls at a time to the pan, to cook in batches. Shallow fry for about 5 minutes until golden all over, moving the balls around the pan so that they brown evenly, topping up with more oil as needed. Drain on kitchen paper.

4 Serve hot with soy sauce and sweet chilli sauce for dipping.

Prepare ahead

The spiced crab paste can be blended up to 4 hours in advance, covered, and refrigerated. Add the egg when ready to continue.

Thai fishcakes

Universally popular, these make a piquant, sophisticated first course.

The fish
Prawns, or cod or monkfish

- **PREP** 15 mins ▪ **COOK** 15 mins ▪ **SERVES** 4

Ingredients

300g (10oz) cooked prawns, peeled and deveined (see page 285)

3 garlic cloves

small handful of fresh coriander

2 hot red chillies, deseeded

splash of Thai fish sauce

splash of dark soy sauce

small handful of basil leaves (preferably Thai basil)

juice of 2 limes

1 egg

salt and freshly ground black pepper

3–4 tbsp vegetable or sunflower oil

sweet chilli sauce, to serve

wild rocket leaves, to serve

1 Put the first 8 ingredients in a food processor, and whizz into a rough paste. Add the egg and plenty of salt and pepper, and whizz again.

2 Heat a little of the oil in a frying pan over a medium-high heat. Scoop out a tablespoon of the mixture, then carefully slide it into the pan and flatten to about 2cm (¾in) thick. Repeat until the pan is full, and shallow-fry for 1–2 minutes each side until golden. You will need to cook in batches, adding more oil as needed. Drain the fishcakes on a plate lined with kitchen paper.

3 Serve hot with a drizzle of sweet chilli sauce and some wild rocket leaves.

Prepare ahead

The fishcake mixture can be blended, covered, and chilled up to 1 day ahead. The flavours will deepen. Return the mix to room temperature before continuing.

Thai crab cakes

These make a delicious starter, or transform into a main course with rice noodles.

The fish
White crab meat, or salmon

- **PREP** 20 mins, plus chilling ▪ **COOK** 5–10 mins ▪ **MAKES** 20

Ingredients

500g (1lb 2oz) white crab meat

115g (4oz) green beans, trimmed and finely chopped

1 green or red chilli, deseeded and very finely chopped

1 tsp lemongrass purée

finely grated zest of 1 lime

1 tbsp Thai fish sauce

1 tbsp finely chopped Chinese chives or garlic chives

1 egg white, lightly beaten

plain flour, to dust

vegetable oil, for deep-frying

lime wedges, to serve

1 Flake the crab meat into a bowl, picking it over carefully to remove any small, sharp pieces of shell. Mix in the green beans, chilli, lemongrass purée, lime zest, fish sauce, and chives.

2 Add the egg white, stirring to bind the mixture together. Dust your hands with flour and shape the mixture into 20 small balls. Flatten them slightly into round cakes, place on a plate or board, spaced slightly apart so they don't stick together, and chill for 1 hour, or until firm.

3 Heat the oil to 160°C (325°F) in a large pan or deep-fat fryer (see page 308). Dust the cakes with flour and deep-fry them in batches for 3 minutes, or until golden. Drain on a plate lined with kitchen paper and serve with lime wedges.

Prepare ahead

The crab cakes can be assembled, covered, and chilled up to 1 day ahead. The flavours will deepen. Return them to room temperature before continuing.

COD FLAVOUR PAIRINGS: Sweet and succulent cod teams well with the sharp flavours of dill, parsley, lemon, capers, and garlic, as well as with gentler bay leaf and butter.

Tuna carpaccio

The fish must be of the very best quality for this recipe, as it will be eaten raw.

The fish

Tuna, or salmon

- **PREP** 10–15 mins - **COOK** 20 mins
- **SERVES** 4

Ingredients

1 sprig of thyme, leaves chopped

2 tsp finely grated lemon zest

5 tbsp extra virgin olive oil

5 Charlotte potatoes, unpeeled

salt and freshly ground black pepper

4 tbsp mayonnaise

1 heaped tbsp small capers, rinsed

2 tbsp olive oil, for frying

400g (14oz) sashimi-grade tuna loin, cut into 8 equal pieces

1 Mix together the thyme, lemon zest, and extra virgin olive oil.

2 Boil the potatoes for 15 minutes, or until tender. Drain, and peel once cool enough to handle. Cut into thick slices and place in a bowl. Season to taste with salt, add a little of the flavoured olive oil, and mix with the mayonnaise; set aside.

3 Pat the capers dry with kitchen paper. Fry them in the olive oil for 2 minutes, or until crisp, then drain off the oil.

4 Pound each piece of tuna between 2 pieces of cling film until uniformly very thin, then peel off the film. Scatter with fried capers, season to taste, and drizzle over the remaining flavoured olive oil. Serve with the potatoes.

Seafood ceviche

A brief, light pickling of raw fish conserves its freshness and brings out the true flavour.

The fish

Any firm-fleshed fish, such as halibut, turbot, salmon, or monkfish

- **PREP** 20 mins, plus freezing and marinating
- **COOK** none - **SERVES** 4

Ingredients

450g (1lb) very fresh, firm-fleshed fish fillets, pinboned and skinned

1 red onion, finely sliced

juice of 2 lemons or limes

1 tbsp olive oil

½ tsp pimentón piccante

1 chilli, finely chopped

salt and freshly ground black pepper

2 tbsp finely chopped flat-leaf parsley

1 Wrap the fish in cling film or foil, and put it in the freezer for 1 hour to firm up the flesh. This will make it easier to slice. With a sharp knife, slice the fish into very thin slivers.

2 Spread the onion evenly in the bottom of a shallow, non-metallic dish. Pour over the lemon juice and olive oil, then sprinkle with the pimentón and chilli.

3 Place the fish on the onion, gently turning to coat with the marinade. Cover and marinate in the refrigerator for at least 20 minutes, preferably more than 1 hour. Season, sprinkle with parsley, and serve with crusty bread.

Prepare ahead

The ceviche can be assembled, covered, and chilled up to 2 hours in advance. Return it to room temperature before serving.

HALIBUT FLAVOUR PAIRINGS: Fresh halibut can be served almost raw; it needs a gentle soaking in citrus first to tenderize the flesh. It's excellent with butter, nutmeg, gherkins, capers, and lemon juice.

Smoked salmon with mustard and dill dressing

Prepared in a trice while chatting to friends.

The fish

Smoked salmon, or very fresh raw salmon or cold-smoked trout

▪ **PREP** 5 mins ▪ **COOK** none ▪ **SERVES** 4

Ingredients

350g (12oz) good-quality smoked salmon

juice of 1 lemon

½ cucumber, finely chopped

For the dressing

90ml (3fl oz) extra virgin olive oil

3 tbsp white wine vinegar

1 tsp wholegrain mustard

1 tsp runny honey

salt and freshly ground black pepper

handful of fresh dill, finely chopped

1 Divide the salmon among 4 serving plates, and squeeze over the lemon juice.

2 Put the olive oil, vinegar, mustard, and honey in a small bowl. Whisk until well combined, then season. Sprinkle in half the dill, and whisk again. Taste, and adjust the seasoning.

3 Toss the cucumber with the remaining dill, then spoon it on to the plates. Drizzle over the dressing, and serve with brown bread.

Prepare ahead

The dressing can be prepared 1–2 hours ahead and kept, covered, in the refrigerator.

Marinated salmon

A Scandinavian favourite, and a refreshing change from smoked salmon.

The fish

Salmon, or trout or sea bass

▪ **PREP** 20 mins, plus marinating ▪ **COOK** none
▪ **SERVES** 6–8

Ingredients

2 salmon fillets, about 140g (5oz) each, skin on

3 tbsp coarse sea salt

3 tbsp sugar

1 tbsp coarsely crushed black peppercorns

3 tbsp aquavit or vodka

4 tbsp chopped dill, plus extra sprigs to serve

1 lemon, cut into wedges, to garnish

For the mustard sauce

4 tbsp Dijon mustard

4 tbsp sunflower oil

3 tbsp sugar

2 tbsp white wine vinegar

1 tsp soured cream

pinch of salt

1 Score the salmon skin, making cuts 3mm (⅛in) deep. Mix the salt, sugar, and pepper, and sprinkle a quarter into a non-metallic dish. Place 1 fillet in the dish, skin-side down, and sprinkle with half the aquavit, another quarter of the salt, and half the dill.

2 Sprinkle the flesh of the second fillet with another quarter of the salt and place it it, skin-side up, on top. Rub the remaining salt over and sprinkle with the remaining aquavit. Cover with cling film, then a large flat plate, and weigh down with cans of food. Refrigerate for 24 hours, draining off any liquid after 5–6 hours, then again after a further 5–6 hours. Turn the salmon and chill for another 24 hours, turning twice.

3 Place the sauce ingredients into a blender and process. Chill for 1 hour, covered. Before serving, add 2 tbsp chopped dill.

4 To serve, scrape the seasonings from the salmon. Place skin-side down on a board. Slice thinly on the slant, away from the skin. Serve with the sauce, lemon wedges, and dill. Good with brown bread, or toasted sourdough.

Prepare ahead

The fish must be prepared 48 hours in advance.

Smoked trout with beetroot, apple, and dill relish

A simple assembly job, but with eye-popping colours and great earthy and smoky flavours.

The fish
Hot-smoked trout, or smoked mackerel

- **PREP** 15 mins ▪ **COOK** none ▪ **SERVES** 4

Ingredients
3–4 tsp creamed horseradish

½ red onion, finely diced

1–2 heads chicory, leaves separated and rinsed

2 large hot-smoked trout fillets, about 225g (8oz) each, flaked

drizzle of olive oil

juice of ½ lemon

salt and freshly ground black pepper

2–3 eating apples

2 whole cooked beetroot, diced

handful of fresh dill, finely chopped

1 In a small bowl, mix together the horseradish and half the onion. Set aside.

2 Arrange the chicory and trout on a serving plate, and drizzle with oil and lemon juice. Sprinkle over a pinch of salt and some pepper.

3 Peel, core, and chop the apple into bite-sized pieces. Put in a separate bowl with the beetroot and dill, and mix together.

4 To serve, spoon the beetroot relish over the leaves and fish. Sprinkle over the remaining onion, and serve with the horseradish on the side.

Smoked trout with pickled cucumber and minted yogurt

A refreshing mix of avocado, yogurt, and fish.

The fish
Hot-smoked trout, or hot-smoked salmon or smoked mackerel

- **PREP** 15 mins ▪ **COOK** none ▪ **SERVES** 4

Ingredients
1 avocado, halved, stoned, and peeled

juice of 1 lemon

2 tbsp white wine vinegar

2 tsp caster sugar

1 fresh red chilli, deseeded and finely chopped

½ large cucumber, peeled and halved lengthways, deseeded, and sliced

4 tbsp Greek-style yogurt

handful of mint leaves, chopped

2 large handfuls of mixed salad leaves

12 green olives, pitted

2 hot-smoked trout fillets, about 200g (7oz) each, flaked

salt and freshly ground black pepper

1 Cut the avocado into slices lengthways, then sprinkle with the lemon juice. Set aside.

2 To make the pickled cucumber, whisk the vinegar, sugar, and chilli in a small bowl until combined. Add the cucumber, and toss. In a separate small bowl, stir the yogurt and mint until well mixed.

3 Arrange the salad leaves and olives in a large salad bowl or on 4 individual plates. Top with the flaked trout and avocado. Season with a pinch of salt and some pepper. Spoon over some of the pickled cucumber, and serve the rest on the side with the minted yogurt.

Scallops with bacon

Bacon, chorizo, and pancetta are all excellent to serve with pan-fried scallops.

The fish

King scallops, or tiger prawns or monkfish cheeks

- **PREP** 5–10 mins **COOK** 15 mins
- **SERVES** 4

Ingredients

4 rashers rindless smoked streaky bacon, sliced

12 king scallops

1 tbsp chopped flat-leaf parsley

squeeze of lemon juice

salt and freshly ground black pepper

handful of rocket, to serve

1 Heat a frying pan and add the bacon. Cook over a medium heat until the bacon is brown and frazzled. Lift on to a plate.

2 Remove the roe from the scallops. Fry the scallops in the bacon fat for 1–2 minutes on each side or until golden brown. Do not put too many in the pan at once, as they will not brown. Lift on to a plate.

3 Reduce the heat in the pan and fry the roes; these are likely to pop in the hot fat. They are cooked when they are firm.

4 Return the scallop muscles and bacon to the pan, add the parsley, and the lemon juice. Season, and serve with rocket leaves.

Fried calamari

A tempting Mediterranean dish, served as a tasty appetizer.

The fish

Squid, or cuttlefish

- **PREP** 15 mins **COOK** 10–15 mins
- **SERVES** 4

Ingredients

2 eggs

2 tbsp chilled soda water

150g (5½oz) plain flour

1 tsp chilli flakes

1 tsp salt

500g (1lb 2oz) small squid, gutted, cleaned, and cut into 1cm (½in) rings (see page 282)

250ml (9fl oz) vegetable or sunflower oil

lemon wedges

1 Break the eggs into a bowl, add the soda water, and whisk well. Put the flour, chilli flakes, and salt on a plate and mix well. Dip each piece of squid into the egg mixture and then into the flour, ensuring they are evenly coated.

2 Heat the oil in a deep-frying pan over a high heat until hot, then carefully add the squid, a piece at a time. Do not overfill the pan. Cook in batches for 2–3 minutes, or until golden brown. Carefully remove with a slotted spoon and place on kitchen paper to soak up excess oil. Keep warm while you fry the rest, then serve with lemon wedges.

KING SCALLOP FLAVOUR PAIRINGS:

Despite their sweetness, scallops can take on bacon, chorizo, red peppers, red onions, and olive oil, or the Asian tastes of sesame oil, black beans, spring onions, ginger, and chilli.

Scallops with sweet chilli sauce

It's so easy to make sweet chilli sauce; almost as quick as opening a jar.

The fish

King scallops, or monkfish or tiger prawns

- **PREP** 10 mins, plus marinating
- **COOK** 5 mins ▪ **SERVES** 4

Ingredients

4 garlic cloves, grated

3 red chillies, deseeded and finely chopped

3 tbsp dry sherry

1 tsp caster sugar

2 tbsp olive oil, plus extra for frying

12 king scallops, roe removed

1 Put the garlic, chillies, sherry, and sugar in a bowl and mix until the sugar dissolves. Add the oil and scallops, toss together, then leave to marinate for at least 30 minutes.

2 Transfer the scallops to a plate, using a slotted spoon. Reserve the marinade. Heat a little olive oil in a non-stick frying pan and cook the scallops over high heat for 1 minute on each side. Remove from the pan and pour in the marinade. Cook over a high heat for 3 minutes, then pour it back over the scallops. Serve with a crisp green salad.

Squid in olive oil and paprika

Use sweet or smoked paprika if you prefer.

The fish

Squid, or cuttlefish, baby octopus, whelks, or winkles

- **PREP** 5 mins ▪ **COOK** 5 mins ▪ **SERVES** 4

Ingredients

450g (1lb) squid, gutted (see page 282)

2 tbsp olive oil

2 garlic cloves, finely chopped

salt

2 tsp hot paprika

1 tbsp fresh juice

lemon wedges, to serve

1 Clean the squid and slice the tubes into rings, and cut each tentacle in half.

2 Heat the oil in a frying pan over a medium heat, add the garlic and fry for 1 minute, stirring, then increase the heat and add the squid. Fry for 3 minutes on a high heat, stirring frequently.

3 Season to taste with salt, then add the paprika and lemon juice.

4 Transfer to small serving plates and serve immediately, with lemon wedges. This is particularly good as part of a spread of other tapas, such as chorizo and olives.

Gefilte fish

Traditionally in this Jewish recipe, the mixture would have been stuffed into the skin of the deboned carp.

The fish

Carp, or pike or cod

- **PREP** 25 mins ▪ **COOK** 6–10 mins
- **SERVES** 4

Ingredients

1kg (2lb) carp fillets, pinboned and skinned

1 tbsp oil

1 onion, finely chopped

2 eggs

1 tsp sugar

salt and freshly ground white pepper

60g (2oz) medium matzo meal

600ml (1 pint) fish stock

beetroot and horseradish relish, to serve

1 Put the fish and oil into a food processor and whizz until very well chopped. Transfer to a bowl.

2 Put the onion, eggs, sugar, salt, pepper, and matzo meal into the food processor, and pulse until well combined. Add to the fish and work into a paste by hand.

3 Shape the paste into balls the size of a small apple, and chill until required.

4 Bring the stock to a gentle simmer in a large saucepan. Drop in the fish balls, and poach gently for 6–10 minutes, or until firm. Serve with a beetroot and horseradish relish.

Prepare ahead

The gefilte fish balls can be made up to 1 day ahead, covered, and refrigerated. Return to room temperature before poaching and serving.

Chilli prawns with coriander and lime

Sharp citrus and hot chilli bring out the sweetness of the prawns.

The fish

Prawns, or scallops

- **PREP** 15 mins ▪ **COOK** none ▪ **SERVES** 4

Ingredients

400g can butterbeans, drained and rinsed

16 cooked prawns, peeled and deveined, tails left on (see page 285)

handful of fresh coriander, finely chopped

1–2 red chillies, deseeded and finely chopped

2 handfuls of wild rocket

juice of 1 lime

salt and freshly ground black pepper

splash of sweet chilli sauce

1 To soften the butterbeans a little, put them in a bowl, and cover with hot water. Leave to stand for 10 minutes, then drain well.

2 Put the prawns in a large bowl. Add half the coriander and all the chillies, and mix well. Tip in the butterbeans, and toss again.

3 Arrange the rocket in a large serving bowl or on 4 individual plates. Sprinkle over a little of the lime juice, a pinch of salt, and some pepper. Add the remaining lime juice to the prawns, stir, then taste and adjust the seasoning.

4 Spoon the prawn mixture over the rocket, then drizzle with sweet chilli sauce, and sprinkle over the remaining coriander. Serve immediately.

Herbed pollock goujons

Fish fingers for grown-ups.

The fish
Pollock, or any white fish, such as haddock, cod, plaice, lemon sole, or coley

- **PREP** 20 mins • **COOK** 10–15 mins
- **SERVES** 4–6

Ingredients
115g (4oz) fresh breadcrumbs

handful of flat-leaf parsley, chopped, plus a few sprigs, to garnish

½ tsp smoked paprika

salt and freshly ground black pepper

85g (3oz) plain flour

1 large egg

225g (8oz) pollock fillets, pinboned and skinned

sunflower oil, for frying

lemon wedges, to serve

1 Place the breadcrumbs, chopped parsley, and smoked paprika in a bowl, season to taste with salt and pepper, and mix thoroughly.

2 Place the flour in a bowl, whisk the egg with 1 tbsp water in another bowl, and spread the breadcrumb mixture into a third.

3 Slice the fish into thin strips. Dust the strips with flour, then dip into the egg, then place in the breadcrumbs, turning to coat completely. Place them on a plate and chill until needed.

4 Heat 2.5cm (1in) sunflower oil in a frying pan until it is hot enough to sizzle when the fish is added. Fry the fish for 1 minute each side, or until crisp, then drain on kitchen paper. Serve with sprigs of parsley and lemon wedges. These are good with a herbed mayonnaise.

Prepare ahead
Prepare the goujons, cover, and refrigerate up to 1 day in advance. Return to room temperature before frying. Or lay the goujons on a baking sheet, cover, and freeze, then tip into a plastic freezer bag to store for up to 1 month.

Grilled sardines on toast

The posh version of a classic snack, great for a late supper, and very healthy.

The fish
Sardines, or herrings, sprats, or small mackerel

- **PREP** 10 mins, plus marinating • **COOK** 6 mins
- **SERVES** 4

Ingredients
8 sardines, scaled, gutted, and boned through the stomach (see page 267) or filleted

4 tbsp olive oil

3 garlic cloves, finely sliced

1 fresh green chilli, deseeded and finely chopped

juice of 1 lemon

1 tsp crushed fennel seeds

2 tbsp finely chopped flat-leaf parsley

salt and freshly ground black pepper

ciabatta, sliced and toasted, to serve

1 Brush the sardines with a little of the oil and cook under a medium grill for 3 minutes on each side. Remove, and allow to cool.

2 Meanwhile, put all the remaining ingredients except the bread in a mixing bowl and combine well. Add the sardines, then leave to marinate for 20 minutes, if you have time.

3 Serve the marinated sardines on the warm, toasted ciabatta.

Prepare ahead
Make the recipe to the end of step 2, cover, and refrigerate for up to 1 day in advance. Return to room temperature before serving on toast.

Variation
Anchovies on toast
Cut 2 baguettes in half lengthways and toast on both sides. Rub with 2 halved tomatoes, squeezing out the seeds and flesh on to the bread. Discard the tomato skins. Lay over 50g (1¾oz) drained anchovy fillets in oil. Slice 2 more tomatoes and arrange on top, drizzle with extra virgin olive oil, season, and scatter with finely chopped shallots and parsley. Top with 50g (1¾oz) more anchovies, and serve.

Salt and pepper prawns

You will find that you can't stop eating these!

The fish

Tiger prawns, or squid or scallops

- **PREP** 10 mins ▪ **COOK** 10 mins ▪ **SERVES** 4

Ingredients

2 tbsp cornflour

1 tbsp sea salt

1 tbsp cracked black pepper

16 raw ting prawns, peeled and deveined (see page 285)

4 tbsp vegetable oil

3 fresh hot red chillies, deseeded and finely sliced

3 garlic cloves, grated or finely chopped

6 spring onions, cut into 5cm (2in) pieces, then halved lengthways

dark soy sauce, to serve

1 In a bowl, mix together the cornflour, salt, and pepper. Add the prawns, and toss until well combined. Set aside.

2 Heat 1 tbsp of the oil in a frying pan over a medium heat. Add the chillies, garlic, and spring onions, and stir-fry for 3–5 minutes. Remove from the heat, and cover with a lid to keep warm.

3 Heat the remaining oil in a separate frying pan over a high heat. Add the prawns, and cook for 3–5 minutes, tossing them gently until they are completely pink.

4 Remove the prawns from the pan with a slotted spoon, and divide among 4 serving plates. Top with the chilli and spring onion mixture, and serve immediately with a splash of soy sauce.

Prawn and courgette balls with caper cream

An unusual and incredibly moreish starter.

The fish

Prawns, or smoked haddock

- **PREP** 30 mins, plus marinating
- **COOK** 20 mins ▪ **SERVES** 6–8

Ingredients

550g (1¼lb) raw prawns, peeled, deveined, and finely chopped (see page 285)

250g (9oz) courgette, grated

1 garlic clove, crushed

2 tbsp finely chopped flat-leaf parsley

grated zest and juice of 1 small lemon

2 eggs, beaten

salt and freshly ground black pepper

250ml (8fl oz) soured cream

1 tbsp capers, rinsed and chopped

1 tbsp finely chopped fresh dill

500ml (16fl oz) olive oil, for frying

1 In a bowl, combine the prawns, courgette, garlic, parsley, lemon zest and juice, and eggs. Season and mix well by hand. Cover with cling film, and marinate in the refrigerator for 1 hour. Meanwhile, put the soured cream, capers, and dill in a separate bowl, and season with pepper. Stir, cover with cling film, and chill until needed.

2 Pour the oil into a wide, heavy frying pan over a medium-high heat. Roll the prawn mixture into walnut-sized balls.

3 When the oil is hot, gently drop in the balls. Fry for 4–5 minutes, or until golden brown, turning. Do not overcrowd the pan; cook in batches if necessary. Remove from the pan with a slotted spoon, and drain on kitchen paper.

4 Serve the prawn and courgette balls with bowls of caper cream.

Prepare ahead

Make the prawn balls and the caper cream up to 1 day in advance. Cover both, and refrigerate until ready to cook.

Crayfish sauté with spicy tomatoes

Crawfish, as they are known in the US, are much-loved in the American South, so in this recipe Creole flavourings add zip to sweet freshwater crayfish.

The fish

Freshwater crayfish, or tiger prawns, squid, or Dublin Bay prawns

- **PREP** 10 mins ▪ **COOK** 15–20 mins
- **SERVES** 4

Ingredients

60g (2oz) butter

1 onion, finely chopped

1 garlic clove, grated or finely chopped

1 carrot, finely diced

1 tbsp creamed horseradish

2 tbsp wholegrain mustard

1 tsp English mustard

½ tsp cayenne pepper

1 tbsp Creole spice mix

400g can tomatoes, chopped

salt and freshly ground black pepper

2 tbsp chopped flat-leaf parsley

5 tbsp mayonnaise

450g (1lb) cooked, peeled, and deveined freshwater crayfish tails, patted dry

1 Melt the butter in a large saucepan, add the onion, garlic, and carrot and cook over a low heat for 4–5 minutes or until the onion is soft. Add the horseradish, mustards, cayenne, and Creole spices. Stir over the heat for 1 minute, then add the tomatoes, bring to a boil and simmer for 7–8 minutes or until thick and pulpy.

2 Season the mixture to taste and add the parsley and mayonnaise. Stir in the crayfish and heat through until piping hot. Do not overheat, or they will become tough.

3 Pile the crayfish into a bowl. For a more substantial dish, serve some boiled rice on the side.

Prepare ahead

The tomato sauce in step 1 can be made up to 2 days in advance, covered, and refrigerated. The flavours will deepen. Return to a simmer before continuing.

Dressed crab

A quintessential English classic, perfect for a summer's day. For the best results, buy the crab live and cook it yourself (see page 289).

The fish

Crab

- **PREP** 35–40 mins ▪ **COOK** none ▪ **SERVES** 2

Ingredients

1 brown edible crab, about 1.3–2kg, cooked

splash of oil

2–3 tbsp fresh white breadcrumbs

English mustard powder, to taste

cayenne pepper, to taste

Worcestershire sauce, to taste

freshly ground black pepper, to taste

1 egg, hard-boiled

chopped flat-leaf parsley, to garnish

lemon wedges, to serve

1 Remove the brown and white meat from the crab and set aside separately. The mouth, stomach sac, and gills must all be discarded (see pages 288–89).

2 Wash the shell well and brush with a little oil. Mix the brown meat with enough breadcrumbs to bind. Add mustard, cayenne, Worcestershire sauce, and pepper, to taste. Flake the white meat into a bowl, taking care to locate and discard any chips of shell.

3 Neatly arrange both white and brown meat back in the cleaned shell and garnish with chopped hard-boiled egg white, sieved hard-boiled egg yolks, and parsley. Serve with bread and wedges of lemon.

Prepare ahead

Pick out the crab meat, put the white and brown meat into separate bowls, cover, and chill for up to 1 day before continuing.

CRAYFISH FLAVOUR PAIRINGS: Enhance sweet crayfish with cayenne pepper or paprika, enjoy simply with lemon, garlic, and tarragon, chives, and dill, or even use Asian ingredients, such as lemongrass, soy sauce, and chilli.

Yam pla fu

This classic Thai recipe is served with a chilli dipping sauce and mango or papaya salad.

The fish

Snapper, or meagre or grey mullet

- **PREP** 15 mins ▪ **COOK** 20–25 mins
- **SERVES** 4

Ingredients

1 large snapper, filleted and scaled

1 tsp oil, plus more for deep-frying

2 tsp salt

75g (3oz) dry roasted peanuts, to serve

nam prik (hot chilli dipping sauce), or sweet chilli sauce, to serve

For the mango salad

2 green mangos or papayas, shredded, or riper fruits, diced

1 carrot, peeled and shredded

2 spring onions, finely sliced

½ cucumber, peeled, deseeded, and shredded

60g (2oz) bean sprouts

For the dressing

1 tbsp palm sugar or dark brown sugar

zest and juice of 1 large lime

1 garlic clove, grated or finely chopped

1 tbsp grated fresh root ginger

splash of Thai fish sauce, to taste

1–2 bird's eye chillies, finely chopped, to taste

large handful of coriander, chopped

large handful of mint, chopped

1 Preheat the oven to 200°C (400°F/Gas 6). Rub the fish with the 1 tsp oil and the salt and arrange on a baking sheet. Roast in the oven for 12–15 minutes, until the skin crisps. Cool.

2 Put the fish in a food processor and whizz until finely chopped. Shape into golf balls. Heat the oil for deep-frying to 180°C (350°F) in a large pan or deep-fat fryer (see page 308).

3 Drop each fish ball into the hot oil and deep-fry in small batches for about 3 minutes until brown and crispy. Lift on to kitchen paper to drain, and keep warm.

4 Toss all the salad ingredients together in a shallow bowl until evenly mixed.

5 Whisk the dressing ingredients together and toss into the salad with the peanuts. Serve with the fish balls, lime wedges, and chilli sauce.

Salade Niçoise

This well-known French salad is substantial enough to serve as a main course for two.

The fish

Tuna, or swordfish

- **PREP** 15 mins ▪ **COOK** 7–8 mins ▪ **SERVES** 4

Ingredients

150g (5½oz) green beans, trimmed

4 tuna steaks, about 150g (5½oz) each

150ml (5fl oz) extra virgin olive oil, plus extra for brushing

salt and freshly ground black pepper

2 tsp Dijon mustard

1 garlic clove, crushed

3 tbsp white wine vinegar

juice of ½ lemon

8 anchovy fillets in olive oil, drained

1 red onion, finely sliced

250g (9oz) plum tomatoes, quartered lengthways

12 black olives

2 romaine lettuce hearts, trimmed and torn into bite-sized pieces

8–10 basil leaves

4 eggs, hard-boiled and quartered

1 Cook the beans in a saucepan of gently boiling water for 3–4 minutes, or until just tender. Drain the beans and quickly tip them into a bowl of iced water.

2 Preheat a ridged griddle pan over a medium-high heat. Brush the tuna steaks with 1–2 tbsp olive oil and season to taste. Sear the steaks for 2 minutes on each side; the centres should be slightly pink. Set aside. Drain the beans again.

3 Meanwhile, whisk together the mustard, garlic, vinegar, lemon juice, and remaining olive oil. Season to taste.

4 Place the beans, anchovies, onion, tomatoes, olives, lettuce, and basil in a large bowl. Drizzle with the vinaigrette and gently toss.

5 Divide the salad among 4 plates and top with the eggs. Cut the tuna steaks in half and arrange on top of each plate.

RED SNAPPER FLAVOUR PAIRINGS:

Snapper is always great with the Asian tastes of sesame oil, soy sauce, ginger, garlic, coriander, palm sugar, and Thai or Vietnamese fish sauces.

Oriental cucumber salad with smoked salmon

Cucumber slices combine well with the flavour of smoked salmon.

The fish

Smoked salmon, or cold-smoked trout

- **PREP** 10 mins ▪ **COOK** none ▪ **SERVES** 6

Ingredients

2 large cucumbers

salt and freshly ground black pepper

400g (14oz) smoked salmon, cut into long strips

1 lime, cut into wedges, to garnish (optional)

For the dressing

1 garlic clove, grated or finely chopped

1 tbsp Thai fish sauce

2 tbsp groundnut oil

60ml (2fl oz) white wine vinegar

1 tbsp Thai sweet chilli dipping sauce

2 tbsp chopped coriander leaves

1 With a vegetable peeler, slice the cucumbers lengthways into ribbons, discarding the central core and seeds. Place the pieces in a bowl.

2 Make the dressing by placing all the ingredients in a jar and shaking well. Ten minutes before serving, pour the dressing over the cucumber and season to taste with salt and pepper. To serve, pile the cucumber on to individual plates, and arrange the smoked salmon on top. Sprinkle with pepper and garnish with lime wedges (if using).

Layered marinated herring salad

For convenience, this recipe uses ready-marinated herring fillets from the supermarket or deli.

The fish

Marinated herring, or marinated anchovies

- **PREP** 15 mins, plus soaking and chilling
- **COOK** none ▪ **SERVES** 6–10

Ingredients

1 sweet onion, finely sliced

250ml (8fl oz) soured cream

120ml (4fl oz) plain yogurt

1 tbsp fresh lemon juice

¼ tsp caster sugar

2 tart dessert apples, peeled, cored, and finely sliced

2 pickled dill cucumbers, sliced or chopped

salt and freshly ground black pepper

300g (10oz) marinated herring fillets, drained

2 cooked potatoes, diced (optional)

1 cooked beetroot, sliced (optional)

1 tbsp chopped dill, to garnish

1 Put the onion in a bowl, cover with cold water, and leave to soak for 15 minutes. Drain well, then toss with the soured cream, yogurt, lemon juice, and sugar. Stir in the apple and pickled cucumber, and season to taste with salt and pepper.

2 Place half the herring in a serving dish and top with the potatoes and the beetroot (if using). Cover with half the soured cream sauce. Layer on the remaining herring, potatoes, and beetroot, then add the remaining sauce.

3 Cover the dish tightly with cling film and refrigerate for at least 5 hours. Sprinkle with dill just before serving. Good with sourdough or pumpernickel bread.

Prepare ahead

The salad benefits from being assembled up to 2 days in advance and chilled.

Smoked trout and pancetta salad

The bitter leaves and radishes combine well with smoky fish in this light lunch or starter.

The fish

Hot-smoked trout, or kiln-roasted smoked salmon, or smoked mackerel

- **PREP** 10 mins • **COOK** 5 mins • **SERVES** 6

Ingredients

350g (12oz) hot-smoked trout fillets

12 thin slices of pancetta

2 bunches of watercress, washed

2 heads of white chicory, leaves divided

140g (5oz) feta cheese, cubed

5 small radishes, finely sliced

2 shallots, finely sliced

For the dressing

1 tbsp red wine vinegar

90ml (3fl oz) extra virgin olive oil

1 tsp caster sugar

juice of ½ lemon

1 tsp Dijon mustard

salt and freshly ground black pepper

1 Skin the trout, if necessary, and carefully remove any bones. Heat a frying pan and fry the pancetta for 5 minutes, or until crisp.

2 Make the dressing by placing all the ingredients in a jar and shaking well. Season. Place the watercress and chicory on to a serving plate, scatter over large flakes of trout, then add the pancetta, feta, radishes, and shallots. Drizzle with the dressing and serve.

Prepare ahead

The dressing can be made, covered, and chilled up to 1 week in advance. Whisk before using.

Salmon salad with mint yogurt dressing

So fresh tasting and glamorous, yet one of the easiest dishes to make.

The fish

Salmon, or trout or tuna

- **PREP** 15 mins • **COOK** 25 mins • **SERVES** 4

Ingredients

2 tbsp red wine vinegar

2 tbsp finely chopped fresh mint, plus extra mint leaves to serve

4 tbsp Greek-style yogurt

salt and freshly ground black pepper

550g (1¼lb) salmon fillets, pinboned and skinned

handful of chopped fresh dill

1 lemon, sliced

1 Preheat the oven to 200°C (400°F/Gas 6).

2 Put the vinegar, mint, and yogurt in a bowl, season, and whisk. Set aside.

3 Lay the salmon on a large piece of foil. Sprinkle with the dill, and overlap a few slices of lemon on top. Season, and loosely seal the foil to make a parcel. Place on a baking tray, and bake in the hot oven for 20–25 minutes. Allow to cool.

4 Transfer the salmon to a plate, drizzle over the dressing, and scatter with fresh mint leaves. Serve with a cucumber salad.

Crab salad with grapefruit and coriander

For a professional finish, tightly pack the crab for each serving into a small pastry cutter, then slide out on to the plates.

The fish
White crab meat, or prawns or cockles

- **PREP** 10 mins ▪ **COOK** none ▪ **SERVES** 4

Ingredients
350g (12oz) fresh white crab meat, or canned white crab meat, drained

handful of baby salad leaves

handful of coriander

2 pink grapefruits, peeled, segmented, and pith removed

For the dressing
3 tbsp extra virgin olive oil

1 tbsp white wine vinegar

pinch of sugar

salt and freshly ground black pepper

1 Make the dressing by placing all the ingredients in a jar and shaking vigorously.

2 Mix the crab with a drizzle of the dressing. Divide the salad leaves and half the coriander leaves among 4 serving plates, and scatter over the grapefruit segments.

3 When ready to serve, drizzle the salad with the remaining dressing. Divide the crab among the plates, spooning it neatly on top of the leaves. Scatter over the remaining coriander, and serve immediately.

Prepare ahead
Make the dressing up to 1 week in advance, and keep in a jar in the refrigerator. Shake to re-emulsify before use.

Variation
Chilli crab with grapefruit and coriander
Add a pinch of chilli flakes or a deseeded and chopped fresh chilli to the dressing.

Crab and mango salad

With fruity mango, this makes a lovely summer lunch. Buy the crab the day you make it.

The fish
Crab, or lobster or Dublin Bay prawns

- **PREP** 15 mins ▪ **COOK** none ▪ **SERVES** 4

Ingredients
a few mint leaves, roughly chopped

handful of coriander leaves, roughly chopped

handful of mixed salad leaves, such as rocket, spinach, and watercress

1 shallot, finely chopped

350g (12oz) fresh crab, white and brown meat separated

1 ripe avocado, sliced lengthways

For the dressing
1 ripe mango, roughly chopped

zest and juice of ½ lime

3 tbsp olive oil

1 To make the dressing, put the mango, lime zest and juice, and olive oil in a food processor and blend until smooth. Add a little water if it's too thick.

2 For the salad, mix together the herbs and salad leaves. Add the shallot and toss in a little of the dressing. Divide the salad between 4 plates and arrange a spoonful each of the white and brown crab meat on top. Serve with the avocado slices and the remaining dressing on the side, and slices of warm soda or brown bread and butter.

Prepare ahead
Make the dressing up to 3 hours in advance, cover, and refrigerate. Whisk well before using.

Prawn, grapefruit, and avocado salad

Simple enough for brunch, but special enough to serve to dinner guests.

The fish

Tiger prawns, or lobster, white crab meat, squid, or scallops

- **PREP** 15 mins · **COOK** none · **SERVES** 6

Ingredients

30 cooked tiger prawns, peeled and deveined (see page 285)

2 large pink grapefruit, peeled, segmented, and pith removed

handful of mint leaves, torn

3 radishes, finely sliced

3 spring onions, finely sliced

2 avocados, peeled and cut into chunks or slices

bunch of watercress

salad leaves

For the dressing

3 tbsp Thai fish sauce

3 tbsp lime juice

2 tbsp caster sugar

2 tbsp olive oil

1 Make the dressing by placing all the ingredients in a jar and shaking vigorously.

2 Pat the prawns dry with kitchen paper, then toss them in a little of the dressing.

3 Place the remaining salad ingredients in a large bowl and toss well with a little more dressing. Divide between 6 plates. Arrange the prawns on top of each plate and drizzle with some of the remaining dressing to serve.

Prepare ahead

The dressing can be made several days in advance and kept refrigerated. Shake the jar to re-emulsify before use.

Vietnamese salad of grilled prawns with papaya

A beautiful mix of fresh, clean flavours.

The fish

Prawns, or squid or scallops

- **PREP** 15 mins · **COOK** 2–3 mins · **SERVES** 4

Ingredients

12 large raw prawns, peeled and deveined, heads and tails removed (see page 285)

2 tbsp vegetable oil

1 tsp rice wine vinegar

1 tsp sugar

1 red chilli, deseeded and very finely chopped

2 garlic cloves, crushed

2 tbsp Vietnamese or Thai fish sauce

1 tbsp lime juice

1 tbsp chopped mint (preferably Vietnamese mint), plus extra sprigs to serve

1 green papaya, deseeded, quartered lengthways, and thinly sliced

½ cucumber, deseeded and shredded

1 Preheat the grill on its highest setting. Spread the prawns out on a foil-lined grill rack, brush with the oil, and grill for 2–3 minutes, or until they turn pink.

2 Meanwhile, whisk the vinegar, sugar, chilli, garlic, fish sauce, lime juice, and 75ml (2½fl oz) cold water in a bowl until the sugar dissolves. Add the prawns and stir to coat in the dressing. Leave to cool completely.

3 Add the mint, papaya, and cucumber and toss. Transfer the salad to a serving platter, with the prawns and mint sprigs on top.

Prepare ahead

Steps 1 and 2 can be completed several hours in advance. Store, covered, in the refrigerator. Return to room temperature before serving.

Tuna and bean salad

This classic recipe calls for canned tuna, although you can sear fresh tuna to serve with these beans, if you prefer.

The fish

Canned tuna, or canned salmon or canned mackerel

▪ **PREP** 20 mins ▪ **COOK** none ▪ **SERVES** 4

Ingredients

2 x 110g can tuna in spring water, drained

1 x 400g can mixed beans, drained

1 red onion, finely chopped

4 tbsp chopped flat-leaf parsley

1 red pepper, deseeded and finely diced

salt and freshly ground black pepper

1 garlic clove, halved

For the dressing

4 tbsp extra virgin olive oil

1 tbsp lemon juice

pinch of sugar

1 Put the tuna into a bowl and break into large chunks with a fork. Add the beans and mix.

2 Stir in the onion, parsley, and red pepper and season generously.

3 Make the dressing by whisking the olive oil with the lemon juice and sugar. Season to taste.

4 Rub the cut side of the garlic around a large salad bowl. Add the dressing to the tuna and beans, toss, and pile into the bowl. Serve with garlic bread.

Prepare ahead

The salad can be made up to 1 day ahead, covered, and chilled. The flavours will deepen. Bring to room temperature before eating.

Herring salad with potatoes and beetroot

Oil-rich and packed with omega 3, herrings have a fairly short shelf life, so preserving them is common.

The fish

Pickled herring, or pickled sprats, marinated anchovies, or smoked mackerel

▪ **PREP** 15 mins ▪ **COOK** 15 mins ▪ **SERVES** 4

Ingredients

450g (1lb) salad potatoes, scrubbed

4 large beetroots, cooked, peeled, and diced

4 spring onions, finely sliced

450g (1lb) cured or pickled herring, or rollmops, cut into 5cm (2in) pieces (see page 297)

sprigs of dill, to serve

For the dressing

150ml (5fl oz) mayonnaise

1 tbsp creamed horseradish

lemon juice, to taste

1–2 tsp German or Dijon mustard

salt and freshly ground black pepper

1 Cook the potatoes in boiling water for about 15 minutes, or until tender, drain and thickly slice. Put into a bowl, and add the beetroot and spring onions.

2 In a separate bowl, mix the mayonnaise, horseradish, lemon juice, and mustard to taste. Season with salt and pepper. Add to the potato and beetroot and toss until well coated.

3 Divide the potato salad between 4 dishes and top with the herrings and dill to serve.

Prepare ahead

You can make the potato salad in advance, cover, and chill for 1–2 days. Bring to room temperature before continuing.

SPRAT FLAVOUR PAIRINGS: These startlingly silver fish are lovely with earthy beetroot, piquant white or red wine vinegars, or with coriander, and spicy coriander seeds.

Lobster salad with watercress

A very special summer salad, ideal for outdoor dining.

The fish

Lobster, or white crab meat, Dublin Bay prawns, or tiger prawns

- **PREP** 20 mins ▪ **COOK** none ▪ **SERVES** 4

Ingredients

½ red onion, finely sliced

1 tsp red wine vinegar

4 cooked lobster tails, halved

1 large bunch of watercress, tough stalks removed

½ fennel bulb, very finely sliced

8 sun-blush tomatoes, chopped

fresh herbs, such as chervil, dill, or chives, to garnish

For the dressing

1 egg

1 egg yolk

2 tsp Dijon mustard

grated zest and juice of 1 lemon

400ml (14fl oz) sunflower oil

10g (¼oz) chervil or chives

salt and freshly ground black pepper

1 To make the dressing, place the egg, egg yolk, mustard, and lemon zest and juice into a blender. Blend on a low speed while slowly adding the oil. Add the chervil. Season to taste with salt and pepper. Set aside.

2 Place the red onion in a bowl with the vinegar, and leave to stand for 10 minutes.

3 Remove all the meat from the lobster tails, keeping the pieces of meat as whole as possible.

4 Arrange the watercress on plates, scatter over the fennel, the drained onion slices, and the tomatoes. Place the lobster meat on top, drizzle with the dressing, and garnish with the herbs.

Prepare ahead

The dressing can be made, covered, and chilled up to 1 day in advance, but only stir in the herbs just before using, to prevent discolouration.

Calamari salad with mint and dill

Fresh herbs and grilled squid make a delicious warm salad.

The fish

Squid, or cuttlefish

- **PREP** 20 mins, plus marinating
- **COOK** 5 mins ▪ **SERVES** 4

Ingredients

1kg (2¼lb) small squid, gutted and cleaned

85g (3oz) lamb's lettuce, or watercress

12 sprigs of mint

1 small red onion, finely sliced

salt and freshly ground black pepper

juice of 1 lime

2 tbsp chopped dill

4 tbsp extra virgin olive oil

For the marinade

2 tbsp chopped flat-leaf parsley

1 tbsp chopped mint

1 garlic clove, crushed

2 tsp ground coriander

1 tsp ground cumin

2 tsp paprika

4 tbsp olive oil

1 Cut off the squid tentacles and remove the beak-like mouth from the centre. Cut the body in half lengthways and score the flesh to form a diamond pattern. Cut the tentacles into bite-sized pieces. Place in a bowl.

2 Combine the marinade ingredients, adding the oil gradually to make a paste. Coat the squid in the mixture. Cover, chill, and marinate for at least 30 minutes.

3 Combine the lamb's lettuce with the mint and onion. Set aside.

4 Preheat the grill on its highest setting. Arrange the squid on a foil-lined grill pan and grill for 4–5 minutes, turning once. Season to taste and sprinkle with a little lime juice.

5 Place the remaining lime juice, the dill, and extra virgin olive oil in a jug, season, then whisk well. Spoon the dressing over the salad and top with the squid. Serve immediately.

Seafood and fennel salad with anchovy dressing

This crisp, sweet, mixed-seafood salad can be assembled in an instant.

The fish

Any mixed seafood, such as prawns, mussels, or squid rings

- **PREP** 15 mins ▪ **COOK** none ▪ **SERVES** 4

Ingredients

handful of mixed crisp lettuce leaves, such as Cos

1 fennel bulb, finely sliced

450g (1lb) ready-cooked mixed seafood, rinsed and dried

6 anchovy fillets in olive oil, drained

1 hot green chilli, deseeded and finely chopped

handful of coriander, roughly chopped

lemon wedges, to serve

rice noodles, to serve

For the dressing

3 tbsp extra virgin olive oil

1 tbsp white wine vinegar

6 anchovy fillets in olive oil, drained and finely chopped

pinch of sugar

handful of flat-leaf parsley, finely chopped

salt and freshly ground black pepper

1 Make the dressing. In a jug, whisk together the oil and vinegar. Add the anchovies, sugar, and parsley, season well, and whisk again.

2 In a bowl, toss together the salad leaves, fennel, seafood, anchovies, chilli, and coriander. Pour over the dressing, and carefully mix together. Pile up in a shallow serving bowl, and serve with lemon wedges for squeezing over, and some rice noodles.

Prepare ahead

Make the dressing up to 1 day ahead, cover and chill. Add the parsley just before serving.

Marinated squid salad

An economical and dramatic-looking dish.

The fish

Squid, or cuttlefish or baby octopus

- **PREP** 15 mins, plus marinating
- **COOK** 3 mins ▪ **SERVES** 4

Ingredients

300g (10oz) small squid, gutted and cleaned

7 tbsp olive oil

salt and freshly ground black pepper

2 tbsp white wine vinegar

3 garlic cloves, crushed

1 tsp paprika

handful of flat-leaf parsley, finely chopped

1 Cut the squid into pieces – a mixture of strips and rings – brush with a little oil and season well.

2 Heat 1 tbsp of the oil in a frying pan, add the squid, and cook over a medium heat, stirring constantly, for 2–3 minutes, or until the squid is cooked. Remove from the heat and transfer to a serving bowl.

3 Mix the remaining oil with the vinegar, garlic, paprika, and parsley, then season with salt and pepper. Pour over the squid, combine well, and leave to marinate for at least 30 minutes. Serve with fresh crusty bread and a green salad.

Soups

New England clam chowder

Clams must be cooked on the day of purchase, so when you find great clams, make sure you also have all the ingredients in your kitchen for this fabulous soup.

The fish

Clams, or mussels

- **PREP** 25–30 mins ▪ **COOK** 35–40 mins
- **SERVES** 4

Ingredients

800g (1¾lb) clams, thoroughly washed

1 tbsp oil

115g (4oz) thick-cut rindless streaky bacon rashers, diced

2 floury potatoes, such as King Edwards, peeled and cut into chunks

1 onion, finely chopped

2 tbsp plain flour

600ml (1 pint) whole milk

salt and freshly ground black pepper

120ml (4fl oz) single cream

2 tbsp finely chopped flat-leaf parsley, to garnish

1 Discard any open clams, then shell the rest, reserving the juices (see page 279). Add enough water to the juices to make 600ml (1 pint). Chop the clams. Heat the oil in a large, heavy saucepan, and fry the bacon over a medium heat for 5 minutes, or until crisp. Remove.

2 Add the potatoes and onion and fry gently for 5 minutes. Stir in the flour for 2 minutes, then add the clam juice and milk, and season. Cover, reduce the heat, and simmer for 20 minutes, or until the potatoes are tender.

3 Add the clams and simmer, uncovered, for 5 minutes. Stir in the cream and reheat without boiling. Serve sprinkled with bacon and parsley, and provide saltines or cream crackers on the side.

Variation

Manhattan cod and mussel chowder
Replace the clams with 1kg (2¼lb) mussels, adding 250ml (8fl oz) dry white wine to the juices before topping up with water. When adding the potatoes, add 2 x 400g (14oz) cans tomatoes, 4 garlic cloves, finely chopped, and 1–2 tbsp tomato purée. Use only half the flour and replace the milk with fish stock. Add 1kg (2¼lb) cod fillets, cut into chunks, at the start of step 3. Omit the cream. Sprinkle with thyme and serve with wholewheat bread.

Brodetto abruzzese

This very plain and simple fish stew heralds from Tuscany and was made by impoverished fishermen landing their catch in the Adriatic.

The fish

Any mixed fish, such as hake, mullet, John Dory, rascasse, or sea bass, and mussels, or clams

- **PREP** 30–40 mins ▪ **COOK** 1 hr ▪ **SERVES** 4

Ingredients

700g (1½lb) white fish fillets, pinboned and skinned

5 tbsp extra virgin olive oil

2 garlic cloves, chopped

½ tsp chilli flakes

8 tomatoes, skinned and chopped, juices reserved (see page 112)

2 tsp tomato purée

150ml (5fl oz) medium white wine

sea salt and freshly ground black pepper

340g (12oz) mussels, prepared (see page 278)

crusty bread, to serve

For the stock

1 tbsp olive oil

1 garlic clove, chopped

1 onion, thickly sliced

4–5 fish heads, gills removed, well washed

4 tbsp white wine vinegar

1 bay leaf

1 Cut all the fish into roughly even 3–5cm (1–2in) pieces, and refrigerate.

2 Heat the oil for the stock in a large saucepan, add the garlic, and onion, and fry for 3–4 minutes, then add the fish heads and stir well for a further 3–4 minutes. Add the vinegar, bay leaf, and water to cover. Bring to a boil, reduce the heat to very low, and simmer gently for 25 minutes. Strain.

3 Heat the oil for the soup in another large saucepan over a medium heat, add the garlic and chilli and fry for 1 minute, then add the tomatoes, juices, and tomato purée. Cook over a medium heat so the tomatoes break down, then add the wine and simmer for 3 minutes. Pour over 1 litre (1¾ pints) of the stock, bring to a boil, reduce the heat, and simmer for 10 minutes. Season.

4 Spoon a little soup into a large casserole, top with the fish and mussels and pour over the remaining soup. Place over a low heat and cook for 12–15 minutes, or until the fish is cooked and the mussels have opened. Serve with crusty bread.

HAKE FLAVOUR PAIRINGS: Economical, and meaty, hake is a great favourite in Spain, so try it with Iberian ingredients such as fruity olive oil, garlic, chorizo, cured ham, and smoked paprika.

Brandied lobster chowder

A luxurious treat, the sweet lobster meat is flattered by warming brandy.

The fish

Lobster, or white crab meat

- **PREP** 20 mins ▪ **COOK** 1 hr ▪ **SERVES** 4

Ingredients

1 small cooked lobster

150ml (5fl oz) dry white wine

1 bay leaf

knob of unsalted butter

2 shallots, finely chopped

4 tbsp brandy

1 large tomato, skinned and diced (see page 112)

2 tsp anchovy essence

4 large new potatoes, scraped and diced

8 baby corn, cut in short lengths

salt and freshly ground black pepper

60g (2oz) mangetout, cut in short lengths

5 tbsp single cream

4 thick slices of lemon, to serve

4 sprigs of parsley, to serve

1 Remove the meat from the lobster (see page 291). Roughly chop the shell and put it in a saucepan with the claw shells and legs. Add 850ml (scant 1½ pints) water, the wine, and bay leaf. Bring to a boil, reduce the heat, cover, and simmer for 30 minutes. Strain and reserve the stock.

2 Melt the butter in a large saucepan over a low heat. Add the shallots and stir for 1 minute. Add the brandy, ignite, and shake the pan until the flames subside. Add the tomato, anchovy essence, potatoes, and corn. Pour in the stock, season, and bring to a boil. Reduce the heat, cover, and simmer gently for 20 minutes.

3 Meanwhile, blanch the mangetout in boiling water for 2 minutes. Drain. Add them to the soup with the cream and lobster meat. Taste and season again. Reheat the soup, but do not boil. Serve with lemon slices and sprigs of parsley, nutty rye bread, and butter.

Prepare ahead

Make the soup base up to the end of step 2, then cool, and chill, covered, for up to 1 day. Bring to room temperature before continuing.

Coley and mussel chowder

A hearty soup laden with chunks of coley, with mussels to add colour and flavour. This is a great, warming dish for the colder months.

The fish

Coley, or cod or pollock and mussels, or clams

- **PREP** 45–50 mins ▪ **COOK** 60 mins
- **SERVES** 8

Ingredients

3 potatoes, about 500g (1lb 2oz) in total

1kg (2¼lb) coley fillets, pinboned and skinned

1.5 litres (2¾ pints) fish stock

2 bay leaves

125ml (4fl oz) medium white wine

175g (6oz) streaky bacon rashers, diced

2 onions, finely chopped

2 celery sticks, finely chopped

1 carrot, finely chopped

2 tsp dried thyme

60g (2oz) plain flour

1kg (2¼lb) mussels, prepared (see page 278)

250ml (8fl oz) double cream

salt and freshly ground black pepper

leaves from 5–7 sprigs of dill, finely chopped, to serve

1 Peel and dice the potatoes into 1cm (½in) cubes. Cut the coley into 2.5cm (1in) cubes.

2 Put the stock and bay leaves into a large saucepan and pour in the wine. Bring to a boil and simmer for 10 minutes.

3 Put the bacon in another large saucepan and stir over a medium heat until crisp. Add the onions, celery, carrot, and thyme. Stir until soft. Sprinkle in the flour and cook for a minute. Add the stock and bring to a boil, stirring until thickened. Add the potatoes and simmer for about 40 minutes, until very tender.

4 Crush some potatoes against the pan and tip in the mussels. Simmer for 1–2 minutes, then add the coley for 2–3 minutes more. Pour in the cream, season, and bring just to a boil.

5 Discard any mussels that have not opened. Ladle into warmed bowls and sprinkle with dill.

Creamy smoked trout soup

This comforting soup is made with a roux-based sauce, so use good stock to make it really sing.

The fish

Hot-smoked trout, or hot-smoked salmon or smoked mackerel

- **PREP** 15 mins ▪ **COOK** 10 mins ▪ **SERVES** 6

Ingredients

50g (1¾oz) butter

35g (1oz) plain flour

750ml (1¼ pints) hot vegetable or fish stock

250ml (8fl oz) whipping cream

4 tbsp medium white wine

2–3 tsp Worcestershire sauce

salt and freshly ground black pepper

squeeze of lemon juice

375g (13oz) hot-smoked trout fillets, skinned and flaked

2 tbsp chopped parsley, to serve

1 Over a low heat, melt the butter in a pan, stir in the flour, and mix until smooth. Cook for 2–3 minutes, stirring constantly. Gradually whisk in the hot stock, making sure there are no lumps. Bring to a boil, then cook, uncovered, over a low heat for about 3 minutes, stirring.

2 Add the cream, wine, Worcestershire sauce, salt and pepper to taste, and lemon juice, then bring back to a boil.

3 Add the fish pieces and heat them through. Sprinkle the soup with parsley and serve.

Prepare ahead

Make the soup base up to the end of step 2, then cool, and chill, covered, for up to 2 days. Bring to room temperature before continuing.

Salmon chowder with whisky

If you would like to thicken up this rich soup, blend in 1 tbsp cornflour with the whisky.

The fish

Salmon, or trout

- **PREP** 20 mins ▪ **COOK** 40 mins ▪ **SERVES** 4–5

Ingredients

1 onion, chopped

1 leek, sliced

15g (½oz) butter

1 large waxy potato, peeled and diced

300g (10oz) salmon, pinboned, skinned, and cut into small chunks

60g (2oz) fresh or frozen sweetcorn

60g (2oz) fresh or frozen peas (optional)

600ml (1 pint) fish or chicken stock

150ml (5fl oz) dry white wine

1 bay leaf

1 large tomato, skinned, deseeded, and chopped (see page 112)

salt and freshly ground black pepper

2 tbsp whisky

4 tbsp double cream

chopped parsley, to serve

1 Fry the onion and leek gently in the butter, stirring for about 5 minutes until soft, but not brown. Add the remaining ingredients except the whisky, cream, and parsley. Bring to a boil, reduce the heat, part-cover, and simmer for 30 minutes until the potatoes are tender.

2 Remove the bay leaf. Stir in the whisky and cream, and simmer for 1 minute. Taste and adjust the seasoning, if necessary. Ladle into warm bowls and sprinkle with parsley.

SUSTAINABILITY CHOICE

Buy local

Buying local supports the local economy and small, independent fishing businesses. Local fleets tend to be responsible fishers because they need to maintain fish stocks to preserve their own livelihoods. Smaller, local boats also produce a high-quality catch – they spend relatively small periods of time at sea (between 2 and 10 hours) and the fish are placed on ice very soon after catching. Also, buying local cuts down on food miles; many fresh fish are air-freighted over large distances. If you buy local it is easy to establish exactly where and how the fish were caught.

Mouclade

An aromatic and wonderfully rich soup from France's Atlantic coast.

The fish
Mussels, or clams

- **PREP** 20 mins ▪ **COOK** 30 mins ▪ **SERVES** 4

Ingredients
1.5kg (3lb 3oz) small mussels, prepared (see page 278)

45g (1½oz) butter

1 large banana shallot, chopped

360ml (12fl oz) dry white wine

several sprigs of flat-leaf parsley

¼ small fennel bulb, roughly chopped

1 bay leaf

sea salt and freshly ground black pepper

pinch of cayenne pepper

1 large egg yolk

5 tbsp soured cream or crème fraîche

1 large garlic clove, crushed

½ tsp mild paprika or 1 tsp mild curry powder

a few strands of saffron or ¼ tsp ground saffron

chunks of fresh warm bread, to serve

1 Put a large sauté pan over a moderate heat. Tip in the mussels with 15g (½oz) of the butter, the shallot, wine, and 350ml (12fl oz) water. Add the parsley, fennel, and bay leaf, season, and add the cayenne. Increase the heat and bring to a boil. Cover and cook for 4–5 minutes, or until the mussels open, shaking a few times.

2 Lift out the mussels, discarding any that haven't opened. Strain the liquor through a muslin-lined sieve and set aside. Shell all but 12 mussels, place in a bowl, and moisten with cooking liquid. Keep warm.

3 In a small bowl, mix the egg yolk and cream. In a separate bowl, mash the remaining butter with the garlic, paprika, and saffron.

4 Put a large saucepan over a low heat. Add the butter mixture and, when it bubbles, the mussel liquor, and bring to a simmer. Remove 3 tbsp of this and whisk it into the egg mixture, then whisk this back into the pan. Divide all the mussels between 4 warmed bowls. Pour the broth over and serve with the bread.

Prepare ahead
You can prepare this ahead, but reheat the mussels as gently as possible or they will become tough and overcooked.

Lobster bisque

A rich and luxurious shellfish soup.

The fish
Lobster, or Dublin Bay prawns or prawns

- **PREP** 35 mins ▪ **COOK** 1 hr 15 mins ▪ **SERVES** 4

Ingredients
1 lobster, about 1kg (2¼lb) in total, cooked

45g (1½oz) butter

1 onion, finely chopped

1 carrot, finely chopped

2 celery sticks, finely chopped

1 leek, finely chopped

½ bulb fennel, finely chopped

1 bay leaf

1 sprig of tarragon

2 garlic cloves, crushed

75g (2½oz) tomato purée

4 tomatoes, coarsely chopped

120ml (4fl oz) Cognac or brandy

100ml (3½fl oz) dry white wine or vermouth

1.7 litres (3 pints) fish stock

120ml (4fl oz) double cream

salt and freshly ground black pepper

pinch of cayenne pepper

juice of ½ lemon

snipped chives, to garnish

1 Split the lobster and remove the meat (see page 291). Crack all the shells with the back of a knife. Chop the shells into coarse pieces and put the meat into the refrigerator.

2 Melt the butter in a large pan over a medium heat, add the vegetables, herbs, and garlic, and cook for 10 minutes, or until softened, stirring occasionally. Add the lobster shells. Stir in the tomato purée, tomatoes, Cognac, white wine, and stock. Bring to a boil and simmer for 1 hour.

3 Let cool slightly, then pulse-blend in a food processor until the shell breaks into very small pieces. Push through a coarse sieve, then pass through a fine sieve. Return to the heat.

4 Bring to a boil, add the lobster meat and cream, then season, adding cayenne and lemon. Serve in warmed bowls, with chives.

Prepare ahead
The bisque can be made to the end of step 3 up to 1 day in advance. Cover, and chill. Finish the recipe just before serving.

MUSSEL FLAVOUR PAIRINGS: The feisty taste of mussels is equally good with dry white wine, butter, cream, parsley, and garlic, and with pungent ginger, lemongrass, chilli, and spices, or even aniseed fennel and Pernod.

Creamy scallop bisque

A rich broth with sweet scallops and spicy chorizo. Serve as a starter at a dinner party.

The fish
Prawns, cod or pollock, and scallops

- **PREP** 20 mins ▪ **COOK** 40 mins ▪ **SERVES** 4

Ingredients
300ml (10fl oz) dry white wine

15g (½oz) butter

1 small onion, finely chopped

1 small shallot, very finely chopped

1 ripe tomato, chopped

200g (7oz) raw prawns, peeled and deveined (see page 285)

100g (3½oz) cod, pinboned, skinned, and cut into chunks

12 small or 6 large scallops

2 tbsp chopped flat-leaf parsley

2 tsp dill seeds

3 tbsp brandy

sea salt and freshly ground black pepper

100ml (3½fl oz) single cream

75g (2½oz) chorizo, diced

1 tbsp finely chopped chives, to garnish

1 Bring 750ml (1¼ pints) water to a boil with the wine. Meanwhile put the butter in a pan over a medium heat. Add the onion and shallot and soften until golden. Add the tomato, prawns, fish, scallop roes, parsley, and dill seeds; stir for 5 minutes. Add the brandy, and cook for 1 minute. Pour in the boiling wine and season. Reduce the heat, and simmer for 10 minutes. Leave to cool, then roughly mash with the back of a spoon. Gently heat the cream.

2 Purée the soup in a blender, strain back into the pan and stir in the cream. Return to a simmer. Remove from the heat, adjust the seasoning, and keep warm.

3 Put a frying pan over a medium heat. Add the chorizo and fry until crisp. Set aside on a plate lined with kitchen paper and keep warm.

4 Quickly add the scallop muscles to the pan for 2 minutes, turn, and cook for 1 minute. Ladle the soup into bowls and add the scallops. Scatter over the chorizo to serve.

Prepare ahead

Make the soup to the end of step 2, cover, and refrigerate for 1 day. Reheat gently.

Fish soup with fennel

Robustly flavoured with brandy and orange.

The fish
Mussels, any firm white fish, such as monkfish, and tiger prawns

- **PREP** 10 mins ▪ **COOK** 1 hr ▪ **SERVES** 4–6

Ingredients
30g (1oz) butter

3 tbsp olive oil

1 large fennel bulb, finely chopped

2 garlic cloves, crushed

1 small leek, sliced

4 ripe plum tomatoes, chopped

3 tbsp brandy

¼ tsp saffron threads, infused in a little hot water

grated zest of ½ orange

1 bay leaf

1.7 litres (3 pints) fish stock

300g (10½oz) potatoes, diced and parboiled for 5 minutes

4 tbsp dry white wine

500g (1lb 2oz) mussels, prepared (see page 278)

salt and freshly ground black pepper

500g (1lb 2oz) firm white fish, cubed

6 raw tiger prawns, deveined (see page 285)

parsley, chopped, to garnish

1 Heat the butter with 2 tbsp of the oil in a large, deep pan. Stir in the fennel, garlic, and leek, and stir over a moderate heat for 5 minutes, or until softened and lightly browned.

2 Stir in the tomatoes and brandy, and boil for 2 minutes, or until reduced slightly. Stir in the saffron, orange zest, bay leaf, stock, and potatoes. Bring to a boil, reduce the heat and skim any scum from the surface. Cover and simmer for 20 minutes, or until the potatoes are tender. Remove the bay leaf.

3 Meanwhile, bring the remaining oil and the wine to a boil in a deep pan. Add the mussels, cover tightly, and shake well over a high heat for 2–3 minutes. Discard any mussels that do not open. Strain, add the liquid to the soup and season. Bring to a boil, add the fish and prawns, reduce the heat, cover, and simmer gently for 5 minutes. Add the mussels and return almost to a boil. Serve sprinkled with parsley.

Prepare ahead

The soup can be made to the end of step 2, covered, and refrigerated up to 3 days in advance. Reheat gently before continuing.

Cotriade

This soup from Brittany was originally a way to use the leftover catch of the day.

The fish
Any mixed fish, such as haddock, pollock, or ling

▪ **PREP** 20 mins ▪ **COOK** 30 mins ▪ **SERVES** 4

Ingredients
2 large floury potatoes, peeled

2 tbsp mild olive oil

30g (1oz) butter

2 Spanish onions, coarsely chopped

1 litre (1¾ pints) light fish stock

3 sprigs of thyme

3 bay leaves

3 sprigs of flat-leaf parsley

sea salt and freshly ground black pepper

800g (1¾lb) mixed fish, skinned, pinboned, and cut into large chunks

4 thick slices country bread, to serve

For the dressing
5–6 tbsp mild olive oil

½ tsp Dijon mustard

sea salt and freshly ground black pepper

1 tbsp white wine or cider vinegar

2 tbsp finely chopped flat-leaf parsley

1 Cut the potatoes into chunks. Put the oil and butter in a large, heavy sauté pan. Add the onions and soften over a moderate heat until just golden, stirring frequently. Add the stock, then tip in the potatoes and herbs. Season lightly, stir, cover and cook for 12–15 minutes or until the potatoes are almost cooked.

2 Place the fish in the pan and season lightly. Gently stir, then cook for 10 minutes, or until the fish just starts to flake when pressed.

3 Meanwhile, in a cup, mix the oil and mustard, and season, then whisk in the vinegar until emulsified. Stir in the parsley.

4 Remove the soup from the heat and adjust the seasoning. Lift out the herbs. Put the bread in 4 warmed bowls and moisten with a little dressing. Ladle over the soup and drizzle on the remaining dressing. Serve hot.

Prepare ahead
Make the dressing up to 6 hours ahead, and cover. Whisk to re-emulsify before use.

Keralan prawn soup

This fragrant soup is from southern India. If you use dried curry leaves, add with the stock.

The fish
Tiger prawns

▪ **PREP** 20 mins ▪ **COOK** 40 mins
▪ **SERVES** 4–6

Ingredients
1 tsp black peppercorns

¾ tsp mustard seeds

2 tsp coriander seeds

½ tsp fenugreek seeds

2–3 large red chillies

4 garlic cloves, chopped

5cm (2in) fresh root ginger, chopped

2–3 tbsp vegetable oil

small handful of fresh curry leaves

2 onions, finely chopped

750ml (1¼ pints) fish stock

250ml (8fl oz) coconut milk

250g (9oz) raw tiger prawns, peeled and deveined (see page 285)

1 tbsp coconut cream

2 tbsp chopped coriander leaves

juice of 1 lime, or to taste

1 Heat a sturdy frying pan over a low heat. Roast the peppercorns, mustard, coriander, and fenugreek seeds together for about 30 seconds, until the mustard seeds start to pop. Grind to a powder, and set aside.

2 Roughly chop the chillies (for a mild flavour, use just 2 chillies and remove the seeds). Put them in a small food processor with the garlic and ginger. Pour in 4 tbsp hot water and process to a paste. Set aside.

3 Heat the oil in a wok or saucepan. When hot, toss in the curry leaves and fry for 20 seconds. Be careful; they will spit. Add the onions, cover, and soften for 10 minutes, stirring occasionally.

4 Stir in the chilli paste and fry for 2–3 minutes, until the water evaporates. Add the ground spices and stir for 30 seconds. Pour in the stock and simmer for 20 minutes, or until reduced by one-third. Stir in the coconut milk and reheat, then add the prawns for a further 4–5 minutes. Add the coconut cream and finish with the coriander leaves and enough lime juice to sharpen.

Prepare ahead
Make this soup up to the point that the fish stock has been reduced, cover, and refrigerate for 1 day. Reheat gently before continuing.

Potage poissonière

This classic cream of whiting soup seems plain, but if using very fresh fish is utterly delicious.

The fish

Whiting, or haddock, coley, cod, or ling

- **PREP** 20 mins ▪ **COOK** 45 mins ▪ **SERVES** 4

Ingredients

1kg (2¼lb) whiting, filleted, with head and bones

1 small carrot, sliced

1 celery stick, sliced

1 onion, finely diced

handful of parsley stalks

sprig of thyme

1 small bay leaf

large pinch of salt

600ml (1 pint) milk

60g (2oz) butter

3 tbsp plain flour

1–2 tbsp creamed horseradish, to taste

grated nutmeg, to taste

freshly ground black pepper

2 tbsp chopped flat-leaf parsley

5 tbsp single cream

croutons, to serve

1 Pinbone and carefully skin the whiting fillets (see page 271). Set aside.

2 To make the stock, put all the whiting skin, the bones, and head (remove the gills) in a large saucepan, pour over 750ml (1¼ pints) of water, and add the carrot, celery, onion, herbs, and salt. Slowly bring to a boil, then cook over a very low heat, uncovered, for 25–30 minutes. Strain.

3 Put the whiting into a large saucepan, add the milk and poach over a low heat for 5–6 minutes. Strain the liquor and reserve. Put the fish into a food processor and whizz to a paste. Set aside.

4 Melt the butter in the rinsed-out saucepan, blend in the flour, and cook over a low heat for 1 minute. Blend in the milk and stock, and bring slowly to a boil. Simmer for 2–3 minutes.

5 Remove from the heat and whisk in the fish and horseradish, adding nutmeg, salt, and pepper. Add the parsley and cream, adjust the seasoning. Serve, with the croutons in a separate bowl.

Prepare ahead

Make the stock 1 day in advance, cover, and chill until needed.

Tom yum goong

Tamarind gives the right piquant note to this key Thai recipe for hot and sour prawn soup.

The fish

Tiger prawns, scallops, or brown shrimps

- **PREP** 10–15 mins ▪ **COOK** 15 mins
- **SERVES** 4

Ingredients

1 tbsp sunflower or peanut oil

1 tsp shrimp paste

2 bird's eye chillies, finely chopped and deseeded, if preferred

2 garlic cloves, finely chopped

2 tsp palm sugar

2 spring onions, finely sliced

60g (2oz) shiitake mushrooms, trimmed and sliced

2 tbsp tamarind paste, to taste

1 litre (1¾ pints) well-flavoured fish stock

1 stalk lemongrass, halved

5cm (2in) piece galangal or fresh root ginger, peeled and finely sliced

a few kaffir lime leaves

1–2 tbsp Thai fish sauce, to taste

1 tsp sesame oil

450g (1lb) raw tiger prawns, peeled but tail intact, deveined and butterflied (see page 285)

squeeze of lime juice, to taste

handful of roughly chopped coriander leaves

1 Heat the oil in a large pan, add the shrimp paste, and cook over a low heat for 1–2 minutes until aromatic. Add the chillies, garlic, palm sugar, spring onions, and mushrooms; stir for 2 minutes.

2 Add the tamarind, stock, lemongrass, galangal, and lime leaves. Bring to a boil and simmer for 2–3 minutes. Season with fish sauce and add the sesame oil and prawns. Poach over a low heat for 3–4 minutes or until the prawns are cooked.

3 Add lime juice, or more tamarind, or fish sauce to taste. Stir in the coriander and serve.

Variation

Tom yum talay

Begin as above, adding 3 chillies, 1 tbsp palm sugar, 3 spring onions, and 1 diced red pepper. Omit the mushrooms. Add a 400g can of coconut milk. Bring to a boil, simmer for 3 minutes. Add 500ml (16fl oz) stock, the lemongrass, galangal and lime leaves; omit the tamarind and sesame oil. Simmer for a few minutes. Add 2–3 tbsp Thai fish sauce and 450g (1lb) mixed seafood (add squid at the last minute), lime, and coriander leaves.

WHITING FLAVOUR PAIRINGS: Enjoy the delicate flavour of whiting with sweet butter, milk, and parsley, as in potage poissonière, or the equally subtle tastes of olive oil, or delicate, aniseed chervil.

Büsumer fish soup

From the German region of Schleswig-Holstein on the North Sea coast.

The fish
Any mixed, firm white fish, such as pollock or haddock, and tiger prawns

- **PREP** 15 mins ▪ **COOK** 20 mins ▪ **SERVES** 6–8

Ingredients
2 large carrots, chopped

1 large potato (King Edward or Maris Piper), peeled and diced

1 large onion, diced

1 litre (1¾ pints) hot vegetable stock

1 bay leaf

salt and freshly ground black pepper

juice of 1 lemon

500g (1lb 2oz) white fish fillets, pinboned, skinned, and cut into bite-sized pieces

200g (7oz) button or chestnut mushrooms, sliced

100g (3½oz) raw tiger prawns, peeled (see page 285)

120ml (4fl oz) double cream

½ bunch of dill, chopped, to garnish

1 Put the carrots, potato, and onion into a saucepan, add the hot stock and bay leaf, and bring to a boil. Reduce the heat and simmer for 10 minutes.

2 Sprinkle a little salt and pepper, and half the lemon juice, over the fish, then add it to the stock with the mushrooms. Simmer for another 5 minutes over a low heat.

3 Add the prawns and the remaining lemon juice, and cook for 3 minutes, or until the prawns turn pink. Remove the bay leaf and season to taste. Stir in the cream and half the dill and serve immediately, using the remaining dill to garnish.

Prepare ahead
Make the soup base up to the end of step 1, then cool, and chill, covered, for up to 3 days. Reheat over a moderate heat to a simmer before continuing.

Potato and clam soup

This is a delicious autumn soup for all the family to enjoy.

The fish
Clams, or mussels

- **PREP** 25 mins ▪ **COOK** 1 hr 15 mins
- **SERVES** 4–6

Ingredients
1kg (2¼lb) clams, thoroughly washed

120ml (4fl oz) dry white wine

2–3 tbsp olive oil

2 celery sticks, finely diced

1 red onion, finely chopped

1 carrot, finely chopped

4 tomatoes, skinned, deseeded, and chopped

2 potatoes, peeled and diced

1 sprig of rosemary

1 tbsp finely chopped flat-leaf parsley or chervil

salt and freshly ground black pepper

4–6 slices country bread

1 Throw away any clams with broken shells and any that are open and won't close when gently tapped. Put them in a large frying pan with the wine, cover, and place on a high heat for 5 minutes or until the shells open. Discard any that remain shut. Drain, reserving the liquid. Remove the clams from their shells, place in a bowl, cover, and refrigerate. Strain the cooking liquid through a fine sieve.

2 Heat the oil in a large, heavy-bottomed pan, add the celery, onion, and carrot, and cook on a low heat for 10 minutes or until light brown. Add the tomatoes, potatoes, reserved cooking liquid, and 1 litre (1¾ pints) water, and bring to a boil. Add the rosemary, then reduce the heat, cover, and simmer for 1 hour.

3 Stir in the clams and parsley or chervil, then season. Remove the rosemary, put a slice of bread in each bowl, and ladle over the soup.

Cullen skink

Named after Cullen, in north-east Scotland, where "skink" is the name for a soup or stew.

The fish

Finnan haddock, or smoked trout or smoked cod

- **PREP** 20 mins **COOK** 25 mins **SERVES** 4

Ingredients

225g (8oz) potatoes, peeled and diced

salt and freshly ground black pepper

30g (1oz) butter

2 whole Finnan haddock (or 4 small smoked haddock fillets)

1 onion, finely chopped

300ml (10fl oz) milk

1 Simmer the potatoes in salted water for 15 minutes, or until tender. Drain, then mash with the butter. Set aside.

2 Put the fish into a sauté pan. Pour in 300ml (10fl oz) water and add the onion. Poach for 8–10 minutes. Lift the fish on to a plate and pull away the flesh in large flakes. Set aside.

3 Return the fish skin and bones to the water and cook for a further 15 minutes. Strain this stock into a large jug, then add as many of the chopped onions as possible. Stir in the milk.

4 Put the milk, stock, and onion back into the saucepan, place over a medium heat and whisk in enough of the mashed potato to form a thick, creamy consistency. Season to taste and add the flaked fish. Serve straight away.

Mango and snapper broth

A complete meal in a bowl. Green mangos add bite to a citrussy, fiery soup.

The fish

Red snapper, or sea bream or sea bass

- **PREP** 15 mins, plus marinating
- **COOK** 10 mins **SERVES** 4

Ingredients

1 tbsp light soy sauce

2 tbsp Thai fish sauce

1 tbsp toasted sesame oil

1 tbsp mirin

1 tsp sugar

juice of 2 limes, or to taste

500g (1lb 2oz) red snapper fillets, pinboned, skinned, and cut into 2.5cm (1in) cubes

2 stalks lemongrass, finely chopped

2 tbsp vegetable oil

4 red bird's eye chillies, finely sliced

4 spring onions, finely sliced

5cm (2in) fresh root ginger, finely shredded

4 garlic cloves, roughly chopped

4 small green (under-ripe) mangos, peeled and finely chopped

2 tsp palm sugar or dark muscovado sugar

2 tbsp rice wine vinegar

1 litre (1¾ pints) fish stock

8 lime leaves, torn

100g (3½oz) egg noodles

100g (3½oz) fine green beans, halved

salt

2 tbsp chopped coriander leaves

1 tbsp shredded mint leaves

1 Combine the soy sauce, half the fish sauce, sesame oil, mirin, sugar, and juice of 1 lime, and spoon over the fish. Refrigerate for 20 minutes. Pound the lemongrass to a paste with a dash of water, using a mortar and pestle. Set aside.

2 Heat the oil in a wok or large pan and fry the chillies, spring onions, ginger, and garlic for 30 seconds over a high heat. Add the mangos and fry for 1 minute. Stir in the sugar until it begins to caramelize. Add the vinegar, lemongrass, stock, lime leaves, and remaining fish sauce. Bring to a boil.

3 Stir in the noodles, beans, and fish pieces (not the marinating liquid). Simmer for 3–5 minutes, until the noodles are cooked and the fish flakes easily. Season with salt, sharpen with lime juice, and add the herbs.

Waterzooi

A delicious Flemish soup in which aniseedy tarragon really lifts the flavours. Perfect on a cold spring day, when asparagus is in season.

The fish

Mussels, or clams, and monkfish, or any firm white fish, and lemon sole, or any flat fish

- **PREP** 20 mins ▪ **COOK** 30 mins ▪ **SERVES** 4

Ingredients

600ml (1 pint) light chicken or fish stock
100ml (3½fl oz) dry white wine
3 large spring onions, finely chopped
1 large waxy potato, peeled and cut into batons
1 large carrot, cut into batons
1 medium-large courgette, sliced on the diagonal
400g (14oz) asparagus, chopped into 5cm (2in) lengths
500g (1lb 2oz) mussels, prepared (see page 278)
100ml (3½fl oz) whipping cream
salt and freshly ground black pepper
300g (10oz) monkfish, cut into chunks
1 lemon sole, filleted and skinned, fillets halved
1 tbsp finely chopped tarragon, to serve

1 Put the stock, wine, and most of the spring onions in a casserole. Bring to a boil over a moderate heat. Add the potato, reduce the heat to a simmer, and cook for 5 minutes, then add the carrot for 5 minutes. Add the courgette and asparagus for 1–2 minutes, or until all is *al dente*. Lift out the vegetables and set aside.

2 Bring the stock to a boil and reduce by a third. Reduce the heat to a simmer, tip in the mussels, cover and cook for 3–4 minutes. Strain through a muslin-lined sieve into a bowl, cool briefly, then discard any that haven't opened. Shell the rest and set aside. Return the stock to a simmer over a moderate heat, then stir in the cream and season. Add the monkfish, cook for 2–3 minutes, add the sole and cook for 1 minute, then return the vegetables and mussels for 2 minutes.

3 Using a slotted spoon, lift the vegetables into 4 warmed bowls. Place the fish on top, ladle over the broth, and scatter with mussels, tarragon, and the reserved spring onion.

COLEY FLAVOUR PAIRINGS: This meaty fish is excellent cooked with beer, or try it with a very creamy white sauce flavoured with leeks, a little parsley, and fennel.

Soupe de poissons

Complement this flavourful soup with garlic croûtes spread with rouille, and topped with Gruyère cheese.

The fish

Any white fish, such as coley, and seafood

- **PREP** 20 mins ▪ **COOK** 1 hr ▪ **SERVES** 6

Ingredients

5 tbsp olive oil
4 onions, chopped
2 leeks, chopped
1.5–2kg (3lb 3oz–4½lb) mixed white fish and seafood
4 pieces of dried fennel stalk, 5cm (2in) long
4 ripe tomatoes, quartered
9 garlic cloves, crushed
5 sprigs of flat-leaf parsley
3 bay leaves
large strip of dried orange peel
1 tbsp tomato purée
salt and freshly ground black pepper
pinch of saffron threads
6 croûtes, to serve

1 Put the oil in a large, heavy saucepan. Add the onions and leeks, and soften over a moderate heat until just golden.

2 Scale and gut the fish. Rinse all the fish and seafood. Stir into the pan, then add the fennel, tomatoes, garlic, parsley, bay leaves, orange peel, and tomato purée. Cook for 8–10 minutes until the fish is just beginning to flake. Pour in 2.5 litres (4 pints) hot water and season. Reduce the heat and simmer for 20 minutes.

3 Remove from the heat. Leave to cool a little, stirring and mashing down the fish with the back of a large wooden spoon. Remove the fennel, orange peel, and bay leaves. Whizz the soup to a rough purée in a blender, then push it through a fine sieve into a clean saucepan. Return to a simmer over a moderate heat.

4 Soften the saffron in a ladleful of the soup, then stir into the rest of the soup in the pan. Taste, and adjust the seasoning. Ladle into bowls, and serve hot, with the croûtes.

Prepare ahead

This soup can be made 1–2 days in advance and kept, covered, in the refrigerator. Reheat gently to serve.

Paella, Pasta, and Risotto

Paella

This Spanish rice dish has many regional variations. This marinera version contains a delicious mix of seafood.

The fish

Tiger prawns, squid, Dublin Bay prawns, cockles, or any mixed seafood

- **PREP** 10 mins ▪ **COOK** 30 mins ▪ **SERVES** 4

Ingredients

1.2 litres (2 pints) hot fish stock

large pinch of saffron threads

2 tbsp olive oil

1 onion, finely chopped

2 garlic cloves, crushed

2 large tomatoes, skinned and diced

12 raw tiger prawns, peeled and deveined (see page 285)

225g (8oz) squid, gutted, cleaned, and sliced into rings (see page 282)

400g (14oz) paella rice

85g (3oz) peas

4 Dublin Bay prawns, or very large raw tiger prawns

12–16 mussels, prepared (see page 278)

1 tbsp chopped flat-leaf parsley, to garnish

1 Pour a little of the hot stock into a jug, add the saffron, and set aside. Heat the oil in a large frying or paella pan, and fry the onion and garlic until softened. Add the tomatoes, cook for 2 minutes, then add the king prawns and squid for 1–2 minutes.

2 Stir in the rice, saffron liquid, peas, and 900ml (1½ pints) of stock. Simmer, uncovered, without stirring, over a low heat for 12–14 minutes, or until the stock has evaporated and the rice is just tender, adding extra stock if necessary.

3 Meanwhile, cook the Dublin Bay prawns in 150ml (5fl oz) simmering stock for 3–4 minutes, or until cooked through. Transfer to a warm plate with a slotted spoon. Tap the mussels and discard any that do not close. Add the mussels to the stock, cover, and cook over a high heat for 2–3 minutes. Remove with a slotted spoon, discarding any that have not opened.

4 Reserve 8 mussels for garnish. Remove the rest from their shells and stir into the paella. Arrange the reserved mussels and Dublin Bay prawns on top, and garnish with parsley.

Risotto al tonno

This creamy fish risotto uses canned tuna, so it's a great store-cupboard recipe.

The fish

Canned tuna

- **PREP** 15 mins ▪ **COOK** 40 mins ▪ **SERVES** 4

Ingredients

30g (1oz) butter

4 tbsp extra virgin olive oil

1 large onion, finely chopped

1 garlic clove, chopped

250g (9oz) risotto rice

120ml (4fl oz) medium white wine

1 litre (1¾ pints) hot fish stock

1 tbsp tomato purée

185g can tuna in spring water, drained and flaked

12 cherry tomatoes, halved

2 tbsp chopped flat-leaf parsley

salt and freshly ground black pepper

1 Heat the butter and half the oil in a large saucepan. Add half the onion and cook over a low heat for 8–10 minutes until soft. Add the garlic and cook for a minute. Tip in the rice and cook for 2 minutes, until it turns translucent. Add half the wine and simmer for a couple of minutes. Stir in the stock a ladleful at a time, stirring frequently, and only adding more when the previous amount has been absorbed, for 20–25 minutes.

2 Meanwhile, in a separate pan, heat the remaining oil and add the remaining onion, cook for 8–10 minutes until soft. Add the tomato purée and stir for 2 minutes. Pour in the remaining wine, bring to a boil, and simmer for 5 minutes. Add the tuna and stir for 2–3 minutes. Add the tomatoes and parsley.

3 When the risotto rice is *al dente* and the stock all absorbed, stir in the tuna mixture, season to taste and serve.

Variation

Risotto nero

This recipe can be turned into risotto nero with the addition of 1 sachet of squid or cuttlefish ink (about 25g/1oz), to the rice, just before the stock.

DUBLIN BAY PRAWN FLAVOUR PAIRINGS:

When cooked very simply Dublin Bay prawns benefit from the gentle flavours of lemon juice or mayonnaise, but can also stand up to bolder garlic, sage, paprika, and chilli.

Prawn risotto

Perfect for a cold night, serve this as soon as it is ready.

The fish

Prawns, or Dublin Bay prawns or scallops

- **PREP** 15–20 mins - **COOK** 25–30 mins
- **SERVES** 6

Ingredients

90ml (3fl oz) olive oil

500g (1lb 2oz) raw prawns, peeled and deveined (see page 285)

2 garlic cloves, grated or finely chopped

leaves from 1 small bunch of flat-leaf parsley, chopped

salt and freshly ground black pepper

4 tbsp dry white wine

1 litre (1¾ pints) fish or chicken stock

1 onion, finely chopped

420g (15oz) risotto rice

1 Heat a third of the oil in a saucepan, and add the prawns, garlic, parsley, and salt and pepper.

2 Cook, stirring, until the prawns turn pink. Pour in the wine and stir thoroughly. Transfer the prawns to a bowl; set aside. Simmer the liquid in the pan for 2–3 minutes, until reduced by three-quarters. Add the stock and 250ml (9fl oz) water, and heat to boiling. Keep the mixture simmering.

3 Heat half the remaining oil in a large saucepan. Add the onion and cook for 2–3 minutes, until soft but not brown. Add the rice, and stir until coated with oil. Add the stock, a ladleful at a time, stirring until it is absorbed before adding more. Continue until the rice is cooked but still has a bit of bite; it should take about 20 minutes.

4 Stir in the prawns and remaining olive oil, and season. Spoon into warmed bowls, and serve immediately.

Haddock, green bean, and artichoke paella

Use paella rice if you can find it for this recipe, instead of the basmati.

The fish

Haddock, or cod or any white fish

- **PREP** 15 mins - **COOK** 30 mins - **SERVES** 4–6

Ingredients

1 tbsp olive oil, plus extra if needed

1 onion, finely chopped

salt and freshly ground black pepper

pinch of turmeric

2 garlic cloves, grated or finely chopped

200g (7oz) green beans, trimmed

280g jar artichoke hearts, drained and rinsed

4 tomatoes, skinned, deseeded, and chopped

pinch of hot or regular paprika

400g (14oz) basmati rice

1.4 litres (2½ pints) hot vegetable stock

675g (1½lb) haddock fillets, pinboned, skinned, and cut into chunky pieces

handful of dill or flat-leaf parsley, finely chopped

juice of 1 lemon

1 Heat the oil in a large, heavy frying pan over a medium heat. Add the onion and a pinch of salt, and sauté for about 5 minutes until soft and translucent. Stir in the turmeric, then add the garlic, beans, and artichokes. Cook gently for about 5 minutes until the beans begin to wilt, adding a little more oil if needed.

2 Now add the tomatoes and paprika, and cook for 5 minutes. Tip in the rice, and stir. Pour in half the hot stock. Bring to a boil, then reduce the heat and simmer for about 15 minutes. Add the remaining stock and the fish, cover, and cook over a low heat for 10 minutes, or until the rice and fish are cooked.

3 Keep the lid on the pan until ready to serve, then stir in the fresh herbs and lemon juice. Taste, adjust the seasoning, and serve.

Prepare ahead

Cook the vegetables up to the point of adding the rice (do not add the rice), cool, cover, and refrigerate up to 6 hours in advance. Reheat gently before continuing.

Smoked fish kedgeree

This classic Anglo-Indian recipe became a popular breakfast dish in Victorian times.

The fish

Smoked haddock, or kippers or smoked mackerel

- **PREP** 15 mins ▪ **COOK** 25–30 mins
- **SERVES** 4

Ingredients

175g (6oz) long-grain rice

125g (4½oz) frozen peas

225g (8oz) smoked haddock fillet

4 eggs

25g (1oz) butter

½ tsp ground cumin

freshly grated nutmeg, to taste

salt and freshly ground black pepper

2 tbsp chopped flat-leaf parsley

2–4 tbsp single cream, to taste

1 Boil the rice according to the package instructions. Drain well, then spread out in a wide dish, and fork through the grains to fluff up. Leave until cold. Boil the frozen peas according to the package instructions, drain, and set aside.

2 Meanwhile, place the haddock in a sauté pan and half-cover with water. Bring slowly to a boil, and simmer gently for 6–7 minutes. Drain well. When cool enough to handle, break the fish into large flakes, discarding any skin.

3 Bring a saucepan of water to a boil, and drop in the eggs. Boil for 7–8 minutes. They will be hard-boiled, but the yolks will remain moist. Drain, and shell. When cold, cut into quarters.

4 Melt the butter in a sauté pan over a medium heat. Add the rice, and stir to coat the grains. Gently mix in the fish and peas. Add the cumin, nutmeg, salt and pepper, and half the parsley. Stir in the cream, and cook, stirring occasionally, until piping hot.

5 Top with the hard-boiled egg quarters, sprinkle over the remaining parsley, and serve.

Prepare ahead

Cook the rice, peas, haddock, and eggs up to 1 day ahead. Cover, and refrigerate separately. Return to room temperature before continuing with the recipe.

Seafood risotto

Replace the scallops and prawns with squid for a more economical dish.

The fish

Prawns and scallops, or squid, and any mixed white fish, such as haddock and pollock

- **PREP** 20 mins ▪ **COOK** 30 mins ▪ **SERVES** 8

Ingredients

2–3 tbsp olive oil

450g (1lb) raw prawns, peeled and deveined (see page 285)

salt and freshly ground black pepper

450g (1lb) mixed white fish, cubed

16 scallops, roe removed

2 knobs of butter

2 onions, finely chopped

4 garlic cloves, grated or finely chopped

2 litres (3½ pints) hot vegetable or fish stock

675g (1½lb) risotto rice

300ml (10fl oz) medium white wine

6 tomatoes, skinned, deseeded, and finely chopped

large handful of flat-leaf parsley, finely chopped

handful of dill, finely chopped

lemon wedges, to serve

1 Heat half the oil in a frying pan, add the prawns and seasoning, and cook for a couple of minutes. Remove and set aside. Add the fish, and more oil, if needed, and cook for a couple of minutes, or until cooked. Remove and set aside.

2 Season the scallops, add to the pan with more oil, if needed, and cook for 2 minutes each side. Remove and set aside. Add a knob of butter to the pan, then the onions, and cook over a low heat for 5–8 minutes, until soft. Stir in the garlic. Put the stock in a large pan and keep on a low simmer.

3 Stir the rice into the onions. Season, then pour in the wine and increase the heat. Allow to boil for a few seconds while the alcohol evaporates. Add the stock, a ladleful at a time, stirring until it is absorbed before adding more. Continue until the rice is cooked but still has a bit of bite; it should take about 20 minutes.

4 Stir in the tomatoes, seafood, and fish, then the herbs and remaining butter. Taste and season, then serve with lemon wedges.

Fideua

This Spanish pasta dish, with a tasty mixture of seafood, is hearty and filling.

The fish
Prawns, scallops, clams, or any shellfish, and any firm white fish, such as cod or monkfish

- **PREP** 15 mins **COOK** 25 mins **SERVES** 4

Ingredients
pinch of saffron threads

750ml (1¼ pints) hot fish stock

2–3 tbsp olive oil

1 onion, finely chopped

2 garlic cloves, crushed

3 ripe tomatoes, skinned, deseeded, and chopped

1 tsp sweet or smoked paprika

300g (10oz) spaghetti or linguine, broken into 5cm (2in) lengths

225g (8oz) raw prawns, peeled and deveined (see page 285)

8 small scallops, cut in half

300g (10oz) clams, thoroughly washed

225g (8oz) firm white fish, cut into 2cm (¾in) pieces

140g (5oz) peas

salt and freshly ground black pepper

2 tbsp chopped flat-leaf parsley

1 Put the saffron in a small bowl and add 2 tbsp of the hot stock. Set aside.

2 Heat the oil in a large frying or paella pan over a medium heat. Add the onion and garlic and fry for 5–8 minutes, or until soft, stirring frequently. Add the tomatoes and paprika and cook for a further 5 minutes. Add the saffron with its liquid and half the remaining stock, increase the heat, and bring to a boil.

3 Add the pasta, reduce the heat, and simmer, uncovered, stirring occasionally, for 5 minutes. Add the prawns, scallops, clams, white fish, and peas, and cook for a further 5 minutes, or until the pasta and fish are cooked. If the mixture begins to dry out, add a little more stock. Season to taste, sprinkle with parsley, and serve hot, straight from the pan. It's good with aïoli and crusty bread.

Prepare ahead
The base of the fideua can be made in advance up to the end of step 2. Pour into a bowl, cool, cover, and refrigerate for up to 2 days. Reheat gently, then return to a boil before continuing.

Linguine alle vongole

Versions of this popular classic are cooked all along the Italian Mediterranean and Adriatic coasts.

The fish
Clams, or mussels

- **PREP** 5 mins **COOK** 20 mins **SERVES** 4

Ingredients
2 tbsp olive oil

1 onion, finely chopped

2 garlic cloves, grated or finely chopped

400g can chopped tomatoes

2 tbsp sun-dried tomato purée

120ml (4fl oz) dry white wine

600g (1lb 5oz) clams, shelled, juices reserved (see page 279)

salt and freshly ground black pepper

350g (12oz) linguine

4 tbsp finely chopped flat-leaf parsley, plus extra to garnish

1 Heat the oil in a large saucepan over medium heat. Add the onion and garlic and fry, stirring frequently, for 5 minutes. Add the tomatoes, tomato purée, wine, and clam juices, and season. Bring to a boil, stirring. Reduce the heat to low, partially cover, and leave to simmer for 10–15 minutes.

2 Meanwhile, bring a large pan of salted water to the boil. Add the linguine, and boil according to the packet instructions, until *al dente*. Drain and shake to remove excess water.

3 Add the clams and parsley to the sauce and simmer for 1–2 minutes. Season to taste.

4 Add the linguine to the sauce and toss to coat. Sprinkle with extra parsley and serve at once with crusty Italian bread and green salad.

Prepare ahead
The tomato sauce in step 1 can be made a day in advance, covered, and refrigerated. Reheat gently before continuing.

Variation
Canned clam linguine
This dish can also be made using canned clams. For this, use 2 x 140g jars clams in natural juice, strained, with the juice reserved. Because they won't be quite as flavoursome, the sauce will benefit from a large pinch of chilli flakes, for added zing.

CLAM FLAVOUR PAIRINGS: Partner this shellfish with a sauce either of cream, onions, herbs, and white wine, or tomatoes, garlic, parsley, bacon, and a touch of chilli.

SQUID FLAVOUR PAIRINGS: When cooked alone, try squid perked up with a sprinkling of chilli, or breadcrumbed and served with garlic mayonnaise, or simply with olive oil and lemon.

Spaghetti puttanesca

A spicy pasta dish popular with everyone.

The fish

Anchovy fillets in olive oil

- **PREP** 15 mins ▪ **COOK** 25 mins ▪ **SERVES** 4

Ingredients

4 tbsp extra virgin olive oil

2 garlic cloves, grated or finely chopped

½ red chilli, deseeded and finely chopped

6 anchovy fillets in olive oil, drained and finely chopped

115g (4oz) black olives, pitted and chopped

1–2 tbsp capers, rinsed and drained

450g (1lb) tomatoes, skinned, deseeded, and chopped (see page 112)

450g (1lb) spaghetti

chopped flat-leaf parsley, to serve

Parmesan cheese, to serve

1 Heat the oil in a saucepan, add the garlic and chilli, and cook gently for 2 minutes, or until slightly coloured. Add the anchovies, olives, capers, and tomatoes, and stir, breaking down the anchovies to a paste.

2 Reduce the heat and simmer, uncovered, for 10–15 minutes, stirring frequently.

3 Meanwhile, cook the spaghetti in lightly salted boiling water according to the packet instructions. Drain.

4 Toss the spaghetti with the sauce, and serve sprinkled with parsley and Parmesan, with a spinach salad and crusty bread.

Prepare ahead

The sauce can be made up to 2 days ahead, covered, and refrigerated. The flavours will deepen. Return to a brisk simmer before adding to the pasta.

Spaghetti frutti di mare

A traditional Italian dish with a hint of spice and the freshest seafood.

The fish

Mussels, baby squid, tiger prawns, or any mixed seafood

- **PREP** 25 mins ▪ **COOK** 20 mins ▪ **SERVES** 4

Ingredients

3 tbsp olive oil

1 small onion, finely chopped

2 garlic cloves, grated or finely chopped

500ml (16fl oz) chunky passata

¼ tsp chilli flakes

450g (1lb) mussels, prepared (see page 278)

450g (1lb) baby squid, gutted, cleaned, and cut into rings (see page 282)

4 tbsp dry white wine

½ lemon, sliced

450g (1lb) spaghetti

12 large raw tiger prawns, peeled and deveined, tails left on (see page 285)

3 tbsp chopped flat-leaf parsley

salt and freshly ground black pepper

1 Heat the oil in a large saucepan and fry the onion and garlic over a low heat, stirring, for 3–4 minutes, or until softened. Add the passata and chilli, then simmer for 1 minute.

2 Tap the mussels and discard any that do not close. Place the mussels and squid in a large pan with the wine and lemon, cover, and bring to a boil. Cook for 3–4 minutes, or until the mussel shells have opened, shaking. Strain the liquid through a fine sieve and reserve. Discard the lemon and any unopened shells. Reserve a few mussels in their shells and shuck the rest.

3 Cook the spaghetti in lightly salted boiling water according to the packet instructions.

4 Meanwhile, add the mussel liquor to the sauce and simmer, uncovered, for 2–3 minutes, or until slightly reduced. Add the prawns and simmer for 2 minutes. Add the mussels and squid, and parsley, and season to taste.

5 Drain the pasta, return to the pan, and toss in the sauce. Tip into a bowl, place the reserved mussels in their shells on top, and serve.

Prepare ahead

The tomato sauce in step 1 can be made up to 3 days in advance, covered, and refrigerated. Return to a simmer before continuing.

Spinach linguine with white clam sauce

Immensely satisfying and quick to make, this dish will soon become part of your regular repertoire.

The fish

Clams, or mussels

- **PREP** 20–25 mins ▪ **COOK** 5–10 mins
- **SERVES** 4–6

Ingredients

800g (1¾lb) clams

1 onion, finely chopped

250ml (8fl oz) dry white wine

salt and freshly ground black pepper

280g (10oz) fresh spinach linguine

4 tbsp olive oil

2 garlic cloves, finely chopped

2 tbsp chopped flat-leaf parsley

1 Scrub the clams well under cold running water. Discard any with cracked shells, or that are open and do not close when firmly tapped. Put them in a large pan that has a lid, with the onion and wine. Place over a high heat, bring to a boil, cover, and shake once or twice. After 2–3 minutes, the shells will have opened.

2 Strain the clams and reserve their liquor. When cool enough to handle, discard any clams that have not opened, and remove most of them from their shells. Return the cooking liquor to the pan over a high heat, and boil to reduce to about 250ml (8fl oz).

3 Bring a large pan of salted water to a boil, add the linguine, and cook according to the package instructions. Meanwhile, heat the oil in another pan over a medium heat, add the garlic, and sauté until aromatic. Add the clams, parsley, and cooking liquor, and season.

4 Drain the linguine, keeping back a tiny amount of the cooking water, and add the pasta to the clams. Mix everything together until piping hot, then serve on warmed plates.

Spaghetti with clams

This simple seafood pasta brings out the best in the fresh, briny clams.

The fish

Clams, or mussels, whelks, periwinkles, or cockles

- **PREP** 20 mins ▪ **COOK** 15 mins ▪ **SERVES** 4

Ingredients

1.1kg (2½lb) clams

15g (½oz) butter

5 tbsp olive oil

2 garlic cloves, coarsely chopped

115g (4oz) fresh breadcrumbs

salt and freshly ground black pepper

350g (12oz) spaghetti

½ tsp chilli flakes

75ml (2½fl oz) dry white wine

1 tbsp extra virgin olive oil, to serve

2 tbsp grated Parmesan cheese, to serve

4 tbsp chopped flat-leaf parsley, to serve

1 Scrub the clams well under cold running water. Discard any with cracked shells, or that are open and do not close when firmly tapped.

2 Heat the butter with 2 tbsp of the oil in a large, heavy frying pan and stir in half the garlic. Add the breadcrumbs and fry gently, stirring, for 2 minutes, or until golden. Remove from the heat and season.

3 Cook the spaghetti in a large pan of lightly salted boiling water according to the package instructions, or until it is cooked, but still has a bit of bite to it. Drain, keeping back a tiny amount of the cooking water.

4 Meanwhile, heat the remaining oil in a large, deep pan, add the remaining garlic and the chilli, and stir over a moderate heat for 1 minute. Add the wine, season to taste, bring to a boil, then add the clams. Cover and cook over a high heat for 4–5 minutes, shaking often, until all the clams have opened.

5 Remove the clams with a slotted spoon, then boil the juices rapidly, uncovered, until reduced by about half.

6 Return the clams to the pan with the pasta; toss lightly. Serve drizzled with extra virgin olive oil, sprinkled with the garlic breadcrumbs, Parmesan, and parsley.

Penne with tuna and roasted onion

This recipe uses fresh tuna steaks, but you can use a 170g can of good-quality tuna in olive oil; add it to the pasta without cooking.

The fish
Tuna, or mackerel or bonito

- **PREP** 10 mins ▪ **COOK** 20 mins ▪ **SERVES** 4

Ingredients
3 red onions, cut into wedges

handful of cherry tomatoes

few sprigs of thyme

3 tbsp olive oil

salt and freshly ground black pepper

2 tuna steaks, about 175g (6oz) each

350g (12oz) penne

grated zest of ½ lemon

pinch of chilli flakes

drizzle of good-quality balsamic vinegar, to serve (optional)

1 Preheat the oven to 200°C (400°F/Gas 6). Place the onions, tomatoes, and thyme in a large roasting tin, drizzle with 2 tbsp olive oil, season with salt, then mix well with your hands. Roast for 15 minutes, or until soft and lightly charred.

2 Meanwhile, heat a grill pan or griddle until hot. Rub the tuna steaks with the remaining oil and season. Fry for 3–4 minutes on each side (depending on thickness and how you like it), remove, and put to one side to rest.

3 Cook the pasta in a pan of boiling salted water for 10 minutes or until it is cooked, but still has a bit of bite to it. Drain, keeping back a tiny amount of the cooking water. Return the pasta to the pan and toss together with the roasted onions and tomatoes.

4 Slice the tuna into chunks, add to the pan with the lemon zest and chilli flakes, and toss gently. Season to taste, then drizzle with balsamic vinegar (if using), and serve.

Pasta with crab and lemon

A light, fragrant, and elegant dish for a summer's evening.

The fish
Crab, or lobster or prawns

- **PREP** 5 mins ▪ **COOK** 10 mins ▪ **SERVES** 4

Ingredients
1 tbsp olive oil

1 large onion, finely sliced

salt and freshly ground black pepper

2 garlic cloves, finely sliced

grated zest and juice of 1 lemon

handful of flat-leaf parsley, finely chopped

200g (7oz) fresh white crab meat, or canned white crab meat, drained

350g (12oz) linguine or spaghetti

chilli oil, to serve (optional)

1 Heat the olive oil in a large frying pan, add the onion and a pinch of salt, and cook over a low heat for 5 minutes, or until soft and translucent. Stir in the garlic and lemon zest, and cook for a few seconds more.

2 Stir in the parsley and crab, then season well with salt and lots of pepper. Add lemon juice to taste.

3 Meanwhile, cook the pasta in a large pan of boiling salted water according to the package instructions, or until it is cooked, but still has a bit of bite to it. Drain, keeping back a tiny amount of the cooking water. Return the pasta to the pan and toss with the crab sauce, drizzle with chilli oil (if using), and serve.

Variation

Piquant pasta with crab and lemon
Add 1 tsp rinsed capers, or a chopped green pepper, to the crab.

Linguine with scallops

A hint of chilli and lime make this a perfect pasta dish for supper, or even entertaining.

The fish
King scallops, or monkfish or prawns

- **PREP** 10 mins ▪ **COOK** 8 mins ▪ **SERVES** 4

Ingredients
400g (14oz) linguine

juice of 1 lime

5 tbsp olive oil, plus extra for brushing

1 red chilli, finely chopped

2 tbsp chopped coriander

salt and freshly ground black pepper

12 king scallops, roe removed

1 Cook the pasta in a large pan of boiling salted water according to the package instructions, or until it is cooked, but still has a bit of bite to it. Drain, keeping back a tiny amount of the cooking water, and keep warm.

2 Meanwhile, whisk the lime juice with the oil Stir in the chilli and half the coriander. Season to taste. Toss the dressing with the linguine, and keep warm.

3 Heat a large griddle pan or heavy frying pan over a high heat. Brush the scallops with oil, place in the pan and sear for 3 minutes, turning once. Do not overcook.

4 Divide the linguine between 4 serving plates and arrange the scallops on top. Serve immediately, with the remaining coriander sprinkled over, with crusty bread and salad.

Spaghetti mare e monti

The ingredients of this well-known dish come from the sea and the mountains.

The fish
Tiger prawns

- **PREP** 15 mins, plus soaking ▪ **COOK** 15 mins ▪ **SERVES** 4

Ingredients
15g (½oz) dried porcini mushrooms, rinsed

6 ripe plum tomatoes

2 tbsp extra virgin olive oil

150g (5½oz) baby button mushrooms

2 garlic cloves, grated or finely chopped

1 bay leaf

150ml (5fl oz) medium white wine

225g (8oz) cooked tiger prawns

salt and freshly ground black pepper

400g (14oz) spaghetti

1 Place the porcini in a bowl and pour over 150ml (5fl oz) boiling water. Leave to soak for 30 minutes. Chop the mushrooms, then strain the liquid through a fine sieve and reserve.

2 Meanwhile, put the tomatoes in a heatproof bowl. Make a nick in the skin of each, then cover with boiling water. Leave for 30 seconds, then drain, peel, deseed, and roughly chop.

3 Heat the oil in a large frying pan. Add all the mushrooms and fry until golden. Add the garlic for 30 seconds. Pour in the porcini liquid, add the bay leaf, and simmer briskly until reduced to a glaze. Reduce the heat to low.

4 Pour in the wine and tomatoes and simmer for 7–8 minutes, or until the tomatoes break down. Remove the bay leaf, add the prawns, and cook for 1 minute. Season to taste.

5 Meanwhile, cook the pasta in a large pan of boiling salted water according to the package instructions, or until it is cooked, but still has a bit of bite to it. Drain, keeping back a tiny amount of the cooking water, then return to the pan. Add the sauce, toss, and serve.

Prepare ahead
Make the sauce up to the point when the tomatoes have broken down up to 2 days in advance, cover, and refrigerate. Reheat gently before continuing.

Pasta with anchovies, chilli, and lemon

You should find white anchovies in oil at the deli counter of the supermarket.

The fish
Anchovy fillets in olive oil

- **PREP** 10 mins **COOK** 10 mins **SERVES** 4

Ingredients
1 tbsp olive oil

2 red onions, finely chopped

salt

2 garlic cloves, grated or finely chopped

1 red chilli, deseeded and finely chopped

1 green chilli, deseeded and finely chopped

grated zest of 1 lemon

350g (12oz) linguine or spaghetti

12 anchovy fillets in olive oil, drained

handful of finely chopped flat-leaf parsley

juice of 1 lemon, to serve

1 Heat the oil in a large frying pan, add the onions and a pinch of salt, and cook over a low heat for 5 minutes, or until soft. Add the garlic, chillies, and lemon zest, and cook for a few minutes more, stirring to make sure the mixture does not brown.

2 Meanwhile, cook the pasta in a large pan of boiling salted water according to the package instructions, or until it is cooked, but still has a bit of bite to it. Drain, keeping back a tiny amount of the cooking water. Return the pasta to the pan.

3 Stir the anchovies into the onion mixture, then toss with the pasta, add the parsley, and toss again. Serve with a squeeze of lemon.

Pasta with seafood and tomatoes

This recipe uses raw seafood, but you can use cooked seafood if it's more convenient.

The fish
Any mixed seafood, such as prawns, squid, and mussels

- **PREP** 5 mins **COOK** 20 mins **SERVES** 4

Ingredients
1 tbsp olive oil

1 onion, finely chopped

salt and freshly ground black pepper

3 garlic cloves, grated or finely chopped

400g can chopped tomatoes

350g (12oz) linguine or spaghetti

350g (12oz) mixed raw seafood

handful of flat-leaf parsley, finely chopped

1 Heat the oil in a large frying pan, add the onion and a pinch of salt, and cook over a low heat for 5 minutes or until soft and translucent. Stir in the garlic and cook for a few seconds more. Add the tomatoes, bring to a boil, then simmer gently for 10–12 minutes.

2 Meanwhile, cook the pasta in a large pan of boiling salted water according to the package instructions, or until it is cooked, but still has a bit of bite to it. Drain, keeping back a tiny amount of the cooking water. Return to the pan.

3 Stir the seafood into the tomato mixture for the last few minutes of cooking. Season well with salt and pepper, stir in the parsley, then toss with the pasta, and serve.

Pies, Tarts, and Bakes

Pollock pie with peas

Easy to make even after a hard day at work, and universally popular.

The fish
Pollock, or any firm white fish, such as haddock, hake, or cod (or even salmon)

- **PREP** 15 mins - **COOK** 25 mins - **SERVES** 4

Ingredients

900g (2lb) floury potatoes, peeled and cut into chunks

450ml (5fl oz) milk, plus 3 tbsp extra

salt and freshly ground black pepper

675g (1½lb) pollock fillets, pinboned, skinned, and cut into chunks

30g (1oz) butter

30g (1oz) plain flour

1 tbsp Dijon mustard

175g (6oz) frozen peas

4 eggs, hard-boiled and coarsely chopped

1 Preheat the oven to 200°C (400°F/Gas 6), or the grill to high. Boil the potatoes in salted

water for 15 minutes, or until soft. Drain well, add 3 tbsp milk, season, and mash. Set aside.

2 Put the fish in a shallow pan. Season well. Pour over enough of the milk to cover (about 150ml/10fl oz), and poach over a medium heat for 3–4 minutes. Remove the fish with a slotted spoon, and transfer to an ovenproof dish.

3 Melt the butter in a pan. Remove from the heat, and stir in the flour with a wooden spoon until smooth. Return to the heat, and stir in the remaining milk, little by little, then cook for 5–10 minutes until thickened. Add more milk if needed. Stir in the mustard, and season. Add the peas and eggs.

4 Spoon the sauce over the fish, top with the mashed potato, and fork to form peaks. Dot with extra butter if you wish, then cook in the oven or under a hot grill for about 10 minutes until crisp and golden.

Prepare ahead
Assemble 1 day ahead and keep, covered, in the refrigerator, before baking or grilling.

Whiting and leek pie

This recipe requires a 1.2-litre (2-pint) pie dish.

The fish
Whiting, or any firm white fish

- **PREP** 15 mins - **COOK** 50 mins - **SERVES** 4

Ingredients

1 tbsp olive oil

1 onion, finely chopped

salt and freshly ground black pepper

4 leeks, finely sliced

1 tsp plain flour

150ml (5fl oz) cider

handful of flat-leaf parsley, finely chopped

150ml (5fl oz) double cream

675g (1½lb) whiting fillets, pinboned, skinned, and cut into chunks

300g (10oz) ready-made puff pastry

plain flour, to dust

1 egg, lightly beaten, for egg wash

1 Preheat the oven to 200°C (400°F/Gas 6). Heat the oil, add the onion and a little salt, and sweat gently. Add the leeks, and cook for 10 minutes. Remove from the heat, stir in the flour, and a little cider. Return to the heat, pour in all the cider, and cook for 5–8 minutes. Stir in the parsley and cream, and spoon into the pie dish with the fish.

2 Roll out the pastry on a floured work surface so it is 5cm (2in) larger all around than the dish. Cut a 2.5cm (1in) strip from the edge. Wet the edge of the dish; fit the pastry strip around, and press down. Brush with egg wash, then top with the pastry. Press the edges to seal. Make 2 slits to allow steam to escape. Brush with egg wash, and bake for 20–30 minutes until puffed and golden.

Prepare ahead
Make the filling 1 day ahead, cover, and chill.

Salmon and prawn fish pie

This luxurious version of everyone's favourite pie is made in a 1.2-litre (2-pint) ovenproof dish.

The fish

Cold leftover salmon, or cold leftover trout, and prawns

- **PREP** 15 mins ▪ **COOK** 35 mins ▪ **SERVES** 2

Ingredients

675g (1½lb) potatoes, peeled and cut into chunks

300ml (10fl oz) milk, plus 2 tbsp extra

salt and freshly ground black pepper

350g (12oz) leftover baked salmon, flaked

200g (7oz) cooked prawns, peeled and deveined

knob of butter, plus extra for topping

1 tbsp plain flour

1 tbsp wholegrain mustard

1 Preheat the oven to 200°C (400°F/Gas 6). Boil the potatoes in salted water for 15 minutes, until soft; drain. Add 2 tbsp milk, season, and mash.

2 Arrange the salmon and prawns in the ovenproof dish. Season, and set aside.

3 Gently melt the butter in a pan. Remove from the heat, and stir in the flour. Add a little milk and beat until smooth. Return the pan to the heat and continue adding the milk, a little at a time, stirring constantly, until thickened. Whisk to get rid of any lumps, then stir in the mustard.

4 Pour the sauce over the salmon, cover with the potato, and dot with extra butter. Bake in the oven for 15–20 minutes until crisp and golden.

Prepare ahead

Assemble 1 day ahead and keep, covered, in the refrigerator.

Fisherman's pie

There are never any leftovers of this great but simple fish pie; the eggs and prawns help to make it incredibly moreish. You'll need a 2-litre (3½-pint) pie dish.

The fish

Any firm white fish, such as haddock, hake, cod, or pollock, and prawns

- **PREP** 35–45 mins ▪ **COOK** 50 mins
- **SERVES** 6

Ingredients

625g (1lb 6oz) potatoes, peeled and cut into chunks

1 litre (1¾ pints) milk, plus 4 tbsp extra

salt and freshly ground black pepper

10 peppercorns

2 bay leaves

1 small onion, quartered

750g (1lb 10oz) white fish fillets, pinboned, skinned, and cut into large chunks

90g (3oz) butter, plus extra for greasing

60g (2oz) plain flour

leaves from 5–7 sprigs of parsley, chopped

125g (4½oz) cooked prawns, peeled and deveined (see page 285)

3 eggs, hard-boiled and coarsely chopped

1 Preheat the oven to 180°C (350°F/Gas 4). Boil the potatoes until tender; drain. Add 4 tbsp milk, salt, and pepper. Mash.

2 Pour the remaining milk into a pan, add the peppercorns, bay leaves, and onion. Bring to a boil, remove from the heat, cover, and let stand for 10 minutes. Add the fish, and simmer for 5–10 minutes. Strain off and reserve the liquid.

3 Gently melt the butter. Whisk in the flour, then the reserved liquid. Return to the heat and stir until thickened. Add the parsley.

4 Butter the pie dish. Spoon in the fish, sauce, prawns, and eggs. Spread over the potato, and bake for 20–30 minutes.

Prepare ahead

Assemble 1 day ahead and keep, covered, in the refrigerator.

Variation

Individual fish crumbles

Make the fish and prawn mixture, but not the potato. Rub 90g (3oz) butter into 150g (5½oz) plain flour. Add 1 tbsp chopped parsley, 45g (1½oz) rolled oats, 1 tbsp grated Parmesan cheese, salt, and pepper. Butter 6 ramekins and fill with the fish, then top with the crumble. Bake for 20–25 minutes.

Salmon coulibiac

A classic Russian speciality. You can vary it, authentically, by using pancakes in place of the rice to layer with the fish filling.

The fish

Salmon, or trout or sturgeon

- **PREP** 40 mins - **COOK** 45 mins
- **SERVES** 4–6

Ingredients

450g (1lb) puff pastry

30g (1oz) butter

1 small onion, finely chopped

60g (2oz) button mushrooms, finely chopped

5 tbsp milk

250g (9oz) cooked salmon (poached or canned), skinned, pinboned, and flaked

2 eggs, hard-boiled and diced

115g (4oz) cooked long-grain rice, chilled

1 tbsp finely chopped flat-leaf parsley

1 tbsp finely chopped dill

salt and freshly ground black pepper

1 egg, beaten, for glazing

1 Roll one-third of the pastry into a 25 x 15cm (10 x 6in) sheet. Lay it on a baking sheet and pierce all over with a fork. Chill for 10 minutes. Preheat the oven to 200°C (400°F/Gas 6). Roll out the remaining pastry to about one-third larger than the base. Chill.

2 Melt the butter in a saucepan, add the onion and cook over a low heat for 4–5 minutes until soft. Increase the heat and add the mushrooms. Fry for 2–3 minutes. Add the milk and simmer until the mushrooms are cooked. Cool.

3 Cook the pastry base in the oven for 5–10 minutes or until crisp; cool on a wire rack.

4 Mix the salmon, hard-boiled eggs, rice, and herbs, season, and add the mushroom mixture.

5 Spoon the salmon mixture over the base. Lay the second sheet of pastry on top, tucking the edges under the cooked pastry to seal.

6 Cut small fishes or leaves from the pastry trimmings. Make a small hole on the coulibiac, brush with beaten egg, and decorate the top. Chill for 15 minutes. Brush again with egg and bake for 25–30 minutes until golden brown.

Prepare ahead

Assemble the coulibiac to the end of step 5, cover, and chill for up to 2 days before baking. Return to room temperature before continuing.

Salmon in puff pastry

Baking salmon en croûte ("in a crust") keeps it moist and succulent.

The fish

Salmon, or trout

- **PREP** 25 mins - **COOK** 30 mins - **SERVES** 4

Ingredients

85g (3oz) watercress, coarse stems removed, very finely chopped

115g (4oz) cream cheese

salt and freshly ground black pepper

400g (14oz) puff pastry

plain flour, for dusting

600g (1lb 5oz) salmon fillet, pinboned, skinned, and halved

oil, for greasing

beaten egg or milk, to glaze

1 Preheat the oven to 200°C (400°F/Gas 6). Place the watercress in a bowl, add the cream cheese, season generously, and mix well.

2 Roll out the pastry on a lightly floured surface to 3mm (1/8in) thick. It should be 7.5cm (3in) longer than the salmon pieces and more than twice as wide. Trim the edges. Transfer to a lightly oiled baking tray.

3 Place 1 piece of salmon in the middle of the pastry. Spread with the watercress cream and place the other piece of salmon on top. Lightly brush the pastry edges with water, then fold the 2 ends over the salmon. Fold in the sides so they overlap slightly and press together. Brush with beaten egg, and make 2 or 3 holes with a skewer to allow steam to escape. Bake for 30 minutes, until well risen and golden.

4 Remove from the oven and allow to stand for a few minutes, then slice and serve.

Prepare ahead

The dish can be assembled up to 12 hours before baking. Cover and chill, then return to room temperature before continuing.

SALMON FLAVOUR PAIRINGS: Classically matched to the fragrance of dill, tarragon, sorrel, lemon, and samphire, salmon also works well with ginger, or even the Indonesian thick soy sauce kecap manis.

Pissaladière

This is a French version of pizza.

The fish

Anchovy fillets in olive oil

- **PREP** 20 mins, plus rising ■ **COOK** 85 mins
- **SERVES** 4 as main course, 8 as canapés

Ingredients

For the topping

4 tbsp olive oil

900g (2lb) onions, finely sliced

3 garlic cloves

a few sprigs of thyme

1 tsp *herbes de Provence*

1 bay leaf

100g jar or can anchovy fillets in olive oil

12 black Niçoise olives, pitted, or Italian olives

For the base

225g (8oz) strong white flour,
plus extra for dusting

salt and freshly ground black pepper

1 tsp soft brown sugar

1 tsp easy-blend dried yeast

1 tbsp olive oil

1 Combine the flour, 1 tsp salt, and pepper in a large bowl. Pour 150ml (5fl oz) tepid water into another bowl, and whisk in the sugar, then the yeast. Set aside for 10 minutes to froth, then pour into the flour with the oil.

2 Mix to a dough, adding more water if it is too dry. Knead on a floured board for 10 minutes, or until elastic. Shape into a ball, return to the bowl, and cover with a tea towel. Leave in a warm place for 1 hour, or until doubled in size.

3 Put the oil in a saucepan over a low heat. Add the onions, garlic, and herbs, cover and simmer for 1 hour, or until the onions become a stringy purée. Set aside, discarding the bay leaf.

4 Preheat the oven to 180°C (350°F/Gas 4). Knead the dough briefly on a floured surface. Roll it out to fit a 32.5 x 23cm (13 x 9in) Swiss roll tin, and prick all over with a fork.

5 Spread the onions over the base. Drain the anchovies, reserving 3 tbsp oil, and halve lengthways. Embed the olives in rows in the dough, and drape the anchovies in a criss-cross pattern on top. Drizzle with the anchovy oil, and sprinkle with pepper. Bake for 25 minutes. Serve warm or cool, cut into rectangles.

Tarte au poissons

Make this cooked fish tart in a flan ring or dish. It's great for leftovers. You will need baking beans for the pastry shell.

The fish

Cooked trout, or cooked salmon, cod, or haddock, cooked smoked fish, or cooked prawns

- **PREP** 45 mins, plus chilling ■ **COOK** 55 mins
- **SERVES** 4

Ingredients

225g (8oz) shortcrust pastry

plain flour, for dusting

1 onion, finely chopped

45g (1½oz) butter

4 ripe tomatoes, skinned, deseeded, and diced
(see page 112)

1 small garlic clove, crushed

2 tsp chopped thyme leaves

large pinch of freshly grated nutmeg

150ml (5fl oz) single cream

2 eggs, beaten

salt and freshly ground black pepper

175g (6oz) cooked trout, pinboned, skinned, and flaked into large pieces

1 tbsp grated Gruyère cheese

1 Roll the pastry on a floured surface to a 25cm (10in) circle and use it to line a 20cm (8in) flan ring or dish. Chill for 15 minutes. Preheat the oven to 180°C (350°F/Gas 4).

2 Line the pastry case with greaseproof paper and baking beans. Bake for 12–15 minutes, or until set. Lift out the paper and beans and return to the oven for a further 5 minutes. Allow to cool. Reduce the oven temperature to 150°C (300°F/Gas 2).

3 Cook the onion in the butter for 4–5 minutes, or until translucent. Add the tomatoes, and garlic, then cool. Stir in the thyme, nutmeg, cream, and eggs, and season well.

4 Put the fish into the pastry case and spoon over the tomato mixture. Sprinkle with the Gruyère. Return the tart to the oven and bake for 25–35 minutes, or until set and golden brown. Serve warm or cold.

Prepare ahead

Bake the pastry shell up to 1 day ahead, cool completely, and store in an airtight container at room temperature.

TROUT FLAVOUR PAIRINGS: Try white wine vinegar, or lemon, to enhance and sharpen the trout's sweet flesh, or match with rich pastry, almonds, or hazelnuts, and highlight with chives.

Smoked haddock, leek, and grainy mustard tart

Use dyed smoked haddock for this recipe, so it shows up well. You'll need a 20–25cm (8–10in) tart case and baking beans.

The fish

Smoked haddock, or smoked cod or canned salmon

- **PREP** 15–20 mins, plus chilling
- **COOK** 1 hr 10 mins–1 hr 20 mins ▪ **SERVES** 4

Ingredients

300g (10oz) shortcrust pastry

plain flour, for dusting

350g (12oz) dyed smoked haddock fillet, with skin

300ml (10fl oz) milk

sprig of thyme

1 bay leaf

60g (2oz) unsalted butter

1 leek (white part only), very finely sliced

1 tbsp plain flour

1 egg, plus 1 egg yolk

salt and freshly ground black pepper

1 tbsp grainy mustard

2 tbsp grated Parmesan cheese

1 Roll out the pastry on a floured surface to line the tart case, and chill for 30 minutes. Preheat the oven to 190°C (375°F/Gas 5). Line the pastry with greaseproof paper and fill with baking beans. Bake for 15–18 minutes. Remove the paper and beans and cool. Reduce the oven temperature to 170°C (340°F/Gas 3½).

2 Put the fish in a sauté pan. Pour over the milk, thyme, and bay leaf. Bring to a boil, reduce the heat, and simmer for 5–6 minutes. Skin, and break into large flakes. Strain the milk.

3 Melt the butter in a saucepan, add the leek, cover, and cook for 6–8 minutes. Stir in the flour and cook for 1 minute. Remove the pan from the heat and slowly blend in the milk. Return to the heat, bring to a boil, then cool. Stir in the egg, yolk, and seasoning.

4 Spread the mustard on the pastry. Arrange the fish on top and spoon on the sauce. Sprinkle with Parmesan and bake for 30–40 minutes. Cool for a moment before serving.

Prepare ahead

Assemble the tart – ensuring all elements are completely cold before placing into the pastry case – up to 1 day ahead, cover, and chill.

Smoked mackerel and spring onion tart

This tart transforms the humble smoked mackerel into a sophisticated and luxurious treat. You will need a 18cm (7in) round, loose-bottomed, straight-sided tart tin and baking beans.

The fish

Smoked mackerel, or smoked salmon

- **PREP** 15 mins ▪ **COOK** 50 mins ▪ **SERVES** 4

Ingredients

250g (9oz) shortcrust pastry

plain flour, for dusting

2 eggs, plus 1 extra for brushing

1 tbsp olive oil

1 bunch of spring onions, finely chopped

salt and freshly ground black pepper

2 smoked mackerel fillets, about 100g (3½oz) each, skinned and flaked

200ml (7fl oz) crème fraîche

handful of flat-leaf parsley, finely chopped

1 bunch of chives, finely chopped

1 Preheat the oven to 200°C (400°F/Gas 6). Roll out the pastry on a floured work surface, and use to line the tin. Trim the excess, line with greaseproof paper, and fill with baking beans. Bake for 15–20 minutes until the edges are golden. Remove the beans and paper, brush with egg wash, and return to the oven for 2–3 minutes to crisp. Reduce the oven temperature to 180°C (350°F/Gas 4).

2 Heat the oil in a frying pan over a low heat. Add half the spring onions and a pinch of salt, and cook gently for 5 minutes. Spoon over the pastry with the raw spring onions. Scatter on the mackerel, and season with pepper.

3 Mix the crème fraîche and the 2 eggs. Add the herbs, season with a little salt, and mix. Carefully pour into the tart case, then bake for 20–30 minutes until set and golden. Leave to cool for 10 minutes before releasing from the tin. Serve with tomato and cucumber salad.

Prepare ahead

The tart shell can be baked 1 day ahead. Cover, and store at room temperature.

Smoked haddock with spinach and pancetta

This deliciously satisfying dish is great for a quick supper.

The fish

Smoked haddock, or smoked cod

- **PREP** 10 mins ▪ **COOK** 15–20 mins
- **SERVES** 6

Ingredients

15g (½oz) butter, plus extra for greasing

1 tbsp olive oil

1 onion, finely chopped

100g (3½oz) pancetta or bacon, chopped

450g (1lb) spinach

100g (3½oz) crème fraîche

salt and freshly ground black pepper

75g (2½oz) Parmesan cheese, grated

800g (1¾lb) smoked haddock fillets, skinned

juice of ½ lemon

30g (1oz) breadcrumbs

1 Preheat the oven to 190°C (375°F/Gas 5) and butter an ovenproof serving dish. Melt the oil and butter together in a frying pan and fry the onion and pancetta for 5 minutes.

2 Add the spinach and stir until wilted, then stir in the crème fraîche, seasoning, and most of the Parmesan. Simmer until slightly thickened.

3 Spoon the spinach mixture into the dish and place the fish on top. Sprinkle with lemon juice. Scatter with breadcrumbs and the remaining Parmesan, and bake for 15–20 minutes, or until the fish is cooked through and flakes easily.

Prepare ahead

Assemble up to 1 day in advance, cover, and refrigerate until ready to bake.

Smoked fish and anchovy gratin

A wonderfully rich and flavoursome recipe for a cold winter evening.

The fish

Smoked mackerel and smoked salmon, or any mix of smoked fish

- **PREP** 10 mins ▪ **COOK** 30 mins ▪ **SERVES** 4

Ingredients

125g (4½oz) smoked mackerel fillet, skinned

125g (4½oz) smoked salmon

8–12 anchovy fillets in olive oil, drained

4 waxy potatoes, peeled, boiled, and sliced

knob of butter, melted

For the sauce

knob of butter

1 onion, finely chopped

1 garlic clove, grated or finely chopped

1 tbsp plain flour

300ml (10fl oz) milk

salt and freshly ground black pepper

handful of curly parsley, finely chopped

1 Preheat the oven to 200°C (400°F/Gas 6). To make the sauce, melt the butter in a pan over a low heat. Add the onion, and sweat gently for about 5 minutes until soft and translucent, then add the garlic and cook for a few seconds more. Remove from the heat and stir in the flour, then add a little of the milk and beat until smooth.

2 Return the pan to the heat, and slowly add the rest of the milk, stirring until thickened. Season well, and stir in the parsley.

3 Layer the smoked fish and anchovies in an ovenproof dish, then spoon over the sauce and gently combine. Top with a layer of potatoes, brush with melted butter, and bake in the oven for 15–20 minutes until golden, crispy, and heated through. Serve with a crisp green salad.

Prepare ahead

Cool the sauce completely, then assemble the dish, cover, and chill up to 2 days in advance. Return to room temperature before baking.

Empanadas

These savoury Spanish pastries make very versatile but substantial nibbles. You'll need a 9cm (3½in) round pastry cutter.

The fish

Canned tuna, or canned sardines

- **PREP** 45 mins, plus chilling
- **COOK** 40–50 mins ▪ **MAKES** 24

Ingredients

450g (1lb) plain flour, plus extra for dusting

salt and freshly ground black pepper

85g (3oz) butter, diced

2 eggs, beaten, plus extra for glazing

1 tbsp olive oil, plus extra for greasing

1 onion, finely chopped

1–2 canned plum tomatoes, drained

2 tsp tomato purée

185g can tuna in spring water, drained

2 tbsp finely chopped flat-leaf parsley

1 To make the pastry, sift the flour into a large mixing bowl with ½ tsp salt. Add the butter and rub in with your fingertips until it resembles fine breadcrumbs. Add the eggs with 4–6 tbsp water and combine to form a dough. Cover with cling film and chill for 30 minutes.

2 Meanwhile, heat the oil in a frying pan, add the onion, and fry over a medium heat, stirring, for 5–8 minutes, or until translucent. Add the tomatoes, tomato purée, tuna, and parsley, and season. Reduce the heat and simmer for 10–12 minutes, stirring occasionally.

3 Preheat the oven to 190°C (375°F/Gas 5). Roll out the pastry to 3mm (⅛in) thick. Using the pastry cutter, cut out 24 rounds. Put 1 tsp of the filling on each, brush the edges with water, fold over, and pinch together.

4 Place the empanadas on an oiled baking tray and brush with egg. Bake for 25–30 minutes, or until golden. Serve warm.

Prepare ahead

Cool the tuna filling completely, then assemble the empanadas, cover and chill for up to 2 days. Bring to room temperature before baking.

Variation

Empanaditas

Cut smaller circles of pastry for bite-sized versions, which make ideal canapés. Bake for just 15–20 minutes.

Coquilles St Jacques

An elegant main course. You'll need 4 scallop shells or ramekins, and a piping bag.

The fish

King scallops, or cockles

- **PREP** 20 mins ▪ **COOK** 50 mins ▪ **SERVES** 4

Ingredients

450g (1lb) floury potatoes, peeled and cut into chunks

85g (3oz) butter

large pinch of grated nutmeg

salt and freshly ground black pepper

3 egg yolks

8 king scallops, roe removed

6 tbsp medium white wine

1 bay leaf

7.5cm (3in) piece of celery stick

4 black peppercorns

small sprig of thyme

225g (8oz) button mushrooms

juice of ½ lemon

1 tbsp plain flour

6 tbsp double cream or crème fraîche

50g (1¾oz) Gruyère or Emmental cheese, grated

1 Boil the potatoes and mash with 30g (1oz) of the butter, nutmeg, and seasoning; beat until fluffy. Stir in the yolks. Spoon into a piping bag and pipe a border around each shell or ramekin.

2 Preheat the oven to 220°C (425°F/Gas 7). Place the scallops in a medium saucepan, add 150ml (5fl oz) water, the wine, bay leaf, celery, peppercorns, thyme, and a pinch of salt. Bring to a boil, cover, and simmer for 1–2 minutes, or until the scallops whiten. Strain, reserve the liquid, and discard the vegetables.

3 Gently cook the mushrooms with the lemon juice, 2 tbsp water, and salt and pepper in a covered pan for 5–7 minutes. Uncover. If any liquid remains, simmer until it evaporates.

4 Melt the remaining butter in a pan. Stir in the flour, and cook for 1 minute. Gradually stir in the reserved scallop liquid. Slowly bring to a boil, and stir until thickened. Season, and simmer over a low heat for 4–5 minutes. Stir in the cream and half the cheese. Cut each scallop in 2, and stir into the sauce with the mushrooms.

5 Spoon the mixture into each shell or ramekin, and sprinkle with the remaining cheese. Bake for 15 minutes, or until golden, and serve.

CANNED TUNA FLAVOUR PAIRING:

The bold taste of canned tuna is great against onion, olives, tomatoes, and garlic. Or make it shine against gentle pasta and creamy cheese sauces.

Salmon, horseradish, and kale bake

When paired with healthy kale, horseradish makes the perfect bake for winter.

The fish

Salmon, or smoked haddock

• **PREP** 10 mins • **COOK** 35 mins • **SERVES** 4

Ingredients

4 salmon fillets, about 150g (5½oz) each, pinboned and skinned

600ml (1 pint) milk

2 handfuls of kale

30g (1oz) butter

1 tbsp flour

115g (4oz) strong Cheddar cheese, grated

1–2 tbsp creamed horseradish

1 Preheat the oven to 200°C (400°F/Gas 6). Put the salmon in a frying pan, and pour in enough milk to cover. Poach gently over a low heat for about 10 minutes until opaque and cooked, then transfer the salmon to an ovenproof dish using a slotted spoon or fish slice. Strain and reserve the milk.

2 Trim the tough stalks from the kale, and roughly chop the leaves. Boil or steam for about 5 minutes until nearly soft, then drain, and add to the salmon. Combine gently.

3 Melt the butter in a saucepan and stir in the flour. Cook for 1 minute, until foaming, then gradually add the poaching milk, whisking constantly to remove lumps. Bring to a boil and cook, stirring, for 4–5 minutes, until thickened. Remove from the heat and add the cheese, stirring, until it melts, then the horseradish.

4 Pour the cheese sauce over the salmon, and bake for about 15 minutes until golden.

Prepare ahead

The whole dish can be assembled, covered, and chilled several hours in advance. Bring to room temperature before baking.

Haddock mornay

With a layer of spinach under the poached haddock, this is a colourful one-pot meal.

The fish

Haddock, or smoked cod or smoked pollock

• **PREP** 10 mins • **COOK** 30 mins • **SERVES** 4

Ingredients

675g (1½lb) haddock fillet, pinboned, skinned, and cut into 4 equal pieces

150ml (5fl oz) fish stock or water

300ml (10fl oz) milk

45g (1½oz) butter, plus extra to grease

45g (1½oz) plain flour

115g (4oz) Cheddar cheese, grated

salt and freshly ground black pepper

250g (9oz) spinach leaves, chopped

pinch of grated nutmeg

60g (2oz) fresh wholemeal breadcrumbs

2 tbsp chopped flat-leaf parsley

60g (2oz) Parmesan cheese, grated

1 Place the fish in a deep frying pan, pour in the stock and milk, and slowly bring to a boil, then cover and simmer for 6–8 minutes, or until the fish is cooked. Lift the fish from the pan and keep warm. Reserve the poaching liquid.

2 Melt the butter in a pan and stir in the flour until smooth. Cook for 1 minute, then gradually whisk in the poaching liquid. Stir over the heat until thickened. Stir in the Cheddar, season, and remove from the heat.

3 Put the spinach in a pan, cover, and cook for 1 minute over a low heat, until wilted. Season with the nutmeg and spread out in a greased, shallow, ovenproof dish. Preheat the grill.

4 Place the haddock on the spinach and pour over the sauce. Mix the breadcrumbs, parsley, and Parmesan, and sprinkle over. Grill until golden, and serve.

Prepare ahead

The whole dish can be assembled, covered, and chilled several hours in advance. Reheat gently before grilling.

Tuna and pasta bake

This is a quick, one-dish, store-cupboard meal that is ideal at the end of a busy day. You'll need a 1.5 litre (2¾ pint) ovenproof serving dish.

The fish
Canned tuna, or canned mackerel

- **PREP** 10 mins ▪ **COOK** 40 mins ▪ **SERVES** 6

Ingredients
salt and freshly ground black pepper
200g (7oz) pasta shells
oil, for the dish
300g can condensed cream of mushroom soup
120ml (4fl oz) milk
200g can tuna in spring, drained
200g can sweetcorn, drained and rinsed
1 onion, finely chopped
1 red pepper, cored and finely chopped
4 tbsp chopped flat-leaf parsley
pinch of chilli powder (optional)
115g (4oz) Cheddar or Cheshire cheese, grated

1 Bring a large saucepan of salted water to a boil over a high heat. Add the pasta, stir, and cook for 2 minutes less than the time specified on the packet. Drain the pasta and set it aside.

2 Preheat the oven to 220°C (425°F/Gas 7) and oil a 1.5-litre (2¾-pint) ovenproof serving dish.

3 Heat the mushroom soup and milk over a low heat in the saucepan used for the pasta. Stir in the tuna, sweetcorn, onion, pepper, parsley, chilli powder (if using), and half the cheese. Once the soup is heated, stir in the pasta. Season to taste.

4 Tip the mixture into the dish and smooth the top. Sprinkle with the remaining cheese. Bake for 30–35 minutes, or until golden brown. Serve hot, straight from the dish, with hot garlic bread and a green salad.

Prepare ahead
The whole dish can be assembled, covered, and chilled several hours in advance. Bring to room temperature before cooking.

Monkfish Americaine

The firm texture of monkfish makes it an excellent candidate for this dish.

The fish
Monkfish, or tiger prawns or lobster

- **PREP** 45–50 mins ▪ **COOK** 1 hr
- **SERVES** 4–6

Ingredients
1.35kg (3lb) monkfish, with its bone
2 onions, chopped
125ml (4fl oz) dry white wine, or juice of ½ lemon
1 tsp peppercorns
3–5 sprigs of parsley
30g (1oz) plain flour
salt and freshly ground pepper
2 tbsp olive oil
125g (4½oz) butter

For the Americaine sauce
1 carrot, diced
2 garlic cloves, finely chopped
400g can chopped plum tomatoes
150ml (5fl oz) dry white wine
3 tbsp Cognac
leaves from 3–4 sprigs of tarragon, chopped, stalks reserved
pinch of cayenne pepper (optional)
1 bouquet garni

4 tbsp double cream
1 tbsp tomato purée
pinch of sugar (optional)

1 Cut the fish into 1cm (½in) slices. Slightly flatten each with the side of a broad knife.

2 Put half the onions in a large saucepan and add the fish bone, wine, peppercorns, parsley, and 500ml (16fl oz) water. Bring slowly to a boil, then simmer, uncovered, for 20 minutes. Strain and reserve.

3 Put the flour on a plate and season. Lightly coat the fish slices. Heat the oil and a quarter of the butter in a sauté pan, add half the fish and sauté for 2–3 minutes. Transfer to a plate. Sauté the remaining fish.

4 Add the carrot, garlic, and remaining onion to the saucepan and cook for 3–5 minutes, or until soft. Add the tomatoes, wine, Cognac, tarragon stalks, salt, pepper, cayenne, and bouquet garni. Pour in the stock. Bring to a boil and simmer for 15–20 minutes.

5 Sieve the sauce into a large saucepan, pressing down with a ladle. Boil for 5–10 minutes, until thickened. Whisk in the cream and tomato purée. Taste, adding sugar if you like.

6 Add the monkfish and simmer for 5–10 minutes. Take from the heat and add the remaining butter in small pieces, shaking. Sprinkle with tarragon and serve.

One Pot

Caldereta asturiana

This iconic stew, from the Asturias region of Spain, traditionally uses fish landed on the day.

The fish

Any mixed white fish, such as hake, monkfish, or red mullet, and shellfish, such as squid, mussels, prawns, or clams

- **PREP** 25 mins ▪ **COOK** 40 mins ▪ **SERVES** 6

Ingredients

1kg (2¼lb) white fish fillets, pinboned and skinned

4 small squid, gutted and cleaned (see page 282)

500g (1lb 2oz) each mussels, prepared (see page 278) and clams, thoroughly washed

150ml (5fl oz) dry white wine

3 tbsp extra virgin olive oil

1 large Spanish onion, chopped

3 garlic cloves, grated or finely chopped

large pinch of cayenne pepper

1 heaped tbsp plain flour

300ml (10fl oz) fish stock

large bunch (8–10 tbsp) flat-leaf parsley, chopped

250g (9oz) large raw prawns, peeled and deveined (see page 285)

2 large red peppers, deseeded and quartered

salt and freshly ground black pepper

lemon juice, to taste

1 Preheat the oven to 180°C (350°F/Gas 4). Cut the fish fillets into large pieces and the squid into large squares. Chill until needed.

2 Check the mussels and clams are shut, or close when tapped sharply. Put the wine in a large saucepan, bring to a boil, add the mussels and clams and cook over a medium heat for 3–4 minutes, or until open. Discard any that remain shut. Strain the liquor and reserve. Remove the shellfish from their shells.

3 Heat the oil in a large casserole, add the onion, and cook until softening. Add the garlic, cayenne pepper, and flour; stir for 1–2 minutes. Add the mussel liquid, fish stock, and parsley.

4 Add the raw seafood and peppers and season. Cover and cook in the oven for 20–25 minutes. Add the mussels and clams, and return to the oven for 5 minutes. Sprinkle with lemon and serve with crusty bread.

Prepare ahead

Make the sauce base in step 3 up to 2 days in advance, cover, and refrigerate. Return to a simmer before continuing.

Ligurian fish stew

An easy, but very impressive stew.

The fish

Red mullet, John Dory, whiting, mahi mahi, clams, or any mixed seafood

- **PREP** 20 mins ▪ **COOK** 20–25 mins
- **SERVES** 6–8

Ingredients

3 medium red mullet, scaled and filleted

4 small John Dory fillets, skinned

225g (8oz) whiting fillet, skinned

225g (8oz) mahi mahi fillet, skinned

150ml (5fl oz) olive oil

1 onion, finely chopped

2 celery sticks, finely sliced

2 small carrots, finely sliced

1 bulb fennel, finely sliced

3 garlic cloves, crushed

1 tsp tomato purée

3 tbsp Pernod

150ml (5fl oz) dry white wine

8 plum tomatoes, deseeded and roughly chopped

2 tsp thyme leaves

2 tsp marjoram leaves, chopped

1 litre (1¾ pints) fish stock

salt and freshly ground black pepper

225g (8oz) clams, thoroughly washed

1 Pinbone the mullet, Dory, and whiting fillets (see page 271) and halve. Trim the mahi mahi fillet and cut into large pieces. Set aside.

2 Heat most of the oil in a large casserole. Add the vegetables and garlic and cook over a low heat for 4–5 minutes. Stir in the tomato purée, then the Pernod, wine, tomatoes, and herbs. Bring to a boil and simmer for 5 minutes. Add the stock, and simmer for 5 minutes. Season.

3 Add the fish and cook over a low heat for 4–5 minutes or until opaque and firm. Add the clams and cook until the shells have opened. Adjust the seasoning and serve with warm ciabatta, drizzled with the remaining oil.

Variation

Seafood and tomato cioppino
Replace the clams with mussels, small scallops, and 2 whole cooked crabs, chopped into pieces. Reduce the total weight of white fish to 500g (1lb 2oz). Omit the celery, carrots, and fennel. Sprinkle with chopped flat-leaf parsley to serve.

JOHN DORY FLAVOUR PAIRINGS:
A tomato accompaniment, as in Ligurian fish stew, suits John Dory, although it's also great with creamy sauces, wild mushrooms, sage, capers, lemon, and rich crème fraîche.

Mussels in fennel broth

A great pick-me-up, aromatic and healthy.

The fish

Mussels, or palourde or hard-shell clams

- **PREP** 10 mins ▪ **COOK** 20 mins ▪ **SERVES** 4

Ingredients

1 tbsp olive oil

1 onion, finely chopped

1 fennel bulb, finely chopped

salt and freshly ground black pepper

2 garlic cloves, grated or finely chopped

2 waxy potatoes, peeled and finely diced

300ml (10fl oz) hot vegetable stock or
fish stock

400g can coconut milk

1.35kg (3lb) mussels, prepared (see page 278)

handful of basil leaves, torn

1 Heat the oil in a large pan over a low heat. Add the onion, fennel, and a pinch of salt, then sweat for about 5 minutes until softened. Add the garlic and potatoes, and cook for a few more minutes, being careful not to allow anything to brown.

2 Pour in the stock, and bring to a boil. Add the coconut milk, reduce the heat slightly, and simmer gently for about 10 minutes, or until the potatoes are cooked. Return to a boil, add the mussels, and cover. Cook for about 5 minutes, until the mussels are open (discard any that remain shut).

3 Stir in the basil, and adjust the seasoning. Serve immediately.

Prepare ahead

Make the broth up to the point when the potatoes are cooked, cover, and refrigerate for up to 2 days. Reheat gently before continuing.

Mussels in ginger and chilli broth

These succulent mussels in a moat of gingery juices are terrific with a mound of fluffy rice.

The fish

Mussels, or palourde or hard-shell clams

- **PREP** 20 mins ▪ **COOK** 25 mins
▪ **SERVES** 2–4

Ingredients

1.5 kg (3lb 3oz) mussels, prepared
(see page 278)

100g (3½oz) butter

2 onions, finely chopped

2 red bird's eye chillies, finely chopped

5cm (2in) fresh root ginger, shredded

5 large garlic cloves, grated or finely chopped

2 stalks lemongrass, split lengthways
and lightly bruised

120ml (4fl oz) ginger wine

400ml (14fl oz) fish stock

150ml (5fl oz) coconut milk

3 tbsp coconut cream

salt and freshly ground black pepper

juice of 1–2 limes, to taste

3 tbsp chopped coriander leaves

1 Tap the mussels and discard any that do not close.

2 Melt the butter in a large pan over a low heat, and gently cook the onions, chillies, ginger, garlic, and lemongrass for 10 minutes until soft but not coloured.

3 Increase the heat to high and add the wine and stock. Bring to a boil before tipping in the mussels. Cover and cook for 5–7 minutes, until they have opened. Discard the lemongrass along with any mussels that remain closed.

4 Pour in the coconut milk and cream, and bring to a boil. Season, sharpen with lime juice, stir in the coriander leaves, and serve.

Mixed fish stew with croutons

A hearty dish ideal for a large gathering.

The fish

Any mixed fish, such as haddock, monkfish, or plaice, and any shellfish, such as prawns

- **PREP** 15 mins - **COOK** 30 mins - **SERVES** 8

Ingredients

2.25kg (5lb) mixed fish fillets, scaled and pinboned, and shellfish, shelled

3 tbsp olive oil

4 garlic cloves, grated or finely chopped

2 tbsp tomato purée

1 onion, finely chopped

8 tomatoes, skinned, deseeded, and chopped (see page 112)

1 tsp fennel seeds

a few strands of saffron

pinch of paprika

1.2 litres (2 pints) fish stock

salt and freshly ground black pepper

1 baguette

125g (4½oz) Gruyère cheese, grated

handful of flat-leaf parsley, finely chopped

1 Wash the fish, then cut it into chunky bite-sized pieces and set aside. Put the oil in a large wide pan, add the garlic, tomato purée, and onion, and cook over a very low heat for 5–8 minutes, or until the onion begins to soften, but not colour.

2 Add the tomatoes, fennel seeds, saffron, and paprika, pour in the stock, and season with salt and pepper. Bring to a boil, then reduce to a simmer, and cook for 10 minutes. Add the fish and shellfish and simmer for 10 minutes more, or until the fish is cooked.

3 Slice the bread on the diagonal and toast. Serve the soup with the croutons, and sprinkle over the cheese, and parsley.

Prepare ahead

Make the soup base up to just before adding the fish, cover, and refrigerate for up to 2 days. Return to a simmer before continuing.

Spicy, saucy monkfish

A satisfying meal for a cold winter's night.

The fish

Monkfish, or grey mullet, mahi mahi, or red snapper

- **PREP** 30–35 mins - **COOK** 30–35 mins
- **SERVES** 6

Ingredients

4 tbsp vegetable oil

2 onions, finely sliced

2 tbsp paprika

300ml (10fl oz) fish stock

2 x 400g cans tomatoes

6 garlic cloves, grated or finely chopped

4 bay leaves

2 celery sticks, peeled and finely sliced

2 carrots, finely sliced

salt and freshly ground black pepper

1kg (2¼lb) monkfish fillets, skinned and cut in 2.5cm (1in) cubes

For the spicy sauce

30g (1oz) butter

1 onion, finely chopped

1 apple, peeled, cored, and diced

1 tsp ground cumin

1 tsp ground coriander

½ tsp ground ginger

½ tsp ground cloves

¼ tsp cayenne pepper, or ½ tsp chilli flakes

½ tbsp cornflour

200ml (7fl oz) coconut milk

150ml (5fl oz) fish stock

1 For the sauce, melt the butter in a saucepan. Add the onion and apple and cook gently for 3–5 minutes, until soft. Add the spices and stir for 2–3 minutes. Blend the cornflour to a paste with 2–3 tbsp of the coconut milk.

2 Add the remaining coconut milk and the stock to the saucepan and bring to a boil. Stir in the cornflour paste; the sauce will thicken. Set aside.

3 Heat the oil in a casserole. Add the onions and cook for 3–5 minutes, until soft. Add the paprika, stock, tomatoes, garlic, bay leaves, celery, and carrots. Season and bring to a boil. Reduce the heat and simmer to reduce by one-third.

4 Add the sauce and return to a boil. Add the fish. Cover and simmer for 12–15 minutes. Discard the bay leaves and serve in warm bowls.

Prepare ahead

Make the spicy sauce and the stew base up to 3 days ahead, mix, cover, and refrigerate. Return to a boil before adding the fish.

SUSTAINABILITY CHOICE
Diversify

Try out less popular fish to take pressure off the more extensively fished species. You can also expect more for your money, as there isn't high demand for them. Aim to vary your choices, however, as less popular species may not yet have been monitored for stock levels and they may quickly become overfished themselves. In the UK, whiting (shown here) is a great example of an underutilized species that should be enjoyed more often. Look out for lesser-known species of fish in responsible supermarkets and restaurants and give them a try.

Prawn gumbo

A classic from Louisiana, this has a brown roux base and is thickened with okra (gumbo).

The fish

Tiger prawns, or cod, scallops, or kingfish, and brown crab meat

- **PREP** 30 mins - **COOK** 1 hr - **SERVES** 6–8

Ingredients

85g (3oz) butter

1kg (2¼lb) raw tiger prawns, peeled and deveined (see page 285)

4 tbsp brown crab meat

2 tbsp plain flour

½ tsp cayenne pepper

1 large onion, finely chopped

2 garlic cloves, grated or finely chopped

115g (4oz) okra, trimmed

1 large red pepper, deseeded and diced

2 x 400g cans tomatoes, or 750g (1lb 10oz) fresh tomatoes, halved

1 litre (1¾ pints) shellfish stock

1 bay leaf

2 sprigs of thyme

grated zest of 1 lemon

1 tbsp filé powder (optional)

salt and freshly ground black pepper

1 Melt the butter in a large saucepan, add the prawns in batches and stir-fry over a medium heat for 2–3 minutes or until cooked. Lift on to a plate and cool.

2 Add the crab and flour to the butter, cook over a low heat for 3–4 minutes or until the flour is golden brown. Add the cayenne, onion, and garlic, and cook for a further 3 minutes.

3 Stir in the okra and red pepper. Pour over the tomatoes, stock, herbs, and lemon zest. Bring to a boil and simmer for 25–30 minutes until thick.

4 Stir the prawns into the gumbo to warm through, add filé powder (if using), and season to taste. Serve with rice and Tabasco sauce.

Prepare ahead

The gumbo can be made, cooled, chilled, covered, and refrigerated up to 1 day in advance of serving. Reheat very gently, or the prawns will toughen.

Bouillabaisse

A delicious soup for a special occasion.

The fish

Any mixed white and oily fish, such as gurnard, John Dory, monkfish, herring, and rascasse, and shellfish, such as prawns and mussels

- **PREP** 20 mins - **COOK** 45 mins - **SERVES** 4

Ingredients

4 tbsp olive oil

1 onion, finely sliced

2 leeks, finely sliced

1 small fennel bulb, finely sliced

6–7 garlic cloves, grated or finely chopped

4 tomatoes, skinned, deseeded, and chopped

2 tbsp tomato purée

250ml (8fl oz) dry white wine

1.5 litres (2¾ pints) fish or chicken stock

pinch of saffron threads

strip of orange zest

1 bouquet garni

salt and freshly ground black pepper

1.35kg (3lb) mixed white and oily fish fillets, pinboned and cut into chunks, and shellfish

2 tbsp Pernod

125g (4½oz) mayonnaise

1 bird's-eye chilli, deseeded and roughly chopped

8 thin slices day-old French bread, toasted, to serve

1 Heat the oil in a large saucepan over a medium heat. Add the onion, leeks, fennel, and 2–3 of the garlic cloves and fry, stirring, for 5–8 minutes, or until the vegetables are softened. Add the tomatoes, half the tomato purée, and all the wine, and stir until blended.

2 Add the stock, saffron, orange zest, and bouquet garni. Season to taste, and bring to a boil. Reduce the heat, partially cover the pan, and simmer for 30 minutes, or until the soup is reduced slightly, stirring occasionally.

3 Remove the orange zest and bouquet garni from the soup and add the firm fish. Reduce the heat to low and let simmer for 5 minutes, then add the delicate fish and simmer for a further 2–3 minutes. Stir in the Pernod, and season.

4 To make the rouille, place the remaining garlic and tomato purée, mayonnaise, chilli, and ½ tsp salt into a food processor and whizz until smooth. Spread each piece of toast with rouille and put 2 slices in the bottom of each bowl. Ladle the soup on top and serve.

CRAB FLAVOUR PAIRINGS: Rich, strong, brown crab meat is great with cayenne pepper or anchovy essence. White crab meat is best with mild egg or mayonnaise.

Italian seafood stew

A simple fish stew from Tuscany, made by impoverished fishermen making the best of their catch in the Adriatic.

The fish

Grey mullet, bogue, or any mixed white fish, and cuttlefish

- **PREP** 10 mins ▪ **COOK** 20 mins
- **SERVES** 6–8

Ingredients

2 grey mullet, scaled and filleted

4 bogue, scaled and filleted

1 cuttlefish, gutted and cleaned (see page 283)

5 tbsp extra virgin olive oil

2 onions, finely sliced

1 red chilli, deseeded and finely diced

3 garlic cloves, chopped

400g can chopped plum tomatoes

150ml (5fl oz) dry white wine

600ml (1 pint) fish stock

2 tbsp chopped flat-leaf parsley

salt and freshly ground black pepper

thickly sliced and toasted Italian rustic bread, to serve

1 Pinbone the fish fillets (see page 271). Cut into large pieces. Thinly slice the cuttlefish and set aside.

2 Heat the olive oil and add the onions; cook over a low heat for 5–6 minutes or until they are translucent. Add the chilli and garlic and fry for a few minutes longer. Stir in the tomatoes, wine, and stock, bring to a boil, and simmer until syrupy. Add the parsley and season to taste.

3 Add the grey mullet and bogue, set the pan over a low heat for 6–8 minutes or until the fish is cooked: it will be opaque. Add the cuttlefish and stir into the broth for a minute or so until it has just lost its translucency.

4 Arrange the toasted bread on 6–8 plates and spoon the broth on top.

Prepare ahead

The broth can be prepared up to 1 day ahead, covered, and refrigerated. Reheat gently before continuing with the recipe.

Monkfish in spicy tomato sauce

This classic recipe has fabulously bold and sunshiney flavours.

The fish

Monkfish, or skate, mahi mahi, or tiger prawns

- **PREP** 20 mins ▪ **COOK** 20 mins ▪ **SERVES** 4

Ingredients

1kg (2¼lb) monkfish tail, filleted and trimmed of membrane (see page 270)

2 tbsp extra virgin olive oil, plus a splash for frying

1 small onion, chopped

2 garlic cloves, chopped

1–2 red chillies, deseeded and chopped

10 plum tomatoes, skinned, deseeded, and chopped (see page 112), or 400g can chopped plum tomatoes

200ml (7fl oz) passata

1 tsp sugar

1 tbsp chopped oregano

12 black olives, stoned and halved

2 tbsp capers, rinsed

salt and freshly ground black pepper

1 Cut the monkfish into 4 even-sized portions; refrigerate until ready to use.

2 Heat the 2 tbsp olive oil in a large sauté pan, add the onion, and cook for 3–4 minutes or until soft. Add the garlic and chilli and fry over a low to medium heat for a further 1–2 minutes.

3 Add the tomatoes, passata, and sugar, bring to a boil, reduce the heat and simmer for 5 minutes, or until the tomatoes begin to break down and soften.

4 In a small frying pan, heat the splash of oil and brown the monkfish for 1–2 minutes. Lift into the tomato sauce and cook over a low heat for 5–7 minutes or until the monkfish is cooked, it will be firm and opaque in appearance.

5 Stir the oregano, olives, and capers into the sauce and season. Serve with rice or pasta.

Prepare ahead

The tomato sauce can be made ahead, covered, and chilled for up to 2 days. Reheat gently, and add the oregano, olives, and capers just before serving.

GREY MULLET FLAVOUR PAIRINGS

The sometimes earthy taste of this firm fish is enhanced by lemon juice, white wine, and white wine vinegar, or any dish containing tomatoes.

Salt cod braised with vegetables

This Spanish recipe is fragrant with the aromas of garlic, bay, and saffron.

The fish

Salt cod, or salt pollock

- **PREP** 20 mins, plus soaking ▪ **COOK** 40 mins
- **SERVES** 4

Ingredients

800g (1¾lb) thick-cut salt cod, soaked, scaled, and cut into 4 pieces

3 tbsp olive oil

1 onion, finely diced

white parts of 2 leeks, finely sliced

3 garlic cloves, grated or finely chopped

3 tomatoes, peeled, deseeded, and chopped (see page 112)

500g (1lb 2oz) potatoes, peeled and diced

salt and freshly ground black pepper

2 bay leaves

large pinch of saffron threads

120ml (4fl oz) dry white wine

2 tbsp chopped flat-leaf parsley

1 Soak the fish for at least 24 hours in enough water to cover, changing the water 2–3 times.

2 Heat the oil in a large, shallow, heatproof casserole. Add the onion and leek, and fry gently, stirring, for 5 minutes, or until soft.

3 Add the garlic and tomatoes, and stir for a further 2 minutes. Add the potatoes, season, and add the bay leaves and saffron.

4 Put the salt cod, skin-side up, on top. Pour in the wine and 250ml (8fl oz) water, then bring to a simmer and cook for 25–30 minutes. Shake the casserole once or twice every few minutes to help thicken the sauce.

5 Sprinkle over the parsley, and serve straight from the casserole.

Prepare ahead

The vegetable base of the braise – steps 2 and 3 – can be cooked up to 2 days ahead, covered, and refrigerated. Return to room temperature before continuing.

Hungarian fish goulash

Seek out responsibly sourced huss for this recipe. Paprika flatters the fish – use more of the spice for greater heat.

The fish

Huss, or carp

- **PREP** 15–20 mins ▪ **COOK** 25 mins
- **SERVES** 4

Ingredients

1kg (2¼lb) huss fillets, skinned

seasoned flour (see page 55)

3 tbsp sunflower oil, plus more if needed

1 large onion, chopped

1–2 red or green peppers, thickly sliced

1–2 tsp paprika, to taste

200–250ml (7–8fl oz) medium white wine

1 tbsp chopped dill

1 tbsp chopped flat-leaf parsley

salt and freshly ground black pepper

250ml (8fl oz) soured cream

1 Cut the huss fillets into 2.5cm (1in) chunks. Roll them in seasoned flour.

2 Heat the oil in a large frying pan and cook the huss in batches for 3–4 minutes or until cooked, adding a little more oil between batches if needed. Lift on to a plate and keep warm.

3 Add the onion and peppers to the pan and fry over a medium heat for 3–4 minutes or until beginning to soften. Stir in the paprika to taste and cook for a further 2 minutes.

4 Add the wine, bring to a boil, and simmer for 2–3 minutes to reduce by one-third. Return the huss and add the herbs. Season to taste.

5 Swirl in the soured cream and heat through until the goulash just comes to a boil. Adjust the seasoning and serve with rice or noodles.

Prepare ahead

The flavours of the goulash will improve if cooled, covered, and refrigerated for up to 36 hours in advance. Reheat gently before adding the soured cream.

HUSS FLAVOUR PAIRINGS: The soft flesh of huss responds well to strong flavours, such as paprika, piquant tartare sauce, salty soy, sesame oil, ginger, and chilli.

OCTOPUS FLAVOUR PAIRINGS: The firm, sweet chunks are great with the Asian tastes of a spicy stir-fry, or try it Italian style with red wine, onions, balsamic vinegar, and sage.

Vietnamese caramel monkfish

The caramel here gives the fish an intense sticky sweetness, which is balanced by salty fish sauce.

The fish

Monkfish, or mahi mahi or tiger prawns

- **PREP** 10 mins ▪ **COOK** 30 mins
- **SERVES** 2–4

Ingredients

750g (1lb 10oz) monkfish tail, filleted and trimmed of membrane (see page 270)

50g (1¾oz) granulated sugar

2 tbsp vegetable oil

2 garlic cloves, chopped

4 small shallots, chopped

3–4 tbsp Vietnamese fish sauce

2 spring onions, finely sliced

freshly ground black pepper

large handful of coriander leaves, to garnish

lime wedges, to garnish

1 Cut the monkfish fillets into 3–4cm (1–1½in) cubes. Set aside.

2 Put 120ml (4fl oz) water and the sugar into a heavy saucepan. Cook over a low heat, stirring very occasionally, until the sugar has dissolved. Increase the heat and boil steadily until the mixture begins to brown. Cover your hand with a cloth, and swirl the pan so the caramel browns evenly; do not stir. Once the caramel is deep brown and smells nutty, quickly add 120ml (4fl oz) more water. It will spit, so take care. Allow the sizzling to subside, then pour into a jug.

3 Heat the oil in a large wok, add the garlic and shallots, and stir over a medium heat until beginning to colour. Add the monkfish and stir-fry over a high heat until brown. Stir in the caramel sauce over a medium heat until the monkfish is white and firm to the touch. Add the fish sauce and spring onions and stir until the onions are slightly soft. Season with pepper.

4 Pile into a serving dish with coriander leaves and lime wedges. Serve with rice or noodles.

Prepare ahead

Make the caramel a day in advance, cover, and store at room temperature. If it hardens, reheat very gently before continuing.

Spicy stir-fried squid

A traditional Thai recipe, although such recipes are legion in many countries and regions across Asia.

The fish

Squid, or cuttlefish, octopus, or prawns

- **PREP** 20 mins ▪ **COOK** 5–6 mins
- **SERVES** 2–4

Ingredients

8 small squid, gutted and cleaned (see page 282)

1 tbsp vegetable oil

1 stalk lemongrass, split into 4 lengthways

2 kaffir lime leaves

1 yellow or orange pepper, deseeded and diced

handful of basil leaves, preferably Thai, shredded

salt and freshly ground black pepper

For the paste

3 garlic cloves, chopped

2 shallots, roughly chopped

1 tbsp grated fresh root ginger

1–2 red chillies, to taste (deseeded for a milder result)

50g (1¾oz) chopped coriander, preferably both leaves and roots

large splash of vegetable oil

1 tbsp palm sugar or dark brown sugar

1 tbsp Thai fish sauce

1 Score the squid tubes (see page 282) and set aside with the tentacles.

2 To make the paste, put the garlic, shallots, ginger, chilli, coriander, vegetable oil, palm sugar, and fish sauce into a food processor. Whizz to form a finely chopped green paste.

3 Heat the 1 tbsp vegetable oil in a large wok, add the paste, and fry over a low to medium heat for 2–3 minutes or until it smells aromatic. Add the squid, lemongrass, lime leaves, and pepper. Stir-fry, tossing over a brisk heat until the squid is opaque and coated in the other ingredients. (Avoid overcooking the squid, as it will become tough.)

4 Stir in the basil and adjust the seasoning, then remove the lemongrass and lime leaves. Serve with rice or noodles and a green salad.

Prepare ahead

The paste can be made up to 1 day ahead, covered, and chilled. It will become hotter.

Sweet and sour prawns

Prawns in a fragrant sauce spiked with chilli, garlic, and ginger makes a great main course.

The fish

Tiger prawns, or squid, scallops, or monkfish

- **PREP** 20 mins ▪ **COOK** 10 mins ▪ **SERVES** 4

Ingredients

3 tbsp rice wine vinegar

2 tbsp clear honey

1 tbsp caster sugar

2 tbsp light soy sauce

2 tbsp tomato ketchup

2 tbsp vegetable oil

3 shallots, peeled and sliced

2cm (¾in) fresh root ginger, grated

1 red chilli, deseeded and finely chopped

1 garlic clove, crushed

1 small carrot, cut into matchsticks

1 celery stick, cut into matchsticks

1 green pepper, deseeded and cut into strips

500g (1lb 2oz) raw tiger prawns, peeled and deveined (see page 285)

2 spring onions, sliced lengthways, to serve

1 Put the vinegar, honey, sugar, soy sauce, and tomato ketchup in a small saucepan, and heat gently until the honey and sugar melt. Remove from the heat and set aside.

2 Heat the oil in a wok, add the shallots, ginger, chilli, garlic, carrot, celery, and green pepper and stir-fry for 4 minutes.

3 Add the prawns and stir-fry for a further 2 minutes or until they turn pink. Pour in the vinegar mixture and stir-fry for 1 minute, or until the prawns and vegetables are coated and everything is heated through.

4 To serve, transfer to a platter and sprinkle with spring onions. Serve with boiled rice.

Pad Thai

One of Thailand's national dishes, this is often served rolled up in a thin omelette.

The fish

Tiger prawns, or squid or monkfish

- **PREP** 20 mins ▪ **COOK** 10 mins ▪ **SERVES** 4

Ingredients

2 tbsp chopped coriander leaves

1 red bird's eye chilli, deseeded and finely chopped

4 tbsp vegetable oil

250g (9oz) raw tiger prawns, peeled and deveined (see page 285)

4 shallots, finely chopped

1 tbsp sugar

4 large eggs, beaten

2 tbsp oyster sauce

1 tbsp Thai fish sauce

juice of 1 lime

350g (12oz) flat rice noodles, cooked according to package instructions

250g (9oz) beansprouts

4 spring onions, sliced

115g (4oz) unsalted roasted peanuts, coarsely chopped

1 lime, cut into wedges, to serve

1 Mix together the coriander, chilli, and vegetable oil. Heat half the mixture in a wok, add the tiger prawns, and stir-fry for 1 minute. Remove and set aside.

2 Add the remaining herb oil to the wok and stir-fry the shallots for 1 minute. Add the sugar and eggs, and cook for 1 minute, stirring frequently to scramble the eggs.

3 Stir in the oyster sauce, fish sauce, lime juice, noodles, and beansprouts, and return the prawns to the wok. Stir-fry for 2 minutes, then add the spring onions and half the peanuts. Toss everything together for 1–2 minutes, or until piping hot.

4 Divide between 4 warmed bowls, scatter the remaining nuts on top, and add a lime wedge. This is excellent with a fresh salad of beansprouts and shredded carrot, tossed with lime juice.

Soba noodles with prawns and avocado

Soba noodles, usually made from buckwheat flour, originate in Japan.

The fish
Tiger prawns, or scallops

- **PREP** 15 mins, plus standing ■ **COOK** 15 mins
- **SERVES** 4

Ingredients
250g (9oz) soba noodles

45g (1½oz) dried wakame (seaweed)

2 tbsp vegetable or groundnut oil

16 raw tiger prawns, peeled and deveined, tails left on (see page 285)

6 shiitake mushrooms, sliced

4 cherry tomatoes, halved

2 tbsp pickled ginger, rinsed and finely chopped

4 tbsp mirin

2 tbsp rice vinegar

2 tbsp Japanese soy sauce

1 avocado, sliced

2 tbsp sesame seeds, to serve

2 tbsp roughly chopped coriander leaves, to serve

1 Cook the noodles in a pan of boiling water according to the package instructions, or until just tender. Drain and rinse under cold water until cool. Drain again, and set aside.

2 Soak the wakame in cold water until soft, then drain, and cut into strips. Set aside.

3 Heat the oil in a wok, add the prawns and mushrooms, and stir-fry for 1 minute. Add the tomatoes and stir-fry for a further minute. Set aside to cool, then add to the noodles.

4 Make a dressing by mixing the pickled ginger, mirin, vinegar, and soy sauce. Add the dressing, wakame, and avocado to the noodles and vegetables, and toss.

5 Divide among 4 serving plates, and sprinkle with sesame seeds and chopped coriander.

Prepare ahead
Make the noodles, without the avocado, up to 1 day ahead, cover, and refrigerate. Return to room temperature, add the avocado, and sprinkle with sesame seeds, and coriander.

Sweet and sour stir-fried fish with ginger

Make sure you buy very firm-fleshed fish for this, so it doesn't fall apart in the wok.

The fish
Any firm white fish, such as haddock

- **PREP** 10 mins ■ **COOK** 20 mins ■ **SERVES** 4

Ingredients
1–2 tbsp cornflour

salt and freshly ground black pepper

675g (1½lb) thick white fish fillets, pinboned, skinned, and cut into strips

1–2 tbsp vegetable or sunflower oil

1 onion, roughly chopped

2 garlic cloves, grated or finely chopped

2.5cm (1in) fresh root ginger, finely sliced

large handful mangetout or sugarsnap peas, sliced into strips

For the sweet and sour sauce
1 tbsp white wine vinegar

1 tbsp tomato purée

1 tbsp sugar

1 tsp cornflour

2 tsp light soy sauce

2 tbsp pineapple juice

1 For the sauce, mix the vinegar, tomato purée, sugar, cornflour, soy sauce, and pineapple juice in a jug, and set aside. Put the cornflour for the fish on a plate, season, and toss in the fish.

2 In a wok, heat half the oil until hot, then add the fish. Stir-fry for 5 minutes until golden. Remove with a slotted spoon, and keep warm. Carefully wipe the wok with kitchen paper, and add a little more oil. When hot, add the onion and stir-fry until it softens, then add the garlic and ginger, and stir-fry for a few minutes more.

3 Pour in the sweet and sour sauce, and let boil for a few minutes, stirring constantly. Reduce the heat to medium, add the mangetout, and stir-fry for 1 minute. Return the fish to the wok, quickly toss together, and serve with rice.

Prepare ahead
Make the sweet and sour sauce up to 2 days ahead and keep, covered, in the refrigerator.

Crab stir-fried with curry powder

This Thai street dish is eaten throughout the country. For eating indoors, you'll need plenty of paper napkins and finger bowls with lemon slices for your diners.

The fish

Crab, or prawns or scallops

- **PREP** 30 mins ▪ **COOK** 15–20 mins
- **SERVES** 4

Ingredients

1 raw crab, about 1kg (2¼lb) in total

1 egg, lightly beaten

2 large garlic cloves, chopped

2.5cm (1in) fresh root ginger, chopped

pinch of salt

500ml (16fl oz) coconut cream

4 tbsp curry powder

4 tsp Thai fish sauce

tiny pinch of white sugar

4 tsp rice vinegar

120ml (4fl oz) coconut milk

30g (1oz) celery sticks (preferably Asian celery), cut into 2cm (¾in) lengths

½ small white onion, sliced

handful of coriander leaves, chopped

1 Clean the crab (see page 287). If you find any orange roe or mustard-coloured tomalley (both are delicacies), set them aside. Segment the crab into about 8 pieces, cracking the claws. Mix any tomalley and roe with the egg.

2 Using a mortar and pestle, pound the garlic, ginger, and salt into a coarse paste. Heat a wok, add 400ml (14fl oz) coconut cream and, when sizzling, add the paste. As the paste mixture is beginning to colour, add the crab and fry for a few moments over a moderate heat. Sprinkle in the curry powder. Continue to fry for a few more moments, stirring. When fragrant, season with the fish sauce, sugar, and vinegar.

3 Add the remaining coconut cream and the coconut milk, stirring well. Cover and simmer until the crab is cooked, tossing regularly.

4 Remove the lid and increase the heat, then stir in the egg mixture until the egg has thickened and begun to separate.

5 Mix in the celery and onion, then sprinkle with coriander and serve with rice, or stir-fried Chinese broccoli with oyster sauce.

Prawn diabolo

Quick and easy prawns in a warming spicy tomato sauce, great to make after a day's work.

The fish

Tiger prawns, or scallops, monkfish, or squid

- **PREP** 5 mins ▪ **COOK** 20 mins ▪ **SERVES** 4

Ingredients

2 tbsp olive oil

1 onion, chopped

1 red pepper, deseeded and sliced

3 garlic cloves, crushed

120ml (4fl oz) dry white wine or stock

250ml (8fl oz) passata

450g (1lb) cooked tiger prawns, peeled and deveined (see page 285)

1–2 tbsp chilli sauce

2 tsp Worcestershire sauce

1 Heat the oil in a large saucepan and fry the onion for 5 minutes. Add the red pepper and fry for another 5 minutes, or until softened.

2 Add the garlic and fry for a few seconds. Stir in the wine and let it bubble away for 1–2 minutes.

3 Stir in the passata and bring to a boil, stirring, then reduce the heat and simmer for 5 minutes.

4 Stir in the prawns just until piping hot, then the chilli and Worcestershire sauces, and serve immediately with boiled rice.

Prepare ahead

Make the tomato sauce 2–3 days ahead, cover, and chill. Return to a simmer before continuing.

Stir-fried yellow curried crabs

The little-known cuisine of Laos is delicious. Once you've tried this dish, you'll be addicted.

The fish
Crab

- **PREP** 25 mins ▪ **COOK** 20–25 mins
- **SERVES** 4

Ingredients

4 tbsp vegetable oil

5 tbsp Laotian kore (see below)

1 tsp Indian curry powder (optional)

8 small crabs, about 225g (8oz) each, halved or quartered

2 spring onions, thinly sliced diagonally

For the Laotian kore

1½ tsp cumin seeds

1 tbsp coriander seeds

1 stalk lemongrass, outer leaves discarded, then chopped

30g (1oz) galangal, chopped

grated zest of 1 kaffir lime

3 large garlic cloves, crushed

1 large shallot, chopped

3 tbsp finely chopped coriander root

½ tsp turmeric

2.5cm (1in) fresh root ginger, chopped

4–6 green or red Thai chillies, deseeded

2 tsp Thai shrimp paste

1 tbsp Indian curry powder (optional)

1 To make the Laotian kore, heat a frying pan over a medium heat and roast the cumin and coriander seeds until fragrant. Put the lemongrass, galangal, kaffir lime zest, garlic, shallot, coriander root, turmeric, ginger, chillies, and roasted seeds in a blender. Blend until smooth, adding water to help. Stir in the shrimp paste and curry powder (if using).

2 Heat the oil in a wok over a high heat and stir-fry the kore for about 5 minutes or until golden and fragrant. Add the curry powder (if using) and stir to blend well.

3 Reduce the heat to medium and add the crab, tossing. Cover and cook for 5 minutes. Uncover, toss, and cook for 5 minutes more. Transfer to a serving platter and sprinkle with spring onions.

Prepare ahead

Make the Laotian kore, cover, and refrigerate up to 2 days ahead. The flavours will deepen.

Fish with tomatoes, potatoes, and onions

Simple, but full of flavour, and hearty.

The fish
Any mixed firm fish, such as red mullet, haddock, bream, sea bass, pollock, or cod

- **PREP** 30 mins ▪ **COOK** 35 mins ▪ **SERVES** 8

Ingredients

3 tbsp olive oil

5 large potatoes, peeled and cut into bite-sized pieces

salt and freshly ground black pepper

4 garlic cloves, grated or finely chopped

handful of flat-leaf parsley, finely chopped

550g (1¼lb) cherry tomatoes, halved

300ml (10fl oz) dry white wine

675g (1½lb) mixed firm-fleshed fish fillets, scaled, pinboned, and cut into bite-sized pieces

16 anchovy fillets in olive oil, drained

1 Heat the oil in a large, shallow, heavy-based pan, add the potatoes, and season well with salt and pepper. Cook over a medium heat, stirring frequently, for 10–15 minutes, or until beginning to turn golden brown. Lower the heat, then stir in the garlic and parsley and cook for a few seconds before adding the tomatoes.

2 Cook for 6–8 minutes, or until the tomatoes begin to split, then increase the heat, add the wine, and allow to boil for a couple of minutes while the alcohol evaporates. Reduce the heat to low, add the fish and anchovies, cover, and cook for 10 minutes.

3 Transfer to a shallow serving dish and serve with crisp dressed salad and crusty bread.

Prepare ahead

Make the tomato base until the alcohol has evaporated from the wine. Cover, and refrigerate for up to 3 days. Return to a simmer before continuing.

Curry

Coconut and turmeric curry of red snapper

This curry should be hot, salty, and a little tart.

The fish

Red snapper, or sea bream or sea bass

- **PREP** Prep 20 mins ▪ **COOK** 10–15 mins
- **SERVES** 4

Ingredients

500ml (16fl oz) coconut milk

250ml (8fl oz) light chicken stock or water

2 stalks lemongrass, bruised

pinch of caster sugar

1 tbsp tamarind paste, or to taste

4 tbsp Thai fish sauce, or to taste

200g (7oz) red snapper fillet or 400g (14oz) whole red snapper, scaled and gutted

handful of torn betel leaves (optional)

120ml (4fl oz) coconut cream

5 kaffir lime leaves, finely shredded

For the curry paste

5–6 dried small red chillies

pinch of salt

2–3 few bird's eye chillies, deseeded if preferred

50g (1¾oz) chopped lemongrass

4 tbsp chopped shallots

2½ tbsp chopped garlic

1 rounded tbsp turmeric

1 rounded tbsp Thai shrimp paste

1 Put all the ingredients for the curry paste into a food processor and whizz, adding just enough water to make a smooth paste.

2 Combine the coconut milk with the stock in a saucepan, add the lemongrass and bring to a boil. Season with the sugar, tamarind, and fish sauce, and add 4 tbsp curry paste. Simmer for a minute before adding the fish and betel leaves (if using). Continue to simmer until the fish is cooked.

3 Check the seasoning, adding more fish sauce or tamarind, if you want, then stir in the coconut cream. Sprinkle with the shredded lime leaves and serve with slices of cucumber, sprigs of mint and coriander, grilled prawns, and rice.

Prepare ahead

Make the curry paste up to 3 days ahead, cover, and refrigerate. The flavours will deepen.

Pineapple curry of mussels

This Thai curry comes from Phetchburi, a prosperous province in southwest Bangkok.

The fish

Mussels, or clams

- **PREP** 20–25 mins ▪ **COOK** 25 mins
- **SERVES** 4

Ingredients

120ml (4fl oz) coconut cream

2–2½ tbsp palm sugar, to taste

2½ tbsp Thai fish sauce

½ tbsp tamarind paste, or to taste

500ml (16fl oz) coconut milk

300g (10oz) finely chopped pineapple

300g (10oz) mussels, prepared (see page 278)

3 kaffir lime leaves, torn

1 long red or green chilli, deseeded if preferred, thinly sliced at an angle

For the curry paste

10 dried large red chillies, soaked and chopped

3 heaped tbsp chopped red bird's eye chillies, deseeded if preferred

pinch of salt

2½ tbsp chopped galangal

5 tbsp chopped lemongrass

2 tsp finely grated kaffir lime zest

1 tsp chopped coriander root

5 tbsp chopped garlic

2½ tbsp chopped shallots

1 rounded tbsp Thai shrimp paste

1 Put all the ingredients for the curry paste into a food processor and whizz, adding just enough water to make a smooth paste.

2 Heat the coconut cream over a moderate heat, add 4 tbsp of curry paste and fry until fragrant. This can take as long as 10 minutes.

3 Season with the palm sugar and fish sauce (not too much, as the mussels will add salt), then the tamarind. Add the coconut milk, then the pineapple and mussels. Simmer until the shells have opened, stirring regularly. (Discard any mussels that remain closed.)

4 Sprinkle with the lime leaves and chilli. Check the seasoning. Serve with steamed rice.

Prepare ahead

Make the curry paste up to 3 days ahead, cover, and refrigerate. The flavours will deepen.

Kenyan fish curry

A fiery, broth-like curry, sharpened with tamarind, and enriched with coconut milk.

The fish

Any white fish, such as haddock, or prawns or squid

- **PREP** 20 mins ▪ **COOK** 35–40 mins
- **SERVES** 4

Ingredients

juice of 1 lime

1 tsp cracked black peppercorns

600g (1lb 5oz) white fish fillet, pinboned, skinned, and cut into chunks

6 tbsp vegetable oil

For the spice mixture

2 dried red chillies

¾ tsp coriander seeds

¾ tsp cumin seeds

1 tsp mustard seeds

¼ tsp turmeric

For the masala

1 red onion, finely chopped

1 red pepper, deseeded and shredded

1 red chilli, finely shredded, deseeded if preferred

4 garlic cloves, grated or finely chopped

250g (9oz) plum tomatoes, skinned, deseeded, and finely chopped (see page 112)

200ml (7fl oz) coconut milk

2 tbsp tamarind paste, or to taste

1 To make the spice mixture, roast the chillies and seeds in a frying pan until aromatic, then grind to a powder and add the turmeric.

2 Combine the lime juice and peppercorns and pour over the fish. Heat the oil in a frying pan. Fry the fish for 1 minute each side, until lightly coloured. Transfer to a plate, and cover.

3 For the masala, add the red onion to the pan. Cover and cook for 5 minutes. Uncover, tip in the red pepper, chilli, and garlic, and fry until the onions are about to turn colour. Stir in the spice mixture and fry briskly for 1 minute. Add the tomatoes, bring to a boil, then pour in 200ml (7fl oz) water. Simmer for 15 minutes. Pour in the coconut milk and enough tamarind paste to lend a tang. The curry shouldn't be too thick; aim for a broth-like consistency.

4 Return the fish to the pan and simmer for 5–10 minutes or until cooked through. Serve hot.

Tamarind fish curry

Giant tamarind trees grow everywhere in southern India, offering both shade and their sweet-sour fruits for cooking.

The fish

Any white fish, such as lemon sole, or prawns or squid

- **PREP** 10 mins ▪ **COOK** 35–40 mins
- **SERVES** 6

Ingredients

2 tbsp vegetable oil

1 tsp mustard seeds

10 curry leaves

pinch of fenugreek seeds

2 garlic cloves, chopped

2 onions, chopped

¼ tsp turmeric

½ tsp chilli powder

3 tomatoes, chopped

1 tsp tomato purée

sea salt

1 tbsp tamarind paste

500g (1lb 2oz) white fish fillets, skinned

1 Heat the oil in a large saucepan. Add the mustard seeds and, when they begin to pop, the curry leaves, fenugreek seeds, and garlic. Sauté for 1–2 minutes or until the garlic turns brown. Stir in the onions and cook over a moderate heat, stirring occasionally, for 10 minutes or until the onions are golden.

2 Add the turmeric and chilli powder and mix well, then add the tomatoes, tomato purée, and some salt and cook for a further 2 minutes. Add the tamarind paste and 200ml (7fl oz) water. Bring to a boil and simmer for 12 minutes, stirring occasionally, until the sauce thickens. Taste, adding more tamarind paste if you wish.

3 Cut the fish into pieces and carefully mix into the sauce. Reduce the heat and cook gently for 4–5 minutes or until just cooked through. Serve with plain boiled rice.

Prepare ahead

The curry sauce can be made up to 2 days ahead, covered very well, and refrigerated. The flavours will deepen. Return to a simmer before adding the fish.

Thai green fish curry with mangetout

Thai curries are wonderful because, although they taste hot, the fire dissipates very quickly.

The fish
Any white fish, such as cod or coley, or prawns, scallops, squid, cuttlefish, monkfish, snapper, or bream

- **PREP** 15 mins ▪ **COOK** 15 mins ▪ **SERVES** 4

Ingredients
2 waxy potatoes, scrubbed, cut into chunks

salt and freshly ground black pepper

115g (4oz) mangetout

400g can coconut milk

2 tbsp Thai green curry paste

550g (1¼lb) white fish, pinboned, skinned, and cut into chunks

1–2 thin green chillies, deseeded and shredded

a few torn basil or coriander leaves

1 Boil the potatoes in lightly salted water for about 5 minutes until almost tender. Steam the mangetout in a metal colander or steamer over the potatoes for 3 minutes. Drain the potatoes.

2 Mix the coconut milk with the curry paste in a pan. Add the fish, potatoes, chillies, and a little seasoning. Bring to a boil, reduce the heat, part-cover, and simmer very gently for 10 minutes until the fish and potatoes are tender.

3 Gently stir in the mangetout. Taste and adjust the seasoning, if necessary. Spoon over Thai jasmine rice in warmed bowls. Sprinkle with basil or coriander leaves.

Variation

With mixed vegetables
This can be cooked with broccoli, French beans, or courgettes instead of the mangetout.

Thai red curry with snapper

Home-made curry paste adds a delicious fragrance and warmth to the curry.

The fish
Snapper, or rabbit fish, meagre, or barracuda

- **PREP** 10 mins ▪ **COOK** 20 mins ▪ **SERVES** 4

Ingredients
2 tbsp sunflower oil

2 tsp shrimp paste

1 large onion, finely chopped

2 garlic cloves, crushed

1 tbsp palm sugar, or dark brown sugar

4 tomatoes, deseeded and diced

400g can coconut milk

300ml (10fl oz) Thai fish or shellfish stock

1–2 tbsp fish sauce, to taste

juice of ½–1 lime

4 snapper fillets, about 175g (6oz) each, scaled, pinboned, and halved

3 tbsp roughly chopped coriander leaves

For the curry paste
4 red chillies, deseeded and chopped

1 red pepper, grilled, skin removed

1 tbsp ground coriander

2 stalks lemongrass, roughly chopped

2 tbsp grated galangal or fresh root ginger

1 tbsp Thai fish sauce

1 tsp shrimp paste

1 tsp palm sugar

1 Place all the ingredients for the curry paste in a food processor and whizz to a paste.

2 Heat the oil in a wok, add the shrimp paste, and stir over a low heat for 1–2 minutes. Add the onion and cook for a further 2 minutes, then the garlic, palm sugar, tomatoes, and curry paste. Stir for 2 minutes, then add the coconut milk and stock. Bring to a boil and simmer for 4–5 minutes; season with fish sauce and lime juice.

3 Add the snapper, return to a boil, then reduce the heat and simmer for 5–6 minutes or until the fish is just cooked; it will be white and beginning to flake. Sprinkle over the coriander and serve with steamed rice.

Prepare ahead
The curry paste will keep, covered, in the refrigerator for up to 1 week.

RABBIT FISH FLAVOUR PAIRINGS:
This subtle-tasting fish is best with the Thai flavours of the curries here, or try it with Afro-Caribbean tastes of coconut, coriander, and warming spices.

Grilled halibut curry

The addition of freshly grated coconut here gives the curry body and substance.

The fish

Halibut, or turbot or brill

- **PREP** 55 mins ▪ **COOK** 40 mins ▪ **SERVES** 4

Ingredients

1–2 large banana leaves, trimmed

500ml (16fl oz) coconut cream

75g (2½oz) Thai basil leaves

6–10 kaffir lime leaves, finely shredded

4 halibut fillets, about 175g (6oz) each, skinned

For the red curry paste

6–10 dried red chillies, soaked and chopped

a few bird's eye chillies, deseeded if preferred

pinch of salt

4 tbsp chopped garlic

5 tbsp chopped shallots

4 tbsp chopped lemongrass

1 rounded tbsp chopped galangal

1 tsp chopped kaffir lime zest

1 tsp chopped coriander root

1 tsp Thai shrimp paste

pinch of freshly ground white peppercorns

pinch of mace (optional)

For the coconut mixture

240ml (8fl oz) coconut cream

2½ tbsp palm or muscovado sugar

4 tbsp Thai fish sauce, or to taste

100g (3½oz) freshly grated coconut

1 Put the curry paste ingredients into a blender, and whizz, adding water to make a paste. For the coconut mixture, simmer 5 tbsp curry paste in half the coconut cream until fragrant, add the sugar, fish sauce, and grated coconut and simmer, adding the remaining coconut cream.

2 Cut the leaf into 8 pieces, 4 about 14cm (6in) wide and 4 about 20cm (8in) wide. Place each small piece on a large one, shiny sides out.

3 Along half of each inner leaf, smear a little coconut cream, then sprinkle with basil leaves. Spread on a layer of coconut mixture, a little basil, lime leaves, and coconut cream. Place the fish on top, then repeat the layering in reverse.

4 Fold the inner leaf over to cover, then wrap tightly in the outer leaf. Secure with cocktail sticks. Grill for up to 30 minutes. The outer leaves will char; the inner leaves are for serving.

Salmon jungle curry

Hot, fresh flavours give new life to salmon.

The fish

Salmon, or monkfish

- **PREP** 10 mins ▪ **COOK** 20 mins
▪ **SERVES** 4

Ingredients

2 tbsp vegetable oil

2 tbsp Thai green curry paste

3 garlic cloves, crushed

5cm (2in) fresh root ginger, grated

2 hot red chillies, deseeded and shredded

400g can coconut milk

good splash of Thai fish sauce

200g (7oz) drained bamboo shoots

2 heaped tbsp pea aubergines (if available)

75g (2½oz) baby corn, halved lengthways

400g (14oz) salmon fillets, pinboned, skinned, cut into chunks

small handful of basil leaves (preferably Thai basil)

1 In a large frying pan, heat the oil, add the curry paste, and stir. Throw in the garlic, ginger, and chillies. Keep stirring for 2–3 minutes.

2 Now pour in the coconut milk. Bring to a boil, then add the fish sauce, bamboo shoots, pea aubergines (if using), and baby corn. Reduce the heat slightly, and simmer for 5 minutes.

3 Add the salmon and basil, and simmer for another 5–10 minutes until the fish is cooked. Season and serve with sticky Thai jasmine rice.

Prepare ahead

The curry sauce can be made 1 day ahead, covered, and refrigerated. Return to a simmer before adding the fish.

Kingfish curry

The rich flavour of kingfish works well with this tamarind and coconut milk combination.

The fish

Kingfish, or swordfish

- **PREP** 15 mins ▪ **COOK** 25 mins
- **SERVES** 4–6

Ingredients

2 tbsp vegetable oil

½ tsp mustard seeds

10 curry leaves

pinch of fenugreek seeds

1 large onion, chopped

2.5cm (1in) fresh root ginger, sliced

½ tsp turmeric

½ tsp chilli powder

1 tsp ground coriander

2 tomatoes, chopped

sea salt

1 tbsp tamarind paste

500g (1lb 2oz) kingfish fillet, pinboned, skinned, and cut into 4cm (1½in) pieces

200ml (7fl oz) coconut milk

pinch of crushed black pepper

1 Heat the oil in a large wok. Add the mustard seeds and, when they start to pop, add the curry leaves and fenugreek seeds. Sauté for 1 minute or until the fenugreek turns golden, then add the onion and cook for 5 minutes over a moderate heat, stirring occasionally.

2 Add the ginger, turmeric, chilli powder, and ground coriander. Mix well, then add the tomatoes and salt to taste. Cook for 5 minutes, stirring constantly. Stir in the tamarind paste and 300ml (10fl oz) water and slowly bring to a boil. Reduce the heat, add the fish and simmer for 5–6 minutes until cooked through.

3 Reduce the heat as low as possible and pour in the coconut milk. Add the pepper. Simmer gently for 2 minutes, then remove from the heat. Serve immediately with boiled rice or potatoes.

Prepare ahead

Make the curry sauce up to just before adding the fish, cover, and refrigerate for up to 2 days. Return to a simmer before continuing.

Seafood curry

This quick curry is flavoured with chillies, coconut, and lime, and is easy to make for a mid-week supper.

The fish

Any firm white fish, such as cod or haddock, and tiger prawns

- **PREP** 15 mins ▪ **COOK** 12 mins ▪ **SERVES** 4

Ingredients

600g (1lb 5oz) white fish, pinboned, skinned, and cut into bite-sized pieces, rinsed and patted dry

½ tsp salt and freshly ground black pepper

½ tsp turmeric

½ onion, chopped

1cm (½in) fresh root ginger, chopped

1 garlic clove, crushed

2 tbsp sunflower oil

1 tsp black mustard seeds

4 green cardamom pods, crushed

2–4 dried red chillies, crushed

100g (3½oz) creamed coconut, dissolved in 500ml (16fl oz) boiling water

12 raw tiger prawns, peeled and deveined (see page 285)

2 tbsp fresh lime juice

coriander leaves, to serve

lime wedges, to serve

1 Put the fish in a non-metallic bowl, sprinkle over the salt and turmeric, and turn to lightly cover. Set aside.

2 Put the onion, ginger, and garlic in a food processor or blender, and process to a paste. Heat a deep frying pan over a high heat until hot. Add the oil and swirl around, then reduce the heat to medium, add the onion paste, and fry, stirring, for 3–5 minutes, or until it just begins to colour. Stir in the mustard seeds, cardamom, and chillies and stir for 30 seconds.

3 Stir in the creamed coconut. Leave to bubble for 2 minutes, then reduce the heat to medium-low, add the fish and any juices in the bowl, and spoon the sauce over the fish. Simmer for 2 minutes, spooning the sauce over the fish once or twice as it cooks, taking care not to break up the pieces.

4 Add the prawns and simmer for 2 minutes, or until they turn pink. Add the lime juice, and serve with coriander leaves and lime wedges.

Laksa lemak

This Malaysian dish is rich with coconut.

The fish

Mahi mahi, and tiger prawns, mussels, and squid

- **PREP** 20 mins ▪ **COOK** 15 mins ▪ **SERVES** 4

Ingredients

400g can coconut milk

450ml (15fl oz) shellfish stock

1 stalk lemongrass

4 kaffir lime leaves

2.5cm (1in) piece galangal or fresh root ginger, peeled and finely sliced

450g (1lb) mahi mahi fillets, pinboned, skinned, and cut into large chunks

12 raw tiger prawns, peeled and deveined, tails left on (see page 285)

450g (1lb) mussels, prepared (see page 278)

2 squid, gutted, cleaned, and cut into rings (see page 282)

350g (12oz) vermicelli, to serve

lime wedges, to serve

For the curry paste

2 tsp vegetable oil

splash of sesame oil

2 tsp palm sugar

3 garlic cloves, halved

½ bunch of spring onions, roughly chopped

1 tsp shrimp paste

2 red chillies, deseeded and chopped

1 large bunch of coriander (with roots, if possible)

1 tsp cumin

1 tsp turmeric

1 tsp salt

1 Put all the ingredients for the curry paste in a food processor and whizz. Blend in half the coconut milk to make a smooth paste.

2 Heat a large wok, add the paste and cook over a low heat for 1 minute. Add the remaining coconut milk and the stock, bring to a boil, and add the lemongrass, lime leaves, and galangal; simmer for 5 minutes. Add the fish, prawns, and mussels, cook for 3–4 minutes. Add the squid.

3 Meanwhile, cook the vermicelli according to packet instructions. Divide between 4 bowls and ladle the laksa on top. Serve with lime wedges.

Prepare ahead

The curry paste can be kept, covered, in the refrigerator for up to 1 week.

Coconut fish curry

This fantastic recipe from southern Kerala is ideal for people who prefer mild curries.

The fish

Any white fish, such as tilapia, or shellfish

- **PREP** 25 mins ▪ **COOK** 20 mins ▪ **SERVES** 6

Ingredients

2 tbsp vegetable oil

200g (7oz) shallots, chopped

10 curry leaves

500g (1lb 2oz) white fish fillets, pinboned and skinned

1 tbsp lemon juice

For the spice paste

100g (3½oz) freshly grated coconut

1 tsp ground coriander

½ tsp chilli powder

large pinch of turmeric

1 To make the spice paste, put the coconut, ground coriander, chilli powder, and turmeric in a blender. Pour in 200ml (7fl oz) water and process to make a smooth paste.

2 Heat the oil in a large frying pan or wok. Add the shallots and curry leaves and cook over a medium-low heat for 5 minutes or until the shallots are soft. Stir in the spice paste with 100ml (3½fl oz) water and bring to a boil. Cook for about 5 minutes, stirring occasionally, until the sauce has thickened.

3 Cut the fish into 2.5cm (1in) pieces and add to the sauce. Pour in the lemon juice and mix carefully. Cook gently for 4–5 minutes or until cooked through. Remove from the heat and serve with boiled rice or Indian bread.

Prepare ahead

The curry base can be made, covered, and refrigerated for 2–3 days. The flavours will deepen. Reheat gently before continuing with step 3.

TILAPIA FLAVOUR PAIRINGS: The sweet, distinctive taste of this fish pairs well with Thai ingredients; try it with bird's eye chillies, kaffir lime, nam pla, shrimp paste, and galangal.

Fish head curry

Fish heads are inexpensive and contain the delicacy of the "pearl" or cheek.

The fish

Salmon, cod, or snapper heads

- **PREP** 15 mins ▪ **COOK** 30 mins ▪ **SERVES** 4

Ingredients

400g can coconut milk

2 tbsp vegetable oil

1 onion, finely sliced

10 cardamom pods, split

2.5cm (1in) piece of galangal or fresh root ginger, thinly sliced

4 tomatoes, deseeded and chopped

1 tbsp tamarind paste

450ml (15fl oz) fish stock

4 large fish heads, gills removed, and washed well

salt and freshly ground black pepper

3 tbsp chopped coriander

For the paste

1 tbsp chopped macadamia nuts

1 garlic clove, chopped

½ bunch spring onions

1 tsp shrimp paste

3 red chillies (more if you like it hot)

1 tsp turmeric

1 tsp ground cumin

2 tsp garam masala

pinch of salt

1 Prepare the paste: put the ingredients into a food processor and finely chop. Add 3 tbsp coconut milk and whizz to a smooth paste.

2 Heat the vegetable oil in a large casserole, add the onion, and cook over a medium heat for 8–10 minutes until slightly golden. Add the paste, cardamom pods, galangal, and tomatoes, and fry for 3–4 minutes. Add the tamarind paste, remaining coconut milk, and stock, bring to a boil, then reduce the heat to a simmer.

3 Add the fish heads, cover, and poach for 12–15 minutes, turning halfway, or until the heads are beginning to break up. Transfer to a serving dish. Bring the cooking liquid to the boil, adjust the seasoning, and stir in the coriander. Pour over the heads to serve.

Prepare ahead

The paste can be made up to 1 day ahead, covered, and chilled until needed.

Goan curry

Red hot with chilli, though this can be tempered to personal taste.

The fish

Snapper, or pomfret or meagre

- **PREP** 10–15 mins ▪ **COOK** 30 mins
- **SERVES** 6

Ingredients

1kg (2¼lb) snapper, scaled and filleted

2 tbsp coriander seeds

1 tsp cumin seeds

6–8 dried red chillies, to taste

3 garlic cloves, chopped

1 tbsp grated fresh root ginger

½ tsp turmeric

½ tsp salt

2 x 400g cans coconut milk

2 tbsp groundnut oil

1 large onion, thinly sliced

2 large tomatoes, deseeded and chopped

1–2 green chillies, deseeded and chopped

2 tbsp tamarind paste

salt and freshly ground black pepper

lime juice, or a handful of chopped coriander

1 Pinbone the snapper fillets and cut each of them into 3, cover, and refrigerate.

2 Put the coriander and cumin seeds in a saucepan; stir over a medium heat until they begin to pop. Remove and cool. Put the seeds, dried chillies, garlic, ginger, turmeric, and salt into a food processor. Whizz until well chopped. Add 4–5 tbsp of the coconut milk and pulse to blend.

3 Heat the oil in a large saucepan, add the onion, and cook over a low heat for 12–15 minutes, until turning golden brown. Add the tomatoes, green chillies, and spice paste and fry over a medium heat for 2–3 minutes until very aromatic. Add the remaining coconut milk, bring to a boil, and simmer for 5–7 minutes. Add the tamarind paste and season.

4 Add the snapper, reduce the heat, and cook for 4–6 minutes or until opaque and firm.

5 Adjust the seasoning and add the lime juice or chopped coriander. Serve with steamed rice.

Prepare ahead

Prepare the spicy sauce up to the end of step 3, cool, cover, and chill for up to 1 day. The flavours will deepen. Return to a simmer before continuing.

BLACK POMFRET FLAVOUR PAIRINGS:

This firm, sweet fish is a natural ingredient in curry, or try it with Middle Eastern tastes such as couscous, orange, plenty of coriander, or chermoula.

Squid curry

In Sri Lanka, fishermen cook freshly caught squid onboard with spices.

The fish

Squid, or cuttlefish or octopus

- **PREP** 15 mins **COOK** 30–35 mins
- **SERVES** 4

Ingredients

3 tbsp vegetable oil

½ tsp mustard seeds

2 large onions, sliced

3 green chillies, slit lengthways

2.5cm (1in) fresh root ginger, finely sliced

½ tsp chilli powder

½ tsp ground coriander

2 large tomatoes, sliced

400g (14oz) squid, gutted, cleaned, and cut into 1cm (½in) rings, with tentacles (see page 282)

1 tbsp chopped coriander leaves, to serve

1 Heat the oil in a large frying pan and add the mustard seeds. When they pop, add the onions and cook for 5 minutes, or until golden.

2 Stir in the green chillies and ginger, then the chilli powder and ground coriander. Mix well and add the tomatoes. Cook over a moderate heat for 5–10 minutes or until the tomatoes break down to give a thick sauce.

3 Add the squid, and mix thoroughly. Cover and cook over a low heat for 15 minutes, stirring occasionally to prevent sticking. If the dish becomes dry, stir in a little water.

4 Serve hot, sprinkled with the coriander, with paratha or chapatti, or any flavoured rice.

Prepare ahead

Make the sauce to the end of step 2, cover, and refrigerate for 2 days. The flavours will deepen. Return to a simmer before adding the squid.

Steamed scallop curry

In Thailand, this is steamed in banana leaves.

The fish

Any white fish, such as turbot, and scallops

- **PREP** 35–40 mins **COOK** 20–25 mins
- **SERVES** 4

Ingredients

50g (1¾oz) white fish fillets, pinboned and skinned

120ml (4fl oz) coconut cream

1½–3 tbsp Thai fish sauce

pinch of caster sugar (optional)

1 small egg

5 kaffir lime leaves, very finely shredded

4 scallops, roe removed, each cut into 3 slices

4 scallop shells, boiled in heavily salted water for several minutes to clean

handful of basil leaves (preferably Thai basil)

1 bai yor leaf, very finely shredded (optional)

few pieces of red chilli, shredded, to serve

few coriander leaves, to serve

For the thickened coconut cream

good pinch of rice flour

5 tbsp coconut cream

pinch of salt (optional)

For the red curry paste

6–8 dried red chillies, soaked and chopped

pinch of salt

2½ tbsp chopped garlic

4 tbsp chopped shallots

4 tbsp chopped lemongrass

1 rounded tbsp chopped galangal

1 tsp chopped kaffir lime zest

1 tsp chopped coriander root

2 tsp Thai shrimp paste

pinch of freshly ground white peppercorns

1 Put the curry paste ingredients in a blender, and whizz with enough water to make a paste.

2 Purée the fish in a blender, then stir in 4 tbsp curry paste, and the coconut cream. Season with fish sauce and sugar (if using). Add the egg. Stir in most of the lime leaves and the scallops.

3 Generously line the scallop shells with the basil and bai yor (if using). Spoon in the scallop curry mixture. Steam gently for about 15 minutes. When the "mousse" is slightly firm, it is cooked. Do not overcook or it will split.

4 Meanwhile, mix the rice flour with 1 tbsp of the coconut cream. Bring the remaining coconut cream to a boil, then stir in the rice flour mixture. Season with salt, if liked. Spoon the thickened coconut cream over the curry and garnish with the reserved lime leaves, the red chilli, and coriander leaves.

Prepare ahead

The curry paste can be prepared up to 3 days ahead, covered well, and refrigerated. The flavours will deepen.

Prawn dhansak

Increase the number of chillies if you like your curry really spicy. The amount here will give a moderate heat.

The fish
Tiger prawns

- **PREP** 15 mins ▪ **COOK** 30 mins ▪ **SERVES** 8

Ingredients
350g (12oz) red lentils

salt and freshly ground black pepper

2 tbsp vegetable oil, or 1 tbsp ghee

6 cardamom pods, crushed

3 tsp mustard seeds

2 tsp medium chilli powder

2 tsp turmeric

2 tsp ground cinnamon

2 onions, finely chopped

10cm (4in) fresh root ginger, finely chopped

4 garlic cloves, grated or finely chopped

3–4 green chillies, deseeded and finely sliced

675g (1½lb) raw tiger prawns, peeled and deveined (see page 285)

1 pineapple, peeled and cut into bite-sized pieces

8 tomatoes, skinned, deseeded, and roughly chopped (see page 112)

handful of fresh coriander, finely chopped

1 Put the lentils in a large, heavy-based pan, season, then cover with cold water. Bring to a boil, reduce the heat to a simmer, and cook for 20 minutes, or until tender. Drain and set aside.

2 Meanwhile, heat half the oil or ghee in a large, heavy-based frying pan, add the dried spices, and cook, stirring, until the seeds pop. Stir in the onions, ginger, garlic, and chillies, and cook for 5 minutes, or until soft and fragrant.

3 Add the remaining oil or ghee to the pan, then add the prawns. Increase the heat and cook, stirring occasionally, for 6–8 minutes. Stir in the pineapple, lentils, and tomatoes and a little hot water so the mixture is slightly sloppy, and simmer for 5 minutes. Season, stir in the coriander, and serve.

Prepare ahead
The curry can be prepared to the end of step 2, covered, and refrigerated for up to 3 days. Reheat gently before continuing.

Green curry of prawns with aubergines and basil

A delicious, thin curry from Thailand.

The fish
Prawns, or scallops, or any firm white fish

- **PREP** 15 mins ▪ **COOK** 20 mins ▪ **SERVES** 4

Ingredients
5 tbsp coconut cream

1½–3 tbsp Thai fish sauce, to taste

250ml (8fl oz) coconut milk, or chicken or prawn stock

3 small aubergines, stalk removed, cut into sixths just before cooking

100g (3½oz) pea aubergines

8–12 large, raw prawns, deveined (see page 285)

3–4 kaffir lime leaves, torn

3 green chillies, deseeded and thinly sliced

handful of basil leaves (preferably Thai basil)

1 rounded tbsp shredded fresh root ginger

For the curry paste
1 heaped tbsp bird's eye chillies, deseeded if preferred

pinch of salt

1 rounded tbsp chopped galangal

2½ tbsp chopped lemongrass

1 tsp grated kaffir lime zest

2 tsp chopped coriander root

1 tsp turmeric

1 rounded tbsp chopped fresh root ginger

2½ tbsp chopped shallots

2½ tbsp chopped garlic

1 tsp Thai shrimp paste

1 tsp white peppercorns

1 tsp roasted coriander seeds

few blades of mace, roasted (optional)

1 Put the ingredients for the curry paste in a blender and whizz; adding just enough water to make a paste.

2 Heat the coconut cream, add 2½ tbsp of the curry paste, and fry over a high heat for about 5 minutes, stirring, until fragrant and oily.

3 Season with fish sauce, then add the coconut milk or stock. Bring to a boil, then add all the aubergines. Simmer for 10–12 minutes, then add the prawns. Simmer for 3–4 minutes until they are cooked.

4 Add all the remaining ingredients, then allow to rest for a minute or so before serving. The curry should have a dappling of separated coconut cream floating on top.

Prepare ahead
The curry paste can be made 3 days in advance. Cover well, and refrigerate. The flavours will deepen.

Green prawn curry
with fresh dill

Dill mellows the intense flavour of lime leaves.

The fish

Tiger prawns, or scallops, monkfish, or sea bass

- **PREP** 30 mins ▪ **COOK** 30 mins ▪ **SERVES** 4

Ingredients

3 tbsp vegetable oil

5 tbsp Thai green curry paste

1 tbsp shrimp paste

1 tbsp palm or granulated sugar

500ml (16fl oz) coconut milk

500ml (16fl oz) chicken or vegetable stock

4–6 kaffir lime leaves, bruised

Thai fish sauce, to taste

2 large waxy potatoes, peeled, and cut into 2.5cm (1in) pieces

675g (1½lb) raw tiger prawns, peeled and deveined (see page 285)

1 bunch of dill

1 Heat the oil in a pan over a medium-high heat and stir-fry the curry paste for about 2 minutes or until fragrant. Add the shrimp paste and sugar, and stir-fry for 1 minute.

2 Reduce the heat and add the coconut milk, stock, kaffir lime leaves, and fish sauce. Add the potatoes, cover, and cook for 20 minutes.

3 Add the prawns and stir well, then cover again and cook for about 5 minutes, or until they turn pink. Sprinkle with dill fronds.

4 You can choose to eat this hot, but in Laos it would be eaten at room temperature with steamed sticky rice on the side: with your fingers, pinch and shape a small amount of rice into a ball and dip into the curry, eating prawn along with dill in the same bite.

Prepare ahead

Make the curry base to the end of step 2 up to 2 days ahead, cover, and refrigerate. Reheat gently before continuing.

Chilli crab

The best way to enjoy this dish is to dress for a mess: cover yourself with a napkin, roll up your sleeves, and tuck in. Prepare bowls of warm water with slices of lemon to rinse fingers.

The fish

Crab, or freshwater crayfish or rock lobster

- **PREP** 10 mins ▪ **COOK** 20 mins ▪ **SERVES** 4

Ingredients

8 raw, small, blue crabs, or other small crabs, weighing about 225g (8oz) each

2 tbsp sunflower oil

2 tsp coriander seeds

2 tsp mustard seeds

1 large onion, finely chopped

4 bird's eye chillies, deseeded if you like, and finely chopped

4 garlic cloves, chopped

2 tbsp grated fresh root ginger

1 tsp turmeric

2 tbsp palm or muscovado sugar

1 bunch of spring onions, finely sliced

3 tbsp tamarind paste

1 tsp cornflour

150ml (5fl oz) shellfish stock

chopped coriander, to serve

1 Clean the crab, if necessary (see page 286). Cook the crabs in a large pan of boiling water for 5 minutes (they may need to be cooked in 2 batches). Cut in half and crack the claws.

2 Heat the oil in a large saucepan, add the coriander and mustard seeds, and cook over a medium heat until they pop. Add the onion and cook for 3–4 minutes or until translucent.

3 Add the chillies, garlic, ginger, turmeric, and sugar, and stir for 2–3 minutes or until aromatic. Tip in the spring onions and cook for 1 minute.

4 Mix the tamarind paste, cornflour, and stock together and blend into the chilli and seed mixture. Bring to a boil, return the crab, and sprinkle with coriander to serve.

Prepare ahead

The sauce for this dish can be made 2 days ahead, covered, and refrigerated. The flavours will deepen. Gently reheat, and cook and cut up the crabs when ready to eat.

Crab and mango curry

This delectable curry from the Maldives marries tropical fruit with spices and seafood.

The fish

Crab claws, or tiger prawns

- **PREP** 15–20 mins • **COOK** 25–30 mins
- **SERVES** 4

Ingredients

juice of 1 lime

¼ tsp ground turmeric

¾ tsp cracked black peppercorns

8 raw crab claws

1 firm, slightly under-ripe mango, cut into 2cm (¾in) cubes

1 tbsp palm or muscovado sugar

For the masala

4 tbsp vegetable oil

¾ tsp mustard seeds

2 sprigs of curry leaves (about 2 tbsp leaves)

4cm (1½in) cinnamon stick

1 large onion, sliced

2 red chillies, deseeded and chopped

3 garlic cloves, finely chopped

2cm (¾in) piece of fresh root ginger, finely chopped

½ tsp ground cumin

½ tsp chilli powder

1 tsp fennel seeds, roasted and ground

4 large plum tomatoes, skinned and finely chopped (see page 112)

1 Mix the lime juice, turmeric, and peppercorns. Coat the crab claws in this mixture and set aside.

2 Heat the oil in a wok and add the mustard seeds; they should pop. Toss in the curry leaves and cinnamon. After 30 seconds, add the onion. Reduce the heat, cover, and soften for 5 minutes.

3 Stir in the chillies, garlic, and ginger and cook for 1 minute. Add the cumin, chilli powder, and ground fennel. Stir, then tip in the tomatoes. Fry until the tomatoes have cooked down.

4 Add the crab claws with the spiced juice, stir, then add the mango and sugar. Fry for 10 minutes over a high heat until the crab claws are cooked. You'll need a small hammer or pair of crackers to break the crab shells; it's messy, but great fun. Serve with flatbreads or rice.

Prepare ahead

Make the spiced tomato sauce 2 days in advance. Cover, and refrigerate.

Prawn balti

More common in the UK than in Pakistan, baltis are a hit with curry aficionados.

The fish

King prawns, or sea bass, sea bream, scallops, or monkfish

- **PREP** 20–25 mins • **COOK** 15–20 mins
- **SERVES** 4

Ingredients

500g (1lb 2oz) raw king prawns, peeled but tails left intact, and deveined (see page 285)

juice of 1 lime

1½ tsp paprika

For the masala

3 tbsp vegetable oil

1 red onion, diced

4cm (1½in) piece fresh root ginger, finely shredded

2 garlic cloves, grated or finely chopped

2 green chillies, shredded

1 red pepper, deseeded and shredded

half a 400g can chopped tomatoes

¼ tsp turmeric

¼–½ tsp chilli powder

¼ tsp ground cinnamon

½ tsp garam masala

½ tsp ground coriander

½ tsp caster sugar

2 tbsp coarsely chopped coriander leaves

1 Put the prawns in a bowl, squeeze over the lime juice and stir in the paprika. Set aside.

2 Heat the oil in a wok over a moderate heat and fry the onion until just beginning to turn golden. Add most of the ginger, the garlic, chillies, and red pepper. Fry for 1 minute.

3 Increase the heat and add the tomatoes, turmeric, chilli powder, cinnamon, garam masala, ground coriander, and sugar. Cook briskly until the tomatoes have thickened. Pour in 150ml (5fl oz) hot water, stir well and reduce the heat to low. Add the prawns, with any lime juice, and simmer until they turn pink.

4 Sprinkle with chopped coriander and the remaining shredded ginger before serving.

Prepare ahead

The masala can be made up to 2 days ahead, covered, and refrigerated. The flavours will deepen. Return to a simmer before continuing.

Pan-fried and Deep-fried

Pan-fried mackerel in rolled oats

The lemon wedges and the hot, sinus-clearing mustard make this dish a cold-weather winner.

The fish

Mackerel, or herring or sprats

- **PREP** 15–20 mins • **COOK** 15 mins
- **SERVES** 6

Ingredients

2 eggs

30g (1oz) plain flour

175g (6oz) rolled oats

salt and freshly ground black pepper

6 large mackerel fillets, pinboned and skinned

75ml (2½fl oz) vegetable oil, plus more if needed

lemon wedges, to serve

watercress sprigs, to serve

For the mustard sauce

60g (2oz) butter

2 tbsp plain flour

juice of ½ lemon

1 tbsp Dijon mustard, or to taste

1 Beat the eggs in a dish and sift the flour into a bowl. Combine the rolled oats and salt and pepper in another bowl. Turn each fish fillet in the flour, dip in the egg, then coat in oats.

2 For the sauce, melt a third of the butter. Add the flour and whisk until foaming. Whisk in 300ml (10fl oz) boiling water. Return to the heat and whisk for 1 minute. Remove from the heat, add the remaining butter, and whisk. Add the lemon juice and mustard, and season.

3 Line a baking sheet with kitchen paper. Heat the oil in a large frying pan. Add half the fish and cook for 2–3 minutes on each side, until crisp and golden. Transfer to the baking sheet and keep warm while you cook the remaining fish. Serve with lemon wedges, watercress, and the sauce.

Shallow-fried masala sardines

These curried fish have a lovely spicy flavour.

The fish

Sardines, or herring or small mackerel

- **PREP** 10–15 mins, plus marinating
- **COOK** 20 mins • **SERVES** 2–4

Ingredients

4 sardines, about 300g (10oz) in total, scaled and gutted

5 tbsp vegetable oil

1 small onion, finely sliced

small handful of chopped coriander leaves, to serve

lemon wedges, to serve

For the spice paste

1 onion, chopped

2 green chillies, chopped, deseeded if liked

1cm (½in) fresh root ginger, finely chopped

10 curry leaves

10 black peppercorns

½ tsp chilli powder

½ tsp turmeric

2 tbsp wine or cider vinegar

1 tsp lemon juice

salt

1 Place all the ingredients for the spice paste in a blender. Process to make a paste. Set aside.

2 Wash the fish, then pat dry. With a very sharp knife, make slashes about 2.5cm (1in) apart along the fish, on both sides. Place on a baking tray and spread the spice paste all over, and into the cuts. Leave for 15–20 minutes.

3 Heat 2 tbsp of the oil in a large frying pan. Add the onion and cook for 5–6 minutes over a very high heat until well browned and crisp. Remove and drain on kitchen paper.

4 Heat the remaining oil in the same pan over a low heat. Place in the fish, cover, and cook for 6 minutes on each side. Lift on to a serving dish. Sprinkle the onions over and serve with coriander and lemon wedges.

Prepare ahead

Make the spice paste 3 days ahead, cover well, and refrigerate until needed.

Crisp salmon with coriander pesto

Lightly cooked, fresh, and fragrant, this is a wonderful way to eat salmon.

The fish

Salmon, or sea bass, tuna, swordfish, John Dory, or skate

- **PREP** 5–10 mins ■ **COOK** 10–15 mins
- **SERVES** 4

Ingredients

4 salmon fillets, about 175g (6oz) each, with skin, scaled and pinboned

3 tbsp vegetable oil

2 tsp sea salt

lemon wedges, to serve

coriander leaves, to serve

For the pesto

leaves from 1 large bunch of coriander

2–3 garlic cloves

2 tbsp pine nuts

75ml (2½fl oz) olive oil

30g (1oz) Parmesan cheese, finely grated

salt and freshly ground black pepper

1 To make the pesto, put the coriander in a food processor with the garlic, pine nuts, and 2 tbsp olive oil. With the blade turning, slowly pour in the remaining oil in a steady stream. Stir in the Parmesan, season to taste, put into a bowl, and cover.

2 Brush the skin side of each salmon fillet with a little vegetable oil. Heat the remaining oil in a frying pan until hot. Add the salmon, skin side down. Cook over medium heat until the skin is crispy. Increase the heat to high, turn and brown the sides and top of each fillet very quickly. The top should remain slightly soft, showing it is rare.

3 Put the salmon on warmed plates, sprinkle with sea salt and spoon on some pesto. Serve with the lemon wedges and coriander leaves.

Prepare ahead

The pesto keeps for 2 days in the refrigerator, if the surface is covered with a thin layer of oil to keep it from the air. (If it is not, the coriander will discolour, and the pesto begin to stale.)

Saltimbocca of salmon

Slices of salmon are marinated, then wrapped around smoked salmon.

The fish

Salmon, monkfish, or tuna, and smoked salmon

- **PREP** 20–25 mins, plus marinating
- **COOK** 1–2 mins ■ **SERVES** 4–6

Ingredients

1kg (2¼lb) salmon fillet, with skin, pinboned

250g (9oz) smoked salmon slices

leaves from 5–7 sprigs of basil

45g (1½oz) butter

For the marinade

juice of ½ lemon

175ml (6fl oz) olive oil

leaves from 3–4 sprigs of thyme

2 bay leaves, crushed

For the tomato-basil garnish

4 tomatoes, skinned, deseeded, and chopped (see page 112)

2 tbsp olive oil

leaves from a small bunch of basil, chopped

salt and freshly ground pepper

pinch of caster sugar

1 With the tail of the salmon fillet facing away from you and working towards it, use a filleting knife to cut 12 diagonal slices, as thin and even as possible. Leave the skin behind.

2 For the marinade, put the lemon juice and oil in a shallow dish with the thyme and bay leaves. Add the salmon slices, cover, and refrigerate for 1 hour.

3 Mix the tomatoes for the garnish with the oil and basil and season, adding sugar to taste. Let stand at room temperature for 30–60 minutes.

4 Lift the salmon from the marinade and pat dry. Cut the smoked salmon slices into pieces the same size as the fresh salmon. Arrange a piece of smoked salmon on top of each fresh salmon slice. Put a basil leaf on top. Roll up as you would a Swiss roll, starting from a long side, and secure with a cocktail stick.

5 Heat the butter in a frying pan and add the salmon, leaving space around each piece. Cook over high heat, turning, for 1–2 minutes. Remove the cocktail sticks and serve with the tomato-basil garnish.

Prepare ahead

The marinade and tomato garnish can both be made, covered, and refrigerated 6 hours ahead. Bring to room temperature before continuing.

Vietnamese crispy fish

This classic dish needs plenty of chilli for an intense heat that is tempered by palm sugar.

The fish

Bream, or snapper or red mullet

- **PREP** 10–15 mins ▪ **COOK** 15 mins
- **SERVES** 2

Ingredients

2 bream, about 450g (1lb) each, scaled, gutted, and trimmed, and heads removed

salt

4 tbsp vegetable oil

3 garlic cloves, chopped

6 tomatoes, deseeded and roughly chopped

2 red chillies (preferably bird's eye), deseeded and finely sliced

1 tbsp palm sugar

2 tbsp nam pla

1 tsp cornflour

2 spring onions, chopped

2 tbsp roughly chopped coriander

1 Slash the fish on each side and season with salt. Heat half the oil in a large frying pan, add the fish, and fry on each side for 6–8 minutes, or until cooked.

2 Heat the remaining oil in a large pan, add the garlic, tomatoes, and chillies, and cook over a high heat until the tomatoes have softened. Add the palm sugar, nam pla, and 6 tbsp water, and cook for a minute or two, or until the mixture is reduced and sticky. Stir in the cornflour, spring onions, and coriander, and cook for another minute.

3 Lift the fish on to a plate and spoon the sweet, sticky sauce over the top. Serve with rice.

Prepare ahead

The sticky sauce – made in step 2 – can be made up to 3 days ahead, covered, and refrigerated. Reheat gently before continuing. It may need a little more water, so adjust the consistency until it is as you prefer.

Shallow-fried red mullet

Pan-frying makes the most of the delicate sweetness of red mullet.

The fish

Red mullet, or grey mullet or sea bream

- **PREP** 5 mins ▪ **COOK** 5 mins ▪ **SERVES** 4

Ingredients

4 red mullet, about 450g (1lb) each, scaled, gutted, and trimmed, and heads removed

sea salt and freshly ground black pepper

cornmeal or polenta, for coating

grapeseed oil, for frying

lemon juice, to serve

1 Season the fish, then coat them on both sides with cornmeal or polenta, shaking off any excess. Set a non-stick or cast-iron frying pan over a moderately high heat and add enough oil to coat the bottom of the pan.

2 Put the prepared fish into the hot oil, presentation-side (the side that will be uppermost when serving) down. Shallow-fry for 2 minutes, or until the fish is golden brown.

3 Carefully turn the fish using tongs and cook until the other side is golden brown. To test if it is cooked, insert a thin-bladed knife into the centre of the fish, then touch the knife tip to your thumb. If it is warm, the fish is ready. Drain briefly on kitchen paper and sprinkle with lemon juice. Serve with sprigs of watercress.

RED SPOT EMPEROR BREAM FLAVOUR PAIRINGS: Try this with tomatoes, garlic, olive oil, marjoram, fennel, and thyme, or with spicier red chilli, fish sauce cumin, and coriander.

Seared tuna with cucumber and fennel

This tuna is served very rare, so it is essential that it is bought as fresh as possible.

The fish

Tuna, or swordfish or marlin

- **PREP** 15 mins, plus cooling ▪ **COOK** 6 mins
- **SERVES** 4

Ingredients

4 tbsp olive oil, plus extra for brushing

4 tuna steaks, about 150g (5½oz)

salt and freshly ground black pepper

1 fennel bulb, sliced

2 shallots, finely chopped

1 cucumber, deseeded, skinned, and finely chopped

30g (1oz) mint, basil, and chervil leaves, torn

juice of 1 lemon

8 anchovy fillets in olive oil, drained

lemon wedges, to serve

1 Rub 2 tbsp of oil over the tuna and sprinkle with plenty of pepper. Set aside.

2 Heat 2 tbsp of oil and sauté the fennel for 4–5 minutes until just tender. Season. Tip the fennel into a large bowl and set aside to cool a little.

3 Add the shallots, cucumber, and herbs to the fennel. Stir in the lemon juice and remaining oil.

4 Heat a heavy frying pan or grill pan until smoking. Lightly brush the tuna steaks with oil, then pan-fry for 30 seconds. Brush with a little more oil, turn, and cook for a further 30 seconds.

5 Place a tuna steak on each plate, with the fennel salad piled on top, and 2 anchovy fillets draped over. Serve with lemon wedges and warm parsley-buttered new potatoes.

Prepare ahead

Sauté the fennel up to 1 day ahead, cover, and chill. Bring to room temperature before continuing with the recipe.

Seared tuna with a black sesame seed crust

A dramatic looking dish, the nutty sesame is a great foil to the juicy tuna.

The fish

Tuna, or swordfish, marlin, or salmon

- **PREP** 10 mins, plus marinating
- **COOK** 1 min ▪ **SERVES** 4

Ingredients

4 tbsp olive oil, plus extra for searing

1 garlic clove, grated or finely chopped

1 small hot red chilli, finely chopped

2 tbsp black sesame seeds, plus extra for sprinkling (optional)

salt

2 tuna steaks, about 300g (10oz) each, halved lengthways

2 radishes

juice of 1 lemon

½ bunch of chives, chopped into 5cm (2in) lengths

1 Mix the oil, garlic, chilli, sesame seeds, and a sprinkling of salt on a large flat dish. Rinse the tuna, and pat dry with kitchen paper. Carefully press them into the sesame seeds so that they stick. Turn, and coat the other side. Cover, and marinate in the refrigerator for at least 1 hour.

2 Meanwhile, cut the radishes into matchsticks, and put them in a bowl with half the lemon juice, to prevent browning.

3 Heat a little extra oil in a frying pan over a high heat. Sear the tuna for 20 seconds on each side. Leave to rest for 5 minutes.

4 Put half a tuna steak on each of 4 serving plates, and drizzle with the remaining lemon juice. Drain the radishes, and scatter over with the chives and extra sesame seeds (if using).

Variation

Black sesame tuna salad

Double the quantities and serve this as a main course with a salad of fresh orange segments, finely sliced cucumber, and sprigs of dill or mint, as well as the radish.

Fish fingers with chunky tartare sauce

You can bake these for 8 minutes at 200°C (400°F/Gas 6) instead of frying, if you prefer. Children love them, too.

The fish

Any firm white fish, such as haddock, cod, or pollock

- **PREP** 15 mins ▪ **COOK** 7 mins ▪ **SERVES** 4

Ingredients

115g (4oz) fresh breadcrumbs

675g (1½lb) thick white fish fillets (loin works best), pinboned and skinned

1–2 tbsp plain flour

1 egg, lightly beaten

60g (2oz) Parmesan cheese, finely grated

salt and freshly ground black pepper

1 tbsp vegetable oil

3 tbsp tartare sauce

1 tsp capers, rinsed, drained, and chopped

3 gherkins, drained and finely chopped

1 Spread the breadcrumbs on a baking tray, and toast in the oven for about 5 minutes, or until golden. Tip them into a food processor, and whizz until fine.

2 Cut the fish fillets into thick, even strips about 2.5cm (1in) wide; you should end up with about 20 "fingers".

3 Tip the flour and egg on to separate plates. Mix the breadcrumbs with the Parmesan, and season. Dredge the fish in the flour, then dip in the egg. Finally, press each into the breadcrumb mixture on all sides.

4 Heat the oil in a large frying pan over a medium heat. Add the fish fingers, in batches so as not to crowd the pan, and fry for 3–4 minutes. Turn and fry for 2–3 minutes. When cooked, they should flake under the gentle pressure of a finger. Remove, drain on kitchen paper, and keep warm while you fry the rest.

5 Put the tartare sauce into a bowl, and stir in the capers and gherkins. Serve with the hot fish fingers.

Prepare ahead

These can be frozen before frying if the fish has not been previously frozen. Freeze on a baking sheet to keep separate then, when frozen solid, tip into a plastic freezer bag to store. Defrost before frying the fish fingers.

Spiced haddock with coconut, chilli, and lime

An unusual and delicious mid-week supper dish for a cold night.

The fish

Haddock, or salmon, cod, pollock, coley, or whiting

- **PREP** 10 mins ▪ **COOK** 20 mins ▪ **SERVES** 4

Ingredients

4 haddock fillets, about 675g (1½lb) in total

salt and freshly ground black pepper

400ml can coconut milk

1 medium-hot red chilli, deseeded and finely chopped

juice of 1 lime

splash of Thai fish sauce

pinch of sugar (optional)

150g (5½oz) green beans, trimmed

1 tbsp groundnut or sunflower oil

For the spice mixture

1–2 tsp cayenne pepper, to taste

1 tsp paprika

1 tsp ground cinnamon

1 tsp ground coriander

1 tbsp cornflour

1 To make the spice mixture, mix together the spices and cornflour in a bowl. Season the haddock fillets, then coat well with the spice mixture. Set aside.

2 Pour the coconut milk into a wide pan, add the chilli, and bring to a boil. Reduce the heat to a simmer, then add the lime juice, fish sauce, and sugar (if using). Throw in the green beans, and simmer for about 5 minutes.

3 Meanwhile, heat the oil in a non-stick frying pan over a high heat. Add the fish, and fry for about 5 minutes on each side until golden.

4 Either add the fish to the sauce, or serve the sauce on the side.

Pan-fried trout with almonds

This all-time classic is served across Europe. Almonds are typically used, but hazelnuts work equally well.

The fish
Trout, or mackerel

- **PREP** 10 mins ■ **COOK** 15 mins ■ **SERVES** 2

Ingredients
2 small trout, scaled, gutted, and gilled

2 tbsp seasoned flour (see page 55)

2–3 tbsp vegetable oil

lemon wedges, to serve

For the almond beurre noisette
50g (1¾oz) unsalted butter

50g (1¾oz) blanched almonds, chopped

1 tbsp chopped flat-leaf parsley

juice of 1 lemon

1 Wash the trout and check the bloodline has been removed completely (see page 266). The head is traditionally left on, as the eye indicates if the fish is cooked (it turns white) and the cheek or "pearl" is the best morsel.

2 Dry the trout well and roll in the seasoned flour. Heat the oil in a large frying pan, add the trout and fry over a low heat for 4–5 minutes. Turn with tongs or fish slices and cook on the second side for 3–4 minutes or until the fish is cooked. Avoid the temptation to keep turning the fish, as it will begin to break up. Lift on to a warmed serving dish and set aside.

3 Wipe out the frying pan and add the butter, heat until hot and foaming, then add the almonds. Fry, stirring, until toasted and golden brown (too dark and they will taste bitter).

4 As soon as the almonds are the right colour, add the parsley and lemon juice. Standing back, as it will spit, swirl the pan, and, while sizzling, pour over the trout. Serve with lemon wedges.

Balinese spicy mackerel

Typical of the cuisine of Indonesia this recipe uses kecap manis, soy sauce, and molasses.

The fish
Mackerel, or salmon, meagre, or mahi mahi

- **PREP** 10 mins, plus chilling ■ **COOK** 15 mins ■ **SERVES** 4

Ingredients
4 small mackerel, skin on, filleted and pinboned

juice and grated zest of 2 limes

½ tsp ground turmeric or 2 tsp freshly grated turmeric

½ tsp salt

3 tbsp vegetable oil

1 stalk lemongrass, split into 4

3 tbsp kecap manis

For the chilli paste
3 red chillies, deseeded (optional) and finely chopped

6 shallots, chopped

2 garlic cloves, crushed

5 roasted candlenuts or macadamia nuts

1 tbsp grated fresh root ginger

1 tbsp tamarind paste

½ tsp caster sugar

salt and freshly ground black pepper

1 Cut the mackerel fillets in half lengthways. Sprinkle with the lime juice, turmeric, and salt, cover and refrigerate for 15–30 minutes.

2 Put the chillies, shallots, garlic, nuts, ginger, tamarind, and sugar into a small food processor, and whizz to chop very finely. Season lightly.

3 Pat the mackerel dry with kitchen paper. Heat the oil in a large frying pan or wok. Fry the mackerel skin side down, a few pieces at a time, until firm, opaque and brown. Avoid stirring to prevent the fish from breaking up. Remove from the pan.

4 Add the spice paste to the pan and fry over a medium heat until fragrant. Add 150ml (5fl oz) of water, and the lemongrass, bring to a boil, and simmer for 2–3 minutes. Return the fish and add the kecap manis, stir over a gentle heat until all ingredients are combined and the sauce reduced and bubbling. Serve with rice and garnish with lime wedges and coriander.

Prepare ahead
You can make the chilli paste up to 1 day ahead, cover, and store in the refrigerator.

MACKEREL FLAVOUR PAIRINGS:
Oil-rich mackerel takes well to the Asian tastes of chilli, shoyu, sesame seeds, mirin, rice vinegar, daikon, cucumber, and coriander, or to Mediterranean basil, olive oil, and garlic.

Sautéed trout with hazelnuts

The crunchy topping makes a delicious contrast to the soft-textured fish.

The fish

Trout, or mackerel

- **PREP** 20–25 mins ▪ **COOK** 20 mins
- **SERVES** 4

Ingredients

4 trout, about 300g (10oz) each, scaled and gutted

60g (2oz) hazelnuts

2 lemons

20–30g (¾–1oz) plain flour

salt and freshly ground black pepper

125g (4½oz) butter

2 tbsp chopped flat-leaf parsley

1 Rinse the trout inside and out, and pat dry with kitchen paper.

2 Preheat the oven to 180°C (350°F/Gas 4). Spread the hazelnuts on a baking sheet and cook for 8–10 minutes, until browned. While hot, rub in a tea towel to remove the skins. Peel the lemons, remove all the pith, and cut into thin rounds. Remove any pips. Set aside.

3 Put the flour on a large plate and season. Press each trout in the flour, turning to coat on all sides. Lift out and gently shake to remove any excess.

4 Heat half the butter in a large frying pan, until foaming. Add 2 trout, and brown over a medium heat for 2–3 minutes. Carefully turn and cook for 3–5 minutes more, until the flesh flakes easily under a fork. Keep warm while you cook the remaining fish in the rest of the butter.

5 Add the hazelnuts to the pan, and sauté for 3–4 minutes, until golden brown. Stir in most of the parsley. Serve the fish on warmed plates, spoon over the hazelnuts, and scatter with lemon slices and the remaining parsley.

Prepare ahead

The hazelnuts can be roasted and skinned 1 day ahead. Store in an airtight container at room temperature.

Pollock with spinach and pine nuts

An extremely healthy dish, and very easy to make quickly.

The fish

Pollock, or any firm white fish, such as turbot, haddock, or cod

- **PREP** 10 mins ▪ **COOK** 15 mins ▪ **SERVES** 4

Ingredients

4 pollock fillets, about 150g (5½oz) each, scaled and pinboned

salt and freshly ground black pepper

2 tbsp olive oil

1 onion, finely chopped

handful of plump raisins

handful of pine nuts, toasted

1–2 tsp capers, rinsed and gently squeezed dry

2 large handfuls of spinach leaves

1 Season the fish with salt and pepper. Salting the fish – ideally with sea salt – before cooking firms the flesh by removing moisture.

2 Heat half the oil in a large non-stick frying pan over a medium heat. Add the fish, skin side down, and cook gently for 5–6 minutes. Turn, and cook on the other side until it just begins to flake when gently pressed; the time this takes will depend on the thickness of the fish, but be careful not to overcook. Remove from the pan, and set aside to keep warm.

3 Carefully wipe out the pan with kitchen paper, then add the remaining oil. Sauté the onion for about 5 minutes until soft and translucent. Add the raisins, pine nuts, and capers, and cook for a few minutes more, breaking up the capers with the back of a fork.

4 Add the spinach, and cook until just wilted. Taste, and season if needed. Serve the fish on a bed of the wilted spinach mixture.

Omelette Arnold Bennett

This famous dish was specially created for the Victorian novelist at the Savoy Grill, London.

The fish

Smoked haddock, or smoked mackerel

- **PREP** 5 mins ▪ **COOK** 20 mins ▪ **SERVES** 4

Ingredients

8 large eggs, separated

150ml (5fl oz) single cream

350g (12oz) smoked haddock fillet, poached, skinned, and flaked

4 tbsp grated Parmesan cheese

freshly ground black pepper

60g (2oz) butter

1 Beat the egg yolks in a bowl with 2 tbsp of the cream, until smooth and creamy. In a separate, clean bowl, whisk the egg whites until they form soft peaks. Add 1 tbsp of the whites to the egg yolk mixture, to loosen it, then fold in the rest with the haddock, half the cheese, and plenty of pepper.

2 Preheat the grill on its highest setting. Melt the butter in a large non-stick frying pan and, when foaming, add the egg mixture. Cook until the eggs have set on the bottom, using a spatula to draw the edges into the middle of the pan as they start to set, so the uncooked mixture can run to the sides of the pan.

3 Once set on the bottom, scatter the remaining cheese on top, and pour over the rest of the cream. Place the pan under the grill until lightly browned and set. Serve at once.

Cod in tomato sauce

The tomatoes and wine add sweetness to this Spanish dish.

The fish

Cod, or haddock, coley, pollock, or whiting

- **PREP** 10 mins ▪ **COOK** 30 mins ▪ **SERVES** 4

Ingredients

1kg (2¼lb) cod fillet, skinned, cut into 4 pieces

2 tbsp olive oil

1 large onion, finely sliced

1 garlic clove, grated or finely chopped

4 large plum tomatoes, skinned, deseeded, and chopped (see page 112)

2 tsp tomato purée

1 tsp caster sugar

300ml (10fl oz) fish stock

120ml (4fl oz) dry white wine

2 tbsp chopped flat-leaf parsley

salt and freshly ground black pepper

1 Preheat the oven to 200°C (400°F/Gas 6). Pinbone the cod fillet. Heat the oil in a flameproof casserole large enough to hold the cod in 1 layer. Fry the fish over a medium-high heat for 1 minute, turn and cook for 1 minute more. Remove and set aside.

2 Add the onion and garlic to the casserole and fry over a medium heat until softened. Add the tomatoes, tomato purée, sugar, stock, and wine, bring to a simmer, and cook for 10–12 minutes. Top with the fish and bake in the oven for 5 minutes. Lift out the cod, and keep warm.

3 Place the casserole over a medium-high heat and simmer the sauce until thickened. Stir in half the parsley and season. Divide the sauce between 4 warmed plates and place the fish on top. Serve sprinkled with the remaining parsley.

Prepare ahead

The tomato sauce can be made up to 2 days ahead, covered, and refrigerated. Return to a simmer before continuing.

Sweet and sour snapper with pineapple

Snapper has a meaty, sweet, and succulent flesh that works well with the classic Chinese sweet and sour flavours.

The fish
Snapper

- **PREP** 25 mins ▪ **COOK** 15 mins ▪ **SERVES** 4

Ingredients
800g (1¾lb) snapper fillets, pinboned and scaled

5 tbsp cornflour

4–5 tbsp sunflower oil, plus extra if needed

1 onion, finely chopped

1 tbsp chopped fresh root ginger

1 garlic clove, chopped

1 red and 1 orange pepper, deseeded and thickly sliced

2 celery sticks, sliced

2 tbsp tomato ketchup

2 tbsp plum sauce

2 tbsp light soy sauce

5 tbsp red wine vinegar

225g can pineapple chunks in natural juice

1 Cut the snapper into 5cm (2in) pieces, and roll in 4 tbsp of the cornflour. Heat half the oil in a large wok, and fry the fish pieces, a few at a time, for 3–4 minutes or until cooked; the flesh will be white and firm. You may need to add more oil between batches. Set aside.

2 Heat the remaining oil in the same frying pan. Add the onion, ginger, garlic, peppers, and celery, and stir-fry over a high heat, tossing all the time, for 3–4 minutes or until the vegetables soften.

3 Mix the ketchup, plum sauce, soy sauce, vinegar, and drained juice from the pineapple together. Stir in the remaining cornflour. Add this to the vegetables and cook over a gentle heat for 2–3 minutes or until lightly thickened. Return the snapper and add the pineapple chunks. Heat through and serve with rice.

Prepare ahead
The sweet and sour sauce can be made up to 2 days in advance, covered, and refrigerated. Reheat gently. It may need more water, so add a little until the consistency is as you prefer.

Red mullet Dieppoise

A Dieppoise garnish usually contains wine and cream, but vitally mussels from that area.

The fish
Red mullet, or rascasse, John Dory fillets, or hake fillets, and mussels, or clams

- **PREP** 20 mins ▪ **COOK** 25 mins ▪ **SERVES** 4

Ingredients
1 shallot, finely chopped

150ml (¼ pint) dry white wine

500g (1lb 2oz) mussels, prepared (see page 278)

30g (1oz) butter

115g (4oz) button mushrooms, thickly sliced

150ml (5fl oz) double cream

salt and freshly ground black pepper

lemon juice, to taste

2 tbsp olive oil

4–8 small red mullet (depending on size), scaled, gutted, and trimmed (liver left in)

1 tbsp seasoned flour (see page 55)

1 Put the shallot and wine into a small saucepan, bring to a boil, and simmer for 2–3 minutes to reduce by one-third. Add the mussels, cover with a well-fitting lid, and cook over a medium heat for 3–4 minutes, or until opened. Try to resist the temptation to lift the lid. Lift on to a plate to cool, and strain the liquid. Discard any mussels that haven't opened and lift the mussels from their shells.

2 Heat the butter in a large saucepan, add the mushrooms, and fry over a brisk heat for 2–3 minutes or until cooked, then add the mussel liquor and simmer for 2–3 minutes to reduce by half. Add the cream, bring to a boil, and simmer until the sauce is a syrupy consistency. Season, adding lemon juice to taste. Tip in the mussels and warm through.

3 Meanwhile, heat the oil in a large frying pan, and coat the fish with the seasoned flour. Fry the fish, in 2 batches, in the hot oil for 3 minutes each side. Lift on to a serving dish and spoon the sauce over.

RED MULLET FLAVOUR PAIRINGS:
This beautiful fish is great with white wine, cream, mushrooms, tomatoes, garlic, and peppers, or with citrus, and herbs such as chervil and tarragon.

Prawns with garlic and chilli

This great recipe is incredibly quick to make – and hard to stop eating!

The fish

Prawns, or scallops or monkfish

- **PREP** 5 mins ▪ **COOK** 10 mins ▪ **SERVES** 4

Ingredients

4 tbsp olive oil

6 garlic cloves, grated or finely chopped

1 tsp chilli flakes

1 tbsp dry sherry

250g (9oz) raw prawns, peeled and deveined (see page 285)

salt and freshly ground black pepper

1 Heat the oil in a frying pan over a medium heat, add the garlic and chilli, and cook gently for 2 minutes.

2 Add the sherry and prawns, increase the heat, and stir for 5 minutes, or until the juices have reduced by half. Season and serve with crusty bread and a crisp salad.

Pan-fried prawns, olives, and tomatoes

The deep tastes of the Mediterranean in this dish highlight the sweet flavour of the prawns.

The fish

Prawns, or monkfish, scallops, or squid

- **PREP** 5 mins ▪ **COOK** 15 mins ▪ **SERVES** 4

Ingredients

1 tbsp olive oil

1 onion, finely chopped

2 garlic cloves, grated or finely chopped

12 large raw prawns, peeled and deveined, tail left intact (see page 285)

splash of dry sherry, or dry white wine

6 tomatoes, skinned, deseeded, and chopped

large handful of mixed olives, pitted

salt and freshly ground black pepper

handful of basil and flat-leaf parsley, chopped

1 Heat the oil in a large frying pan over a medium heat. Add the onion, and sauté for about 5 minutes until soft and translucent. Add the garlic, and cook for a few seconds, then tip in the prawns and cook over a high heat, until they are just turning pink.

2 Add the sherry, and continue cooking for 5 minutes, stirring, until the alcohol has evaporated. Add the tomatoes and olives and cook for a further couple of minutes, stirring occasionally, until the tomatoes start to break down. Season well, and stir in the herbs. Serve immediately with fresh crusty bread.

Pan-fried clams with parsley and garlic

Simple tastes here for a healthy winter feast.

The fish

Clams, or mussels

■ **PREP** 10 mins ■ **COOK** 20 mins ■ **SERVES** 4

Ingredients

1 tbsp olive oil

1 onion, finely chopped

salt

2 garlic cloves, grated or finely chopped

1–2 green peppers, deseeded and finely chopped

150ml (5fl oz) dry white wine

450g (1lb) clams, prepared

handful of flat-leaf parsley, finely chopped

lemon wedges, to serve

1 Heat the oil in a large frying pan over a medium heat. Add the onion and a pinch of salt, and sweat for about 5 minutes until soft and translucent. Add the garlic and peppers, and gently sweat until the peppers begin to soften. Increase the heat to high, and add the wine. Cook for a couple of minutes until the alcohol has evaporated.

2 Add the clams, shaking the pan occasionally, and cook for 5–6 minutes until the clams open (discard any that remain shut). Add the parsley, and stir to combine. Serve piping hot with fresh crusty bread to mop up the juices and some lemon wedges.

Pan-fried scallops with chilli, ginger, and an anchovy dressing

An extravagant treat with strong flavours for an adventurous crowd.

The fish

King scallops, or squid or monkfish

■ **PREP** 10 mins ■ **COOK** 30 mins ■ **SERVES** 4

Ingredients

2–3 tbsp olive oil

675g (1½lb) waxy potatoes, peeled and thinly sliced

12 king scallops, roe removed

salt and freshly ground black pepper

1 hot red chilli, deseeded and finely chopped

2.5cm (1in) fresh root ginger, grated

juice of ½ lemon

handful of flat-leaf parsley, finely chopped

For the anchovy dressing

3 tbsp extra virgin olive oil

1 tbsp white wine vinegar

8 anchovy fillets in olive oil, drained and finely chopped

pinch of sugar (optional)

1 Heat 1–2 tbsp of the olive oil in a large non-stick frying pan over a medium-high heat. Add the potatoes, and sauté for 15–20 minutes until golden and cooked through. Drain on kitchen paper, and set aside to keep warm.

2 Meanwhile, make the anchovy dressing. In a jug, whisk together the extra virgin olive oil, vinegar, and anchovies until well combined. Taste, and add a pinch of sugar if it needs it. Season with pepper.

3 Pat the scallops dry with kitchen paper, and season with salt and pepper. Put the remaining olive oil in the frying pan over a high heat. When hot, add the scallops. Sear for about 1 minute, then turn them over. Add the chilli and ginger, and squeeze over the lemon juice, being careful, as it will spit. Remove the pan from the heat, and sprinkle over the parsley.

4 Serve immediately with the sautéed potatoes and a drizzle of the anchovy dressing.

Prepare ahead

Make the anchovy dressing up to 2 days ahead, cover, and refrigerate. Return to room temperature, and whisk before use.

SUSTAINABILITY CHOICE

Buy seafood outside the spawning season

Fish and shellfish spawn at different times of the year, though many spawn in spring and early summer. Avoid buying any fish that are full of roe to give the species the chance to reproduce. Lobster, for example, produces millions of eggs, and only very few will survive, so this slow-growing crustacean needs time to replenish the stock. During the latter stages of roe production and immediately after spawning, fish can also be disappointing to eat, lacking flavour and texture, as their muscles are not exercised as often as at other times of the year.

Pan-fried prawns in garlic butter

The prawns can be peeled or not; provide finger bowls and plenty of paper napkins if you leave the shell on.

The fish

Tiger prawns, or scallops, monkfish, or cod cheeks

- **PREP** 5 mins ▪ **COOK** 10 mins ▪ **SERVES** 4

Ingredients

85g (3oz) unsalted butter

juice of 1 lemon, plus more to serve

2 garlic cloves, crushed

2 tbsp finely chopped flat-leaf parsley, plus extra, to serve

salt and freshly ground black pepper

2 tbsp olive oil

16–20 raw tiger prawns, peeled, deveined, and butterflied (see page 285)

lemon wedges, to serve

1 Mix the butter, lemon juice, garlic, and parsley together, and season to taste with salt and plenty of pepper.

2 Heat the oil in a large frying pan, add half the prawns and pan-fry over a medium heat for 2 minutes, or until they have lost their translucency and turned pink. Lift on to a large serving platter and keep warm while you cook the remaining prawns in the same way.

3 Wipe out the frying pan if necessary and add the garlic butter. Heat until hot and foaming and the garlic is soft, but not brown. Add a splash of lemon juice to stop the cooking and immediately pour over the prawns.

4 Garnish with parsley and lemon wedges, and provide lots of crusty bread to mop up the delicious garlic butter.

Prepare ahead

The garlic butter can be made up to 2 days ahead. Wrap it in greaseproof paper and store in the refrigerator.

Plaice with smoked bacon

A recipe for a romantic dinner, as it's difficult to pan-fry more than two fish.

The fish

Plaice, or any flat fish such as dab, flounder, or lemon sole

- **PREP** 10 mins ▪ **COOK** 20 mins ▪ **SERVES** 2

Ingredients

2 medium plaice

115g (4oz) thick-cut smoked streaky bacon, rind removed, diced

1 tbsp seasoned flour (see page 55)

lemon wedges, to serve

chopped flat-leaf parsley, to serve

1 Remove the gills, the bloodline, and trim the plaice (see page 272).

2 Heat a large frying pan, add the bacon, and cook until brown and crispy. Lift out on to a plate, but keep the fat in the pan.

3 Dust the fish with the seasoned flour. Pan-fry the plaice one at a time in the bacon fat for 3–4 minutes on each side. Once cooked, lift on to a plate and keep warm.

4 Once both fish are cooked, arrange them on a large plate, and spoon the bacon over the top. Garnish with lemon wedges and parsley. Serve with steamed green beans, or a tomato salad.

PLAICE FLAVOUR PAIRINGS: This subtle-flavoured, delicate-fleshed fish is best with mild partners; try butter, lemon, parsley, breadcrumbs, sage, chestnut mushrooms, or mashed potatoes.

Sole meunière

Pan-frying in clarified butter (*à la meunière*) is a classic French way to cook fish simply.

The fish

Lemon sole, or brill, turbot, or plaice

- **PREP** 5 mins - **COOK** 10 mins - **SERVES** 2

Ingredients

2 lemon sole, skinned and filleted

2 tbsp seasoned flour (see page 55)

6–8 tbsp butter

2 tbsp finely chopped flat-leaf parsley

juice of ½ lemon

1 Roll the sole fillets in the seasoned flour until well coated. Arrange them in a single layer on a plate (do not stack, as they will stick together and the flour will become soggy).

2 To clarify the butter, melt it in a heavy-based saucepan over very low heat. When it stops spitting, carefully pour it into a dish, leaving the white sediment (the milk solids) behind in the bottom of the pan.

3 Heat half of the clarified butter in a large frying pan until it is no longer sizzling. Lower in the fish, and press down gently with a spatula. Pan-fry for 1 minute. Turn the fish over and cook on the second side for a further 30 seconds or so; the fish is cooked when it is firm and white. Lift on to a plate and keep warm. (You may need to fry in two batches.)

4 Wipe out the frying pan and add the remaining butter. Allow to cook for a few seconds until it turns golden brown, then add the parsley and a squeeze of lemon juice, and pour, still sizzling, over the fish.

Samak maquli

This is typical Egyptian street food. If you can't find small red mullet, use fillets instead.

The fish

Red mullet, or small grey mullet, sardines, small mackerel, or small pomfret

- **PREP** 15 mins - **COOK** 5–10 mins
- **SERVES** 2

Ingredients

6–8 small red mullet, scaled, gutted, and gills removed

8 garlic cloves, crushed

4 tbsp chopped flat-leaf parsley

grated zest of 1 lemon

salt and freshly ground black pepper

olive oil, for deep-frying

3 tbsp seasoned flour (see page 55)

lemon wedges, to serve

For the sauce

3–4 tbsp tahini paste

4 garlic cloves, crushed

juice of 1–2 lemons, to taste

1 tbsp chopped flat-leaf parsley

1 Rinse the fish to ensure all traces of blood are removed; pat dry on kitchen paper.

2 Mix the garlic, parsley, and lemon zest and season generously. Use this to rub all over and inside the cavity of the fish.

3 Heat the oil to 180°C (350°F) in a large pan or deep-fat fryer (see page 308).

4 When the oil is hot, dust the fish with seasoned flour and fry 2–3 fish at a time. Once cooked (their flesh will be white and opaque), lift on to a warmed serving dish while you cook the remaining fish.

5 For the sauce, mix the tahini paste, garlic, lemon juice to taste, and parsley. Add water if the mixture is too thick. Serve the fish with the tahini sauce and lemon wedges.

Prepare ahead

Rub the fish with the garlic, parsley, and lemon, and make the tahini sauce, 1 day in advance. Cover both separately, and refrigerate. Bring to room temperature before continuing.

LEMON SOLE FLAVOUR PAIRINGS:

Lemon sole is much-prized for its delicate, yet definite sweet flavour and soft flesh. Treat it simply, and pair with seasoned flour or herbed breadcrumbs.

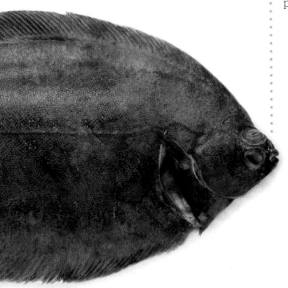

Pollock and pumpkin chips

Pollock is a great alternative to cod. Deep-frying it is quick and simple.

The fish
Pollock, or any white fish, such as coley, bass, or tilapia

- **PREP** 25 mins ▪ **COOK** 30–40 mins
- **SERVES** 4

Ingredients
1 pumpkin, about 1.25kg (2¾lb)

olive oil, for drizzling

115g (4oz) plain flour, plus more to coat

a pinch of salt

2 tbsp vegetable oil, plus extra for deep-frying

150ml (5fl oz) milk

1 large egg white

4 pollock fillets, about 175g (6oz) each, pinboned and skinned

1 Preheat the oven to 240ºC (475°F/Gas 9), or its highest setting. Peel the pumpkin and cut into chips. Put them on a baking sheet, drizzle with oil, and cook for 30 minutes, turning halfway, until crisp, but tender inside.

2 Meanwhile, sift the flour into a bowl. Make a well in the middle, add the salt with 2 tbsp oil and the milk, and whisk until smooth. Whisk the egg white until stiff, then fold it in.

3 Heat the oil to 180°C (350°F) in a large pan or deep-fat fryer (see page 308). Coat the fish in a little seasoned flour, then dip it in the batter. Fry the fish, 1 piece at a time, in the oil for 8 minutes until crisp and golden brown. Carefully remove and drain on kitchen paper. Keep warm whilst cooking the rest.

4 Serve immediately with the pumpkin chips, and peas steamed with fresh mint.

Mixed fried fish

You can use squid rings in this recipe but be careful not to overcook them.

The fish
Any mixed fish, such as cod, salmon, and snapper, and tiger prawns or squid rings

- **PREP** 20 mins ▪ **COOK** 10 mins ▪ **SERVES** 4

Ingredients
4 tbsp plain flour

2 eggs, lightly beaten

85g (3oz) dried white breadcrumbs, or Panko breadcrumbs

3 mixed fish fillets, about 115g (4oz) each, pinboned and skinned

12 raw tiger prawns, peeled and deveined, heads removed (see page 285)

oil, for deep frying

For the sauce
60g (2oz) rocket, plus extra to serve

1 garlic clove, crushed

100ml (3½fl oz) mayonnaise

1 tsp lemon juice

salt and freshly ground black pepper

1 Place all the sauce ingredients in a food processor, season, and blend until smooth.

2 Season the flour. Place the flour, eggs, and breadcrumbs in 3 separate dishes. Cut each fish fillet into 4. Toss the fish and prawns in the flour, dip in the egg, then coat in breadcrumbs.

3 Heat the oil to 180°C (350°F) in a large pan or deep-fat fryer (see page 308). Fry the fish in batches for 2–3 minutes, or until crisp and golden. Drain on kitchen paper.

4 Place a few rocket leaves on each serving plate and lay the fish on top. Serve immediately, with the sauce alongside.

Egg fu yung

Light and tasty, these Chinese patties are made with prawns and stir-fried vegetables.

The fish

Prawns, or any firm white fish

- **PREP** 15 mins ▪ **COOK** 20 mins ▪ **SERVES** 4

Ingredients

200ml (7fl oz) vegetable stock

1 tbsp oyster sauce

1 tbsp light soy sauce

1 tbsp Chinese rice wine

vegetable oil, for deep-frying

3 shallots, thinly sliced

2 garlic cloves, crushed

1 green pepper, deseeded and chopped

1 celery stick, chopped

85g (3oz) beansprouts

115g (4oz) raw prawns, peeled and deveined (see page 285)

5 eggs, beaten

2 tsp cornflour

1 Pour the stock, oyster sauce, soy sauce, and rice wine into a small saucepan. Set aside.

2 Heat 2 tbsp of oil in a wok and stir-fry the shallots, garlic, green pepper, and celery for 3 minutes. Add the beansprouts and prawns. Stir-fry for 2–3 more minutes, until they turn pink. Transfer to a bowl and set aside.

3 When the mixture is cool, stir in the eggs. Wipe the wok with kitchen paper.

4 Return the wok to the heat and pour in 5cm (2in) oil. When hot, ladle in one-quarter of the mixture and fry for 2 minutes, until browned, spooning over the oil so the top starts to set. Carefully turn and cook the other side. Place on kitchen paper and keep warm while you cook the rest of the mixture.

5 Mix the cornflour with a little water until smooth and stir into the stock mixture in the saucepan. Bring to a boil, stirring, and simmer for 1 minute, until thickened. Spoon over the patties and serve with the rice.

Prepare ahead

Make the sauce 1 day ahead, cover, and refrigerate. Reheat gently to serve, adding a little more water if it has become too thick.

Breaded fried prawns

Easy, and far tastier than shop-bought.

The fish

Tiger prawns, or squid or scallops

- **PREP** 20 mins, plus chilling ▪ **COOK** 15 mins ▪ **SERVES** 4

Ingredients

12 tbsp dried breadcrumbs

6 tbsp polenta

2 tsp dried marjoram or oregano

2 tsp dried thyme

freshly ground black pepper

24 raw tiger prawns, peeled and deveined, tails left on (see page 285)

plain flour, to dust

3–4 eggs, beaten

sunflower oil, for deep-frying

1 Mix the breadcrumbs, polenta, marjoram, thyme, and pepper, and spread out on a plate.

2 Pat the prawns dry with kitchen paper and dust with flour, leaving the tails clear. Brush with beaten egg, then press into the breadcrumb mixture to evenly coat. Chill for 30 minutes.

3 Heat the oil to 180°C (350°F) in a large pan or deep-fat fryer (see page 308). Deep-fry the prawns in batches for 2–3 minutes, until the coating is golden and crisp. Drain on kitchen paper and serve at once, with sweet chilli sauce. For a special occasion, add herb- and chilli-flecked thin rice noodles.

Fritto misto di pesce

In coastal Naples and Liguria, *Fritto misto* (little fried morsels) is made with fish, other regions use offal and vegetables instead.

The fish

Any small mixed fish, such as sardines, sprats, anchovies, red mullet, and shellfish, such as squid

- **PREP** 10 mins ■ **COOK** 10–15 mins
- **SERVES** 4

Ingredients

8 sardines or sprats, scaled and gutted

16 fresh anchovies, if available, or fresh sprats, scaled and gutted

4 small red mullet, scaled and gutted

8 small squid, gutted, cleaned, and cut into rings (see page 282)

6 tbsp seasoned flour (see page 55)

olive oil, for deep-frying

lemon wedges, to serve

1 Prepare the fish, ensuring they are gutted well, the gills are removed, and any trace of blood is cleaned away. Pat dry on kitchen paper. Dredge all the fish and squid well in seasoned flour.

2 Heat the oil to 180°C (350°F) in a large pan or deep-fat fryer (see page 308).

3 Cook the fish in small batches for 3–4 minutes, depending on species and size (fry batches of same-sized fish together for even cooking), then drain on kitchen paper.

4 Pile on to a serving dish with lemon wedges for people to help themselves.

DAB FLAVOUR PAIRINGS: Sharpen the subtle taste of this flat fish with white wine vinegar, capers, and lemon juice, or bake with potatoes, sage, and mushrooms.

Sole colbert

This French Escoffier classic is traditionally served with *pont neuf* (very thin chips).

The fish

Dover sole, or any small flat fish, such as dab, flounder, plaice, or lemon sole

- **PREP** 25 mins ■ **COOK** 5–7 mins ■ **SERVES** 2

Ingredients

2 small Dover sole, skinned

vegetable oil, for deep-frying

2 tbsp seasoned flour (see page 55)

1 egg, beaten

6 tbsp dried white breadcrumbs, sieved

For the maître d'hôtel butter

60g (2oz) unsalted butter, softened

3 tbsp finely chopped flat-leaf parsley

lemon juice, to taste

salt and freshly ground black pepper

1 Prepare the Dover sole, but do not snip away the backbone (see page 276).

2 Heat the oil to 180°C (350°F) in a large pan or deep-fat fryer (see page 308).

3 Dust the fish evenly with the seasoned flour. Brush thoroughly with the egg and roll in the breadcrumbs. Set aside.

4 Mix all the ingredients for the maître d'hôtel butter, adding lemon juice and seasoning to taste. Roll into a sausage shape, wrap in cling film, and chill.

5 Fry the sole for 5–7 minutes, it will curl slightly and be golden brown. Lift on to kitchen paper and carefully remove the backbone by snipping at either end and pulling away, so the fillets are separated.

6 Arrange the fish on a serving dish. Slice the butter into 0.5cm (¼in) slices and put 2–3 in the middle of each of the fish. It will melt to create a lovely, if rich, dressing. Serve with chips and a flower salad.

Prepare ahead

The maître d'hôtel butter can be made and refrigerated for 2–3 days before use.

Deep-fried haddock in beer batter

Skin on or off is down to personal taste, though purists say it should be removed.

The fish

Haddock, or any white fish, such as cod, pollock, coley, tilapia, or smoked haddock (a revelation)

- **PREP** 10 mins
- **COOK** 7–10 mins
- **SERVES** 4

Ingredients

oil, for deep-frying

4 haddock fillets, about 175–225g (6–8oz) each, pinboned and skinned

4 tbsp seasoned flour (see page 55)

For the batter

115g (4oz) plain flour

1 tsp baking powder

½ tsp salt

250–300ml (8–10fl oz) pale ale

salt and freshly ground black pepper

1 Sift the plain flour, baking powder, and salt into a bowl. Make a well in the centre and add half the ale. Gradually stir in the flour so the batter remains smooth. As it thickens, blend in more ale until the batter is the consistency of single cream, and season.

2 Heat the oil to 180°C (350°F) in a large pan or deep-fat fryer (see page 308). Dust the fish with seasoned flour. Using tongs, lower the fish into the batter to coat completely, then lift out and let any excess drip back into the bowl. Swish the fish through the hot oil to allow the batter to start to "set", then let the fish go.

3 Fry for 7–10 minutes or until the batter is golden brown. Lift the fish on to kitchen paper and sprinkle with salt. Serve with chips and tartare sauce.

Tempura

Unusually, a good tempura batter should have many small lumps.

The fish

Any white fish, such as snapper, lemon sole, or sea bass, or salmon and a selection of seafood

- **PREP** 25 mins
- **COOK** 10–15 mins
- **SERVES** 4

Ingredients

For the batter

600ml (1 pint) cold sparkling water

1 egg, beaten

60g (2oz) cornflour

225g (8oz) self-raising flour

For the seafood

oil, for deep-frying

175g (6oz) white fish fillet, pinboned and skinned

115g (4oz) raw tiger prawns, peeled and deveined (see page 285)

8 scallops

2 squid, gutted, cleaned, and cut into rings (see page 282)

For the traditional dipping sauce

150ml (5fl oz) boiling water infused with 2 tbsp bonito flakes, and strained

150ml (5fl oz) Japanese soy sauce

1 tbsp caster sugar

1 tsp grated fresh root ginger

For the new-style dipping sauce

2 tbsp syrup from stem ginger

2 tbsp red wine vinegar

2 tbsp dark soy sauce

1 tbsp clear honey

2 spring onions, finely sliced

1 To make the batter, put the water into a large bowl, add the egg and flours and whisk together to form a batter with lots of fine lumps. Cover and refrigerate for 20–30 minutes.

2 Mix together the ingredients for both the traditional and new-style dipping sauces in two separate bowls.

3 Heat the oil in a deep-fat fryer to 180°C (350°F) (see page 308). Dip the prepared fish, shellfish, and squid in the batter and fry a few pieces at a time until crisp. The batter should remain quite pale in colour. Lift on to kitchen paper and keep warm while you fry the rest. Serve with both dipping sauces.

HADDOCK FLAVOUR PAIRINGS: The briny, fresh flavour of haddock is complemented with rich batter and piquant tartare sauce, or even salty dulse seaweed, or Cheddar or mozzarella cheeses.

Roasted and Baked

Baked salmon with salsa verde and cucumber

This is also an excellent way to use up leftover salmon.

The fish

Salmon, or sea bass, sea bream, or grey mullet

- **PREP** 20 mins ▪ **COOK** 10 mins ▪ **SERVES** 4

Ingredients

350g (12oz) salmon fillet, pinboned and skinned

1 tbsp olive oil

1 cucumber

For the salsa verde

handful of basil leaves

handful of mint leaves

handful of flat-leaf parsley

2 tbsp white wine vinegar, plus extra to taste

2 tsp capers, rinsed and finely chopped

2 garlic cloves, grated or finely chopped

8 anchovy fillets in olive oil, drained and finely chopped

2 tsp wholegrain mustard

salt and freshly ground black pepper

6 tbsp extra virgin olive oil, plus extra to taste

1 Preheat the oven to 200°C (400°F/Gas 7). Rub the fish with the olive oil, place on a baking sheet, and bake for 10 minutes, or until opaque, and the flesh begins to flake under the pressure of a finger. Set aside to cool.

2 To make the salsa verde, chop all the herbs finely and put in a bowl. Drizzle with the vinegar and stir. Tip in the capers, garlic, and anchovies, and stir again. Add the mustard and season well. Slowly stir in the olive oil. Taste, and add more vinegar or oil as required. Transfer to a bowl.

3 Peel the cucumber, slice in half lengthways, and scoop out the seeds. Dice the flesh. Put the salmon on a platter. Spoon the salsa verde over, and place the cucumber on the side.

Prepare ahead

Make the salsa verde 1 day in advance, cover, and refrigerate. The flavours will deepen. Return to room temperature before serving.

Sole with basil and pinenuts

The success of this simple Venetian recipe lies in the quality of the fish, the basil, and Italian olive oil.

The fish

Dover sole, or lemon sole, flounder, or plaice

- **PREP** 10–15 mins, plus marinating
- **COOK** 15 mins ▪ **SERVES** 4

Ingredients

4 small Dover sole, about 350g (12oz) each

2 tbsp extra virgin olive oil, plus extra for the baking sheet

juice of ½ lemon

1 tbsp shredded basil leaves

salt and freshly ground black pepper

lemon wedges, to serve

For the sauce

4 tbsp pine nuts

2 tbsp extra virgin olive oil

1–2 tbsp shredded basil, plus extra for garnish

juice of ½ lemon

1 Skin and trim the Dover sole (see page 276) taking care to remove the bloodline. Arrange on a tray and drizzle with the olive oil and lemon juice. Sprinkle with the basil and season lightly. Cover and refrigerate for 30 minutes.

2 Preheat the oven to 210°C (415°F/Gas 6½). Arrange the marinated fish on a lightly oiled baking sheet, pouring over the marinade. Roast in the oven for 8–10 minutes or until the flesh of the fish has lost its translucency.

3 Meanwhile, dry roast the pine nuts in a frying pan until just beginning to brown, add the olive oil and basil, and frazzle together for a few seconds. Add the lemon juice, standing back, as the pan may spit, and immediately pour over the fish.

4 Return the sole to the oven for a further 2–3 minutes then lift on to warmed plates. Serve with the juices from the baking sheet, and lemon wedges.

DOVER SOLE PAIRINGS: The delicate, firm flesh is wonderful with lemon, or try mint and cucumber to lift the tastes. It is also excellent, and indulgent, with truffle oil and wild mushrooms.

Salmon with mushrooms and pak choi

The piquant flavours of Asian ingredients are beautiful with the salmon in this easy dish that you can bung-it-in-the-oven on a weeknight.

The fish

Salmon, or snapper

▪ **PREP** 15 mins ▪ **COOK** 25 mins ▪ **SERVES** 4

Ingredients

1 tbsp olive oil

1 tbsp dark soy sauce

½ tbsp mirin (Japanese rice wine), or dry sherry

5cm (2in) fresh root ginger, finely chopped

2 garlic cloves, grated or finely chopped

salt and freshly ground black pepper

4 salmon fillets, about 150g (5½oz) each

2 pak choi, quartered lengthways

200g (7oz) chestnut mushrooms, halved if large

1 Preheat the oven to 200°C (400°F/Gas 6). Put the olive oil, soy sauce, mirin, ginger, and garlic in a bowl, mix well, and season with salt and pepper.

2 Put the salmon, pak choi, and mushrooms in a roasting tin, then drizzle over the oil mixture. Roast in the oven for 20–25 minutes, or until the salmon is cooked through. Serve with rice.

Roasted salmon with Swiss chard and herb butter

This would be equally delicious with curly kale or spinach instead of the chard.

The fish

Salmon, or trout, turbot, or brill

▪ **PREP** 10 mins ▪ **COOK** 30 mins ▪ **SERVES** 4

Ingredients

4 salmon fillets, about 150g (5½oz) each

1 tbsp olive oil

salt and freshly ground black pepper

2 handfuls of Swiss chard, trimmed and chopped

juice of 1 lemon

pinch of chilli flakes

For the herb butter

125g (4½oz) butter

handful of curly parsley, finely chopped

handful of dill, finely chopped

1 First, make the herb butter. Put the butter and herbs in a mixing bowl, and beat well. Spoon on to greaseproof paper, then roll into a log. Twist the edges of the paper, and put the roll in the refrigerator.

2 Preheat the oven to 200°C (400°F/Gas 6). Sit the salmon fillets in a non-stick roasting tin, drizzle with the olive oil, and season. Bake for 15–20 minutes until cooked through.

3 Meanwhile, cook the Swiss chard in a large pan of boiling salted water for 5–8 minutes, until it still has a bite to it. Drain well, and transfer to a serving dish. Squeeze over the lemon juice, and stir in the chilli flakes. Divide between 4 warmed plates.

4 Place the roasted salmon on top of the Swiss chard, lay a slice of herb butter on each piece, and serve immediately.

Prepare ahead

The herb butter can be made ahead, and stored in the refrigerator for 1–2 days.

Salmon en papillote

Cooking "en papillote" – in a tightly sealed parchment packet – ensures the fish is moist.

The fish
Salmon, or sea bass, bream, red mullet, or snapper

- **PREP** 25 mins ▪ **COOK** 15 mins ▪ **SERVES** 4

Ingredients
4 salmon fillets or steaks, about 175g (6oz) each

olive oil, for greasing

4 tomatoes, sliced

2 lemons, sliced

8 sprigs of tarragon

freshly ground black pepper

1 Cut 8 circles of greaseproof paper large enough for the salmon steaks to fit on half of the circle. Use 2 circles per steak to create a double thickness. Lightly grease the top circle with olive oil. Repeat with the rest.

2 Preheat the oven to 160°C (325°F/Gas 3). Divide the tomatoes among the circles, placing them on one half. Place the salmon on top, then the lemon slices and tarragon. Season with pepper. Fold up the paper to enclose the fish. Crimp the edges to create a tight seal. Place on a baking tray and bake for 15 minutes.

3 Place on warm plates, and serve immediately, with beurre blanc (see page 245).

Prepare ahead
The paper cases can be assembled, and stored in the refrigerator for 2 hours.

Asian halibut en papillote

Because of the paper cases, this dish retains all of its delicious fragrance.

The fish
Halibut, or turbot or brill

- **PREP** 15–20 mins ▪ **COOK** 10–12 mins
- **SERVES** 4

Ingredients
125g (4½oz) mangetout, trimmed

30g (1oz) black fermented Chinese beans, or 2 tbsp black bean sauce

4 garlic cloves, grated or finely chopped

2.5cm (1in) fresh root ginger, finely chopped

3 tbsp light soy sauce

2 tbsp dry sherry

½ tsp granulated sugar

1 tbsp sesame oil

2 tbsp vegetable oil

1 egg

½ tsp salt

4 halibut fillets or steaks, 175g (6oz) each, skinned

4 spring onions, thinly sliced

1 Preheat the oven to 200°C (400°F/Gas 6). Simmer the mangetout in salted water for 1–2 minutes. Drain. If you are using fermented black beans, rinse and coarsely chop.

2 Stir together the black beans or black bean sauce, garlic, ginger, soy sauce, sherry, sugar, and sesame oil. Set aside.

3 Fold a sheet of greaseproof paper in half and cut out a curve to make a heart shape when unfolded. It should be large enough to leave a 7.5cm (3in) border around a fish fillet. Repeat to make 4. Open each out and brush with oil, leaving a 2.5cm (1in) border. Beat the egg and salt together. Brush on the borders.

4 Arrange the mangetout on one side of each paper heart and set a halibut fillet on top. Spoon over the black bean seasoning and sprinkle with spring onions. Fold the paper over and seal the edges.

5 Lay the cases on a baking sheet and bake for 10–12 minutes, until puffed. Allow each diner to open their own aromatic package.

Prepare ahead
The paper cases can be assembled, and stored in the refrigerator for 2 hours.

Sea bream en papillote

A classic method of cooking fish; wrapped in paper with a selection of aromatics.

The fish

Sea bream, or sea bass or snapper

- **PREP** 10 mins • **COOK** 12–15 mins
- **SERVES** 1

Ingredients

1 small sea bream, scaled, filleted, and trimmed

a few slices of spring onion or fennel

herbs of your choice (try dill, tarragon, rosemary, or oregano)

knob of butter or splash of olive oil

splash of Pernod or white wine

sea salt and freshly ground black pepper

lemon or lime wedges, to serve

1 Pinbone the fish fillets (see page 271). Heat the oven to 210°C (415°F/Gas 6½). Arrange the fillets, skin-side up, on a large sheet of greaseproof paper.

2 Arrange the vegetables and herbs around the fish and season lightly. Add the butter or oil, and drizzle with Pernod or wine. Season lightly.

3 Wrap the fish securely, but not too tightly, so that the steam can circulate. Roast in the oven for 12–15 minutes or until cooked through. The flesh will be firm and opaque.

4 Serve directly from the greaseproof paper. To eat, open the parcel and squeeze the lemon or lime juice over the fish.

Prepare ahead

Assemble the parcel up to 1 day in advance, and refrigerate. Return to room temperature before baking.

Roast hake with remoulade

Remoulade is similar to tartare sauce and both work equally well with deep-fried, pan-fried, or roasted white fish.

The fish

Hake, or Patagonian toothfish, plaice, lemon sole, pollock, or coley

- **PREP** 5–10 mins • **COOK** 6–8 mins
- **SERVES** 4

Ingredients

4 hake fillets, about 175g (6oz) each, pinboned and skinned

1 tbsp extra virgin olive oil

salt and freshly ground black pepper

4 small sprigs of thyme

sprigs of watercress, to serve

lemon wedges, to serve

For the remoulade

5 tbsp mayonnaise

5 tbsp half fat crème fraîche

1 tsp Dijon mustard

2 tsp chopped capers

2 tsp chopped gherkins

1 tbsp chopped tarragon

1 tbsp chopped chervil, or flat-leaf parsley

½–1 tsp anchovy essence, to taste

1 Preheat the oven to 200°C (400°F/Gas 6). To make the remoulade, mix all the ingredients in a small bowl and season to taste with anchovy essence and pepper.

2 Brush the hake with the olive oil and season lightly. Arrange on a baking sheet and put the thyme on top. Bake in the oven for 6–8 minutes, or until cooked; it will be opaque and the flesh white and firm. Lift out the fish and drain well on kitchen paper.

3 Lift the fish on to a warmed serving dish and garnish with the watercress and lemon wedges. Serve the remoulade separately.

Prepare ahead

The remoulade can be made, covered, and chilled up to 1 day ahead. Return to room temperature before serving.

PATAGONIAN TOOTHFISH FLAVOUR PAIRINGS:

The dense, sweet flesh of this fish responds well to mayonnaise spiked with capers, or try it with Asian soy sauce, sesame, chilli, and coriander.

Stuffed squid, Naples-style

Squid stuffed with pine nuts and sultanas, then casseroled in a tomato sauce.

The fish

Squid, or cuttlefish or baby octopus

- **PREP** 35 mins - **COOK** 1 hr 10 mins
- **SERVES** 4

Ingredients

4 large squid, gutted and cleaned, with tentacles (see page 282)

5 tbsp extra virgin olive oil

2 garlic cloves, chopped

1 tbsp chopped marjoram

1 tbsp chopped flat-leaf parsley

2 tbsp sultanas

2 tbsp pine nuts

12 Italian green olives, chopped

2 anchovy fillets in olive oil, drained and chopped

salt and freshly ground black pepper

5 tbsp fresh white breadcrumbs

For the sauce

2 tbsp extra virgin olive oil

1 small onion, finely chopped

5 tbsp medium white wine

¼ of a 400g can tomatoes

pinch of sugar (optional)

1 Prepare the squid, but do not open the tubes out flat. Lightly score the tubes and set aside. Chop the tentacles.

2 Heat the olive oil, add the tentacles, garlic, and herbs, toss for 1 minute. Stir in the sultanas, pine nuts, olives, and anchovies, and season. Add the breadcrumbs, then cool. Preheat the oven to 170°C (340°F/Gas 3½).

3 For the sauce, heat half the oil and cook the onion until translucent, add the wine and tomatoes, and simmer for 5 minutes. Season, adding sugar if it tastes acidic.

4 Stuff the squid tubes with the stuffing and seal with cocktail sticks. Heat the remaining oil in a flameproof casserole and lightly brown the squid. Pour on the sauce, cover, and bake for 1–1½ hours.

5 Lift the squid on to a warmed dish, and remove the cocktail sticks. Reduce the tomato sauce if necessary, then pour it over, and serve with noodles or rice.

Sea bream with tomato sauce

Make sure you use well-flavoured tomatoes, as they make all the difference to the finished dish.

The fish

Sea bream, or hake or sea bass

- **PREP** 10 mins - **COOK** 25 mins - **SERVES** 4

Ingredients

4 small sea bream, about 340g (12oz) in total, scaled, gutted, and trimmed

1 tbsp seasoned flour (see page 55)

5 tbsp Italian extra virgin olive oil

1 onion, finely chopped

2 celery sticks, finely sliced

2 garlic cloves, chopped

8 plum tomatoes, roughly chopped

5 tbsp dry white wine

salt and freshly ground black pepper

pinch of sugar

2 tbsp chopped flat-leaf parsley

1 Preheat the oven to 190°C (375°F/Gas 5). Slash the sea bream 3–4 times on each side. Dust with the seasoned flour and arrange in a baking tray.

2 Heat the olive oil in a frying pan, add the onion, celery, and garlic, and cook over a low heat for 2–3 minutes, until softening. Add the tomatoes and wine, and cook for 3–4 minutes, until the juices run. Season and add the sugar.

3 Spoon the tomato sauce over the sea bream and bake in the oven for 15–20 minutes or until cooked. The flesh will be white and opaque.

4 Slide the fish on to a large, warmed serving dish and sprinkle with parsley. Don't forget to take the cheeks from the fish heads; these are particularly delicious.

Prepare ahead

The tomato sauce can be made 2–3 days in advance. Cover, and refrigerate. Bring to room temperature before continuing.

GILT-HEAD BREAM FLAVOUR PAIRINGS:

Try this firm, meaty fish with Mediterranean tastes, such as tomatoes, fennel and Pernod, lemon, saffron, parsley, and garlic. It also works well with coriander.

Baked coley in wine and herbs

Wholesome and so quick to make.

The fish

Coley, or any white fish, such as haddock, pollock, turbot, or cod

- **PREP** 5 mins ▪ **COOK** 20 mins ▪ **SERVES** 4

Ingredients

675g (1½lb) coley fillets, pinboned, skinned, and cut into 4 pieces

salt

200ml (7fl oz) dry white wine

12 cherry tomatoes

handful of flat-leaf parsley, finely chopped

1 Preheat the oven to 190°C (375°F/Gas 5). Sprinkle the coley with salt, then lay it in an ovenproof dish. Pour over the wine, and add the tomatoes and herbs.

2 Cover the dish tightly with foil, then bake in the oven for 15–20 minutes, until the fish is cooked through and the alcohol has evaporated. Serve with salad and fresh crusty bread for a summery dish, or creamy mashed potato in winter.

Swordfish baked with herbs

Rosemary and thyme perfectly complement the strong flavours of this dish.

The fish

Swordfish, or marlin, tuna, or skate

- **PREP** 20 mins ▪ **COOK** 15–20 mins
- **SERVES** 4

Ingredients

4 swordfish steaks, 175g (6oz) each, skinned

freshly ground black pepper

2 tbsp extra virgin olive oil, plus extra for greasing

1 fennel bulb, thinly sliced

4 tomatoes, sliced

1 lemon, sliced

4 tbsp chopped flat-leaf parsley

1 tbsp chopped mint

4 sprigs of thyme

2 tsp chopped rosemary leaves

100ml (3½fl oz) dry white wine

1 Preheat the oven to 180°C (350°F/Gas 4). Season the swordfish steaks with plenty of pepper. Lightly grease an ovenproof dish with oil and evenly place in the fennel.

2 Lay the fish in the dish in a single layer and top with the tomatoes and lemon. Sprinkle with the herbs, and pour over the wine. Drizzle with the olive oil and cover the dish tightly with foil.

3 Bake for 15–20 minutes, or until just cooked. Serve immediately, spooning the juices in the dish over the fish. New potatoes and broccoli or French beans are good on the side.

Lemon sole with herbs

The very delicate flavours here perfectly suit this subtle-tasting fish.

The fish
Lemon sole, or plaice, brill, or any other flat fish

• **PREP** 10 mins • **COOK** 20 mins • **SERVES** 4

Ingredients
3 tbsp extra virgin olive oil

1 tbsp white wine vinegar

1 tsp Dijon mustard

small handful of herbs, such as parsley, thyme, and dill, chopped

salt and freshly ground black pepper

4 lemon sole fillets, about 175g (6oz) each

1 Preheat the oven to 200°C (400°F/Gas 6). To make the dressing, whisk together the oil and vinegar in a jug. Add the mustard and herbs, and mix well. Season well, and mix again.

2 Lay the fish in a roasting tin, then cover with about 0.5cm (¼in) water. Season well. Bake in the oven for 15–20 minutes, until the fish is cooked through and the water has almost evaporated. To check whether the fish is cooked, poke it to make sure the flesh lifts from the bone easily. It should be white with no traces of pink.

3 Using a fish slice or spatula, carefully lift the fish on to a warmed serving dish or individual plates. Spoon over some of the dressing. Serve hot with sautéed potatoes and broccoli.

Butterflied sardines stuffed with tomatoes and capers

Cheap, healthy, and completely delicious.

The fish
Sardines, or herring or mackerel

• **PREP** 15 mins • **COOK** 10 mins • **SERVES** 4

Ingredients
4–6 tomatoes, skinned and finely chopped

2 tsp capers, drained and rinsed

handful of flat-leaf parsley, finely chopped, plus extra to garnish

2 garlic cloves, grated or finely chopped

salt and freshly ground black pepper

12 fresh sardines, boned through the stomach

a little olive oil

juice of 1 lemon

1 Preheat the oven to 200°C (400°F/Gas 6). Put the tomatoes, capers, parsley, and garlic in a bowl. Season well, and stir.

2 Lay the sardines out on some plates, skin-side down, and spoon on the tomato mixture. Either roll up the sardines or just fold them over, then sit them all in a baking tray. Drizzle with the olive oil and lemon juice.

3 Bake in the oven for 10–15 minutes until cooked through. Garnish with extra parsley, if you wish, and serve with a crisp green salad.

Halibut in rosemary and garlic crust

Versatile and quick, this crispy recipe with its couscous crust is popular with children.

The fish

Halibut, or cod, haddock, monkfish, turbot, brill, or salmon

- **PREP** 20 mins ▪ **COOK** 15 mins ▪ **SERVES** 4

Ingredients

60g (2oz) couscous

1 tsp turmeric

1 tbsp chopped rosemary, plus extra small sprigs to garnish

1 large garlic clove, grated or finely chopped

60g (2oz) pecorino or Parmesan cheese, finely grated

salt and freshly ground black pepper

sunflower oil, for greasing

1 egg, beaten

3 tbsp seasoned flour

4 halibut fillets, about 150g (5½oz) each, scaled

200ml (7fl oz) passata

½ tsp clear honey

1 Preheat the oven to 190°C (375°F/Gas 5). Stir 5 tbsp boiling water into the couscous in a bowl. Cover for 5 minutes, then spread on a plate, and leave to cool. Stir in the turmeric, chopped rosemary, garlic, cheese, and seasoning. Oil a roasting tin and heat it in the oven.

2 Put the egg on one plate, and the flour on another. Dip the fish in the flour, then the egg, then the couscous. Put it in the hot roasting tin. Bake for 15 minutes until golden and cooked through, turning once.

3 Meanwhile, heat the passata and honey together in a pan. Season to taste. Spoon on to 4 warmed plates and top with the halibut. Garnish with sprigs of rosemary and serve with baby potatoes and French beans.

Baked bream

This classic Iberian dish, *besugo al horno*, combines fish and potatoes.

The fish

Sea bream, or snapper or sea bass

- **PREP** 10 mins, plus marinating
- **COOK** 1 hour ▪ **SERVES** 4

Ingredients

2 sea bream, about 600g (1lb 5oz) each

1 tbsp tapenade

2 lemon slices, thickly sliced

juice of 1 lemon

3 tbsp olive oil

675g (1½lb) potatoes, finely sliced

1 onion, finely sliced

2 peppers, deseeded and sliced into thin rings

4 garlic cloves, chopped

2 tbsp chopped parsley

1 tsp hot paprika

120ml (4fl oz) dry white wine

salt and freshly ground black pepper

1 Scale and gut the fish. Make 2 diagonal cuts on each side of the thickest part of both fish. Place in a non-metallic dish and spread the tapenade over the inside and outside. Tuck a lemon slice into the gills, drizzle with lemon juice, and place in the refrigerator for 1 hour.

2 Preheat the oven to 190°C (375°F/Gas 5). Grease an ovenproof dish with 1 tbsp of the oil. Layer half the potatoes in the dish, then the onion and peppers. Scatter with the garlic and parsley, and sprinkle with the paprika, then layer the remaining potatoes on top. Drizzle over the rest of the oil, and sprinkle with 2–3 tbsp of water. Cover with foil and bake for 40 minutes, or until cooked through and golden.

3 Increase the oven temperature to 220°C (425°F/Gas 7). Place the fish on the potatoes, pour over the wine, season, and return to the oven, uncovered, for 20 minutes, or until cooked. Serve immediately.

Prepare ahead

The fish can be prepared to the end of step 1, covered, and chilled 6 hours in advance. Bring to room temperature before continuing.

Teriyaki fish with noodles

Impress your friends with this deceptively easy meal. The aromatic flavours of teriyaki sauce are a popular and delicious combination with sweet, thick fish fillets.

The fish

Cod loins, or thick fillets of salmon or mahi mahi

- **PREP** 10 mins ▪ **COOK** 15 mins ▪ **SERVES** 4

Ingredients

4 cod loins, about 150g (5½oz) each, scaled and pinboned

250g (9oz) thick or medium udon noodles, or thin rice noodles

4 spring onions, sliced

handful of coriander, leaves only

lime quarters, to serve

For the teriyaki sauce

1–2 tbsp dark soy sauce

1 tbsp clear honey

2.5cm (1in) fresh root ginger, grated

pinch of sugar

1 tbsp mirin or dry sherry

1 Preheat the oven to 200°C (400°F/Gas 6). Mix the ingredients for the teriyaki sauce in a bowl. Pour over the fish, and leave for 10 minutes.

2 Sit the fish and sauce in a roasting tin, and bake for 15 minutes, until cooked through.

3 Meanwhile, prepare the noodles according to the packet instructions. Leave for a few minutes, then drain and toss with the spring onions and coriander. Serve with the fish and lime quarters.

Skewered swordfish with caperberries

A very easy, yet satisfying and piquant dish. You'll need 12–15 short wooden skewers, or cocktail sticks.

The fish

Swordfish, or tuna, mahi mahi, or marlin

- **PREP** 15 mins ▪ **COOK** 10 mins ▪ **SERVES** 4

Ingredients

450g (1lb) swordfish steaks, cut into bite-sized pieces

salt and freshly ground black pepper

3 tbsp olive oil

1 tbsp white wine vinegar

2 tbsp caperberries

2 garlic cloves, finely sliced

splash of chilli oil, to serve

1 Soak the wooden skewers in cold water for 30 minutes before using. Preheat the oven to 200°C (400°F/Gas 6). Thread 3 pieces of swordfish on to each skewer. Place in a baking dish and season with salt and pepper.

2 Mix the oil, vinegar, caperberries, and garlic in a small bowl, crushing half the caperberries with the back of a fork. Pour evenly over the swordfish and bake for 10 minutes. Serve with a splash of chilli oil and fresh crusty bread.

Pike with herb crust

This recipe works well with many fish that have a reputation for a slightly earthy taste. Pike has lots of large pinbones so make sure you take care to remove them all.

The fish

Pike, or zander, freshwater perch, carp, grey mullet, or trout

- **PREP** 15 mins ▪ **COOK** 12–15 mins
- **SERVES** 4

Ingredients

4 pike fillets, about 175g (6oz) each, pinboned and skinned

45g (1½oz) butter

1 tbsp chopped flat-leaf parsley

juice of ½ lemon

salt and freshly ground black pepper

sprigs of sage, to garnish

lemon wedges, to garnish

For the crust

8 tbsp fresh breadcrumbs

2 tbsp melted butter

1 tbsp chopped sage

1 tbsp chopped chives

grated zest of ½ lemon

1 Preheat the oven to 200°C (400°F/Gas 6). Arrange the fish on a baking sheet.

2 Mix the butter, parsley, and lemon juice, and season with salt and plenty of pepper. Spread a thin layer of butter over each fish.

3 Mix together the breadcrumbs, melted butter, sage, chives, and lemon zest, season lightly, and sprinkle over the fish, pressing to stick to the butter.

4 Roast in the oven for 12–15 minutes or until the fish is cooked – it will be white, firm, and opaque.

5 Transfer to a warmed serving dish, garnish with the sage and lemon wedges, and serve with green beans.

Sea bass in a salt crust

This classic North Italian dish is usually served with aïoli or mayonnaise. It is one of the very few recipes where the fish is not scaled before cooking, as the scales help to prevent the fish from absorbing the salt.

The fish

Sea bass, or sea bream or grey mullet

- **PREP** 25 mins ▪ **COOK** 22–25 mins
- **SERVES** 4

Ingredients

1 whole sea bass, about 1.35–2kg (3–4½lb), trimmed

1kg (2¼lb) coarse sea salt

1–2 egg whites

1 Preheat the oven to 220°C (425°F/Gas 7). Gut the fish through the gills (see page 266). Clean well and rinse, but do not scale.

2 Spread a layer of salt on to a large piece of foil on a baking tray. Arrange the fish on top. Moisten the remaining salt with the egg whites, adding a splash of water if necessary. Pack this mixture on the fish to completely encase it.

3 Bake in the oven for 22–25 minutes. Lift the fish on to a serving dish. Take to the table and carefully chip off any remaining salt crust. Peel away the skin and serve the fish straight from the bone with aïoli or mayonnaise.

PIKE FLAVOUR PAIRINGS: The fine flavour of pike is flattered by unsalted butter, pungent sage, cream, and bay leaf. Any earthy taste can be cut with lemon and white wine.

Mackerel roasted with harissa and lime

Hot harissa pasta and citrus are perfect partners for mackerel, which takes assertive flavours well.

The fish

Mackerel, or herring or trout

- **PREP** 10 mins ▪ **COOK** 30 mins ▪ **SERVES** 4

Ingredients

4 large or 8 small mackerel, scaled, gutted, and washed

3–4 tsp harissa paste

1½ tbsp olive oil

2 limes, quartered

1.1kg (2½lb) baby new potatoes, halved if large

handful of fresh coriander, finely chopped

1 Preheat the oven to 200°C (400°F/Gas 6). Lay the mackerel in a roasting tin, then mix the harissa paste with half the oil. Drizzle this over the fish, making sure the mackerel are covered inside and out. Add the limes to the tin, then toss the potatoes with the remaining oil and add them to the tin, too.

2 Roast in the oven for 20–30 minutes, or until the potatoes and fish are cooked through. Scatter with the coriander, and serve with a crisp green salad.

Halibut with chunky romesco

Romesco is a classic sauce from Catalonia, Spain, made from tomatoes, garlic, onion, peppers, almonds, and olive oil.

The fish

Halibut, or John Dory or mahi mahi

- **PREP** 10 mins ▪ **COOK** 30 mins ▪ **SERVES** 6

Ingredients

3 tbsp extra virgin olive oil, plus extra for greasing

1kg (2¼lb) halibut fillets, 2cm (¾in) thick, scaled

salt and freshly ground black pepper

2 garlic cloves, grated or finely chopped

75g (2½oz) almonds, coarsely chopped

125g (4½oz) breadcrumbs

3 tbsp chopped flat-leaf parsley

For the romesco sauce

350g jar roasted red peppers, rinsed, patted dry, and coarsely chopped

1 tbsp sherry vinegar

¼ tsp cayenne pepper

pinch of smoked paprika

1 Preheat the oven to 230°C (450°F/Gas 8). Brush the bottom of an ovenproof dish with olive oil, and add the fish, skin-side down. Season to taste.

2 Heat 2 tbsp oil in a heavy frying pan. Add the garlic, almonds, and breadcrumbs, and fry over a medium heat, stirring, for 6–8 minutes, until just golden. Do not let the nuts burn. Stir in the parsley, then spoon the mixture over the fish.

3 Bake the fish uncovered for 5 minutes, then loosely cover with foil, and bake for 15 minutes, or until just cooked through. The fish will flake easily when it is ready. Remove from the oven and sprinkle with the remaining olive oil.

4 Meanwhile, to make the romesco sauce, combine all the ingredients. Either serve the fish topped with the sauce, or serve the romesco separately in a bowl.

Prepare ahead

The romesco sauce can be made, covered, and refrigerated for 2 days. The flavours will deepen. The nut and breadcrumb topping can be made 6 hours ahead and stored in an airtight container at room temperature.

Mackerel with garlic and tomatoes

A very speedy superfood supper.

The fish

Mackerel, or sardines, herring, or trout

▪ **PREP** 10 mins ▪ **COOK** 25 mins ▪ **SERVES** 4

Ingredients

24 cherry tomatoes on the vine

4 garlic cloves

few sprigs of thyme

grated zest of 1 lemon

pinch of chilli flakes

1–2 tbsp olive oil

salt and freshly ground black pepper

4 mackerel fillets, about 115–150g (4–5½oz) each, scaled

1 Preheat the oven to 200°C (400°F/Gas 6). Put the tomatoes, garlic, and thyme in a roasting tin. Sprinkle over the zest and chilli. Drizzle with oil, and season. Roast in the oven for 10 minutes, until the tomatoes soften and shrivel.

2 Remove from the oven, sit the mackerel on the tomatoes, then cover with foil. Return to the oven for a further 10–15 minutes, until the fish is cooked through. Serve hot with salad and fresh crusty bread.

Roasted squid and potato with spiced coriander pesto

Herby and immensely satisfying, this is a different way to cook squid.

The fish

Squid, or tuna, swordfish, John Dory, or skate

▪ **PREP** 10 mins ▪ **COOK** 20 mins ▪ **SERVES** 4

Ingredients

1.1kg (2½lb) waxy potatoes, peeled and cubed

2 tbsp olive oil

salt and freshly ground black pepper

350g (12oz) squid, gutted, cleaned, and scored (see page 282)

pinch of chilli flakes (optional)

For the pesto

large handful of coriander leaves

large handful of basil leaves

2 garlic cloves, chopped

large handful of pine nuts

60g (2oz) Parmesan cheese, freshly grated

pinch of chilli flakes

150ml (5fl oz) extra virgin olive oil

1 Preheat the oven to 200°C (400°F/Gas 6). To make the pesto, put the herbs, garlic, pine nuts, most of the Parmesan, and the chilli flakes in a food processor, and whizz to grind. Slowly add the olive oil in a stream, until it forms a smooth paste. Stir in the remaining Parmesan.

2 Put the potatoes in a roasting tin. Drizzle over half the oil, and toss. Season, and roast in the oven for 15–20 minutes until golden.

3 Meanwhile, mix the squid with the remaining oil and chilli (if using). Add to the potatoes for the last 10 minutes of cooking. Toss everything together, and serve with the coriander pesto.

Prepare ahead

Make the pesto up to 3 days ahead, cover with a film of extra virgin olive oil, seal, then refrigerate. (If not completely covered with oil, it will discolour and begin to stale.)

Roast cod with garlic

Cooked at a very high temperature, the flour seasons the fish well.

The fish

Cod, or any firm, meaty white fish, such as pollock, haddock, ling, snapper, or Patagonian toothfish

- **PREP** 5 mins • **COOK** 15 mins • **SERVES** 4

Ingredients

5 tbsp extra virgin olive oil

2 sprigs of rosemary

4 garlic cloves, unpeeled

4 cod loins, about 170g (6oz) each, skin on, scaled and pinboned

2 tbsp seasoned flour (see page 55)

1 Preheat the oven to 230°C (450°F/Gas 8). Put the olive oil in a large, heavy-duty, flameproof roasting tin, add the rosemary and garlic and cook in the oven for 2–3 minutes. Remove from the oven.

2 Dry the cod with kitchen paper. Dust with the seasoned flour and shake to remove excess.

3 Put the fish skin side down in the hot oil, place the roasting tin over a medium heat and fry for 2–3 minutes or until the skin is crisp. Turn the fish over and put in the oven. Roast for 6–7 minutes or until just cooked – the flesh should be white and flake easily – and the garlic is soft. Serve straight away.

Roast gurnard with bacon

This fish has a very special flavour, and is best cooked on the bone.

The fish

Gurnard, or monkfish

- **PREP** 5 mins • **COOK** 7–10 mins • **SERVES** 4

Ingredients

4 small to medium gurnard, scaled, gutted, and trimmed

salt and freshly ground black pepper

4 smoked streaky bacon rashers, cut in half

4 sprigs of thyme

1 tbsp extra olive oil

lemon wedges, to serve

flat-leaf parsley, to serve

1 Preheat the oven to 200°C (400°F/Gas 6). Arrange the fish on a baking sheet and season.

2 Remove the rind from the bacon and stretch each rasher with the back of a kitchen knife.

3 Arrange a sprig of thyme over each fish and drape with 2 half rashers of bacon; do not tuck them under the fish. Drizzle with olive oil and roast in the oven for 7–10 minutes or until the bacon is brown and the fish cooked; it should be white and opaque.

4 Lift on to a warmed plate and serve with lemon wedges and parsley.

GURNARD FLAVOUR PAIRINGS: Sweet-tasting gurnard is great with plenty of olive oil, or with pancetta, bacon, or chorizo – salty flavours that will flatter the fish and keep it moist during cooking.

Monkfish wrapped in prosciutto

This popular meaty fish takes robust flavours well and is also low in fat.

The fish

Monkfish, or gurnard, catfish, or salmon

- **PREP** 5 mins • **COOK** 12–15 mins • **SERVES** 2

Ingredients

2 monkfish fillets, about 140g (5oz) each, trimmed of membrane (see page 270)

splash of olive oil

½ tbsp chopped flat-leaf parsley

½ tbsp chopped basil

4 slices of prosciutto or pancetta

freshly ground black pepper

1 Preheat the oven to 220°C (425°F/Gas 7). Arrange the monkfish on a lightly oiled baking sheet, sprinkle with the herbs, and drape the prosciutto slices over. Brush with more olive oil and season with pepper.

2 Roast in the oven for 12–15 minutes or until the fish is firm and opaque and the prosciutto is crisp. Serve with a green salad.

MONKFISH FLAVOUR PAIRINGS:

This sturdy, firm, sweet fish stands up as well to punchy chorizo, sage, and rocket, as it does to basil, and prosciutto. Or try it rubbed with spices.

Baked salt cod

Salt fish including cod and Alaskan pollock are excellent store-cupboard staples for fishcakes and baked dishes.

The fish

Salt cod, or salt pollock or salt ling

- **PREP** 40 mins, plus overnight soaking
- **COOK** 40 mins • **SERVES** 4

Ingredients

450g (1lb) strips of boneless, skinless salt cod

3 tbsp extra virgin olive oil

450g (1lb) potatoes, peeled and diced

1 large onion, finely sliced

2 garlic cloves, crushed

2 red peppers, thickly sliced

freshly ground black pepper

300ml (10fl oz) fish stock

handful of black olives

2 tbsp chopped flat-leaf parsley

1 Soak the salt cod in several changes of water for 24 hours.

2 Preheat the oven to 190°C (375°F/Gas 5). Heat the oil in a large casserole over a medium heat, add the potatoes, and stir for 5–6 minutes or until beginning to brown. Add the onion and fry for a further 3–4 minutes. Stir in the garlic and red peppers. Season with pepper, pour over the stock, cover, and bake in the oven for 15 minutes.

3 Tuck the salt cod into the potatoes and red peppers and return to the oven for a further 15–20 minutes, or until the salt cod is white and flakes easily.

4 Remove from the oven and stir in the olives and parsley. Serve with a green salad.

Prepare ahead

While the salt cod must be soaked 24 hours in advance of cooking, the potato base made in Step 2 can also be made 1 day ahead, cooled, covered, and refrigerated. Reheat in the oven for 10 minutes before continuing.

Hungarian roast carp

The world's most extensively farmed fish, carp is popular in countries with no easy access to the coast, including Hungary and China.

The fish

Carp, or sea bass, sea bream, or freshwater perch

- **PREP** 25 mins, plus soaking ▪ **COOK** 30 mins
- **SERVES** 4

Ingredients

1.25kg (2¾lb) carp, scaled, gutted, and trimmed

3 tbsp white wine vinegar

2 tbsp seasoned flour (see page 55)

1 tsp paprika

For the topping

450g (1lb) floury potatoes, peeled and cut into 1.5cm (¾in) cubes

salt and freshly ground black pepper

splash of vegetable oil

110g (3¾oz) bacon lardons

3 tbsp roughly chopped gherkins or dill pickles

2 tbsp chopped flat-leaf parsley

1 Preheat the oven to 190°C (375°F/Gas 5). Put the carp into a sink of cold water with the vinegar for 10 minutes. Lift on to the draining board and pat dry with kitchen paper.

2 Mix the seasoned flour and paprika and dredge over the fish to coat evenly. Arrange on a baking sheet and cook in the oven for 15 minutes.

3 Meanwhile, parboil the potatoes in boiling salted water for 3–4 minutes. Drain and reserve 300ml (10fl oz) of the cooking water.

4 In a separate frying pan, heat the oil and cook the potatoes until beginning to brown. Add the bacon and fry for another 2–3 minutes. Add the gherkins and parsley, and season well.

5 Spoon this mixture over the carp and pour over the reserved potato liquid. Return to the oven for 15–20 minutes or until the carp is completely cooked: the flesh should be white and opaque and will easily pull away from the bone. Serve with roasted red peppers.

Simple Italian roast lobster

This Neapolitan dish is easy to prepare and makes an excellent celebration dish.

The fish

Lobster, or Dublin Bay prawns or tiger prawns

- **PREP** 15 mins ▪ **COOK** 15 mins ▪ **SERVES** 4

Ingredients

2 cooked lobsters, preferably rock lobsters, split and prepared (see pages 290–291)

4 tbsp Italian extra virgin olive oil

4 tbsp finely chopped flat-leaf parsley, plus extra sprigs, to serve

2 garlic cloves, crushed

3–4 tbsp fresh breadcrumbs

salt and freshly ground black pepper

lemon wedges, to serve

1 Preheat the oven to 190°C (375°F/Gas 5). Put the split lobsters on to a large baking tray or baking dish.

2 Heat the olive oil in a small saucepan, add the parsley and garlic, and sizzle for 30 seconds, then stir in the breadcrumbs and season well.

3 Spoon the mixture over the cut lobster flesh. Bake in the oven for 7–10 minutes, or until the lobsters are piping hot. Remove from the oven and arrange on a large, warmed serving dish with lemon wedges.

CARP FLAVOUR PAIRINGS: This fish is best with central European tastes of paprika, butter, capers, dill, garlic, parsley, and cornmeal, or Chinese fresh root ginger, rice wine, and sesame.

Poached and Steamed

Sole bonne femme

A delicious old-fashioned recipe.

The fish

Dover sole, or any flat fish

- **PREP** 30 mins • **COOK** 30 mins • **SERVES** 4

Ingredients

15g (½oz) butter, plus extra for the baking dish

250g (9oz) mushrooms, sliced

salt and freshly ground black pepper

2 shallots, finely chopped

2 Dover sole, about 1kg (2¼lb) each, filleted, heads and bones reserved

For the fish stock

1 onion, sliced

3–5 sprigs of flat-leaf parsley

1 tsp peppercorns

250ml (8fl oz) dry white wine or juice of 1 lemon

For the velouté sauce

30g (1oz) butter

2 tbsp plain flour

3 tbsp double cream

3 egg yolks

juice of ½ lemon, or to taste

1 Put the fish heads and bones in a saucepan. Add the onion, 500ml (16fl oz) water, parsley, peppercorns, and wine. Simmer for 20 minutes.

2 Preheat the oven to 180°C (350°F/Gas 4). Melt the butter in a pan, add the mushrooms, salt, and pepper. Cook for 5 minutes. Set aside.

3 Butter a baking dish and add the shallots. Fold each fillet in half, skinned side in, and put on top. Half-cover with stock. Top with foil. Poach in the oven for 15–18 minutes. Drain, reserving the liquid, and keep warm.

4 Add the cooking liquid and shallots to the remaining stock; boil down to 360ml (12fl oz). Melt the butter in a separate saucepan. Whisk in the flour. Cook for 1–2 minutes, strain in the reduced stock, then simmer for 5 minutes. Remove from the heat and add the mushrooms.

5 Whisk the cream and egg yolks in a small bowl. Whisk in a little hot sauce, then stir it all back into the sauce. Stir over a gentle heat for 2–3 minutes. Add lemon juice, salt, and pepper.

6 Heat the grill on its highest setting. Arrange the fillets on flameproof plates. Ladle the sauce over, grill for 1–2 minutes, then serve at once.

Sole veronique

This dish, with white grapes, is part of the classic French repertoire.

The fish

Lemon sole, or petrale sole, brill, or turbot

- **PREP** 30 mins • **COOK** 20 mins • **SERVES** 4

Ingredients

4 lemon sole, skinned and filleted

½ onion, thinly sliced

6 black peppercorns

1 bay leaf

100ml (3½fl oz) dry white wine

175g (6oz) seedless white grapes

For the sauce

45g (1½oz) butter

1 rounded tbsp plain flour

5 tbsp warm milk

5 tbsp double cream

salt and freshly ground white pepper

1 Preheat the oven to 180°C (350°F/Gas 4). Fold the sole fillets into 3, skinned-side in. Arrange in an ovenproof dish, and sprinkle around the onion, peppercorns, and bay leaf. Mix the wine with 100ml (3½fl oz) water, pour over, and cover with buttered greaseproof paper.

2 Poach in the oven for 10–12 minutes or until the fish is cooked; it will be white and opaque. Remove the fish and keep warm. Strain the cooking liquor into a saucepan and boil rapidly to reduce to 150ml (5fl oz). Peel the grapes (a paperclip assists greatly), and set aside.

3 In another saucepan, melt half the butter, remove from the heat, and stir in the flour. Cook over low to medium heat for 30 seconds. Remove from the heat and blend in the milk, then the fish liquor. Return to a low heat and bring to a boil, stirring. Stir in the cream, remove from the heat, and whisk in the remaining butter. Season, add the grapes, and heat through.

4 Lift the fish on to warmed plates. Carefully spoon the sauce over to serve.

Prepare ahead

Peel the grapes up to 4 hours in advance, cover and chill. Return to room temperature before adding to the sauce.

PETRALE SOLE FLAVOUR PAIRING:

A fine, sweet fish, lovely when bathed in a cream sauce, or try it more simply with butter and lemon, or even deep-fried.

Truite au bleu

For this recipe, you need to use just-caught, unwashed trout, gutted through the gills. The trout's blue colour is a result of the reaction between the vinegar and the slime on the skin.

The fish

Trout, or any freshwater fish, such as carp or perch

- **PREP** 10 mins **COOK** 35 mins **SERVES** 2

Ingredients

270ml (9fl oz) white wine vinegar

1 onion, sliced

1 carrot, sliced

2 bay leaves

4 sprigs of thyme

4 sprigs of flat-leaf parsley

6 black peppercorns

2 small trout, freshly caught, unwashed, scaled, and gutted through the gills (see page 266)

50g (1¾oz) butter, to serve

salt and freshly ground black pepper, to serve

squeeze of lemon juice, to serve

1 Pour 1 litre (1¾ pints) water, 120ml (4fl oz) of the vinegar, the onion and carrot, half the herbs, and the peppercorns into a saucepan. Simmer for 15 minutes. Strain this court bouillon into a clean saucepan and return to a boil.

2 Prepare the trout and place in a flameproof roasting tin. Bring the remaining vinegar to a boil, and pour directly over the fish, then pour over the court bouillon. It should be just covered. Add the remaining herbs.

3 Bring to a boil and poach for 12–15 minutes or until the fish is cooked. The eye of the fish will be white and the dorsal fin will peel away easily. The flesh will be flaky and a delicate pink. Lift the fish from the roasting tin and allow to drip dry for a moment or two, then transfer to a serving dish.

4 Heat the butter in a separate saucepan with a little salt and pepper, allow the milk solids in the butter to brown, and immediately add the lemon juice, it will sizzle. Now pour straight over the trout, and serve with boiled potatoes and a simple salad.

Poached turbot with champagne and oysters

Rich and decadent, this is an all-time Escoffier classic from the French culinary repertoire.

The fish

Turbot, or halibut or brill, and oysters, or mussels or scallops

- **PREP** 35 mins **COOK** 30 mins **SERVES** 4

Ingredients

4 turbot fillets, about 175g (6oz) each, scaled

300ml (10fl oz) Champagne or sparkling Saumur

150ml (5fl oz) fish stock

1 tsp black peppercorns

2 sprigs of thyme

1 bay leaf

sprigs of flat-leaf parsley

4 tsp Sevruga caviar (optional), to garnish

For the sauce

30g (1oz) butter

1 tbsp plain flour

150ml (5fl oz) double cream

salt and freshly ground black pepper

2 tbsp snipped chives

6 oysters, preferably native, removed from the shell

1 Skin the turbot and fold in half. Put the Champagne, stock, peppercorns, and herbs into a large sauté pan, bring to a boil, and simmer for 1 minute. Remove from the heat.

2 Put the turbot into the hot liquid, cover with buttered greaseproof paper, and slowly bring to a boil. Reduce the heat until it just quivers and poach for 6–7 minutes, or until opaque.

3 Melt the butter in a small saucepan, remove from the heat, and blend in the flour.

4 When the fish is cooked, lift it from the liquid and keep warm. Add a splash of the liquid at a time to the butter and flour over low heat, stirring constantly. Once it has all been added, bring to a boil, stirring. Simmer for 4–5 minutes until thickening. Blend in the cream and simmer until the sauce coats the back of a spoon. Season.

5 Add the chives and oysters, and poach for 1 minute or until the oysters are firm. Arrange the turbot on a warmed plate and coat with the sauce and oysters. Top each fillet with a small spoon of caviar, if using.

TURBOT FLAVOUR PAIRINGS: The fine, firm flesh of turbot is delicious with wild mushrooms, cream, Gruyère or Parmesan cheeses, and butter, or a sauce made from shellfish stock with lemon.

Skate with beurre noire and capers

Skate is subject to overfishing so choose a sustainable smaller, fast-growing species, such as spotted or cuckoo ray, for this recipe. It is poached in a lightly acidulated court bouillon in this classic French dish.

The fish
Skate wings, or any flat fish

- **PREP** 15 mins ▪ **COOK** 30 mins ▪ **SERVES** 2

Ingredients
1 onion, sliced

1 carrot, sliced

1 celery stick, sliced

300ml (10fl oz) medium white wine

1 bay leaf

2 skate wings, about 175g (6oz) each, skinned (see page 277)

60g (2oz) unsalted butter

2 tbsp white or red wine vinegar

2 tsp capers

2 tsp chopped flat-leaf parsley

1 Put 3 litres (5¼ pints) of water, the onion, carrot, celery, white wine, and bay leaf into a large sauté pan, bring to a boil, and simmer for 15 minutes. Remove from the heat and cool for a few minutes.

2 Lower the skate into the court bouillon, bring to a boil, reduce the heat, and poach for 10–12 minutes. It is cooked when the thick part of the cartilage at the "shoulder" of the wing will pull away easily. Lift on to a plate and pat dry with kitchen paper.

3 Melt the butter in a large frying pan, allow it to sizzle and then keep cooking until it is nut brown, but not smoking. Add the vinegar, capers, and parsley, and pour the furiously sizzling sauce over the skate wings to serve.

Prepare ahead
Make the court bouillon up to 2 days ahead, cover, and refrigerate. Return to just under a simmer before continuing.

Bourride

Rich, creamy, and served in many French restaurants, this recipe uses mussels, but other fish are great here, too.

The fish
Mussels, or haddock, cod, or Patagonian toothfish

- **PREP** 35 mins ▪ **COOK** 20 mins ▪ **SERVES** 4

Ingredients
2kg (4½lb) mussels, prepared (see page 278)

30g (1oz) unsalted butter

2 shallots, finely chopped

3 garlic cloves, crushed

large pinch of saffron

1 tsp medium curry powder

2–3 strips of orange zest

150ml (5fl oz) dry white wine

150ml (5fl oz) mayonnaise

2 tbsp chopped flat-leaf parsley

squeeze of lemon juice

salt and freshly ground black pepper

warm baguette, to serve

1 Check the mussels are all closed, discard any that are broken or will not shut when sharply tapped.

2 Melt the butter in a very large saucepan or casserole over very low heat, add the shallots and 1 garlic clove and cook for 1–2 minutes to soften. Add the saffron, curry powder, and orange zest, stir, then pour in the wine. Bring to a boil and simmer for 1–2 minutes.

3 Add the mussels. Cover with a well-fitting lid and steam for 4–5 minutes, or until they are fully opened. Lift the mussels into a large soup tureen or divide between 4 individual bowls and keep warm.

4 Bring the cooking liquor to a boil and reduce to half the original quantity by boiling rapidly over high heat. Mix 3–4 tbsp of the liquid into the mayonnaise and stir in the remaining garlic, the parsley, lemon juice, and seasoning. Whisk the mayonnaise back into the hot cooking liquid, set over a low heat and stir until it comes to just under a boil. (Do not boil or it will separate). Spoon over the mussels and serve with the baguette.

SKATE FLAVOUR PAIRINGS: Sharp, piquant tastes match brilliantly with skate. Try vinegar, capers, parsley, and lemon juice, and marry those flavours with lashings of butter.

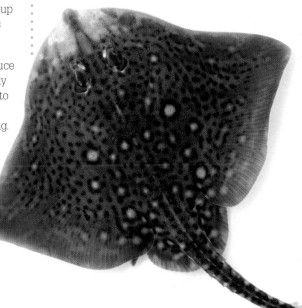

Poached salmon with dill butter

Poaching is one of the simplest methods of cooking salmon, and it produces a succulent result.

The fish

Salmon, or char, trout, or pollock

- **PREP** 10 mins • **COOK** 10 mins • **SERVES** 4

Ingredients

4 skinless salmon fillets or steaks, about 175g (6oz) each, scaled and pinboned

600ml (1 pint) court bouillon (see page 302)

50g (1¾oz) butter, softened

2 tbsp finely chopped dill

grated zest and juice of ½ lemon

salt and freshly ground black pepper

sprigs of dill, to serve

lemon wedges, to serve

1 Put the salmon into a sauté pan. Add the court bouillon, with some water to ensure the fish is just submerged. Bring slowly to a boil, reduce the heat, and cook over low heat so that the liquid just blips. Cover and cook for 4–6 minutes or until the fish has lost its translucency and is pale pink in colour.

2 Meanwhile put the butter, dill, and lemon zest into a small bowl and beat until smooth. Then gradually beat in the lemon juice, and season well.

3 Lift the fish from the court bouillon and pat dry with kitchen paper. Melt the dill butter in a frying pan and add the fish, turning it once to ensure it is evenly coated. Lift on to a warmed serving dish and drizzle over the remaining butter. Garnish with dill and lemon wedges, and serve with new potatoes and steamed asparagus.

Variation

Poached salmon with coriander and lime butter

Make as above, but mix the butter with a large handful of chopped fresh coriander, and 2 peeled, segmented, and roughly chopped limes, instead of the dill and lemon. Serve hot with new potatoes.

Whole poached and dressed salmon

A classic for cold buffets, traditionally served with hollandaise sauce.

The fish

Salmon, or sea trout, large brown trout, or large rainbow trout

- **PREP** 40 mins • **COOK** 45 mins
- **SERVES** 8–10

Ingredients

2–3kg (4½–6½lb) salmon, scaled, gutted through the gills (see page 266), and trimmed

3–4 litres (5¼–7 pints) court bouillon (see page 302)

For decoration

1 cucumber, thinly sliced

24 unpeeled, cooked, prawns, deveined

handful of sprigs of dill

300ml (10fl oz) aspic jelly (optional)

To serve

grated zest of 1 lemon, and a squeeze of juice

300ml (10fl oz) mayonnaise

1 Make sure the fish is clean and the bloodline has been removed. Trim the tail into a "V" shape with scissors.

2 Arrange the fish in a suitable flameproof baking tray or on the trivet of a fish kettle. Pour over the court bouillon. Cover and bring to a boil, then reduce the heat so the liquid barely quivers. Cook for 15 minutes, then remove from the heat, and leave the fish in the liquid for a further 15 minutes. Lift from the fish kettle and allow to cool completely.

3 Very carefully peel away the top skin of the fish, carefully turn, and remove the skin from the other side. Slide on to a serving dish. Arrange slices of cucumber over the fillets and decorate with prawns and dill. If it is not to be served within an hour or two, a coating of aspic can keep it glossy. Follow the package instructions to make the aspic, cool completely, then spoon over the top of the garnish and fish.

4 Mix the lemon into the mayonnaise and serve separately, with potato and side salads.

Prepare ahead

Poach the fish up to 6 hours ahead, cover, and refrigerate. Return to room temperature before garnishing and serving.

CHAR FLAVOUR PAIRING: Excellent poached with butter and dill, or highlight the taste with white wine vinegar and lemon, or even pair with toasted hazelnuts and almonds in a sauté.

Steamed halibut with dill butter sauce and cucumber

There is a good supply of farmed Atlantic halibut and excellent supplies of Pacific halibut (often frozen).

The fish

Halibut, or turbot or salmon

- **PREP** 40 mins, plus soaking ▪ **COOK** 20 mins ▪ **SERVES** 4

Ingredients

2 tbsp sea salt

4 halibut steaks or thick-cut fillets, about 175g (6oz) each, scaled

For the dill butter sauce

115g (4oz) unsalted butter, plus 30g (1oz) to serve, plus extra for steaming

1 shallot, finely chopped

150ml (5fl oz) fish stock

5 tbsp dry white wine

2 tbsp aquavit or vermouth

2 tbsp chopped dill

squeeze of lemon juice

freshly ground black pepper

1 large cucumber, peeled, deseeded, and thinly sliced

1 Heat the salt and 300ml (10fl oz) of water over medium heat, stirring until dissolved. Cool.

2 Put the halibut into a deep dish, pour over the cold salt solution, and soak for 15 minutes.

3 Lift the fish from the liquid and arrange in a steamer lined with buttered baking parchment (you may need 2 steamers). Steam for 10–12 minutes or until white and opaque.

4 Melt a small knob of the butter in a small saucepan and add the shallot; cook over low heat for 3–4 minutes. Add the stock, wine, and aquavit, bring to a boil and simmer until the liquid has reduced by one-third. Pull the pan a little off the heat and beat in the butter, a knob at a time, until the sauce is creamy and buttery. Add the dill, lemon, salt, and pepper. Set aside.

5 In a frying pan, melt the 30g (1oz) butter until beginning to brown, add the cucumber and toss for 1–2 minutes until very hot.

6 Spoon the cucumber on to a large dish and arrange the fish on top. Spoon the dill butter sauce over to serve.

Sea bass with black bean sauce

A wonderful combination. The well-flavoured bass works well with the saltiness of the sauce.

The fish

Sea bass, or sea bream, pomfret, or snapper

- **PREP** 25 mins ▪ **COOK** 30 mins ▪ **SERVES** 4

Ingredients

3 tbsp black fermented beans (available at Oriental supermarkets)

2 tbsp sunflower oil

2 spring onions, finely chopped

5cm (2in) fresh root ginger, cut into matchsticks

1 garlic clove, very finely sliced

3 tbsp dark soy sauce

2 tbsp Chinese rice wine or dry sherry

1 tsp caster sugar

300ml (10fl oz) fish stock

1 tsp cornflour

4 sea bass fillets, about 175g (6oz) each, scaled and pinboned

sprigs of coriander, to garnish

splash of sesame oil

1 Rinse the black beans very thoroughly under cold running water. Heat the oil in a large frying pan over low heat. Add the spring onions and ginger, fry over low heat until aromatic. Add the garlic and stir-fry for another minute.

2 Remove from the heat and add the soy sauce, rice wine, and sugar; bring to a boil. Add three-quarters of the stock and return to the heat. Bring to a boil and simmer for a couple of minutes. Mix the cornflour with the remaining stock in a small bowl.

3 Arrange the fish on a bamboo steamer and cook for 7–8 minutes, covered, over a large saucepan of simmering water.

4 Meanwhile, stir the cornflour mixture into the hot stock with the beans, stir up to a boil, and simmer for 2–3 minutes until thickened slightly.

5 Arrange the fish on a platter with the coriander. Spoon the sauce over and drizzle with sesame oil. Serve with rice.

Prepare ahead

The black bean sauce can be made 1 day ahead, covered, and refrigerated. Return to a simmer before continuing. Add a splash of water, until the consistency is as you prefer.

SEA BASS FLAVOUR PAIRINGS: Chinese flavours are great with sea bass, but also try Mediterranean tomatoes, garlic, olive oil, and red pepper, or even Pernod.

Steamed carp in beer sauce

If you would like a spicier dish, add a few juniper berries, peppercorns, or cloves to the fish before steaming.

The fish

Carp, or sea bass, sea bream, scallops, or monkfish

- **PREP** 10 mins ▪ **COOK** 15 mins ▪ **SERVES** 4

Ingredients

1 carp, about 1.35kg (3lb), filleted, pinboned, and skinned

330ml (11fl oz) sweet malt or dark beer, or wheat beer

1 onion, finely sliced

1 celery stick, finely sliced

1 carrot, finely sliced

4–5 thick flat-leaf parsley stalks

1 bay leaf

1 tsp salt

110g (3½oz) unsalted butter

110g (3½oz) gingerbread crumbs

2–3 tsp cornflour (optional)

freshly ground black pepper

2 tbsp chopped flat-leaf parsley

1 Cut any large carp fillets into portion-sized pieces. Arrange the fillets on a steamer.

2 Put the beer, onion, celery, carrot, parsley stalks, bay leaf, and salt into a large saucepan. Bring to a boil and simmer for 2–3 minutes. Arrange the steamer over the bubbling beer. Steam for 7–10 minutes or until the carp is cooked: it will be firm and opaque.

3 Lift the carp from the steamer and keep warm. Strain out and discard the vegetables from the beer, then return it to the heat. Whisk in the butter a little at a time. Stir in enough of the gingerbread crumbs to form a smooth and creamy sauce. (If you prefer, you can sieve the sauce.) If the sauce seems too thin, mix the cornflour with enough water to make a paste, and slowly whisk it into the sauce, over a low heat, until it thickens. Season to taste with pepper.

4 Arrange the carp in a deep-sided dish, pour over a little sauce, and sprinkle with parsley. Serve the remaining sauce on the side.

Chinese-style steamed bass

An impressive but easy dish that brings out the clean, delicate flavours of sea bass.

The fish

Sea bass, or snapper or bream

- **PREP** 15 mins ▪ **COOK** 20–24 mins
- **SERVES** 4

Ingredients

8 tbsp dark soy sauce

8 tbsp Chinese rice wine or dry sherry

6 tbsp shredded fresh root ginger

4 small sea bass, scaled, gutted, and rinsed

2 tbsp sesame oil

1 tsp salt

4 spring onions, trimmed and shredded

8 tbsp sunflower oil

4 garlic cloves, grated or finely chopped

2 small red chillies, deseeded and shredded

finely grated zest of 2 limes

1 Prepare a steamer, or position a steaming rack above a wok containing water. Bring to a boil.

2 Stir together the soy sauce, rice wine, and 4 tbsp ginger, and set aside. Using a sharp knife, make slashes in the fish, 2.5cm (1in) apart and not as deep as the bone, on both sides. Rub the fish inside and out with the sesame oil and salt.

3 Scatter one-quarter of the spring onions over a heatproof serving dish that will hold 2 fish and fit in the steamer. Place 2 fish on the dish and pour over half the sauce.

4 Place the dish in the steamer, cover, and steam for 10–12 minutes, or until the fish flakes easily when tested with a knife. Remove the fish, cover, and keep warm. Repeat with the remaining fish.

5 Meanwhile, heat the sunflower oil in a small saucepan over a medium-high heat until it shimmers. Scatter the fish with the remaining spring onions and ginger, the garlic, chillies, and lime zest. Drizzle the oil over the fish and serve.

Steamed sea saibling filled with herbs

Saibling is the German name for Bavarian char, from the salmon group. The cheek is a delicacy.

The fish
Sea saibling, or salmon, trout, or mackerel

- **PREP** 5 mins **COOK** 15–20 mins
- **SERVES** 2 generously

Ingredients
1 sea saibling weighing about 1kg (2¼lb), scaled and gutted

sea salt and freshly ground black pepper

small bunch of herbs including flat-leaf parsley, dill, chervil, and sage

150ml (5fl oz) medium white wine

30g (1oz) unsalted butter, melted

lemon wedges, to serve

1 Wash the fish well and check the belly cavity shows no traces of blood. Season the cavity, and fill with the herbs.

2 Pour 5cm (2in) of water into a large saucepan, add the wine, and bring to a boil. Arrange the fish on a large plate or steamer. Cover with a tight-fitting lid and steam for 15–20 minutes or until the eye has turned white and you can feel the fish flake when you press the skin.

3 Lift the fish on to a warmed plate and spoon the melted butter over the top. Serve with lemon wedges and slow-roasted red peppers for a lovely summer lunch.

Prepare ahead
Stuff the fish with herbs up to 12 hours in advance, cover, and refrigerate. The herb flavours will permeate the flesh.

Steamed trout in lettuce

Steaming is the ultimate way of enjoying very fresh trout, as well as keeping it low in fat. Cooked lettuce is a slightly bitter revelation.

The fish
Trout, or monkfish or gurnard

- **PREP** 15 mins **COOK** 10 mins **SERVES** 2

Ingredients
8 large Iceberg lettuce leaves

4 trout fillets, pinboned and skinned

salt and freshly ground black pepper

1 tbsp sunflower oil

4 spring onions, finely sliced

8 shiitake mushrooms, finely sliced

2 tbsp chopped tarragon

splash of lemon juice

For the dressing
150ml (5fl oz) Greek-style yogurt

1 tbsp chopped capers

2 tbsp chopped parsley

1 shallot, finely chopped

1 Blanch the lettuce leaves in boiling water for 20–30 seconds. Rinse under running cold water and pat dry with kitchen paper. Trim out the thick centre veins so it is possible to lay the leaves flat. Overlap 2 leaves together, arrange a trout fillet on each, and season.

2 Heat the oil in a small saucepan, add the spring onions and mushrooms, and fry over a brisk heat for 3–4 minutes until cooked. Add the tarragon and lemon juice, then cool.

3 Divide the mushroom mixture over each trout fillet. Fold the lettuce over to encase.

4 Lift the trout on to a large bamboo steamer. Do not allow the parcels to touch. Steam for 5–6 minutes, until the fish flakes to the touch.

5 Meanwhile, mix the yogurt, capers, parsley, and shallot together and season lightly. Lift the fish parcels on to a large serving dish and serve the dressing separately.

Prepare ahead
Assemble the trout parcels, cover, and refrigerate for up to 1 day. Bring to room temperature before continuing.

Steamed lobster with herbed lemon butter

Lobster is often included in a steamed clam bake. This is a quick version.

The fish

Lobster, or mussels or clams

- **PREP** 5 mins, plus freezing ■ **COOK** 10 mins
- **SERVES** 2

Ingredients

salt and freshly ground black pepper

1 live lobster, about 1kg (2¼lb)

60g (2oz) butter, softened

grated zest and juice of ½–1 lemon, to taste

2 tbsp chopped flat-leaf parsley, plus extra sprigs to serve

2 tbsp chopped tarragon

1 Put the lobster in the freezer to render it unconscious (see page 290). Fill a very large pan three-quarters full with water, and salt well. Bring to a boil. Cook the lobster in the boiling water for 5 minutes. Split the lobster in half and remove the digestive tract.

2 Arrange the lobster halves, cut side up, in a steamer over a large saucepan of simmering water. Cover with a well-fitting lid and steam for a further 5 minutes.

3 Meanwhile, put the butter, lemon zest and juice in a bowl, and add the herbs. Season lightly with pepper.

4 Lift the lobster on to a warmed serving dish and spoon some of the butter over the top. Serve with warm crusty bread and the parsley.

Prepare ahead

You can make the herbed lemon butter up to 2 days in advance. Wrap in greaseproof paper, and refrigerate until needed.

Leaf-wrapped Asian sole

Wrapping fish in leaves helps it to retain moisture. Add a little chilli for more heat.

The fish

Lemon sole, or red mullet or halibut

- **PREP** 15 mins ■ **COOK** 10 mins ■ **SERVES** 4

Ingredients

4 lemon sole fillets, about 175g (6oz) each, scaled

4 tsp lemon juice

4 tsp dark soy sauce

2 tsp grated fresh root ginger

¼ tsp ground white pepper

sesame oil, to drizzle

16–20 large pak choi leaves, tough stalks removed

1 Drizzle each sole fillet with the lemon juice, soy sauce, ginger, pepper, and a light, even drizzle of sesame oil. Gently roll the fillets lengthways and arrange on a heatproof plate.

2 Fill a large saucepan fitted with a steamer with 2.5cm (1in) water, bring to a boil, then reduce the heat to a simmer.

3 Blanch the pak choi for 30 seconds in boiling water, then refresh in iced water. Drain.

4 Wrap each fillet in 4–5 leaves, securing with cocktail sticks if necessary. Set on a plate, then place on the steamer rack, cover, and steam for 8–10 minutes, or until the fish is opaque. Serve with stir-fried vegetables, or boiled white rice.

Prepare ahead

Assemble the fish parcels 1 day in advance, cover, and refrigerate. Bring back to room temperature before continuing.

Variation

Spinach-wrapped sole
Use spinach instead of pak choi without blanching it. Replace the soy sauce, ginger, and sesame oil with a little butter over the fillets, and sprinkle with dried mixed herbs.

Garlic and rice wine steamed razor clams

Take care not to overcook razor clams. As soon as the shells open, lift them on to a serving dish.

The fish

Razor clams, or scallops, sea bass, sea bream, or monkfish

- **PREP** 5 mins ▪ **COOK** 10 mins ▪ **SERVES** 2

Ingredients

1.25kg (2¾lb) razor clams

2 tbsp sunflower oil

2 garlic cloves, chopped

1 red chilli, deseeded and finely chopped

1 tbsp grated fresh root ginger

4 tbsp rice wine

salt and freshly ground black pepper

2 tbsp roughly chopped coriander

1 Wash the razor clams and check that they are alive: the shell will either be tightly shut or will shut if you run a knife along the open edge. Discard any that are cracked or broken.

2 Heat the oil in a large casserole, add the garlic, chilli, and ginger, and stir over a low heat for 2–3 minutes. Add the rice wine, bring to a boil and add the clams. Cover with a well-fitting lid and cook over a medium heat for 2–3 minutes or until the clams have opened.

3 Lift the clams on to a large, warmed serving dish. Reduce the cooking liquid by boiling for 1 minute, season to taste and add the coriander. Spoon over the razor clams to serve.

Steamed fish with warm vinaigrette

The different-coloured skins of mackerel, lemon sole, and snapper look beautiful together in this recipe.

The fish

Red snapper, lemon sole, and mackerel, or salmon, lemon sole, and plaice

- **PREP** 35–40 mins ▪ **COOK** 20–30 mins ▪ **SERVES** 6

Ingredients

For the court bouillon

1 bouquet garni

6 peppercorns

2 cloves

1 carrot, quartered

1 onion, quartered

For the fish

375g (13oz) red snapper fillets, with skin, scaled

375g (13oz) lemon sole fillets, with skin, scaled

375g (13oz) mackerel fillets, with skin, scaled

salt and freshly ground black pepper

For the vinaigrette

120ml (4fl oz) red wine vinegar

2 tsp Dijon mustard

2 shallots, very finely chopped

75ml (2½fl oz) olive oil

150ml (5fl oz) vegetable oil

leaves from 5–7 sprigs of tarragon or thyme, finely chopped, plus more to garnish

leaves from 7–10 sprigs of flat-leaf parsley or chervil, finely chopped, plus more to garnish

1 Combine 1 litre (1¾ pints) water, the bouquet garni, peppercorns, cloves, carrot, and onion in a pan over which you can fit a large steamer. Bring to a boil and simmer for 20–30 minutes.

2 Trim the fish fillets so they are roughly the same length. Cut each into 6 strips. Transfer to the steamer and sprinkle with salt and pepper. Set the steamer over the court bouillon. Cover and steam for 8–10 minutes, until the fish just flakes easily.

3 In a small saucepan, whisk together the vinegar, mustard, and shallots, then the oils. Heat gently until warm, whisking constantly. Remove from the heat and whisk in the herbs and salt and pepper to taste. Spoon on to 6 warmed plates and put the fish on top. Garnish with the herb sprigs.

Variation

Steamed fish with warm sherry vinaigrette Make the court bouillon. Cut the fish into even diamonds. Steam for 5–7 minutes, depending on thickness. Prepare the warm vinaigrette, substituting sherry vinegar for red wine vinegar and walnut oil for olive oil. Spoon a little over the fish and serve the remainder separately.

On the Grill

Chargrilled swordfish

Meaty fish are best chargrilled or barbecued, rather than grilled. They need fierce heat to colour the exterior.

The fish

Swordfish, or tuna, marlin, or mahi mahi

- **PREP** 5 mins ▪ **COOK** 5 mins ▪ **SERVES** 2

Ingredients

2 swordfish steaks, about 140g (5oz) each, about 2.5cm (1in) thick is best

splash of olive oil

salt and freshly ground black pepper

1 Preheat a well-seasoned griddle pan until it is just beginning to smoke. Meanwhile, brush the swordfish with olive oil and season.

2 Press the steaks on to the hot griddle with a palette knife. Allow to cook for 1–2 minutes, or until the steak will lift cleanly off the griddle. Flip over and press flat with the palette knife. Cook for a further 1–2 minutes, or until they will lift cleanly from the pan. Reduce the heat and turn again, trying to position them so that the chargrill marks are at an angle with those of the first cooking. Cook for a further 1 minute before turning on to the second side.

3 Avoid turning the steaks a third time, but cook until firm to the touch. Leave to rest for 1 minute before serving with a simple salad or a flavoured butter.

SWORDFISH FLAVOUR PAIRINGS:

This substantial fish is great simply chargrilled, or try it smoked over mesquite chips (see page 307), or rubbed with spices such as paprika, ground cumin, and ground coriander.

Chargrilled snapper in banana leaves

Grilling fish in banana leaves allows the fish to steam in its own moisture. The leaves also give a wonderful smoked flavour.

The fish

Red snapper, or meagre, black sea bass, or Patagonian toothfish

- **PREP** 20 mins, plus marinating
- **COOK** 20 mins ▪ **SERVES** 4

Ingredients

1 red snapper, about 1.5kg (3lb 3oz), scaled and gutted

2–3 large banana leaves

1 tsp sesame oil, plus more for the banana leaves

lime wedges, to serve

For the marinade

2 tbsp roughly chopped coriander

½ tbsp grated fresh root ginger

2 garlic cloves, chopped

2 tbsp dark soy sauce

1 tbsp rice wine vinegar

grated zest of 1 lime

1 red chilli, deseeded and chopped

salt and freshly ground black pepper

1 Make 3–4 slashes on each side of the fish, nearly to the bone.

2 Put the marinade ingredients into a blender, and chop. Press into the slashes in the fish, and the cavity. Set aside for 15–20 minutes.

3 Blanch the banana leaves in boiling water for 30 seconds to soften. Remove with tongs and rinse under cold running water. Cut the thick vein from the centre, and arrange them overlapping on a large chopping board, shiny side down. Brush with sesame oil. Put the fish on the leaves and wrap to encase the body (the head and tail can be visible). If necessary, secure the leaves with cocktail sticks.

4 Preheat the barbecue until glowing red and the coals are ash grey. Cook the fish, turning often, to prevent the leaves from burning. It will take around 18–20 minutes. Insert a metal skewer into the centre of the fish, through the leaves, for 30 seconds. If the fish is cooked, the skewer will emerge piping hot.

5 Transfer to a serving dish and garnish with lime wedges. Unwrap at the table, and serve with boiled rice.

Trout with orange-mustard glaze

Grilled whole fish is a dream for the cook, as it is quick to prepare, and easy to present.

The fish
Trout, or John Dory or sea bass

- **PREP** 15–20 mins • **COOK** 20–30 mins
- **SERVES** 6

Ingredients
6 trout, each weighing 375g (13oz), scaled and gutted through the gills (see page 266)

leaves from 6–8 sprigs of tarragon

3–4 tbsp vegetable oil, for the grill rack

3 large sweet onions, thickly sliced

250g (9oz) mushrooms, trimmed

3 ripe tomatoes, cored and halved

For the orange-mustard glaze
4 tbsp Dijon mustard

2 tsp honey

juice of 2 oranges

4 tbsp vegetable oil

salt and freshly ground black pepper

1 Slash the fish diagonally 3–4 times on both sides. Tuck a tarragon leaf into each slash. Set aside.

2 Whisk the mustard, honey, and orange juice. Gradually whisk in the oil, until thickened. Season to taste.

3 Preheat the grill on its highest setting. Brush the rack with oil. Arrange the onion, mushrooms, and tomatoes on the rack. Brush with glaze and season. Grill, brushing with glaze and turning, allowing 3 minutes for mushrooms, and 5–7 minutes for onions and tomatoes; they should char. Keep warm.

4 Grill the fish for 4–7 minutes, until brown. Carefully turn, and brush generously with glaze. Grill until the flesh flakes easily (it should take 4–7 minutes more). Serve with the vegetables and any remaining glaze.

Prepare ahead
The glaze can be made 1 week ahead and kept, covered, in the refrigerator. Whisk before use.

Variation
Grilled cod steaks with maitre d'hotel butter
Omit the glaze. Cream 75g (2½oz) butter. Mix in 1 finely chopped shallot and a large handful of finely chopped parsley, the juice of ½ lemon, salt, and pepper. Shape into a roll; chill until firm. Brush 6 scaled cod steaks with olive oil, and grill for 3–5 minutes each side. Set a slice of the butter on top and serve.

Griddled swordfish with fennel and sun-dried tomatoes

Beautifully scented with aniseed from the fennel and Pernod, this is an elegant dish for a party.

The fish
Swordfish, or tuna, marlin, or mahi mahi

- **PREP** 25–30 mins, plus marinating
- **COOK** 55 mins • **SERVES** 4

Ingredients
leaves from 2–3 sprigs of thyme

2 tbsp vegetable oil, plus extra for the griddle

juice of ½ lemon

salt and freshly ground black pepper

4 swordfish steaks, about 250g (9oz) each, skinned

60g (2oz) butter, plus extra for the foil

3 fennel bulbs, sliced

60g (2oz) sun-dried tomatoes in oil, drained and chopped

1–2 tbsp Pernod, or other aniseed liqueur

1 Put the thyme, oil, and lemon juice into a shallow, non-metallic dish. Season the swordfish and coat in the marinade. Cover and refrigerate for 1 hour.

2 Melt the butter in a saucepan, add the fennel, season, and press a piece of buttered foil on top. Cover and cook over low heat until very soft; it will take 40–45 minutes.

3 Stir in the sun-dried tomatoes with the Pernod. Cook for about 10 minutes, then season to taste.

4 Heat a griddle pan. Brush the griddle with oil, and add the swordfish. Brush with the marinade, and cook for 2–3 minutes, without turning, until a steak comes away from the griddle without tearing. Turn, brush with the remaining marinade, and griddle for 2–3 minutes more. Serve with the fennel mixture on the side.

Prepare ahead
Make the fennel mixture up to 2 days ahead, cover, and refrigerate. Reheat very gently.

Grilled sea bream with spice rub

The firm flesh of bream is wonderful with the strong flavours in this recipe.

The fish

Sea bream, or sea bass, meagre, or snapper

- **PREP** 15 mins **COOK** 6–8 mins **SERVES** 4

Ingredients

4 sea bream fillets, about 150g (5½oz) each, scaled and pinboned

lemon wedges, to serve

For the spice rub

3 tbsp walnut or olive oil

4 tbsp chopped coriander leaves

2 garlic cloves, crushed

1 tsp crushed coriander seeds

1 tsp lemon juice

1 small green chilli, very finely chopped

salt

For the tomato salad

1 tbsp walnuts

4 plum tomatoes, chopped

1 tbsp chopped coriander leaves

1½ tsp walnut or olive oil

sea salt and freshly ground black pepper

1 Mix all the ingredients for the spice rub together and season with salt. Preheat the grill on its highest setting.

2 Line a baking sheet with foil and place the fish fillets on it, skin-side down. Brush the spice rub over the fish. Place under a hot grill for 6–8 minutes, until cooked through and lightly golden. Remove from the heat and keep warm.

3 Meanwhile, toast the walnuts by stirring them in a dry frying pan over medium heat for 2–3 minutes, then remove and lightly crush. Mix with all the other ingredients for the tomato salad and season. Serve the fish with the salad and lemon wedges.

Prepare ahead

Make the spice rub and toast the walnuts up to 6 hours ahead and store in separate airtight containers at room temperature.

Herrings in oatmeal with gooseberry sauce

Gooseberry sauce is traditional with grilled mackerel but is served here with herring.

The fish

Herring, or mackerel

- **PREP** 10 mins **COOK** 15 mins **SERVES** 4

Ingredients

4 herrings, scaled, gutted, and trimmed

125g (4½oz) fine oatmeal

For the gooseberry sauce

350g (12oz) fresh or frozen gooseberries

30g (1oz) butter

30g (1oz) sugar

¼ tsp nutmeg, freshly grated

salt and freshly ground black pepper

1 Cook the gooseberries in a pan with 1–2 tbsp water and cook for 4–5 minutes, or until tender.

Purée in a food processor, add the butter, sugar, and nutmeg, and season.

2 Cut off and discard the herring heads and slit the fish along the belly right down to the tail. Open the herrings out flat and place, skin-side up, on a chopping board. Press firmly all along the backbone with the heel of your hand. Turn over and pull away the backbone, snipping it off at the tail with scissors. Remove any bones left behind with pinboners or a pair of tweezers.

3 Preheat the grill on its highest setting. Spread the oatmeal on to a large plate and season well. Press the herrings firmly into the oatmeal. Arrange them in a grill pan and grill for 6–8 minutes, or until tender and flaky, turning once.

4 Meanwhile, gently reheat the sauce over a very low heat, and serve with the herrings. Serve with a green salad.

Prepare ahead

Make the sauce several hours in advance, or freeze for up to 6 months.

SUSTAINABILITY CHOICE

Buy line-caught fish

Line-fishing, when baited lines are placed in the water, is a more selective method of fishing that produces a much smaller bycatch than other methods, such as trawling and beam trawling. The most sustainable forms of line-fishing are rod and handline. Handline fishing from small boats (shown here) is particularly sustainable, as only a few fish, such as mackerel and sea bass, are caught. The fish are often in premium condition, as each fish is individually landed. Handlined fish will usually be labelled as such but you can also identify them by damage to their jaw.

GIANT BLACK TIGER PRAWN FLAVOUR PAIRINGS:

These are hardy enough to stand up to fierce heat and Asian flavours, or sharpen the sweet flesh with lemon juice and capers.

Sesame barbecue prawns

Meaty prawns are excellent for barbecuing, but are best left in the shell to protect them from the fierce heat. You'll need 8 wooden skewers, soaked in water for 30 minutes.

The fish

Tiger prawns, or monkfish or scallops

- **PREP** 40 mins, plus marinating
- **COOK** 10 mins ▪ **SERVES** 4

Ingredients

16 large raw unpeeled tiger prawns, about 50g (1¾oz) each

handful of coriander leaves, to serve

lime wedges, to serve

For the marinade

2 tbsp sunflower oil

2 tsp toasted sesame oil

2 tbsp dark soy sauce

1 tbsp runny honey

2 tsp Thai fish sauce

1 large red chilli, deseeded and chopped

1 tbsp grated fresh root ginger

1 garlic clove, crushed

salt and freshly ground black pepper

2 tbsp sesame seeds

1 Snip off the small legs and feelers from the prawns. Snip down the back of the shell and remove the digestive tract if visible (sometimes it isn't, especially if the prawns are farmed).

2 Put all the ingredients for the marinade except the sesame seeds into a small blender and whizz until smooth. Stir in the sesame seeds. Put the prawns in a non-metallic dish and pour the marinade over; marinate for 30 minutes.

3 Preheat the barbecue until the coals are glowing and grey in appearance.

4 Thread 2 prawns on each skewer. Barbecue, brushing with marinade, for 2–3 minutes each side. Pile on to a large plate and garnish with the coriander and lime wedges. Serve with a dressed salad of bitter green leaves such as rocket and watercress.

Prepare ahead

Make the marinade up to 2 days in advance, cover, and refrigerate. Only marinate the prawns for 30 minutes, or the texture will change.

Barbecued prawn satay

You'll need 8 wooden skewers, soaked in water for 30 minutes.

The fish

Tiger prawns, or monkfish, mahi mahi, or scallops

- **PREP** 40 mins, plus marinating
- **COOK** 20 mins ▪ **SERVES** 4

Ingredients

16 large raw unpeeled tiger prawns, about 50g (1¾oz) each

lime wedges, to serve

For the marinade

2 garlic cloves, crushed

1 tbsp grated fresh root ginger

1 large red chilli, deseeded and chopped

2 tbsp tamarind paste

2 tbsp kecap manis

salt and freshly ground black pepper

For the satay sauce

1 tbsp vegetable oil

1 small onion, finely chopped

1 garlic clove, chopped

2 tbsp grated fresh root ginger

1 tsp shrimp paste

115g (4oz) smooth peanut butter

150ml (5fl oz) coconut milk

2–3 tsp dark brown sugar

1 tbsp kecap manis

1 Snip off the small legs and feelers from the prawns. Snip down the back of the shell and remove the digestive tract if visible (sometimes it isn't, especially if the prawns are farmed).

2 Place the ingredients for the marinade into a small blender and whizz until smooth. Put the prawns in a non-metallic dish and pour the marinade over; marinate for 30 minutes.

3 Heat the oil in a saucepan, add the onion, garlic, and ginger, and cook over a low heat for 3–4 minutes. Add the shrimp paste, peanut butter, coconut milk, and sugar. Stir over a low heat until you have a smooth paste. Add the kecap manis and season. Remove from the heat.

4 Preheat the barbecue until the coals are glowing and grey in appearance. Thread 2 prawns on each skewer. Barbecue, brushing with marinade, for 2–3 minutes each side. Pile on to a platter with the lime wedges. Serve the sauce separately.

Marinated sweet and hot tuna steaks

Juicy, healthy, quick, and wonderfully moreish.

The fish

Tuna, or swordfish or salmon

- **PREP** 10 mins, plus marinating
- **COOK** 5 mins • **SERVES** 4

Ingredients

2 tbsp dark soy sauce

2 tbsp olive oil

juice of 2 limes

2 garlic cloves, grated

2.5cm (1in) fresh root ginger, grated

2 tbsp dark muscovado sugar

1 tsp cayenne pepper

salt and freshly ground black pepper

4 skinless tuna steaks, about 200g (7oz) each

1 Put the soy sauce, oil, lime juice, garlic, ginger, sugar, and cayenne pepper in a bowl. Season with salt and pepper, and mix together well. Put the tuna steaks in a plastic freezer bag, tip in the marinade, and seal. Massage the fish through the bag, making sure it is well coated. Marinate in the refrigerator for 30 minutes.

2 Heat the barbecue, or a charcoal grill or griddle pan, until hot. Griddle the tuna steaks over a high heat for 2 minutes on each side. Remove to a plate, and rest in a warm place for 2 minutes. Serve with a fresh green salad.

Griddled prawns with hot pepper sauce

You can make this dish even more quickly by substituting a pinch of chilli flakes for the fresh chilli.

The fish

Prawns, or squid or scallops

- **PREP** 10 mins • **COOK** 4 mins • **SERVES** 4

Ingredients

250g (9oz) large raw prawns, unpeeled

2 tbsp olive oil

1 hot red chilli, deseeded and finely chopped

For the hot pepper sauce

1 garlic clove, grated or finely chopped

1 tsp hot chilli powder

1 tsp paprika

pinch of ground cumin

juice of 1 lime

4–5 tbsp mayonnaise

salt and freshly ground black pepper

1 Put the prawns in a bowl, and combine with half the oil and the chilli. Toss well. Set aside.

2 To make the hot pepper sauce, stir together the remaining oil, garlic, chilli powder, paprika, cumin, lime, and mayonnaise. Taste, and adjust the seasoning.

3 Heat a large, heavy frying pan or ridged cast-iron grill pan over a high heat. Tip in the prawns, and cook for about 2 minutes on each side until they turn pink. Serve with the hot pepper sauce, salad, and fresh crusty bread.

Prepare ahead

Make the hot pepper sauce up to 6 hours ahead, cover, and refrigerate. It will get spicier. Return to room temperature before serving.

Variation

Skewered prawns with hot pepper sauce
Thread the prawns on to skewers, and serve 2 or 3 per person. (If using bamboo skewers, soak them in water for 30 minutes first.)

Grilled sardines with salsa verde

A quick and very healthy recipe with a sparkling, piquant Italian herb dressing.

The fish

Sardines, or sprats

- **PREP** 20 mins · **COOK** 6–8 mins · **SERVES** 4

Ingredients

1 bunch of watercress

3 sprigs of flat-leaf parsley

2 sprigs of marjoram

30g (1oz) breadcrumbs

120ml (4fl oz) olive oil

3 tbsp lemon juice

1 tbsp capers in vinegar, rinsed

salt and freshly ground black pepper

8 large sardines, scaled and gutted

1 Trim the coarse stalks from the watercress. Place in a blender with the parsley, marjoram, breadcrumbs, oil, lemon juice, and capers. Blend until the mixture forms a sauce, scraping down the sides as necessary. Season to taste.

2 Place the sardines on a sheet of foil on the grill rack. Grill for 3–4 minutes on each side until sizzling brown and cooked through. Serve with the salsa verde spooned over.

Prepare ahead

Make the salsa verde up to 3 hours in advance, coat with a film of oil to prevent discolouration, cover, and refrigerate.

Variations

Barbecued mackerel, or herring, with salsa verde

Put mackerel or herring in a hinged wire rack and cook them over a preheated barbecue; the coals should be white-hot. The fish will need to cook for 5–8 minutes on each side. Serve with the salsa verde.

Oysters with salsa verde

The salsa is also good spooned over oysters just before eating.

Mediterranean-style grilled sardines

Popular all over southern Europe, this is the way to enjoy these oily fish at their very best.

The fish

Sardines, or small mackerel and herring, or sprats

- **PREP** 15 mins, plus marinating
- **COOK** 4–6 mins · **SERVES** 4

Ingredients

8 large sardines, scaled and gutted

8 sprigs of thyme or lemon thyme, plus extra to garnish

4 lemons

3 tbsp olive oil

2 garlic cloves, crushed

1 tsp ground cumin

1 Rinse the sardines inside and out, and pat dry. Put a sprig of thyme inside each fish, and place them in a shallow non-metallic dish.

2 Grate the zest and squeeze the juice from 3 of the lemons and place in a small bowl. Add the oil, garlic, and cumin, and whisk together. Pour this mixture over the sardines, cover, and refrigerate for at least 2 hours.

3 Preheat the grill on its highest setting. Put the sardines in a grill pan, allowing space between each fish, and grill for 2–3 minutes on each side, basting with the marinade.

4 Cut the remaining lemon into wedges. Place the sardines on a warmed serving plate and serve with lemon wedges and sprigs of thyme.

Prepare ahead

The sardines will benefit from marinating for 2–4 hours before cooking. Cover, and refrigerate.

Grilled halibut with beurre blanc

Halibut has a delicate flesh that is low in fat. Simple flavours suit its texture and flavour well.

The fish

Halibut, or John Dory, salmon, or turbot

▪ **PREP** 5 mins ▪ **COOK** 15 mins ▪ **SERVES** 2

Ingredients

2 halibut steaks, about 140g (5oz) each, scaled

115g (4oz) unsalted butter, plus extra, melted, for the fish

1 shallot, finely chopped

5 tbsp fish stock

1 tbsp white wine vinegar

salt and freshly ground black pepper

lemon juice, to taste

1 Preheat the grill to its highest setting, or heat a griddle pan over a high heat. Brush the halibut steaks with the melted butter. Cook for 3–4 minutes on each side.

2 Cut the remaining butter into small chunks. Melt 25g (scant 1oz) in a small saucepan, add the shallot and cook for 2–3 minutes, or until soft. Add the stock and vinegar, bring to a boil, and simmer until the liquid has reduced to about 3 tbsp.

3 Reduce the heat to very low and add the remaining butter, a few pieces at a time, whisking vigorously between each addition. It is important to keep the stock hot, but don't allow it to boil. Once all the butter has been added, the sauce should be creamy and fairly thick. Remove from the heat, season, add lemon juice to taste, and serve, poured over the halibut, with peas.

Grilled sea bass with roast artichokes and fennel

Some of the best globe artichokes are grown in Lazio, Italy, and they make an excellent combination with sea bass.

The fish

Sea bass, or black bream, gilt-head bream, or meagre

▪ **PREP** 45 mins ▪ **COOK** 25 mins ▪ **SERVES** 4

Ingredients

6 tbsp extra virgin olive oil

4 sea bass fillets, scaled and pinboned

salt and freshly ground black pepper

8 small or 3–4 large artichoke bottoms

squeeze of lemon juice

1 large fennel bulb, finely sliced

3 garlic cloves, finely sliced

large handful of basil, shredded

1 Preheat the oven to 200°C (400°F/Gas 6). Brush a griddle with 2 tbsp of the oil. Slash the skin of each fillet 3 times, and season. Set aside.

2 Cut the artichoke bottoms into quarters and blanch in boiling water with the lemon juice for 3–4 minutes. Drain and put into a large roasting tin with the fennel and garlic. Toss with the remaining olive oil. Season generously and roast in the oven for 15–18 minutes, or until the fennel is roasted and the artichokes are soft.

3 Heat the griddle until just smoking, add the fish, skin side down, and cook for 2–3 minutes on each side: the skin will be charred and the flesh white and firm.

4 Toss the basil into the roasted artichokes and pile on to a serving dish. Arrange the sea bass on top and serve.

Prepare ahead

Roast the vegetables up to 6 hours ahead and keep, covered, at room temperature. Reheat gently before continuing.

BLACK BREAM FLAVOUR PAIRING:

Delicious with braised fennel, or complement it with Pernod, or spice the fish up with saffron, coriander, and plenty of garlic.

Jerk salmon

Jerk seasoning is Jamaican in origin. Traditionally used to marinate both poultry and meat, it works well with fish, too.

The fish
Salmon, or mahi mahi, snapper, tuna, or swordfish

- **PREP** 20 mins, plus marinating
- **COOK** 10 mins • **SERVES** 4

Ingredients
4 thick salmon fillets, about 175g (6oz) each, scaled and pinboned

1–2 tbsp sunflower oil

For the jerk seasoning
1 tbsp ground allspice

½ tsp ground cinnamon

½ tsp freshly grated nutmeg

2 tbsp dark brown sugar

4 garlic cloves, chopped

2 Scotch bonnet chillies, deseeded

½ tbsp thyme leaves

4 spring onions, white part only, roughly chopped

2 tbsp lime juice

1 tbsp sunflower oil

salt and freshly ground black pepper

1 Put the ingredients for the jerk seasoning together in a small blender and whizz until well chopped. Rub some of the seasoning on to the fish; you may decide not to use it all.

2 Brush a griddle pan with the sunflower oil and heat until smoking. Add the fish and reduce the heat. Griddle for 3–4 minutes on each side until charred on the outside and the flesh is cooked: it will flake and be paler in appearance with no sign of translucency.

Prepare ahead
Make the jerk seasoning 1–2 weeks in advance and store in a sealed jar in the refrigerator.

Griddled tuna steaks with salsa

Always be careful with tuna to keep the centre of the fish moist and slightly rare.

The fish
Tuna, or swordfish or mahi mahi

- **PREP** 25–30 mins, plus marinating
- **COOK** 4–6 mins • **SERVES** 4

Ingredients
4 skinless tuna steaks, about 250g (9oz) each

salt and freshly ground black pepper

4 tomatoes, skinned, deseeded, and chopped (see page 112)

200g canned sweetcorn, drained

leaves from 1 bunch of coriander, finely chopped

1 onion, chopped

1 red pepper, diced

2 limes

For the marinade
2–3 sprigs of thyme

2 tbsp vegetable oil

juice of ½ lemon

1 For the marinade, strip the thyme leaves into a non-metallic dish with the oil and lemon juice. Season the tuna, then add to the dish. Cover and marinate for 1 hour, turning once.

2 Put the tomatoes, sweetcorn, coriander, onion, and pepper in a bowl. Squeeze 1 of the limes into the mixture and season. Leave to stand.

3 Heat a griddle pan. Cook the tuna for 2–3 minutes, turn, and brush with marinade. Griddle for 2–3 minutes more. The tuna should be rare in the centre.

4 Put the tuna on to 4 warmed plates. Serve the salsa and lime wedges on the side.

Prepare ahead
Make the salsa 1 day in advance, cover, and refrigerate. Serve at room temperature.

MAHI MAHI FLAVOUR PAIRING:
This dense, meaty fish takes equally well to chilli heat and Caribbean spices, and to Asian fish sauce, lime, garlic, and coriander.

Grilled brill with anchovy butter

Brill has a sweet flavour that works very well with the salty anchovy butter.

The fish

Brill, or turbot, halibut, lemon sole, or flounder

▪ **PREP** 15 mins ▪ **COOK** 4–6 mins ▪ **SERVES** 4

Ingredients

4 brill fillets, about 175g (6oz) each, skinned

butter, for greasing

115g (4oz) rocket leaves, to serve

lemon wedges, to garnish

For the butter

50g (1¾oz) unsalted butter, softened

2 salted anchovy fillets, rinsed and patted dry

1 tsp anchovy essence

squeeze of lemon juice

freshly ground black pepper

1 Preheat the grill on its highest setting. Put the fish, skinned side down, on a large sheet of lightly buttered foil on a baking sheet.

2 Put the butter, anchovies, and anchovy essence into a mortar and pestle or small food processor. Work together until well combined. Beat in the lemon juice and season with pepper.

3 Grill the brill for 2–3 minutes, turn, and spread each fillet with a generous layer of anchovy butter. Return to the grill on a lower shelf and grill for a further 2–3 minutes or until golden brown on top.

4 Arrange the rocket leaves on a large serving dish and arrange the grilled fish on top. Garnish with the lemon wedges.

Prepare ahead

The anchovy butter can be made, wrapped in baking parchment, and refrigerated 1–2 days in advance.

Grilled herring with mustard butter

Many breakfast herring recipes use bacon and oatmeal, but the mustard here makes this recipe a great way to start the day.

The fish

Herring, or sprats, mackerel, sardines, or trout

▪ **PREP** 10 mins ▪ **COOK** 4–6 mins ▪ **SERVES** 4

Ingredients

8 herrings, scaled, gutted, and trimmed, heads removed

1 tbsp vegetable oil

salt and freshly ground black pepper

115g (4oz) bunch of watercress, to garnish

lemon wedges, to garnish

For the butter

75g (2½oz) butter, softened, plus extra for grilling

1 tbsp wholegrain mustard

1 tsp thyme leaves

splash of lemon juice

1 Preheat the grill on its highest setting. Pat the herrings dry with kitchen paper, brush with oil, and season lightly. Place on a large sheet of lightly buttered foil on a baking sheet.

2 Mix the butter, mustard, and thyme together. Add a little lemon juice and season.

3 Grill the herrings for 2–3 minutes on each side or until cooked; it will be firm to the touch.

4 Lift the herrings on to a large, warmed serving dish and dot with the mustard butter to melt over the fish. Garnish with watercress and lemon wedges.

Prepare ahead

The mustard butter can be made, wrapped in baking parchment, and refrigerated 1–2 days in advance.

BRILL FLAVOUR PAIRINGS: The fine, firm flesh of brill is a treat with a buttery sauce, or a sauce made from white wine or Champagne and cream, or wild mushrooms and Parmesan cheese.

Lobster Thermidor

Another version of this classic lobster recipe is where the raw lobster is split along the centre (see page 290) and roasted then grilled, with the sauce poured over.

The fish

Lobsters, or Dublin Bay prawns

- **PREP** 20 mins ▪ **COOK** 10–15 mins
- **SERVES** 4

Ingredients

2 lobsters, about 675g (1½lb) each, cooked

paprika, to garnish

lemon wedges, to serve

For the sauce

30g (1oz) butter

2 shallots, finely chopped

120ml (4fl oz) dry white wine

120ml (4fl oz) fish stock

150ml (5fl oz) double cream

½ tsp ready-made English mustard

1 tbsp lemon juice

2 tbsp chopped flat-leaf parsley

2 tsp chopped tarragon

salt and freshly ground black pepper

75g (2½oz) Gruyère cheese, grated

1 Cut the lobsters in half lengthways. Remove the meat from the claws and tail, along with any roe or meat from the head (see page 291). Cut the meat into bite-sized pieces. Clean out the shells and reserve.

2 To prepare the sauce, melt the butter in a small saucepan, add the shallots, and fry gently until softened but not browned. Add the wine and boil for 2–3 minutes, or until reduced by half.

3 Add the stock and cream and boil rapidly, stirring, until reduced and slightly thickened. Stir in the mustard, lemon juice, and herbs, then season to taste. Stir in half the cheese.

4 Preheat the grill on its highest setting. Add the lobster meat to the sauce, then divide among the lobster shells. Top with the remaining cheese.

5 Place the lobsters on a foil-lined grill pan and grill for 2–3 minutes, or until bubbling and golden. Sprinkle with a little paprika and serve hot with lemon wedges.

Barbecued sardines in harissa

Very fresh sardines, still stiff with rigor mortis, have a sweet and delicate flavour.

The fish

Sardines, or mackerel, sprats, or herrings

- **PREP** 25 mins ▪ **COOK** 2–3 mins ▪ **SERVES** 4

Ingredients

12–16 sardines, scaled, gutted, and trimmed

1–2 tbsp olive oil

salt and freshly ground black pepper

1 tsp ground coriander

For the harissa dressing

2 tbsp extra virgin olive oil

2 tbsp harissa paste

2 tsp runny honey, to taste

grated zest and juice of 1 lime

For the salad

large handful of coriander leaves

2 Little Gem lettuces, finely sliced

grated zest and juice of 1 lemon

pinch of sugar

3 tbsp extra virgin olive oil

1 Preheat a barbecue until the coals are glowing and grey in appearance.

2 Cut 3 slashes in either side of each sardine. Brush with olive oil and season generously with salt, pepper, and ground coriander. Set aside.

3 To make the dressing, whisk together the oil, harissa, honey, and lime zest and juice, season, and add more honey if necessary to balance the acidity of the lime. Set aside.

4 Prepare the salad: toss the coriander with the lettuce and pile into a large, flat serving dish. Whisk together the lemon zest, juice, sugar, and olive oil. Season and drizzle over the salad.

5 Cook the sardines on the barbecue (or under a preheated grill) for 2–3 minutes or until the flesh is white and opaque. Brush with the harissa paste and barbecue the other side for a further 30 seconds. Pile on to the coriander salad and serve with warm crusty bread.

Prepare ahead

Make the harissa dressing 1 day ahead, cover, and refrigerate. The flavours will deepen.

SARDINE FLAVOUR PAIRINGS: The definite tastes of oil-rich sardines can take almost any strong flavours. Try it with harissa, or Sicilian olive oil, garlic, sultanas, pine nuts, and oregano.

TECHNIQUES

Tools

Stock your kitchen with this kit, which includes the essentials you need for preparing all manner of seafood. After using your tools, rinse and scrub them thoroughly in cold running water to remove any trace of scale and flesh. Follow this with a thorough hot, soapy wash. Handles and chopping boards should then be rinsed in a sterilizing solution (baby bottle sterilizer is a good option) and dried. This will keep your equipment scrupulously clean and odour-free.

Fish scaler
A fish scaler makes scaling fish easy and the scales tend to collect in one place. There are several varieties around; choose one that feels comfortable to grip. In the absence of a scaler, use the back of any kitchen knife but take care, as the scales tend to flick further around the kitchen. For scaling, see page 264.

Steaking knife
A steaking knife is a long-bladed, rigid knife (around 30cm/12in) that is excellent for cutting through bones, and so perfect for steaking large fish (see pages 270 and 275). It is also good for skinning larger fillets. If you do not have a steaking knife, you can use a large chef's knife in its place.

Filleting knife
A flexible knife with a 15–25cm (6–8in) blade is essential for filleting. Choose a knife that has good flexibility without being too bendy. Use the tip to slip under fillets, and the mid-section to cut through skin and to make the long cuts required to remove the fillet. The mid-section can also be used to skin small fillets. Apply pressure to the heel, the least flexible part of the knife, to cut through bones.

Steel
Knives require steeling on a regular basis in order to keep them sharp. Once blunt, it is virtually impossible to sharpen the blade yourself. To steel a knife, place the tip of the steel on a work surface and hold it firm. Run the blade from the heel to the tip, at a 30° angle. It should feel gritty when being drawn over the steel.

Scissors
A good, sturdy pair of kitchen scissors makes light work of some tough jobs, such as removing the head from a flat fish, trimming fins, and cutting through soft bones. Many fishmongers generally use a knife for these jobs, but scissors make easier work of it.

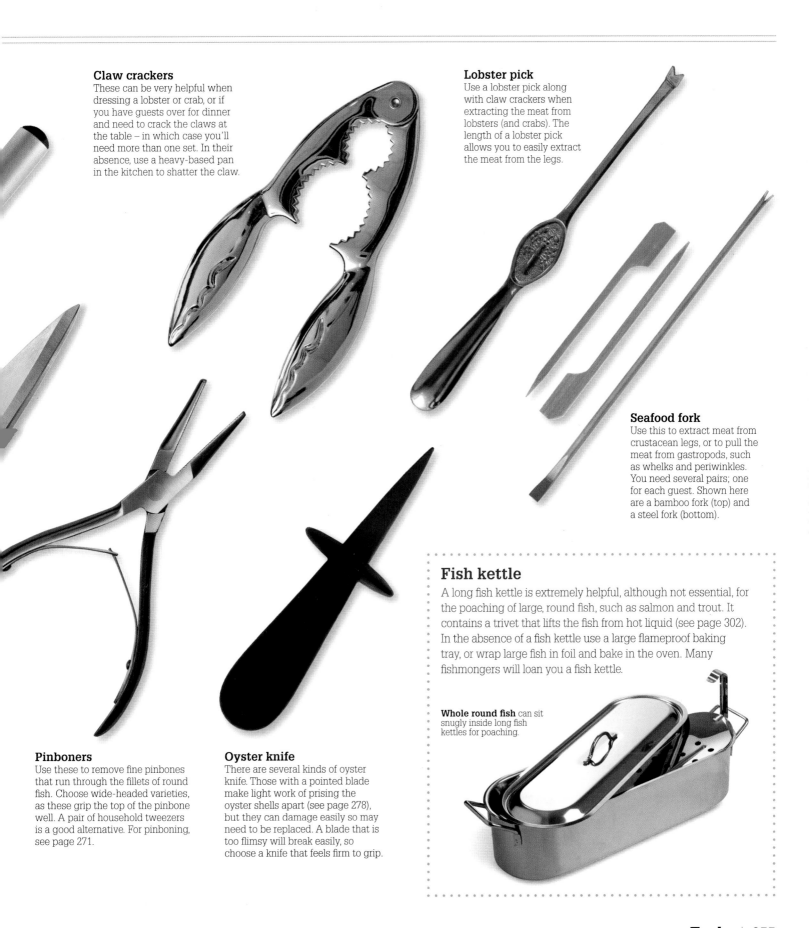

Claw crackers

These can be very helpful when dressing a lobster or crab, or if you have guests over for dinner and need to crack the claws at the table – in which case you'll need more than one set. In their absence, use a heavy-based pan in the kitchen to shatter the claw.

Lobster pick

Use a lobster pick along with claw crackers when extracting the meat from lobsters (and crabs). The length of a lobster pick allows you to easily extract the meat from the legs.

Seafood fork

Use this to extract meat from crustacean legs, or to pull the meat from gastropods, such as whelks and periwinkles. You need several pairs; one for each guest. Shown here are a bamboo fork (top) and a steel fork (bottom).

Pinboners

Use these to remove fine pinbones that run through the fillets of round fish. Choose wide-headed varieties, as these grip the top of the pinbone well. A pair of household tweezers is a good alternative. For pinboning, see page 271.

Oyster knife

There are several kinds of oyster knife. Those with a pointed blade make light work of prising the oyster shells apart (see page 278), but they can damage easily so may need to be replaced. A blade that is too flimsy will break easily, so choose a knife that feels firm to grip.

Fish kettle

A long fish kettle is extremely helpful, although not essential, for the poaching of large, round fish, such as salmon and trout. It contains a trivet that lifts the fish from hot liquid (see page 302). In the absence of a fish kettle use a large flameproof baking tray, or wrap large fish in foil and bake in the oven. Many fishmongers will loan you a fish kettle.

Whole round fish can sit snugly inside long fish kettles for poaching.

Choosing and storing

Choosing

Sight, smell, and touch are used to assess the quality of all seafood. Fish and shellfish should be bought and cooked as fresh as possible, preferably when in season. Choose the freshest, best-looking fish available – one that has bright eyes and smooth, glistening skin. There are particular signs of quality all over the body of a fish and a shellfish (shown here are a brook trout and a Dungeness crab) that are worth knowing before you buy.

Fish

Most fish can be assessed in the same way. Round fish have a round body and produce a fillet either side of the backbone. Flat fish start life as small round fish, turning on to their side as they grow. Fish can also be categorized by their texture: white or oil-rich. White fish have low-fat flesh that turns white and opaque when cooked, and the liver contains most of the oil. The flesh can be very dense and meaty, as with monkfish, or flaky, as with cod and snapper. Oil-rich species have fat distributed throughout their body and have high levels of omega-3 fatty acids. These include mackerel, herring, trout, and salmon.

Scales
On a whole fish these should be bright and glistening and firmly attached to the skin. Dull and dry scales that detach easily indicate the fish is not fresh.

Skin
Look for fish with bright skin with evenly distributed surface slime that appears clear and colourless. The fish's colour fades as it decomposes and the slime becomes sticky and discoloured.

Feel
A fresh fish may still show signs of rigor mortis (be stiff and rigid), indicating that it has been out of the water for no more than 24–48 hours. Once there are no signs of rigor, a good-quality fish should feel firm and elastic and the flesh should be firmly attached to the backbone. Press down along the fish's back to assess firmness.

Eyes
These should be bright, convex, and black with a translucent cornea. As a fish loses condition the eyes look sunken, the pupil appears grey or milky, and the cornea opaque.

Gills
A fresh, gutted fish has bright red gills. As the fish loses condition the colour fades to brown and the mucous becomes sticky.

Smell
Fresh fish should either have no smell at all or should smell pleasantly of the sea, with no underlying offensive aroma. Fish that are beginning to decompose will smell stale and sour.

Shellfish

The term "shellfish" refers to many edible species that are covered by a shell. Crustaceans are a group of mainly aquatic shellfish, such as lobsters and prawns, that have segmented bodies, no backbone, jointed legs/claws, and two antennae, and that can move independently. Molluscs are soft-bodied invertebrates with a hard shell. They can be subdivided into many groups as follows: gastropods/univalves, typically found in one coiled shell, include whelks, periwinkles, snails, and conch; bivalves or filter feeds, typically found in two hinged shells, include oysters, clams, mussels, and scallops; cephalopods are a group of invertebrates, such as octopus, squid, and cuttlefish, that have tubular heads and many arms with suckers.

Look
All live shellfish should show signs of life, most obviously movement. Never buy dead, uncooked molluscs, as decomposition begins immediately after death (see box, page 279). The tubular part of octopus, cuttlefish, and squid should be white in appearance; avoid flesh that has become pink.

Smell
Cooked shellfish should have a fresh smell with the sweet aroma of sea ozone. Avoid any that smell stale, musty, and of ammonia, as they are beginning to decompose and are not safe to eat.

Feel
When cooked or raw, the limbs of crabs and lobsters should hold firmly and snap back into position if extended. Floppy or loose limbs may indicate the crab is dead or dying, and so may not be safe to eat.

Shell
The shell should feel heavy and should not be seeping water; a crab or lobster that feels light may have recently shed its shell, and may lack brown meat. Shells should be hard and dry.

Refrigerating

Try to buy seafood on the day you intend to cook it, but if you have to store it for a short period of time you need to ensure it is safe to eat. Ideally, fish should be stored at 0°C (32°F) (5°C/41°F cooler than a domestic fridge). Ice helps to create a cooler environment. Refrigerate shellfish at 3°C (37°F) or under, for the timings given below. Never submerge any shellfish in water and always check molluscs for signs of life before cooking (see page 279).

Whole fish

Surround whole fish with ice and place it in the coldest part of the refrigerator (the lowest shelf). Fishmongers pack whole fish directly over ice and you can replicate this using ice or picnic ice packs. Storage times vary between species, but all fish is best eaten within 24–36 hours.

Fillets

Ensure the fillet's flesh side doesn't come into direct contact with ice, as this will give the fish bleached patches. Either store the fillets skin side in contact with ice, or in a plastic container, loosely covered with cling film, with ice packed around it. Best eaten within 24–36 hours.

Shellfish

Refrigerate mussels and clams in a covered bowl for 36 hours. (Oysters and scallops may last for 1 week, stored round side down.) Live lobsters and crabs, wrapped in a damp cloth, will keep for 48 hours. Cooked or raw prawns will keep for 24 hours. Squid and cuttlefish will store for 3 days.

Freezing

If you intend to use fish after 24 hours of purchase, freeze it as soon as you get it home. Freezing fresh fish slows the changes that occur as spoilage takes place and, if carefully done, it can be impossible to tell the difference between fresh and frozen. First, pat the fish (fillets, steaks, or whole fish) dry with kitchen paper. If freezing whole fish, remove the scales, guts, and fins before freezing. To defrost fish, remove it from the freezer bags and place in a colander set over a plate. Place the fish in the refrigerator and allow to defrost very slowly – rapid defrosting can result in loss of moisture, ruining the texture of the fish. For home-freezing, only freeze cooked shellfish.

Whole fish and fillets

To freeze surplus fresh fish at home, pack fillets, steaks, or small whole gutted fish individually (or no more than two at a time), in a double layer of plastic freezer bags. Then exclude the air, label, and freeze. Freeze for up to 6 weeks.

Shellfish

Once cooked and cold, wrap the shellfish in a double layer of cling film and then a freezer bag, and label. Freeze for up to 6 weeks. Cooked lobsters and prawns, and cooked mussels, whelks, and periwinkles (removed from the shell) can be frozen in this way.

Cuts of a large round fish

Most round fish are cut into two long fillets, which run along either side of the backbone. These are portioned into individual servings. Large round fish (over 1.5kg/3lb 3oz), such as salmon (shown here), cod, pollock, and coley, can be divided into other cuts as well as fillets. Some species, including snapper, breams, and mahi mahi, have a laterally compressed body, which is best simply filleted.

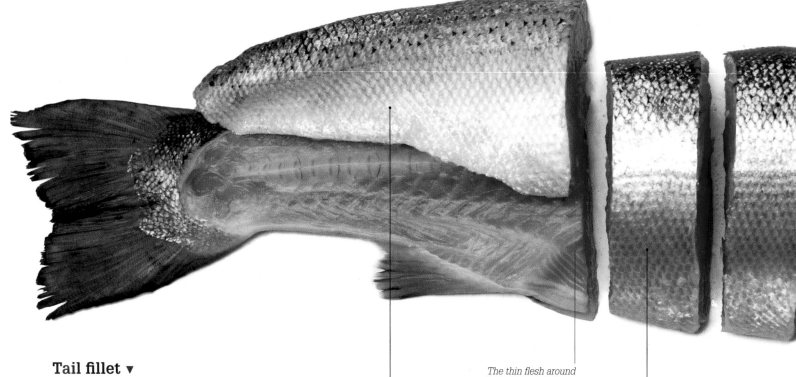

The thin flesh around the belly is sometimes sold separately.

Tail fillet ▼

This thin triangular fillet spans from the base of the tail to the base of the anal fin. It does not contain pinbones and rarely takes more than 5 minutes to pan-fry, bake, barbecue, roast, or poach. For a more unusual dish, skin the fillet and lightly bat it out between two pieces of greaseproof paper. It can then be rolled with a stuffing to cook as paupiettes (rolls of tail fillet).

Steaks ▶

Steaks (or darnes) are cross sections, about 2.5–4cm (1–1¾in) thick, that contain a section of backbone. The bone helps the flesh retain moisture when cooked, and, in turn, lengthens the cooking time slightly. Grill, pan-fry, braise, microwave, or barbecue steaks in oil or herb butter.

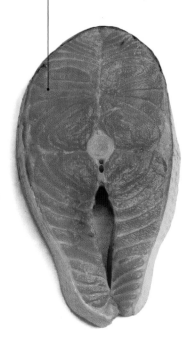

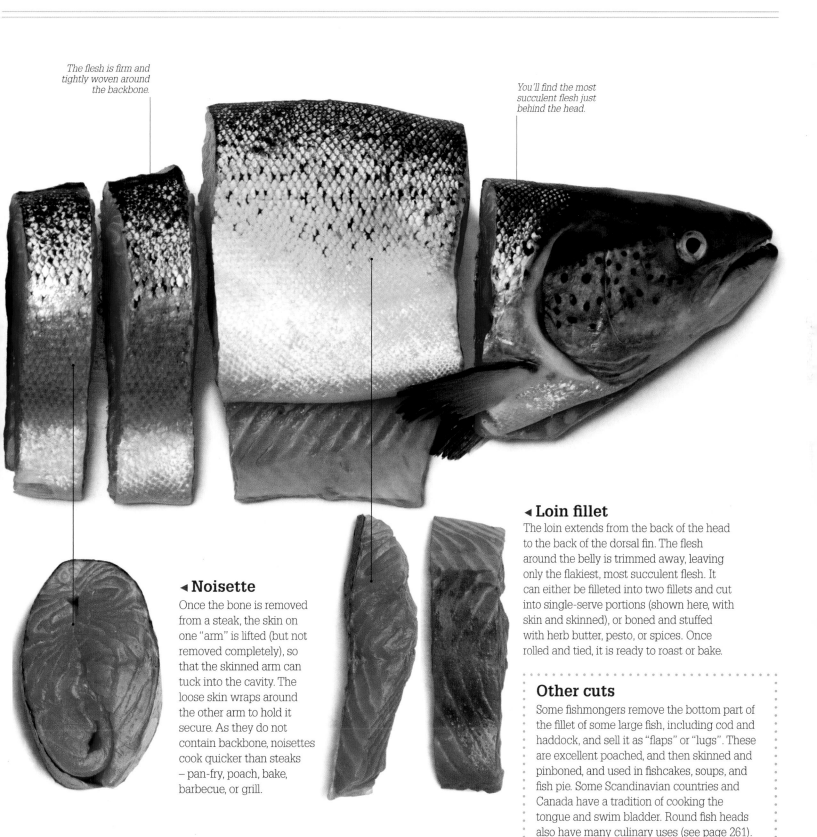

The flesh is firm and tightly woven around the backbone.

You'll find the most succulent flesh just behind the head.

◄ Noisette

Once the bone is removed from a steak, the skin on one "arm" is lifted (but not removed completely), so that the skinned arm can tuck into the cavity. The loose skin wraps around the other arm to hold it secure. As they do not contain backbone, noisettes cook quicker than steaks – pan-fry, poach, bake, barbecue, or grill.

◄ Loin fillet

The loin extends from the back of the head to the back of the dorsal fin. The flesh around the belly is trimmed away, leaving only the flakiest, most succulent flesh. It can either be filleted into two fillets and cut into single-serve portions (shown here, with skin and skinned), or boned and stuffed with herb butter, pesto, or spices. Once rolled and tied, it is ready to roast or bake.

Other cuts

Some fishmongers remove the bottom part of the fillet of some large fish, including cod and haddock, and sell it as "flaps" or "lugs". These are excellent poached, and then skinned and pinboned, and used in fishcakes, soups, and fish pie. Some Scandinavian countries and Canada have a tradition of cooking the tongue and swim bladder. Round fish heads also have many culinary uses (see page 261).

Cuts of a large round fish | 259

Cuts of a large flat fish

The shape of flat fish is better suited to filleting rather than other methods of cutting. However, large flat fish of over 1.7kg (3½lb), such as halibut (shown here) and turbot, are thick enough to be cut into single steaks (taken from one side of the backbone) or double steaks (where the cut spans the width of the fish). Unlike those taken from a round fish, flat fish fillets do not contain pinbones; filleted correctly and carefully, they are bone free.

Single fillets ▼

Flat fish can either be filleted into four quarter-cross fillets, where the fillet is taken from either side of the backbone on both sides of the fish (one of these is shown below), or as "cross-cut" or double fillets, one on each side of the fish (see page 274). The fillets can be skinned and portioned or just portioned; a large fish produces thick boneless fillets, great for pan-frying, grilling, and baking.

Tail fillet ▲

The triangular tail fillet extends from the anal fin to the base of the fish. It is best to fillet the tail, as it is too thin for steaks. The tail end piece of the fillet can be skinned or left as it is for quick pan-frying or baking. As with all fish, the tail fillet contains no pinbones and is quick to cook.

Their scale covering is much more modest than that of round fish.

A fillet is taken from each quarter of the fish.

Steaks ▶

Usually 2.5–4cm (1–1¾in) thick, steaks are cut up to two-thirds along the body. Flat fish steaks are more triangular than those taken from a round fish because the guts of a flat fish sit just behind the head area, rather than along the fish's body. The skin protects the flesh during cooking, but pulls away easily once the fish is cooked. Large flat fish offer meaty, dense steaks that are suitable for grilling, pan-frying, microwaving, or barbecuing.

Fish heads

The head contains the cheek or "pearl", which is worth removing, either before or after cooking. It is considered a delicacy in Scandinavia, North America, Southern Europe, and some other parts of the world, where it is deep-fried, poached, or pan-fried. Use the head to make fish head curry and to flavour fish stock, or simply poach and remove the flesh to use in fishcakes and pies. If using the head in this way, remove the gills and rinse the head first to wash away any traces of blood.

The cheeks are extracted from larger fish and are particularly delicious. Ask your fishmonger for them.

Dense cheeks are removed from both sides of the head of a large flat fish.

Portions of a cooked crab

All species of crab are comprised of the same parts: two claws, eight legs, a carapace, and the main body. Shown below is a brown edible crab and the components where you will find the brown and the white meat. Start by removing the claws and the legs and then pull the main body away from the carapace. Make sure you remove all of the inedible parts, all of which are easily identified (see box, below). For more information on how to dress a crab, see pages 288–289.

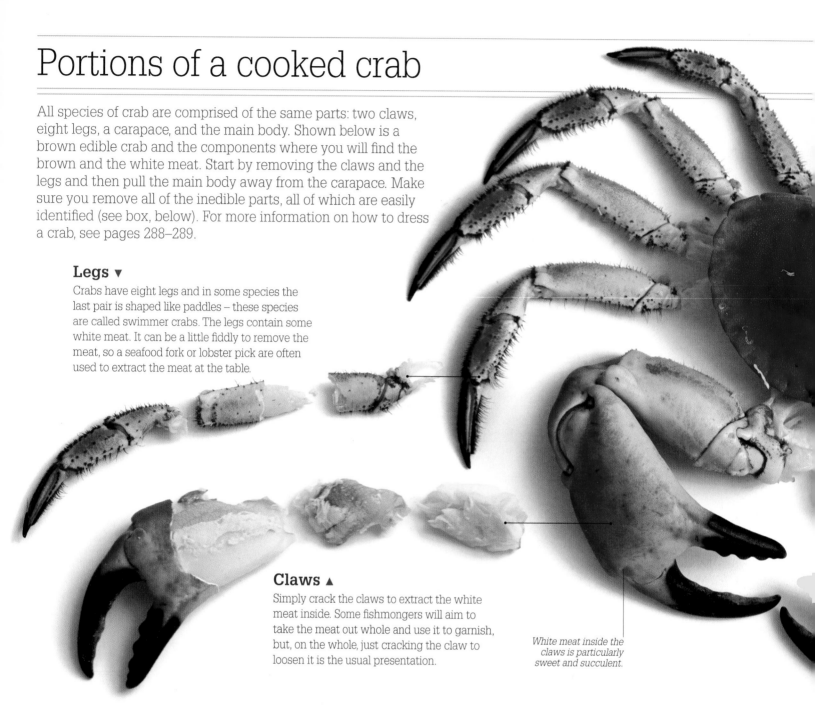

Legs ▼
Crabs have eight legs and in some species the last pair is shaped like paddles – these species are called swimmer crabs. The legs contain some white meat. It can be a little fiddly to remove the meat, so a seafood fork or lobster pick are often used to extract the meat at the table.

Claws ▲
Simply crack the claws to extract the white meat inside. Some fishmongers will aim to take the meat out whole and use it to garnish, but, on the whole, just cracking the claw to loosen it is the usual presentation.

White meat inside the claws is particularly sweet and succulent.

Inedible parts
The gills, or "dead man's fingers", are attached to the main body, but a few may be left in the carapace during preparation. Their dry, spongy texture makes very unpleasant eating. The mouth and stomach sac are found in the carapace and also need to be removed. The crab's tail, or apron, located on the underside of the main body, is inedible. Male crabs have thin aprons, while hens have wider, more rounded aprons (see page 378). Shards of shell can ruin white meat. To locate any, put the meat into a metal bowl and shake it around. Listen for the shell pinging against the side of the bowl.

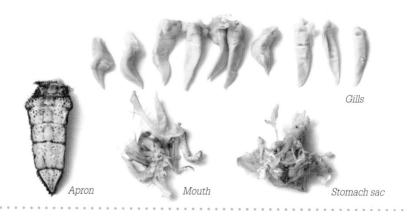

Apron *Mouth* *Gills* *Stomach sac*

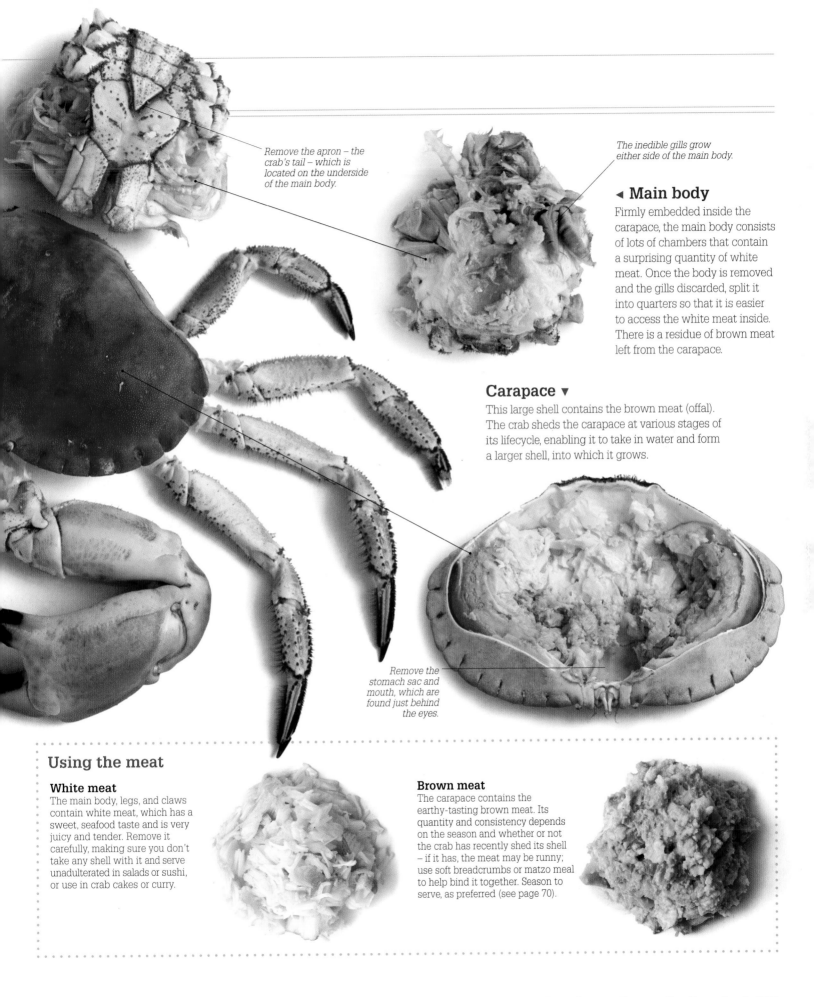

Remove the apron – the crab's tail – which is located on the underside of the main body.

The inedible gills grow either side of the main body.

◄ **Main body**

Firmly embedded inside the carapace, the main body consists of lots of chambers that contain a surprising quantity of white meat. Once the body is removed and the gills discarded, split it into quarters so that it is easier to access the white meat inside. There is a residue of brown meat left from the carapace.

Carapace ▼

This large shell contains the brown meat (offal). The crab sheds the carapace at various stages of its lifecycle, enabling it to take in water and form a larger shell, into which it grows.

Remove the stomach sac and mouth, which are found just behind the eyes.

Using the meat

White meat

The main body, legs, and claws contain white meat, which has a sweet, seafood taste and is very juicy and tender. Remove it carefully, making sure you don't take any shell with it and serve unadulterated in salads or sushi, or use in crab cakes or curry.

Brown meat

The carapace contains the earthy-tasting brown meat. Its quantity and consistency depends on the season and whether or not the crab has recently shed its shell – if it has, the meat may be runny; use soft breadcrumbs or matzo meal to help bind it together. Season to serve, as preferred (see page 70).

Preparing round fish

Scaling and trimming

Always remove the scales if you intend to cook fish with its skin, so they don't spoil the dish. Scaling is messy, so put the fish (salmon is shown here) in a plastic bag or in a sink to stop the scales flicking around the kitchen. Trimming the fins neatens the fish. Fins also stick to a baking sheet or foil, making it hard to release a fish intact after cooking.

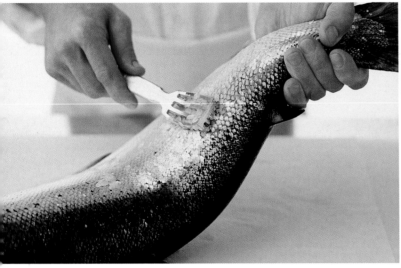

1 Holding the fish by the tail, run a scaler or the back of any kitchen knife along its length, from tail to head, to lift off the scales. Don't forget to scale the back and the belly as well as the side flanks of the fish.

2 Use scissors to trim the fins close to the body. In some cases, this should be done before scaling, as the fins can get in the way. Some species have sharp fins, so it is safe to remove them before scaling.

Removing the gills

If you plan to cook a fish with the head on (a mackerel is shown here), remove the gills as soon as possible, as they contain bacteria, which cause the fish to decompose. It is best to cook fish whole, as bones retain moisture and flavour, and prevent the fish from drying out. Remove the bones, head, and tail once the fish is cooked, if you prefer.

1 Firmly lift the gill flap with your thumb and forefinger and cut the throat with the tip of a sharp filleting knife. Lifting the gill makes it easier to get a clean cut through the fish.

2 Insert a thumb and index finger around the gills, and pull. They should come out fairly easily. If not (they can be tough on large fish), cut through the gills where they attach to the head, then pull them out.

Removing the head

There is no real reason to remove the head of a fish before cooking, but many people prefer to. It's important to cut into the fish on a sharp diagonal behind the fins to avoid wasting any of the flesh, which is at its most succulent just behind the head and nearest to the bones. Use the head to flavour soups and stews.

1 Using a sturdy, sharp knife, make cuts on a sharp diagonal behind the fins and into the back of either side of the head. This ensures maximum flesh stays on the fish.

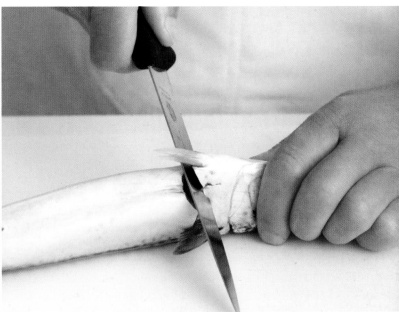

2 Make a cut underneath the head, behind the ventral fins, to join up with the two head cuts. This also removes the ventral fins that would otherwise be trimmed away before cooking.

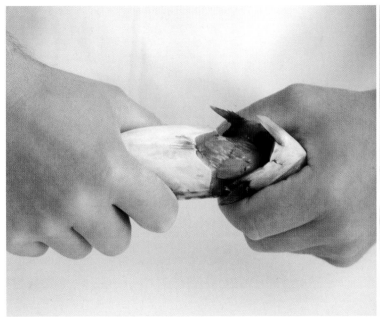

3 Firmly gripping the fish body in one hand and the head in the other, bend the head backwards away from the belly. Be quite forceful; you should be able to hear a few distinct cracks.

4 Turn the fish around, and swiftly and firmly bend the head back in the opposite direction, towards the belly of the fish. You should now be able to pull the head clear from the body.

Gutting through the stomach

You need to remove the guts (the internal organs) of the fish, as they quickly decompose. Once you have removed the guts, loosen and remove the dark bloodline running along the spine near the head, then thoroughly rinse the belly cavity to remove any remaining traces of blood or viscera. A mackerel is shown here.

1 Insert a slim filleting knife into the vent (you will see a small hole), and with a single stroke cut along the belly to the chin.

2 Lift the belly flap with your thumb and cut all the way down into the fish until you reach the dark-coloured bloodline near the spine.

3 With the back of the knife, release the bloodline (see page 272), then scrape it away with the guts. Rinse, then firmly wipe the belly cavity clean.

Gutting through the gills

This technique is far trickier than gutting through the stomach, but is great for recipes where it is important to keep the fish as intact as possible, such as for Whole Poached Salmon (see page 224). It is also the ideal way to gut any round fish that you plan to cut it into steaks. A rainbow trout is shown here.

  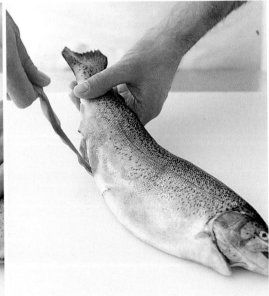

1 Cut the gills with scissors at the base of the head, and pull them out. Take care as these can be sharp.

2 Using an index finger, hook the entrails through the hole left by the gills and pull to release them from the body cavity.

3 Snip the vent end, and pull out the remaining guts. Run a finger inside the fish to loosen the bloodline, then rinse the cavity well to remove it.

Boning through the back

Often referred to as "canoeing", this technique keeps the fish in shape so it can take flavouring or stuffing before cooking. It removes the backbone, dorsal fin, and some pinbones. Once boned, remove the guts and pull away the gills. Finally, rinse the fish only briefly, as the delicate flesh absorbs water easily. A black sea bass is shown here.

1 With a filleting knife, cut along the back of the fish on one side of the backbone. Using a long, sweeping action, run the knife over the bones.

2 Turn the fish and do the same on the other side, keeping the knife flat over the bones. If the knife is angled, you could cut through to the second side.

3 Once the fillets are released, snip the backbone at the head and tail and pull it free. Pinbone the fillets (see page 271).

Boning through the stomach

If you intend to stuff a fish, this is the ideal method of boning. It is also the usual technique used to prepare herrings (shown here) for Rollmops (see page 297), and for baking fish. A fish that has been boned through the stomach will lie flat during cooking and will need to be turned only once, so is great for pan-frying and barbecuing.

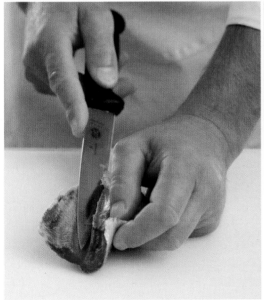

1 Remove the head and guts. Lie the fish on its back and run a filleting knife along one side of the backbone from top to tail.

2 Run the knife along the other side of the bone and release the second fillet, keeping the knife flat to the bone to avoid wasting too much flesh.

3 Carefully pull away the backbone and snip it free at the tail with scissors, or cut it with a sharp knife. Pinbone the fillets (see page 271).

Classic filleting

A round fish such as red mullet (shown here) is typically cut into two fillets. A sharp, flexible filleting knife and good control of the blade are vital. Keep the blade flat against the bone and use long, sweeping cuts to prevent damage to the fillet. Use this technique to remove the head and bones. Fillets are quick to cook, but overcook easily.

1 Release the fillet close to the head: using a sharp, flexible filleting knife, insert the blade at an angle into the head to prevent losing too much flesh. Make a cut until you reach the bone.

2 With the knife flat, stroke the blade along one side of the backbone to open up the skin and reveal the backbone underneath. One or two strokes are all that are needed.

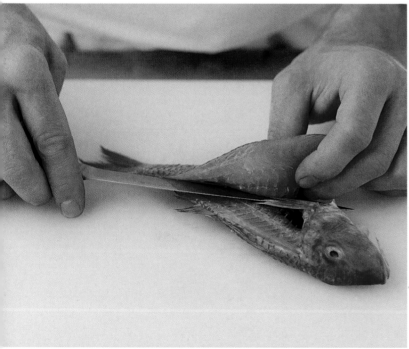

3 Keeping the knife flat, cut over the rib cage and out the other side of the fish. Using stroking, sweeping cuts of the knife, continue to the tail end to release the whole fillet.

4 Turn the fish over and do exactly the same on the other side. Support the fish with your free hand and remember to keep the knife flat, and the cuts firm, but long and stroking. Pinbone the fillets (see page 271).

Block filleting

Fishmongers use this technique to remove both fillets at the same time, leaving the rib cage behind on the bone. It is achievable at home and, although a little wasteful, gives a particularly neat fillet as well as a "cage" (carcass), which is great for fish stock. This technique works best on small, round fish such as whiting (shown here).

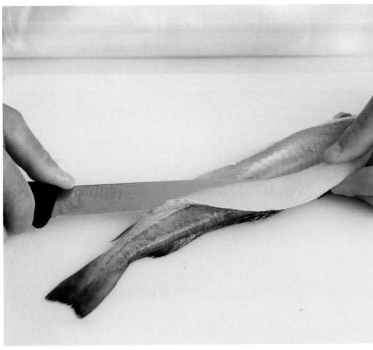

1 Starting from the belly, lay a sharp, flexible filleting knife flat against the ribcage and – using the ribcage as a guide – cut in a sweeping action from head to tail, keeping the tip of the blade on the backbone.

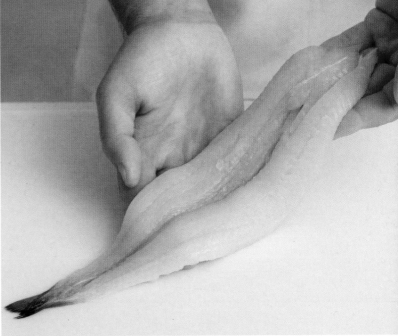

2 Turn the fish over and repeat on the other side, holding the released fillet with your other hand. Keep the blade of the knife flat against the bones to avoid too much wastage, and use long, sweeping strokes.

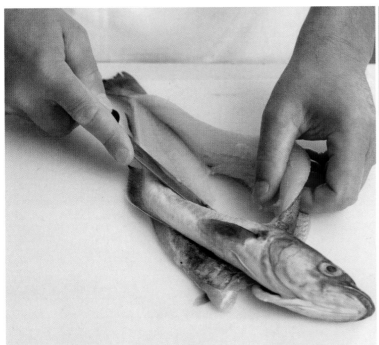

3 Run the tip of the knife along the back of the fish. Pull the two fillets from the bones with your free hand. With scissors, snip the backbone close to the tail to free the fillets. Pinbone the fillets (see page 271).

The double fillet achieved by the block technique gives you the chance to work with a large, neat amount of boneless fish. Try baking with a herb stuffing for an unusual, impressive dish.

Filleting a monkfish tail

Monkfish is usually sold by the tail. Once filleted, monkfish is boneless and the flesh is sweet and dense. Although a fishmonger will often skin the fish, there will be a couple of layers of grey-brown membrane under the skin that you will need to remove. If left attached, they shrink around the fish during cooking, making it a little tough.

1 Lay the monkfish tail on its belly. Using a sharp, flexible filleting knife, cut along one side of the backbone with long, sweeping strokes, straight through to the belly. Turn the fish and repeat on the other side.

2 Lay the fillet on a board, membrane down. With the knife at a sharp angle, cut between membrane and fillet. Grip the end of the membrane firmly, and continue to cut it away from the length of the fillet.

Cutting steaks

Steaks are cut straight through the fish and have bone in the centre. The bone retains flavour and moisture in the fish during cooking. If the fish is large, with dense bones, hit the back of the knife with a wooden mallet to break the backbone. This prevents the flesh from being crushed under too much pressure. A salmon is shown here.

1 Remove the head of the gutted fish by cutting with a sturdy, sharp knife at a diagonal behind the fins. Repeat on the other side, hitting the back of the knife with a mallet to break through the neck.

2 Using a large, sharp chef's knife, score the skin at 2.5cm (1in) intervals along the length of the fish to ensure even steaks. Once marked, cut the steaks straight through the fish. Wipe the knife between each cut.

Pinboning and skinning a fillet

When skinning, keep the knife flat against the board, or you will leave too much flesh on the skin. You don't always have to skin a fillet, as the skin helps to retain moisture during cooking. It also looks attractive, and will peel away easily once the fish is cooked. A salmon fillet is shown here. Always pinbone fish fillets, to avoid choking hazards.

1 Run your thumb along the pinbones to make them stand out. Grasp the bone with pinboners and pull it out towards the head. Pinbones are usually found at the thickest part of the fillet, and not at the tail end.

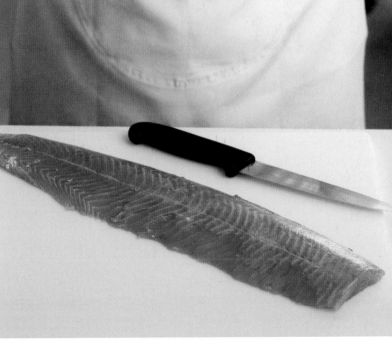

2 Choose a knife that is long and flexible enough to work up the whole fillet. Starting at the tail (the thinnest part of the fillet), and keeping the knife close to the skin, make a cut between the flesh and the skin.

3 Grip the flap of skin with your free hand. Keeping the skin taut, and the knife at a 30° angle to – and in contact with – the board, saw and push the knife towards the head. Discard the skin.

Traces of iridescent "silverskin" left on a fillet is the clearest sign that you have skinned it well, as the wastage of flesh is negligible.

Preparing flat fish

Removing the gills

Before handling flat fish, rinse them under cold, running water, as they are often slimy making them slippery to handle. If necessary, use a brush to scrub off the slime.

If the head is to be left on for cooking, the gills need to be removed as one of their roles was to trap bacteria, which would now cause the fish to spoil. A plaice is shown here.

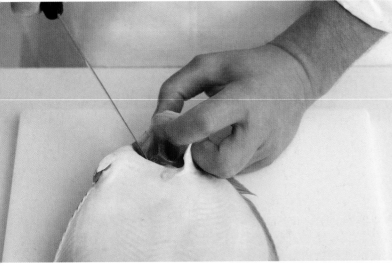

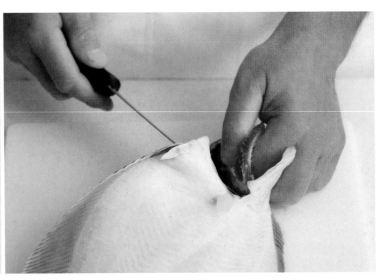

1 Lift the gill flap with your finger and cut behind the gills with the tip of a sharp, slim knife. Pull the gills up, and run the knife around their base. Release them by making one small cut with the tip of the knife.

2 Pull the gills free with your fingers, remove, and discard. Rinse the fish briefly under cold running water, checking to ensure all traces of blood from the gills have disappeared.

Removing the bloodline

As flat fish are gutted once caught, the only viscera you need to remove is the bloodline, which is the main artery, and runs down the backbone. Fish blood has an unpleasant, bitter taste, and it should be banished from the cavity. When rinsing fish, do so as briefly as possible, or the delicate flesh will begin to absorb the water.

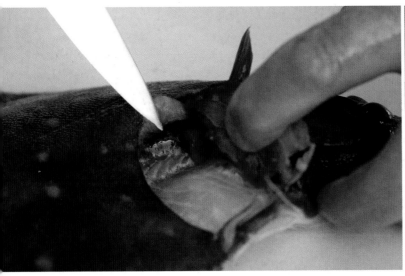

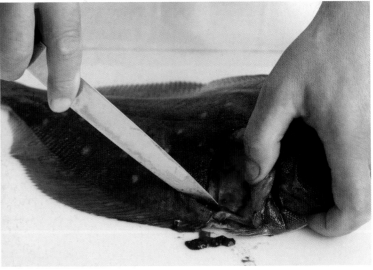

1 Insert the tip of a sharp, slim knife to break the membrane holding the bloodline in place. This is found in a small pocket at the head of the fish, attached to the thickest part of the backbone.

2 Pull or scrape away the dark, congealed bloodline, checking carefully that you have removed it entirely. Finally, rinse the cavity of the fish briefly under cold running water.

Trimming

Some flat fish need scaling (see page 264). If you are unsure whether a fish needs scaling, scrape a sharp knife from tail to head. If nothing much comes off, scaling isn't necessary.

Although a flat fish's fins and tail tend to be wider and less obvious than those of a round fish, they are no less inedible for that, and need trimming.

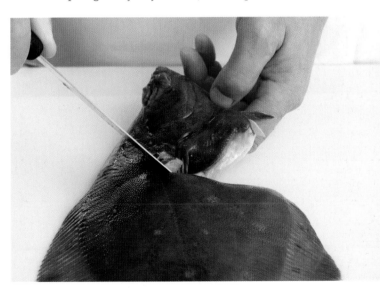

1 Cut away the fins with scissors, working from tail to head. Removing fins makes the fish look neat. If you leave them attached, they can be pulled away after cooking.

2 Trim away the tail; this is both to make the fish neat and because it will stick to whatever the fish is cooked on. Removing the tail means you will easily be able to lift the fish from a baking sheet or grilling pan.

Removing the head

Most fishmongers would offer to remove the head of a flat fish as part of trimming, so the fish is ready to cook. If you are attempting the job yourself, it is important to aim for minimum waste. With a sharp knife, score a guiding mark around the back of the head, close to the bone, to avoid wasting the thick piece of fillet nearest the head.

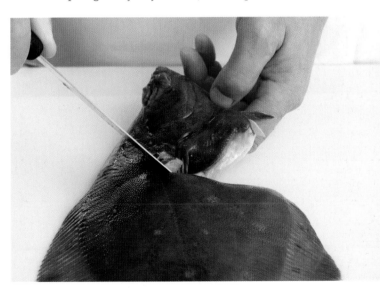

1 Lift the head from the board with your free hand, being careful to tuck your fingers away from the blade. With a sturdy, sharp knife, cut across the fillet where the fish has been gutted.

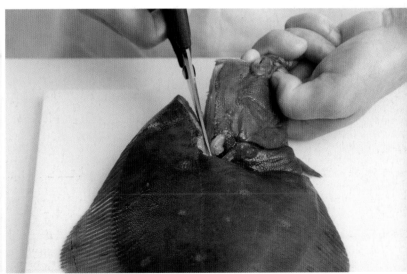

2 Following the natural bone line of the head, mark the flesh by scoring with a knife close to the bone. Using sturdy scissors, snip through the fish, following the guide mark, to remove the head.

Cutting two fillets

Fillets are great for pan-frying, roasting, baking, grilling, steaming, or barbecuing. Remember that flat fish fillets are thin and delicate and can overcook easily. When filleting small flat fish, use this technique of "cross-cut" – or double – filleting, to transform the fillets into more substantial portions. A lemon sole is shown here.

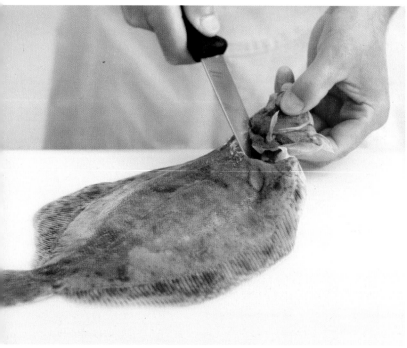

1 Remove the head. Lift it with your hand, and score around it with a sharp knife close to the head, for minimum wastage. Using the scoring mark as a guide, cut the head off with sturdy scissors.

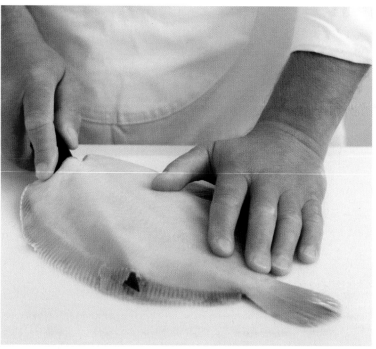

2 Turn the fish over. Insert a long, flexible filleting knife between flesh and one side of the backbone in the centre of the fish, keeping it close to the bone. With a sawing action, cut to the edge of the fillet.

3 Holding the released fillet gently with one hand, run the knife in a long, sweeping action from the tail to the head, until you come into contact with the backbone.

4 Release the fillet at the backbone. Continue to use a long, stroking action with the knife, to release the fillet at the opposite fins. Turn the fish over and repeat on the other side.

Cutting four fillets

This is the easiest technique for filleting flat fish and the most commonly used. There are two key points to remember: first, keep the knife as close to the bone as possible (you should hear the blade "pinging" against the bones); second, use long, sweeping strokes to prevent damage to the delicate fillet. A turbot is shown here.

1 Using a long, flexible filleting knife, cut down the centre of the fish to the bone, using the whole length of the blade. Work on the dark side first.

2 Using the tip of the knife, release the fillet along the backbone. With long, sweeping strokes, remove the fillet from the bone right to the edge of the fish.

3 Repeat on the second half of the dark side. Turn the fish over, and remove the two fillets from the white side in the same way.

Steaking a flat fish

Steaks are an easy way to get the most from a large flat fish. Each has a small piece of bone in the middle, so the flesh retains moisture and will easily lift from the bone once cooked. Using a heavy mallet to push the blade through the central bone prevents damage to the delicate flesh. Wipe the blade between cuts. A turbot is shown here.

1 Trim the fish and, using a sharp, sturdy knife, remove the head (see page 273). Remove the bloodline (see page 272).

2 Split the fish with a sharp, sturdy steaking knife down both sides of the backbone. Rinse the cavity briefly to remove traces of blood.

3 Score the fish into steaks using the tip of the knife, then cut them out. A mallet will help to push the knife through the bone.

Skinning and boning sole

This technique is almost impossible to do well with very fresh fish because the skin will not separate easily from the flesh, which will tear. So choose a fish that is a few days old and can "kiss its tail" (where the fish can be bent so its mouth reaches its tail), as it will be far easier to skin, and the flesh will be firmer and tastier.

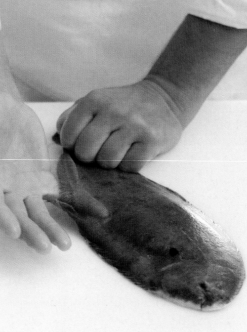

1 Cut the skin from the flesh at the tail, with a sharp, slim knife. Peel back 2.5cm (1in) of skin. You may need to grip it with a cloth.

2 Insert a finger under the skin at the edge of a fillet and gently but firmly run it up to the head. Repeat with all four fillets.

3 Grasp the skin firmly in one hand (use a cloth if it is slippery), and pull the skin towards the head slowly to avoid ripping the flesh.

4 Cut down the middle of the fish with a filleting knife. Cut the fillets away with long, sweeping strokes. Turn the fish and repeat.

5 Using sturdy scissors, and keeping close to the edge of the fillet, cut the main bone from the fish. It can be used for fish stock (see page 310).

The boneless sole can be reassembled simply by folding back the bottom and top fillets. It will be very quick to cook, but take care not to dry it out.

Skinning and filleting a skate wing

Skate "wings" are the large fins of various species of ray. The rest of the body is usually discarded, except the round, tasty skate "knobs", found just behind the wings, which are similar to scallops in shape and sweetness. The skin of these cartilaginous fish can be rough so, to protect your hands, you may prefer to use a cloth when removing skin.

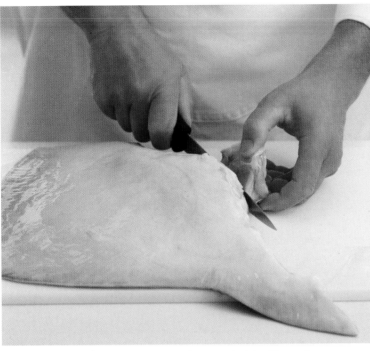

1 Cut the bony "knuckle" off at the thickest end of the fillet, using a chef's knife. This makes it far easier to see where the top of the cartilage begins, so making it simpler to fillet.

2 Trim the edges of the skate with a sharp, heavy knife, or with sturdy scissors. Insert a sharp, slim filleting knife between the top of the fillet and the skin, and move the knife across the flesh to the edge.

3 To remove the skin completely, move the knife to the thickest part of the wing. Using a sweeping action and cutting away from yourself, sweep the knife across the fillet to the edge to release the skin.

4 Starting at the thickest part, insert the tip of the knife between the flesh and the central cartilage. Release the fillet, keeping the knife close to the cartilage and using a long, sweeping action. Turn, and repeat.

Preparing shellfish

Cleaning and de-bearding mussels

Mussels need more preparation than other bivalve molluscs. If dredged, they have a coating of barnacles that you need to scrape off with a knife. The byssus thread ("beard") needs to be removed, too. Prepare mussels just before cooking. If you need to prepare them earlier, always check when ready to cook that the shells will still close.

1 Scrub the mussels with a stiff brush under cold running water, to remove any stubborn grit, sand, or seaweed, that will spoil the finished dish. Check each mussel for signs of life (see box, facing page).

2 Remove the hairy "beard" from each mussel, by pulling it away sharply with your fingers, and discard. If it is thin, grasp it close to the mussel shell, to prevent it from snapping in two.

Opening oysters

Despite their reputation, oysters are easy to open, or "shuck", if you use a good, firm oyster knife. Oysters are traditionally served in the half shell and should be enjoyed straight away, either cooked or simply raw. You can open them from the round end, too, using a type of pincer that cracks the shell easily, but shards of shell may break off.

1 Hold the oyster firmly in a thick cloth to protect your hand. Insert the tip of an oyster knife at the hinge end of the oyster. Twist the knife to get a good hold in the shell, release pressure, and prise off the top shell.

2 Discard any chips of the shell that have fallen inside the oyster. Run the knife under the oyster to release it from the shell, taking care not to spill any of the juices.

Opening clams

Clams are most often served raw or cooked (steamed or baked) directly in the shell. Served from the shell they are as easy to eat as mussels. If you want to eat raw clams, or if you're removing the meat to make chowders or stuffings, you need to prise the shell apart. Check the shell is tightly closed before doing this; if not, discard the clam.

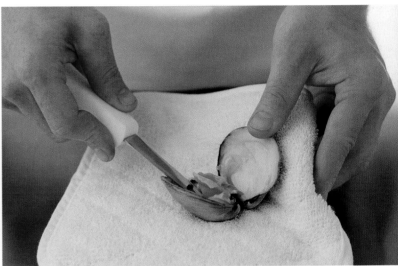

1 Hold the clam in a thick cloth to protect your hands. Insert the tip of a narrow, pointed oyster knife into the shell, opposite the hinge. Twist the knife to separate the shells.

2 Once prised open, pull back the top shell, and carefully release the clam from the bottom shell using the tip of the knife, trying to ensure that you do not cut into the flesh.

Opening razor clams

Razor clams are often steamed or grilled in their shells, but the delicate meat is also excellent raw in a ceviche. Like all bivalves, they must be alive at the time of shelling.

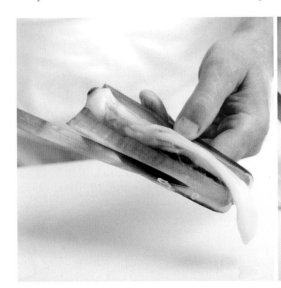

1 Run a sharp, thin-bladed knife along the shell opening and prise the clam apart with your thumb. Take care, as the shell is sharp.

2 Remove the clam from the shell and separate the white muscle from the intestine. The muscle can be either thinly sliced or left whole for cooking.

Opening scallops

Once the scallop is removed, both parts of the shell (valves) can be boiled for a few minutes and used as a container in which to cook the scallop. You can grill scallops on the rounded shell or seal the two shells together with pastry and either bake or barbecue. Lightly rinsed, both roe and muscle can be cooked: pan-fry, poach, barbecue, or grill.

1 With the round shell down, run a sturdy knife around the shell's groove to release it, keeping the knife close to the round shell.

2 Discard the rounded shell, or reserve it for cooking. Use a sharp knife to remove the skirt (or frill), located around the muscle, and discard.

3 Remove the black stomach and intestines. Using the tip of the knife, remove the small sac of mud attached to the thick white muscle.

4 Hold the shell at an angle and cut away the scallop, keeping the knife as close to the shell as possible to minimize waste.

5 Cut away the thick white piece of muscle on the edge of the scallop and discard. This is firmer and can be tough when cooked.

Freshly prepared scallops look luscious when returned to their cooked shell. Simply slice off the roe, if preferred.

Removing whelks and periwinkles from their shells

You can buy whelks and periwinkles live or cooked. To cook them at home, wash them in several changes of water, soak in a little salt water for a few minutes, then boil until cooked. Periwinkles will only take 3–5 minutes, while whelks require 12–15 minutes. Once cooked, they are easy to extract from the shell with a small seafood fork or pin.

Whelks

1 Insert a seafood fork into the meat and gently twist the shell to extract all the meat. Avoid pulling, or some of the meat will be left behind.

2 Peel back the muscle at the top of the whelk to reveal a small piece of tough, inedible meat. Gently pull this away.

Periwinkles

Insert a clean pin into the meat and gently twist it from the shell. Remove the operculum (the horny "foot") before eating.

Opening sea urchins

It is worth wading your way through the prickly shell of a sea urchin to locate the creamy roe (or uni), which has an intensely salty and seaweedy flavour. Serve it raw, poach, or purée to add to a cream-based sauce and serve with grilled fish or pasta. Look out for sea urchins in spring and in autumn when they are in season.

1 Hold the sea urchin in a towel, prickles down, and locate the small hole on the underside. Insert sturdy scissors into this hole and snip around the underside of the sea urchin. Discard the cut-away shell.

2 Using a teaspoon, lift out the orange-coloured sacs of roe, which are attached to the top of the shell, and collect them in a bowl. Take care not to break them, as they are very delicate.

Cleaning and preparing squid

The edible parts of squid are the tube, tentacles, and wings, and they are eaten all over the world. Over high heat, they cook in just seconds, becoming translucent; overcooked they become rubbery. Squid also suits slow and gentle cooking. The texture of slow-cooked squid is wonderfully different from the quick-seared version.

1 Hold the mantle (body) in one hand and gently pull the tentacles away from it to separate them. The eyes, some viscera, and beak (mouth-piece) will come away with the head.

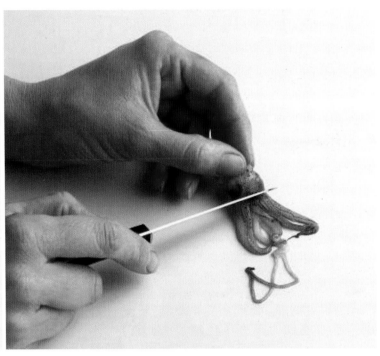

2 Cut the tentacles with a small, sharp knife just below the eyes to separate the viscera and trim the two long arms level with the remaining tentacles. Discard the head, beak, eyes, and viscera.

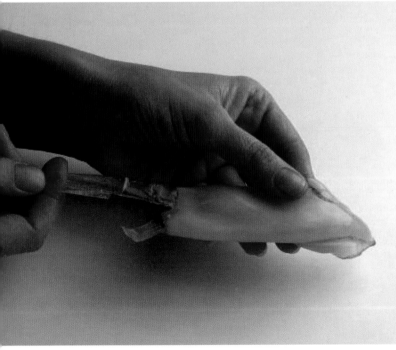

3 Locate the hard quill attached to the inside of the mantle and pull it away. Pinch the two fins (wings) together and pull away, with the purple membrane. Pull the membrane from the wings and discard.

4 Leave the tube whole for stuffing, cut into rings for deep-frying, or open flat (as shown), and lightly score with a sharp knife. This enables heat to travel quickly to the centre and prevents overcooking.

Cleaning and preparing cuttlefish

Once skinned of its thick membrane, a cuttlefish's white flesh can be opened out flat and scored in the same way as squid. Either cook it as a whole "steak" or slice it very thinly and flash-fry, poach, or deep-fry. The tentacles are often very tough and don't respond well to quick methods of cooking, but are best casseroled or braised.

1 Insert your hand inside the head, gently grasp the viscera, and pull away with the tentacles. Avoid breaking the pearly-grey ink sac, as the ink will stain. You can use the ink to flavour and colour many dishes.

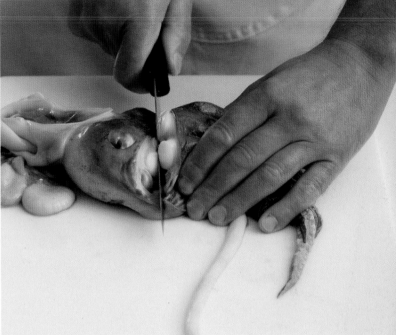

2 Cut the head away from the tentacles below the eyes with a sturdy, sharp knife, and discard, then cut off and discard the hard beak from the middle of the tentacles. Trim the two long arms level.

3 Nick the membrane, stand the cuttlefish head upright, and press down firmly to release the internal shell, peeling back the outer skin. It should come out cleanly. Discard the shell.

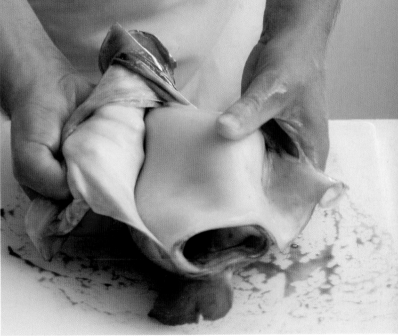

4 Peel away the thick, inedible membrane from the body by virtually turning it inside out. Discard the membrane and prepare the flesh for cooking as for squid tubes (see facing page).

Cleaning and preparing octopus

Unlike squid and cuttlefish, octopus has no internal shell (quill). Baby octopus can be simply fried and served whole. Larger specimens are better suited to longer methods of cooking; although the head can cook quickly, the tentacles need to be slow-cooked to become tender. Octopus makes a wonderful rich stew when cooked in its own ink.

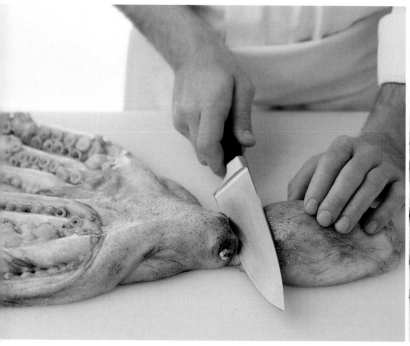

1 With a sharp, heavy chef's knife, cut the head from the body above the eye. The head can be opened out, gutted, skinned of its membrane, and cooked along with the tentacles.

2 Remove the beak (mouth-piece) from the centre of the tentacles, using a small, sharp knife. Wash the tentacles thoroughly in two or three changes of water to remove any traces of mud or grit.

3 Cut off the individual tentacles and – for a larger octopus – cut the tentacles into short sections, or leave them whole until after cooking (see box, right). Trim off and discard the hard parts of the suction pads.

Tenderizing octopus

To cook a large octopus, you have to tenderize it by very slowly simmering in a court bouillon (see page 302), adding enough water to cover the octopus, and simmering gently in a very large saucepan for 15 minutes.

Weigh the cleaned octopus. Add the octopus to the pan, return the liquid to the boil, reduce the heat, and gently simmer for about 50 minutes for an octopus weighing less than 1.5kg (3lb 3oz). A larger octopus may take longer; simmer until tender. Leave in the liquid until completely cool.

Remove the octopus from the liquid, and drain on kitchen paper. Cut into chunks, and dress with olive oil, lemon juice, and white wine vinegar. Frozen octopus will have been further tenderized by freezing.

Cleaning and preparing prawns

All prawns have a black intestinal vein, which should be discarded, without removing the shell if need be. If the prawn is to be grilled or barbecued, leave the shell on to protect it from the heat. Opening the prawn out across its back is called butterflying. In farmed prawns, often the intestinal vein is so insignificant it is invisible so will not need to be removed, but always check. The same technique can be used for Dublin Bay prawns.

Peeling and deveining

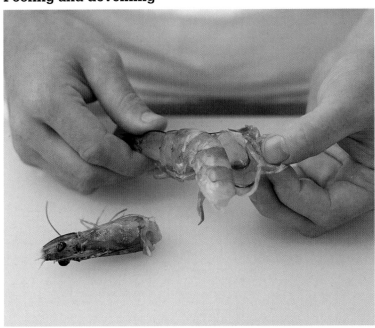

1 Pull the head from the prawn, then carefully peel away the shell, starting from the underside, without damaging the flesh. Both head and shell can be used for stock. Leave the tail on, if preferred.

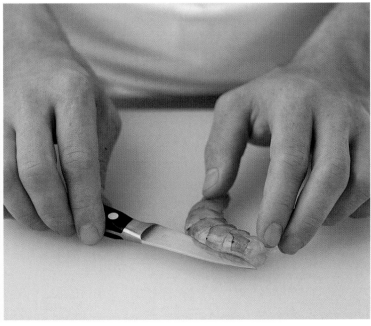

2 To remove the vein, lay the prawn flat and, using a small, sharp knife, make an incision down the back of the prawn a few millimetres deep. Pull out the black vein.

Deveining without cutting

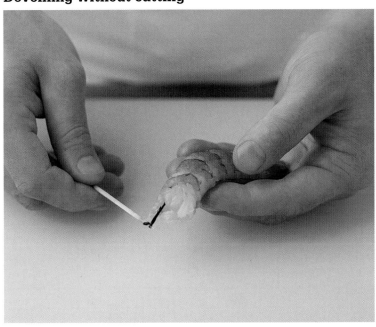

You will see the beginning of the black vein where the head once was. Using a cocktail stick, stab the vein and very gently pull it out, to avoid it breaking and remaining inside the prawn.

Butterflying

To butterfly a prawn, make a deep cut into the back three-quarters of the way through to the belly, using a small, sharp knife. The prawn will open up attractively during cooking.

Picking cooked crayfish

Crayfish and other similar crustaceans – including slipper lobsters and Dublin Bay prawns – are most often served directly in the shell with a finger bowl of hot water and lemon. They are boiled in a court bouillon, fish stock, or salted water for 6–8 minutes. The heat-sensitive pigment in the shell turns them an intense colour.

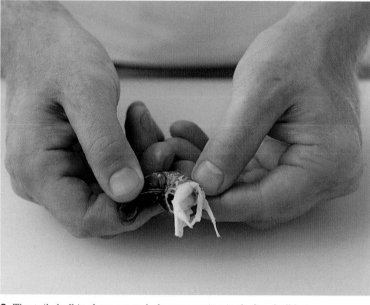

1 Twist the head away from the body shell and remove. In the head of all crustaceans there are sweet juices and trimmings of meat that can be extracted with a small teaspoon.

2 The tail shell is sharp so, to help remove it, pinch the shell between your thumb and index finger until it snaps. Peel it away carefully to prevent tearing the meat.

Cleaning a live soft-shelled crab

All crabs moult their hard shell (carapace) at various stages of their life, enabling the main body to grow. It is at this stage that they are called "soft-shelled". The whole crab is eaten and the slightly crunchy carapace is particularly good. When using a live crab, chill it in the freezer for at least an hour before preparing, to render it dormant.

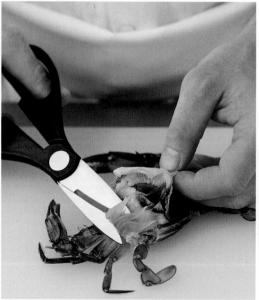

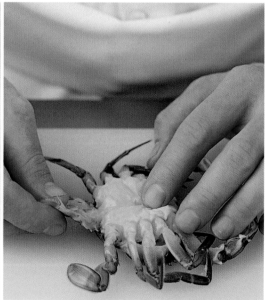

1 Using sturdy kitchen scissors, cut across the front of the crab to remove the eyes and mouth, and discard.

2 Pull back the soft carapace to reveal the gills (dead man's fingers), snip these away, and discard. There are around four gills each side of the body.

3 Turn the crab on to its back and pull away the tail flap (apron). The guts should come out with the apron. The crab is now ready to cook.

Cleaning a live crab

Crabs that have not moulted their hard carapace can be slightly more tricky to clean. When using a live crab, chill it in the freezer for at least an hour before preparing, to render it dormant. It is unsafe to cook a dead crab unless you know exactly when it died. Once dormant, a crab is much easier to prepare than you might imagine.

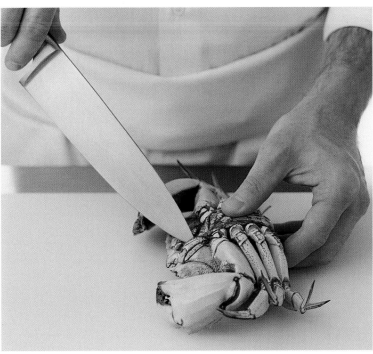

1 Lay the dormant crab on its back. With a very sturdy, sharp knife, pierce the crab firmly through the mouth, between and below the eyes, bringing the knife sharply down to the board.

2 Lift up and pull off the triangular tail flap (apron). Hen crabs have rounded aprons; the male apron is long and thin. It is useful to know if you have a hen, so you can watch out for any roe (a delicacy) later.

3 Turn the crab on to its front. At the head end, firmly press down on the shell, then pull the shell up and away from the legs and body.

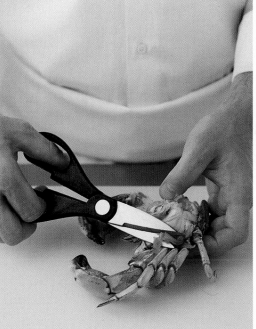

4 With sturdy scissors, trim off the gills (dead man's fingers) from the body. Locate and discard the spongy bag (the stomach) behind the eyes.

5 With a very sturdy, sharp knife, cut the crab body into halves or quarters, depending on size and the cooking method.

Removing the meat from a cooked crab

Whatever the species of crab, the same parts need to be located and removed during the "dressing" process. As the meat is pre-cooked (see box, facing page), any reheating needs to be done with care to prevent losing the sweet flavour. Collect the white and brown meat in separate bowls and return to the cleaned shell to enjoy as a dressed crab.

1 Lay the crab on its back on a chopping board and firmly grip a claw. Twist it away from the main body cleanly and forcefully. Repeat with the other claw, and with the legs. Set aside.

2 Set your thumbs between the carapace and main body at the head of the crab. Firmly lever the main body away from the carapace. It should come away cleanly in one piece. Pull away the apron (tail) from the body.

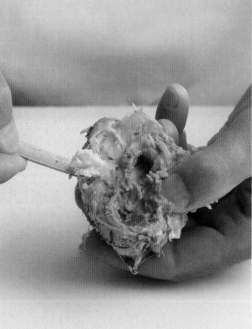

3 Pull away the gills (dead man's fingers) from the main body and discard any that have been left behind in the carapace.

4 Cut the main body into halves or quarters. Using the back of a small teaspoon or a seafood fork, pick the white meat from the body chambers.

5 Gently press the mouth shell down to break it from the carapace. Pull away the mouth and the stomach sac should come with it.

6 Position a large, sharp knife on the groove on the underside of the carapace and carefully crack the edges. Remove the excess shell.

7 Scoop out the brown meat from the carapace with a teaspoon. Watch out for buttery tomalley (liver) or yellow roe, as they are both delicacies.

8 Use the back of a heavy knife to crack the legs at their narrowest point. Pick away the white meat with a seafood fork.

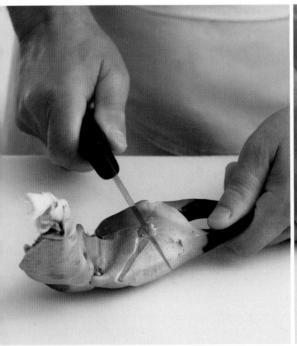

9 Crack the claws using a heavy implement, or claw crackers. Take care not to use too much force, as this will damage the delicate meat.

10 Remove the piece of thick cartilage from the claws with your fingers and extract the white meat with a seafood fork.

Boiling crab

Boil the crab for 15 minutes per 500g (1lb 2oz) in a very large saucepan with enough heavily salted water or court bouillon (see page 302) to cover. Ensure the liquid is rapidly boiling when you add the crab and start timing when the liquid returns to the boil. Large crabs may take slightly longer to cook, as they have a thicker carapace.

Once cooked, if the crab is to be eaten cold it should be cooled rapidly, not only for safety reasons but also to help the meat draw away from the shell, making it easier to remove. Place the cooked crab in the bottom of the refrigerator, well away from other perishables.

Preparing shellfish | **289**

Preparing a live lobster for grilling

For grilling, use a raw lobster. Re-heating cooked lobster toughens and dries the meat and it loses flavour. When using a live lobster, chill it in the freezer for at least an hour before preparing, to render it dormant. It is unsafe to cook a dead lobster unless you know exactly when it died. This is one of the techniques for suitable for Lobster Thermidor.

1 Place the dormant lobster on a chopping board and hold the tail with one hand. Using a large, heavy chef's knife, cut down the centre of the head shell to cut it in half. For a better grip, secure the tail with a cloth.

2 Turn the lobster around and split the tail shell right to the bottom, keeping the knife in as straight a line as possible, so that the lobster is cut in half evenly.

3 Locate the intestine that runs along the back, and remove. In the centre of a female lobster, there will be a dark green roe. The pale green-brown tomalley (the liver) can also be left in place, and grilled.

4 Remove the stomach sac, situated behind the eyes. It is not necessary to remove the gills. These are located close to the carapace and you'd need to remove the upper part of the shell to dislodge them.

Removing the meat from a cooked lobster

Unlike crab, a lobster contains essentially only white meat, found in the tail and the claws. If purchasing a boiled lobster, you need to make sure it was cooked when fresh. Pull open the tail shell: it should snap back into position. If the shell stays floppy, it indicates that the lobster has been dead for some time prior to cooking, and should be avoided.

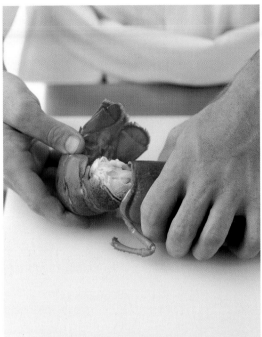

1 Twist the tail away from the main carapace. The carapace can be used for stock, but scoop out any greyish-green tomalley (the liver) first.

2 Using sturdy kitchen scissors, cut open the tough tail shell on the underside, being careful of your fingers as it is sharp.

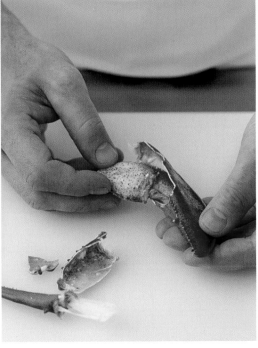

3 Open up the shell and carefully extract the meat in one piece. Remove the dark intestine, which runs along the back of the tail meat.

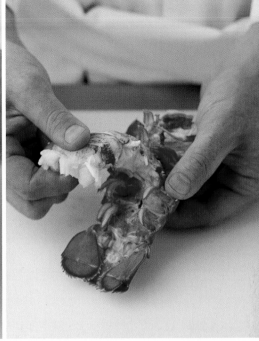

4 Using a heavy implement, or claw crackers, split the claws. Take care not to use too much force, as this will damage the delicate meat.

5 Open the claws and extract the meat carefully from the shell, removing the piece of thick cartilage. Locate any shards of shell and discard.

Boiling lobster

Boil the lobster for 10–12 minutes per 500g (1lb 2oz) in a very large saucepan with enough heavily salted water or court bouillon (see page 302) to cover. Ensure the liquid is rapidly boiling when you add the lobster and start timing when the liquid returns to the boil. Large lobsters have thicker shells and may need longer in the boiling pot.

Leave the lobster to cool rapidly in the refrigerator once cooked.

Sushi techniques

Slicing fish fillets

Always use supremely fresh fish that has been commercially frozen specifically for sushi and sashimi. Freezing kills parasites that are present in raw fish. Oil-rich species, such as mackerel and tuna, are sliced slightly thicker than other fish used for sushi, such as lemon sole, snapper, and sea bass, because they have a softer texture. When preparing salmon, remove the dark muscle close to the skin. Use a long, flexible sashimi knife or a very sharp smoked salmon knife.

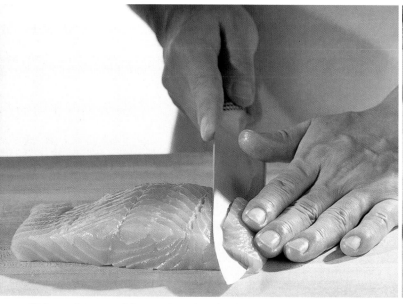

Using a long stroking action, slice the fillet into 5mm (¼in) slices on the angle through the bias (diagonally). Don't apply too much pressure or the flesh will tear. These are ideal for Nigiri Sushi (see page 48).

Slice a fillet into slices (see left), then slice again into even 1cm (½in) wide sticks using the tip of the knife. These are ideal to place inside Nori Maki Sushi (see page 48).

Make wafer-thin 3mm (⅛in) cuts across the top of the fillet, keeping the blade parallel to the board. Drape over Nori Maki Sushi, or scatter into Chirashi Sushi (see pages 48–51).

Cut the trimmed fillet into even slices, each about 1cm (½in) thick. Use the slices to top Nigiri Sushi, scatter into Chirashi Sushi, or use for Sashimi (see pages 48–53).

Preparing fish steaks

Steaks require boning and skinning before using for sushi and sashimi. Trim away any fatty tissue from the boned and skinned steaks to form a neat block. Cut the block into slices of around 1cm (½in) to use in Chirashi and Nigiri Sushi, or Sashimi, (see pages 48–53). Cut these strips in half again to form small finger-sized strips, useful for all rolled sushi, such as Nori Maki Sushi (see page 48). A salmon steak is shown here.

1 Lay the steak on its side and slice it in half: work the knife into the steak just under the main backbone and through the other side. Keep the blade flat, and avoid too much pressure on the blade in case it slips.

2 Turn the fish over and make a second cut underneath the backbone in one action, you will feel the knife cut through pinbones. Remove the pinbones and skin the fish as necessary (see page 271).

Sushi rice

Make fresh rice to accompany sushi and serve it at room temperature. For best results use a rice cooker, but this method also works well. This recipe makes enough for 10 sushi rolls.

1 Put 600g (1lb 5oz) Japanese short-grain sushi rice in a sieve and lower it into cold water, rinse thoroughly, and discard the water. Repeat until the water runs clear.

2 Put the rice and 660ml (1 pint 2fl oz) water in a very heavy saucepan or casserole. Add 2 small strips of kombu (dried seaweed) and cover with a tight-fitting lid. Slowly bring to a boil and, once bubbling, reduce the heat and simmer for 11–12 minutes. Remove from the heat, leaving the lid on, and leave to steam for 10 minutes. Remove the kombu.

3 Put 8 tbsp Japanese rice vinegar, 4 tbsp sugar, and 1 tsp salt into a saucepan, and heat slowly until the grains have dissolved.

4 Turn the rice on to a large shallow dish or plastic tray. Drizzle the warmed vinegar mixture over and turn to coat until all the grains look glossy. Fan the rice as you go (ideally with an electric fan). Once cool, it is ready to use.

Turn the rice with a wooden spatula to make sure it is evenly coated with the vinegar mixture. Try to keep the rice quite thin so it cools quickly.

Curing fish fillets for sushi

Small fish fillets with a high oil content and soft flesh, such as mackerel (shown here), benefit from marinating before use in sushi. The fish is salted, then marinated briefly in rice wine vinegar, firming up the flesh and creating an added dimension to the taste. It is excellent used to top Nigiri Sushi (see page 48).

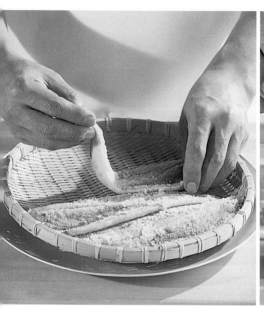

1 Place 4 mackerel fillets in a bowl and rub with 8 tbsp coarse sea salt. Arrange in a bamboo strainer. Leave for 30 minutes.

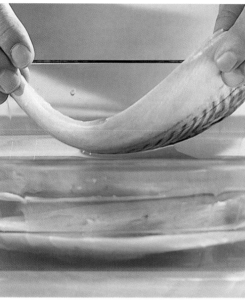

2 Rinse the fillets and pat dry. Submerge them in 500ml (16fl oz) rice wine vinegar mixed with 2 tbsp mirin, and 2 tsp salt, and marinate for 1–2 hours.

3 Remove the fillets from the vinegar and pat dry. Slowly peel off the papery thin outer skin. Place the fillets on a board, and pinbone (see page 271).

Tenderizing skin

The skin of some species, such as snapper (shown here), sea bass, and bream, is tough and difficult to remove even after scaling. This technique is very quick, so it is important to have boiling water and a bath of iced water to hand. The blanching can start to cook the flesh if it isn't chilled and refreshed immediately after contact with boiling water.

1 Arrange a scaled and pinboned fillet, skin side upwards, on an upturned bamboo strainer set over a shallow dish.

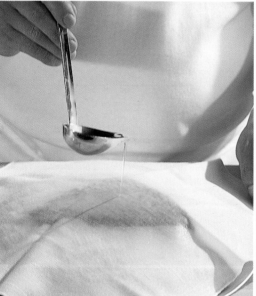

2 Cover the fillet with muslin or a tea-towel. Using a ladle, splash a small amount of boiling water on to the skin.

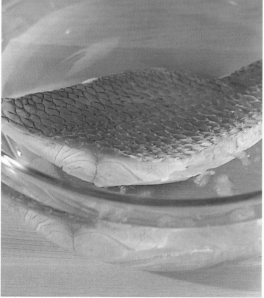

3 Immediately remove the muslin and lower the fish into the ice bath. Drain, pat dry, and proceed to slice as preferred (see page 292).

Preparing prawns for sushi

Large warm water prawns are hugely popular in Japan for use in sushi, sashimi, and tempura. They do require cooking, unlike many other species. For Nigiri Sushi, or whenever the prawn is to be presented flat, they need preparation before cooking to prevent them curling into their natural shape during the initial poaching.

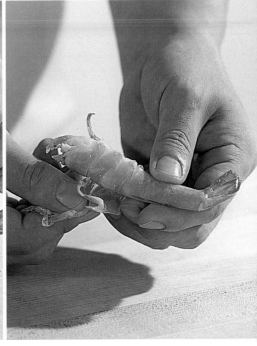

1 Insert a wooden skewer through the centre of a raw prawn to hold it flat. Put into a large saucepan. Pour over boiling water and poach for 2–3 minutes.

2 Carefully pull away the head of the prawn, keeping the tail flesh intact, and discard, or use to make fish stock (see page 310).

3 Starting on the underside of the prawn, peel the body shell away. Some chefs prefer to leave the tail shell in place.

4 Lay the prawn flat on its back and make a neat incision along the centre, nearly through to the back, enough to show any digestive tract.

5 Remove the digestive tract with a cocktail stick or your fingers, being firm but careful that it does not break, and discard.

6 If the tail shell has been left on, trim it to make a neat "V". Japanese food is all about attention to detail.

Preserving

Curing in salt

Gravadlax, which means "buried salmon" in Swedish, is a classic recipe. Salmon is swathed in a blanket of salt, dill, and sugar that draws out moisture. You can also use sea bass and trout. The curing takes 48 hours and leaves the fish firm. Serve with a sweet dill mustard sauce. Refrigerate and eat within 3–4 days, or freeze for up to 2 months.

1 Combine 85g (3oz) caster sugar, 30g (1oz) chopped dill, 1 tbsp lemon juice, 75g (2½oz) fine sea salt, and 1 tsp freshly ground black pepper in a small bowl. Mix all the ingredients together well.

2 Lay one thick, scaled and pinboned fillet of salmon (approx 500g/1lb 2oz), skin side down, in a clean, non-metallic shallow dish or tray. Spread all the curing mix evenly over the whole fillet.

3 Place another fillet on top. Wrap tightly in cling film and weigh them down with a plate and cans of food. Refrigerate for 48 hours.

4 Turn the fish every 12 hours to compress each side, and to drain the fluid so the fillets firm up. Remove, unwrap, and pat dry with kitchen paper.

Use a sharp knife to slice the salmon at an angle from the tail end into thin slices, discarding the skin.

Curing in vinegar

Pickling fish in vinegar, or citrus, in effect "cooks" the flesh and dissolves tiny bones. Here, vinegar is used to make classic rollmop herrings. Seafood Ceviche (see page 60) uses citrus as the pickling element. Feel free to experiment with either recipe, making the flavourings as mild or as sharp as you want, using your favourite spices.

1 Put 175g (6oz) sea salt and 750ml (1¼ pints) water into a pan, bring to a boil, and stir until dissolved. Cool completely. Pour over four scaled and filleted herrings, to submerge. Cover and refrigerate for 24 hours.

2 Put 1 litre (1¾ pints) distilled malt vinegar, 4 black peppercorns, 4 allspice berries, 1 mace blade, 3 bay leaves, and 1 dried chilli into a large saucepan, bring to a boil, then simmer for 5 minutes. Cool.

3 Rinse the herrings and pat dry. Lay on a board, skin side down, and arrange a few fine slices of red onion and a pickled gherkin over the top of each. Roll up and secure with a cocktail stick.

4 Pack the rollmops into a small plastic or glass container, and pour the cold spiced vinegar over to cover. Refrigerate for a minimum of 12 hours, or up to two or three days.

Cooking

Baking

Baking is ideal for fish fillets, some fish steaks (including salmon, snapper, halibut, and turbot), and whole fish. You can bake fish in a paper case, in a salt crust, in banana leaves, and in pastry; all seal in flavour and moisture.

The fish can also be baked with the skin on, skin side up, which protects it from the oven heat. If it's skinned, the fish needs a coating of butter or oil to protect it. Baking is usually done at 180°C (350°F/Gas 4).

Fillets

1 Lay the fish fillets in a lightly buttered ovenproof dish or baking tray. Season with salt, finely ground black pepper, and chopped herbs (optional). Brush with melted butter and place in a preheated oven.

2 Bake for 6–8 minutes, until opaque, and the flakes separate when lightly pressed. Some fish also become a lighter colour once cooked. If the fish still has its skin, it will peel away easily once cooked.

Whole fish

If fish is to take a marinade, slash the sides into the flesh. This allows flavours to penetrate. Place aromatics in the gut cavity and wrap in aluminium foil. Bake until the eye turns white, and, if you press the skin, you can feel the flakes separate.

Baking times

Fish is very quick to bake, but it is hard to give a specific time as the thickness and density of different fish varies so greatly.

Small, low-fat, flaky fillets such as whiting will take just a few minutes to bake, while a thick salmon steak takes up to 12 minutes and a whole sea bass may take 35 minutes. Once cooked, the fish loses translucency, becomes paler in appearance, and the flakes separate easily.

When any fish is cooked, protein comes to the surface: look for a white curd. If you baked the fish with its head on, one of the most reliable signs that it is ready is that the eyes have turned white.

Baking en papillote

Cooking fish in paper produces succulent, moist flesh and, if no oil or butter is used, is low in fat. Use aromatics and vegetables to flavour the fish as you wish. Serve the parcel, still wrapped, to be opened at the table to release all of its wonderful aromas. Make the parcel with greaseproof paper so you can see the fish cook inside. While preparing the fish, preheat the oven to high 230°C (450°F/Gas 8) with a baking sheet placed inside to heat up.

1 Cut out a large heart shape from greaseproof paper, big enough to enclose the fish plus a border. Arrange the fish on sautéed vegetables, or simply add a sprig of herbs and a squeeze of citrus juice.

2 Fold the paper over the top, and pleat the edges tightly to seal, twisting the end. Make sure it is wrapped well, but has space inside so hot air can circulate around the fish in the oven.

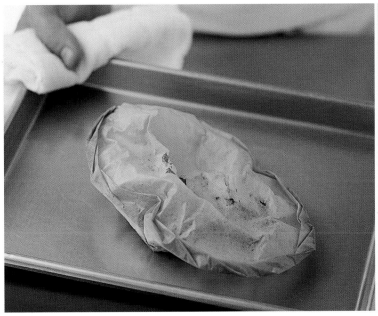

3 Place on the hot baking sheet and bake for 10–15 minutes. Don't open the parcel, but insert a metal skewer through the paper into the fish for 15 seconds. The tip should be piping hot when removed.

4 Lift the parcel on to a serving dish and present it to your guests. They should open the parcel at the table to enjoy the fabulous aroma released with the first breath of steam.

SUSTAINABILITY CHOICE

Buy pot-caught shellfish

This is a relatively unobtrusive fishing method where sturdy pots are placed on the seabed for a few days. The pots are baited with pieces of fish that entice the selected species, such as crab, prawns, and lobster, into the pot through a hole. Once in the pot the creature finds it virtually impossible to escape. This method is very selective and has the advantage that if the shellfish is undersized or carrying roe, it can be returned to the water. Other selective methods of shellfish fishing include diver-caught scallops, where divers search for individual scallops.

Poaching

This gentle method of cooking produces succulent flesh. The fish is submerged in liquid and cooked over low heat, or covered, and oven-poached at 180°C (350°F/Gas 4).

The liquid barely simmers throughout the process, which prevents the fish from breaking up. Skate wings (shown here) are excellent poached, as the fish retains moisture.

1 To make a court bouillon, put 1 litre (1¾ pints) water, 120ml (4fl oz) white wine vinegar, sliced onions and carrots, fresh herbs, and a few black peppercorns into a saucepan. Simmer for 15 minutes.

2 Arrange the fish in a suitable flameproof baking tray or fish kettle. Ladle over enough hot court bouillon to cover the fish. It should be completely submerged, so top up with hot water, if necessary.

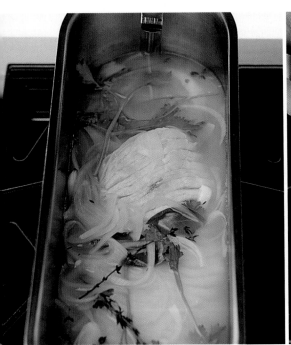

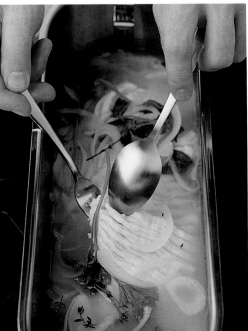

3 Set over a low heat (you may need two hobs). Bring to a boil. Reduce the heat until bubbles blip the surface. Cover, ensuring the liquid doesn't boil.

4 After 10–15 minutes, check the fish is cooked. It will flake easily. (For skate wings, the thick shoulder cartilage will pull away easily).

5 Lift the fish from the liquid and drain. Pat dry. Slide on to a serving dish and spoon over some of the cooking aromatics.

Microwaving

A fish fillet or steak can be cooked in a microwave in a very short time. It cooks in its own juices, just like steamed fish. Don't season with salt, as the flavour becomes intense very easily. The microwaving technique works very well with small fish fillets or steaks, white, textured species, and salmon (shown here).

1 Season the fish with black pepper and place in a microwaveable dish. Brush with oil, add 1–2 tbsp water, cover with cling film and microwave according to the manufacturer's instructions (usually 2–3 minutes).

2 Allow the fish to stand for 1 minute once it is cooked, then remove the cling film, being careful of your hands, as the steam is very hot. Lift on to a serving dish.

Braising

Braising is a mix of steaming and baking. It's best to leave the fish whole or in one large piece, and arrange it on aromatic herbs and vegetables. Add liquid, and cook the dish, covered, at a low temperature (160°C/325°F/Gas 3). Braising is ideal for whole fish including salmon, trout, and skate wings, and for the monkfish tails shown here.

1 Lay sliced vegetables in a large casserole or roasting pan. Cut the vegetables thinly if you are cooking a smaller piece of fish, as they need to cook simultaneously. Add herbs, such as rosemary, sage, or tarragon.

2 Arrange the fish on top and spoon over hot stock just to cover the vegetables. Cover and cook in the oven for 12–15 minutes, or until the centre of the fish is white. Serve with the reduced cooking juices.

Steaming

Steaming is ideal for small fish such as snapper, and for seafood including clams, both shown below. It is a fast, but gentle technique, that is very low in fat. Fish is arranged in a steamer over boiling liquid, or in a saucepan with a very small amount of liquid. You can also use another technique called "indirect steaming", as used in Steamed Trout in Lettuce (see page 229), when the fish is placed in a dish or bowl within a steamer, so it cooks entirely in its own juices.

Shellfish in a pan

1 Pour in enough water to cover the base of a large saucepan with about 0.5cm (¼in) of liquid. Add a splash of lemon juice or wine, and finely chopped aromatic herbs, such as oregano and parsley. Bring to a boil.

2 Add the seafood, cover, and cook over a medium heat until the shells have opened (2–3 minutes). Shake the pan occasionally, and avoid lifting the lid so the steam doesn't escape.

Whole fish in a steamer basket

1 Choose a saucepan or wok with a well-fitting lid. Pour in enough water to come just below the base of the steamer. Add preferred aromatics, such as lemongrass and coriander. Arrange the fish in a steamer basket.

2 Place over a medium heat and bring to a simmer. Place the steamer over the liquid, cover, and keep the liquid at a boil for 7–8 minutes. Don't lift the lid, as this allows the steam to escape.

Making seafood quenelles

A quenelle is a classic fish recipe: a dumpling made with cream and egg white. It is poached in stock or court bouillon. Although whiting and pike are traditional, you can use most fish or seafood. Always use fresh fish, as defrosted fish gives a coarse texture. All the ingredients must be cold. In fact, quenelles are often prepared in a bowl set directly over ice and water, as shown here. Do not overwork the mixture, as the cream may split.

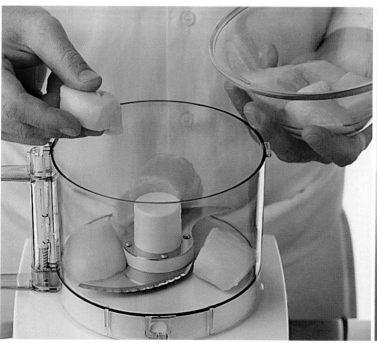

1 Whizz 500g (1lb 2oz) chilled seafood in a food processor until smooth (scallops trimmed of roe are shown here). Chefs use a fine-meshed sieve for this, which is hard work, but does produce a particularly fine result.

2 Put the puréed fish into a glass bowl over a bowl of ice. Start stirring in 600ml (1 pint) cream and then fold in 3 whisked egg whites. Do not overwork, as the mixture can curdle easily.

3 Dip two dessertspoons into hot water, scoop out a spoonful of the mixture, and shape into lozenges, to give three sides to each quenelle. Dip the spoons in hot water after forming each one.

4 Lower the quenelles into simmering water. Initially they sink to the bottom. Once cooked, in about five minutes, the quenelles rise to the surface and feel firm to touch. Serve with a cream or white wine sauce.

Grilling

Fish becomes golden and succulent under the heat of a grill. This technique is great for steaks, fillets, such as the red mullet shown here, and small whole mackerel, and herring. Make sure the grill is red-hot and the rack preheated, and leave the skin on the fish, to protect it. You'll need to turn whole fish halfway through; fillets won't need turning, as they are thin, but it helps to slash the skin. The side you cook last should be uppermost on the plate.

1 Arrange the fish on a pre-heated grill rack, skin side up. Brush generously with seasoned melted butter or oil. Arrange under the grill and cook for 3–4 minutes.

2 Check the fish is cooked: the skin will become loose, and the flesh lose its translucency and become white. Lift on to a serving dish and pour some of the cooking juices over the top.

Barbecuing and char-grilling

This technique is good for many types of robustly textured fish, including tuna, halibut, swordfish, marlin, and salmon, and shellfish, such as squid and scallops (shown here). More delicate fish are not suitable, as they will break easily. Both the barbecue and griddle must be very hot (barbecue coals should be glowing and grey). Fish often benefits from a marinade to prevent it from drying out. You can also brush the fish with oil to stop it sticking to the grill pan or rack.

1 Marinade prepared scallops in oil, herbs, and seasoning. If using citrus, marinate for only 30 minutes, or the texture will change.

2 Thread the scallops on to skewers. This aids in turning the fish. If using wooden skewers, soak in water for 30 minutes first, to prevent scorching.

3 Place on a griddle pan. Turn after 2–3 minutes. Once cooked, scallops will be bar-marked and the fish firm. Drizzle with a splash of lemon to serve.

Hot-smoking

This simple technique imparts a subtle smokey flavour into fish. Use hardwood shavings, such as oak or fruit, and add other aromatics to give flavour. Add a little water or wine to create a moist atmosphere and stop scorching. Small fish, such as rainbow trout (shown here) and mackerel, steaks, thick fillets, and many types of seafood, including prawns and mussels, are ideal for home-smoking. This is best done on a barbecue outside, as the smoke is very invasive.

1 Line a wok that has a well-fitting lid with aluminium foil, being sure to cover the whole inside of the pan, and fold the foil tightly over the sides. Sprinkle over some wood shavings and add a splash of water or wine.

2 When smoking whole fish, score them through the skin nearly to the bone with a sharp knife. This enables the fish to take on all the flavours of the smoke well. Place the fish on a trivet that fits inside the wok.

3 Light the shavings with a long match, splash with water or wine, add the fish, and cover. Seal with a foil collar to trap the smoke, and place over medium heat; whole fish will take 15–18 minutes.

Hot-smoked fish are a glorious golden brown, with a deep, satisfying flavour, and excellent in salads, pies, or mousses.

Deep-frying

There are a few rules for perfect deep-fried fish. It should be coated in batter or breadcrumbs to protect it from the heat. Once cooked, drain on kitchen paper and season with salt. The frying pan must not be more than half-filled with oil. Once the pan is on the heat, keep a lid at hand to cover it, in case of fire. Never leave a deep-fat fryer unattended.

1 Dip the seafood in well-seasoned flour and shake off the excess. Now dip it in beaten egg to coat it evenly.

2 Roll in breadcrumbs. These are often dried and sieved to make sure that they are fine and also that they give an even coating.

3 When the oil reaches 180°C (350°F), add the seafood and cook for about 2 minutes, or until golden brown. Do not overcrowd the pan.

Pan-frying

Small whole fish, fillets, steaks, and some shellfish are ideal for pan-frying. It is not suitable for large fish, as they must fit into the frying pan. The fish can be rolled in seasoned flour, breadcrumbs, or polenta before cooking to create a golden brown jacket. If you're not using a coating, pan-fry the skin first and serve skin-side up.

1 Roll the fish in a coating, ensuring it is evenly covered. If using flour, do this just before frying the fish or it will become soggy.

2 Lower the fish into hot oil, and cook for several minutes until the flesh is opaque (see box, right). Carefully turn with tongs halfway through cooking.

Heating the oil

For deep-frying, the oil must be at the correct temperature, usually 180°C (350°F). If it is too hot, the coating will turn brown before the fish is cooked. If it is too cool, the coating will soak in oil, making it soggy, and the fish will not brown.

If you don't have an oil thermometer, use a cube of bread to test the oil: if it turns golden brown within 60 seconds, it is hot enough. If it browns much more quickly, the oil is too hot; if it does not brown within a minute, it's too cool.

For pan-frying, heat the oil or butter (butter gives an excellent flavour), until hot. When the oil is hot, it expands in the pan and becomes free-running just before it starts to smoke. Butter will foam and sizzle as it melts. When it stops sizzling and begins to brown, it is hot enough.

Pan-frying fish in oil that is too cool stops the fish browning well and can make it pale and unappetizing.

Frying information

Deep-frying

Fish	Cut	Frying time	Coating
Large, flaky fish, such as cod, haddock, coley, pollock, and hake	Fillets	6–8 mins	Breadcrumbs, batter
Small, flaky fish, such as tilapia, sea bass, and river cobbler	Fillets	4–6 mins	Breadcrumbs, polenta, batter
Scallops	Prepared out of the shell; white muscle only	1–2 mins	Tempura batter, breadcrumbs
Tiger prawns	Deveined (with or without shell)	1–2 mins	Tempura batter, breadcrumbs
Squid, small octopus, and cuttlefish	Thin slices	1–2 mins	Tempura batter, breadcrumbs

Pan-frying

Fish	Cut	Frying time	Flavouring
Large, flaky fish, such as, cod, haddock, coley, pollock, salmon, halibut, and turbot	2.5cm (1in) bone-in steaks (large fish only)	3–4 mins per side	Brush with oil. Add dill, or tarragon, capers, and lemon juice at the end of cooking. Treat both steaks and fillets in the same way.
	Fillets	2–3 mins per side	
Small, flaky fish, such as sea bass, bream, snapper, carp, gurnard, and John Dory	Fillets	3–5 mins per side	Roll in seasoned flour or brush with oil. Finish with herb butter, soy sauce, sesame oil, and rice wine or citrus juice.
	Small, whole, gutted fish	3–5 mins per side (adjust depending on size of fish)	Slash the fish, roll in flour or brush with oil. Finish with citrus juice, fish sauce, soy sauce, and rice wine.
Firm-textured fish, such as tuna, swordfish, and mahi mahi	2.5cm (1in) boneless steak	2–4 mins per side. Thicker steaks and denser textured fish will require longer	Brush with seasoned oil. Deglaze the pan after cooking with soy sauce, sesame oil, and rice wine or sherry.
Flat fish, such as sole, plaice, and flounder	Skinned fillets	30 secs–1 min per side	Roll in seasoned flour. Deglaze the pan after cooking with lemon, parsley, and capers.
Small oil-rich fish, such as trout, mackerel, anchovies, sardines, and herring	Small, whole, gutted fish	3–5 mins per side (adjust depending on size of fish)	Roll in seasoned flour. Deglaze the pan after cooking with lemon, parsley, capers, and add flaked or chopped nuts.
Skate and rays	Wing	4–6 mins per side (adjust depending on size of fish)	Roll in seasoned flour. Wipe pan clean after cooking and add extra butter, heat until it turns brown or nutty, and add capers, lemon, and parsley.
Scallops	Prepared out of the shell. Cook the roe separately, as it "pops" or bursts easily, over a high heat	30 secs–1 min per side	Roll in seasoned flour or brush with oil. Finish with citrus juice, or soy or Worcestershire sauces.
Tiger prawns	Deveined (with or without shell)	In the shell: 2–3 mins per side. Shelled: 1–2 mins per side	Brush with oil or dust in dry spice mix. Finish with citrus juice, soy sauce, or rice wine vinegar.
Squid, small octopus, and cuttlefish	Thin slices	30 secs–3 mins, or until opaque	Brush with oil and seasoning or dust with cornflour. Finish with sesame oil, citrus juice, soy sauce, or fish sauce.

Making fish stock

Homemade fish stock is far better than shop-bought, and freezes well. You can make a basic stock with the raw bones of white, non-oily fish. Classically, the bones of flat fish are used, but salmon (shown here) makes excellent stock. Shellfish stock requires raw prawn shells, or cooked crab or lobster shells. Reduce stock by rapid boiling after straining, to intensify the flavour. Stock will keep in the refrigerator for a few days, or freeze for up to 3 months.

1 Break the fish frames (bones with fillets removed) into pieces. If using fish heads, remove the gills and rinse well to wash off any traces of blood, which will make the stock bitter.

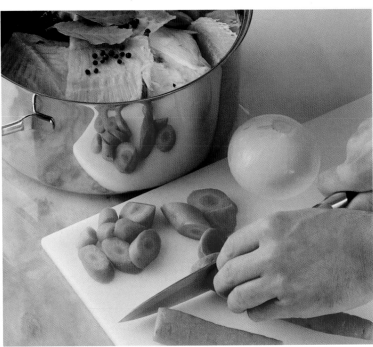

2 Add a balanced selection of sliced root vegetables, such as onion, carrot, leek, and celery, and bay leaves, parsley stalks, and thyme, and peppercorns. Don't add salt, as the flavour will intensify during cooking.

3 Cover the ingredients with cold water and bring to a boil, then use a skimmer or flat spoon to remove the scum from the surface (this is just fat and impurities that need to be removed).

4 Reduce the heat and allow the stock to simmer for 25–30 minutes. Do not boil. Remove the stock from the heat and allow it to cool for a few minutes before straining.

Serving whole cooked fish

Serving fillets is easy, but a whole fish is more challenging. If serving a large fish to more than one person, you'll need to remove the flesh to share. Fillets can be removed just as cleanly from a cooked fish as they can from a raw fish. If the fish is skinned before cooking, remove the fillets in the same way as the technique below. Don't forget to remove the delicious morsels of flesh located inside and just behind the head. Red snapper and Dover sole are shown here.

Round fish

1 Remove any untrimmed fins and gently peel away the skin; discard. If the skin won't peel away easily, it could indicate that the fish isn't quite cooked. Return the fish to the oven and cook for a few minutes more.

2 Run a table knife along the centre of the fish to separate the two fillets, then slide it under to lift them off. Snip the backbone at the head with scissors, then lift the bone free to reveal the fillets beneath.

Flat fish

1 Run a table knife around the edge of the fillet and firmly push away the loose fin bones. Slide the knife under the fillet, above the rib cage, and lift it away from the bone.

2 Pull the bone away. This should be easy, as the flesh releases from the bone once it is cooked. The head should also come away with the bone. Push away any fin bones from the bottom fillet, and serve.

FISH GALLERY

Cod _Gadidae_

Fished throughout the cold waters of the Atlantic, Pacific, and Arctic oceans by both line and trawl, cod is one of the most important commercial fish in the Northern Hemisphere. Members of the cod or Gadidae family can be identified by a distinct three-fin-dorsal pattern. They are white fish, with the main concentration of oil being found in the liver, so the flesh is low in fat. The flesh colour varies, but cod is renowned for having well-flavoured flesh that, when cooked, offers succulent and sweet flakes.

SUSTAINABILITY Cod, especially Arctic cod, is endangered in some parts of the world. For many members of this group there is a maximum catch quota in place and landed fish must be of a minimum size to preserve stocks. Sustainability issues are a cause for concern, so cod farming has recently begun to develop as an industry. The following fish are good alternatives to cod: haddock, pollock, coley, whiting,

and pouting. Pacific cod is a suitable alternative to Arctic cod.

CUTS Whole (gutted, with head on or off), fillets, steaks; Atlantic cod: head, cheek, tongue, roe, liver, swim bladder/"sounds".

EAT Cooked: Deep-fry or pan-fry in batter or breadcrumbs, bake, poach in stock or milk, use chopped flesh for soup or chowder, grill fillets or whole fish. **Preserved:** Cold smoked (dyed and undyed), salted, dried.

FLAVOUR PAIRINGS Dill, parsley, bay leaf, lemon, olive oil, tomatoes, olives, capers, garlic, breadcrumbs, butter.

CLASSIC RECIPES Deep-fried fish and chips; brandade de morue; taramasalata; cod in parsley sauce.

Poor cod ▶
Trisopterus minutus capelanus
Also known as pelan, poor cod can grow to 40cm (16in) and is fished commercially across the Eastern Atlantic as far as the Atlantic coast in the Mediterranean. It is popular in southern Europe. Much like whiting, it is soft, white, and delicate, with a low fat content. Good pan-fried, steamed, or baked.

Look out for the three-fin dorsal pattern that is typical of the Gadidae family.

This fish is distinguished by an olive-green skin and yellow freckling with a white lateral line.

Atlantic cod has white flesh with a firm texture that chunks and flakes well.

Atlantic cod ▲
Gadus morhua
Also known as codling, sprag, or scrod, Atlantic cod is one of the largest members of the Gadidae family. It is identified by a white lateral line, green-yellow marbled skin that fades to white on the belly, and a square tail. This species can grow to 1.5m (5ft). Atlantic cod is fished extensively by North America, many European countries, and Scandinavia. This fish has white, chunky flakes with a sweet seafood taste. Commonly used deep-fried in fish and chips, but excellent poached for fish pie or baked with a crust.

Firm, sweet, and well flavoured, Pacific cod is a popular fish for cooking.

Belly flaps are often trimmed away from large members of the cod group and sold separately for use in fish pies and fishcakes.

Pacific cod
Gadus macrocephalus

Also known as Alaskan cod, grey cod, true cod, or treska brown, Pacific cod has dark mottled skin and a pale belly. It can grow to over 2m (6ft 6in) and is found in the North Pacific and Pacific Rim. It is fished by the US, China, Japan, Canada, and Korea, is exported to Europe, and is enjoyed in North and South America and the Caribbean. Excellent for fish and chips, poaching, and grilling. Pacific cod is a good alternative to Arctic cod, which has been heavily over-fished.

Coley *Gadidae*

The cheeks, considered a delicacy, are sold ready prepared and can be poached or fried.

Coley is also known as saithe, coalfish, black cod, green cod, and sometimes as pollock in the US. This key member of the cod family is considered an inexpensive alternative to cod but for many years has been viewed as good only for cat food, as it is only palatable if eaten very fresh. Young fish live in the top layers of the sea and swim deeper as they mature. Coley is caught in the Northern Atlantic, both in the US and Europe, and is available all year round, though it is not at its best during the summer months.

CUTS Whole (gutted, with head on or off), fillets.
EAT Cooked: Deep-fry, pan-fry in batter or breadcrumbs, bake, poach in a court bouillon, steam, use poached flesh for fish pie and fishcakes. Inexpensive addition to fish soups. **Preserved:** Cold and hot smoked (dyed and undyed), dried, salted, cured, smoked.
FLAVOUR PAIRINGS Butter, milk, beer, parsley, chives.
CLASSIC RECIPES Norwegian fish soup; *frikadeller* (fish rissoles).

Fresh coley will have firm and tightly knitted flakes.

Coley has a heavily scaled iron-grey or black back with a thick, white lateral line.

Coley
Pollachius virens

The flesh of this fish has been described as coarse, but it has been undervalued. It looks grey-pink when raw but, on cooking, whitens well and becomes flaky and well flavoured. It works in a fish casserole or curry, as it takes robust flavours well.

The lower jaw protrudes slightly, and the fish has a large prominent eye.

Haddock *Gadidae*

Fishmongers refer to haddock, from the Gadidae family, as ping, chat, kit, gibber, and jumbo (in ascending order of size). Haddock is found in the Northeast Atlantic and neighbouring seas. It is second to cod in popularity, particularly when it is smoked.

SUSTAINABILITY There is a maximum catch quota in place and landed fish must be of a minimum size, so that stocks remain sustainable.

CUTS Whole (gutted, with head on or off), fillets, roe.

EAT Cooked: Deep-fry or pan-fry in batter or breadcrumbs (considered sweeter than cod), grill, bake, poach in a court-bouillon or milk, steam. **Preserved:** Hot smoked (Arbroath smokies), cold smoked (undyed and dyed fillet), traditional Finnan haddock.

FLAVOUR PAIRINGS Parsley, milk, bay leaf, dulse seaweed, Cheddar cheese.

CLASSIC RECIPES Haddock Mornay; kedgeree; haddock and chips; Cullen skink.

Haddock
Melanogrammus aeglefinus
Haddock has a black lateral line on a grey back and a silver flank. Traditionally used for fish and chips, and preferred in this dish in Scotland, but also poached for fish pie and baked for Haddock Mornay. It is creamy-white, and has a delicate, sweet flavour.

Quality haddock has creamy-white flesh.

Haddock has a black spot on the shoulder known as St Peter's mark or thumbprint.

The thick, scaly skin is easy to remove, but can be left on while poaching and removed afterwards.

Pollock and Alaskan pollock *Gadidae*

Pollock, also known as green pollock and lythe, rivals cod in flavour and texture. Not of great importance commercially, it is a sport fish for recreational sea anglers. It is caught in the coastal waters throughout the North Atlantic and extensively spans the coast from Newfoundland right down to the Iberian Peninsula. It is often found in shallow inshore waters and grows up to 1m (3ft 3in) in length. With an olive-green back fading to a silver belly, pollock has a fine lateral line that has the appearance of being stitched in place, as it is slightly puckered. Alaskan pollock, a related species, is similar to cod in colour (with yellow speckles on the skin) and in the texture of the fillets (lean, snow white, and succulent). Found in the North Pacific and caught by Alaska, Russia, and Japan, it is prolific in the Bering Sea.

CUTS Whole (gutted, with head on or off), fillets.

EAT Cooked: Roast, deep-fry, bake, poach, steam. **Preserved:** Salted, smoked.

FLAVOUR PAIRINGS Tomatoes, chilli, pancetta, basil.

CLASSIC RECIPE Fish and chips.

Alaskan pollock
Theragra chalcogramma
Also known as Pacific pollock and walleye pollock, this fish is the largest food-fish resource in the world, and is thought to make up nearly half of all white-fish stocks. It is white and firm with a medium texture. Excellent for deep-frying as well as poaching to put into fish pie.

Fresh pollock has a very firm texture and cooks to a white, delicate sweetness.

If cooking with the skin on, remove the heavy layer of scales first.

Ling and Tusk *Gadidae*

These fish are two similar members of the Gadidae family. Ling is a highly commercial fish found in temperate waters spanning the Northwest and Northeast Atlantic, and the Northwest Mediterranean. It has a long body, reaching a maximum of 2m (6ft 6in). The skin can be marbled reddish-brown along the back and flanks, fading to a white belly. There is a distinct black spot at the back of the first dorsal fin. Ling has a long history, particularly as a salted fish to add to pies and soup. It is at its best when line caught. Tusk, also known as torsk, cusk, and moonfish, is found in the temperate waters of the Northwest and Northeast Atlantic. It can be 1.2m (4ft) long, but is mostly found at around 50cm (20in). It varies from dark red-brown to olive green along the back with a pale yellow belly.

SUSTAINABILITY For both ling and tusk, there is a maximum catch quota in place and landed fish must be of a minimum size.
CUTS Whole, fillets, steaks.
EAT Cooked: Steam, pan-fry, grill, bake.
Preserved: Dried, salted.
FLAVOUR PAIRINGS Olive oil, cream, potatoes, garlic.
CLASSIC RECIPE Salted ling with mashed potatoes.

Ling
Molva molva
Also known as common ling, it is excellent in fish pies, soups, and stews. This white fish cooks to an excellent firm and white, textured, sweet flesh. Salt ling is a traditional Irish feast.

Australian whiting *Sillaginidae*

A wide range of important whiting from the Sillaginidae family are caught in the waters surrounding Australia, Tasmania, and New Zealand. These fish are long and tapered in shape, with two dorsal fins, each with a differing number of spines and soft rays. They are unrelated to the whiting from the Gadidae family (see page 318). Various methods of fishing are used to harvest these fish commercially, and they all have differing habitats. All members have a bony structure and white, flaky flesh.

CUTS Whole (gutted); fillets (single and block/butterfly).
EAT Cooked: Steam, pan-fry, grill, bake. **Preserved:** Smoked, dried, salted.
FLAVOUR PAIRINGS Olive oil, butter, milk, parsley, chervil.
CLASSIC RECIPE Fish pie.

School whiting
Sillago bassensis
There are several "school whiting" caught in the waters around the Australian coast. They are similar in appearance, each with some distinguishing marks on a silver skin. They have a delicate, sweet flavour, similar to other whiting, and are low in fat, with a fine texture. Best when fresh, and excellent when steamed, poached, or pan-fried.

School whiting has firm flesh and a subtle flavour.

The skin is a coffee brown with a delicate lateral line that curves over the shoulder of the fish.

Sand whiting has a dark area at the base of the pectoral fin, and the anal and ventral fins are yellow in colour.

Sand whiting
Sillago ciliate
Also known as silver or summer whiting, this elegant fish is being considered for aquaculture. It is caught along the east coast of Australia by beach seine, haul nets, and gill nets, and is a highly regarded angling fish.

The flesh of a sand whiting is firm, flaky, and well flavoured.

Whiting

Whiting is the name used to describe several species from a variety of unrelated groups of fish, including the Gadidae, Merlucciidae, and Sillaginidae families. The taste of the fish varies from one species to the next, but the flesh of whiting is always white. The Gadidae whiting is found in the North Atlantic and surrounding seas, and the related southern blue whiting is caught in the Southwest Atlantic. Both these species have an easily digestible flesh. Hake (Merlucciidae family) is sometimes referred to as whiting. The fish is undervalued by many, as it has a delicate taste (it becomes almost tasteless when the fish is past its best). It is often popular with fishmongers, as it tends to be less expensive than some other members of the cod group. The skin of a whiting is particularly thin and care should be taken when skinning the fish, although leaving the skin on, particularly for grilling, protects the delicate flesh.

CUTS Whole (gutted); fillets (single and block/butterfly).
EAT Cooked: Steam, pan-fry, grill, bake. **Preserved:** Smoked, dried, salted.
FLAVOUR PAIRINGS Olive oil, butter, milk, parsley, chervil.
CLASSIC RECIPE Fish pie.

Whiting flesh is delicate and should be enjoyed very fresh, as it deteriorates quickly.

Atlantic whiting ▼
Merlangius marlangus
Whiting can grow up to 70cm (28in), although its usual size is around 25–30cm (10–12in). It has a light yellow-brown back, sometimes with hues of blue and green, and a grey to silvery-white belly. It has a light and delicate texture and is very low in fat.

Pout whiting ▼
Trisopterus luscus
Also known as bib, pout, or pouting, this fish is found as far south as the Mediterranean and up to the North Sea. It has a delicate texture, and spoils easily, so should be eaten very fresh.

Soft and delicate, pout whiting has a subtle texture and is low in fat.

Pout whiting is identified by a black spot behind the pectoral fins.

Hake *Merlucciidae*

Although hake is often associated with cod and the Gadidae family, it comes from the Merlucciidae family. It is caught in many waters around the world, but particularly in the Atlantic and Northern Pacific. Silver hake (also known as Atlantic hake or New England hake) is caught in the Northwest Atlantic. European hake is fished throughout Europe, but is particularly popular in Spain. Often regarded as a "cod-like" fish, the white flesh is very similar to cod, but the bone, fin pattern, and skeleton all differ. This species of fish is deceptively soft – in many other fish, soft, delicate flesh would indicate bad quality, but hake cooks to a firm and meaty texture.

SUSTAINABILITY Some areas have been over-fished and strict catch quotas – and even bans – are in place in some countries. Other members of the cod family can be used interchangeably.
CUTS Whole, fillets, steaks.
EAT Cooked: Pan-fry, roast, poach, sauté, grill. **Preserved:** Dried, smoked.

FLAVOUR PAIRINGS Olive oil, garlic, smoked paprika, butter, lemon.
CLASSIC RECIPE Hake in green sauce with clams (Basque recipe).

European hake
Merluccius merluccius
Also known as hake, colin, or in France, merluche, this species comes from North Africa, the Mediterranean, and as far north as Norway. A large, deep-water fish, it has been greatly affected by over-fishing.

Morid cod and Blue cod

There are a few types of morid cod, including New Zealand red cod and ribaldo, found in waters around South and Southeastern Australia, and New Zealand. They have a long dorsal fin running the length of the back, and the fillet tapers towards the caudal fin. Their size ranges from 40cm to 1.5m (16in to 5ft). They have white, textured, soft flesh. Like whiting, these fish are best eaten very fresh. Sandperch or blue cod (from the Pinguipedidae family) are temperate marine fish found in the Atlantic and along the coasts of South America and Africa. They are also found in the Indo-Pacific, from Hawaii to New Zealand, and off Chile. New Zealand blue cod are part of this group.

SUSTAINABILITY Both morid cod and blue cod are endangered in some parts of the world. Use Pacific cod or as an alternative.

CUTS Whole (gutted), fillets (single and block/butterfly).

EAT Cooked: Steam, bake en papillote, poach, fry, microwave.
Preserved: Smoked.

FLAVOUR PAIRINGS Batter, capers, gherkins, parsley, soft-leaf herbs.

New Zealand blue cod
Parapercis colias
Other names for this fish include Boston blue cod, sandperch, and, in Maori, rawaru or pakirikiri. It is a species that is exclusive to New Zealand and is commercially harvested by the South Island. This is a white, textured fish with similarities to other white fish from the true-cod group, but slightly more coarse in texture. Good for deep-frying, grilling, steaming, and roasting.

White, sweet, and succulent, New Zealand blue cod is a popular fish.

Adult blue cod have a blue-green back, fading to white on the belly. Young fish are dappled.

Roughy *Trachichthyidae*

Roughy refers to an unusual family of fish (*Trachichthyidae*) that include several roughys, slimeheads, and sawbellys. They have a wide global distribution and are landed by many countries. Orange roughy is the main species to receive international acclaim and it has been marketed intensely as an alternative to cod. Also known as sea perch or deep-sea perch, orange roughy is an important commercial fish in Australia, where it is found around the south coast of the continent, and New Zealand. The layer of oil under the skin is routinely used in the cosmetics industry.

SUSTAINABILITY Orange roughy was fished extensively until it was discovered that they mature and develop slowly. They have become seriously threatened and are endangered in some parts of the world. Pacific or Atlantic cod can be used as alternatives.

CUTS Occasionally whole, commonly skinned fillets.

EAT Cooked: Pan-fry, grill, deep-fry, bake.

FLAVOUR PAIRINGS Olive oil, chilli, lime, butter, beer batter, crème fraîche, cream.

Orange roughy
Hoplostethus atlanticus
The soft, moist, white, textured flesh of orange roughy has a sweet flavour. It is usually "deep skinned", to remove the skin, and also the layer of fat directly under the skin.

The flesh of this fish is soft, moist, and white, with a sweet, mild taste.

Hake has a deep blue or steel-grey back and silvery skin. Its lateral line has black edging.

Bream *Sparidae*

The extensive bream family (Sparidae) is distributed globally in temperate and tropical seas. The members of this group (known as porgies in the US) are important commercial fish for many countries. Most bream have a round, deep, laterally compressed body with a long, single, spiny dorsal fin. They have a good covering of large scales across the body and head. Different species are identified by the teeth as a general rule. Many are marine fish, but some dwell in estuarine brackish waters or fresh water. Most are fairly small, about 40–70cm (16–28in) in length. They require careful trimming and scaling. Their white, well-textured flesh, is at its best when simply pan-fried.

SUSTAINABILITY There is a minimum landing size in place for many species around the world, which varies from region to region. Alternatives can be responsibly farmed bream or sea bass.

CUTS Whole, fillets, often with skin on (after scaling), thick steaks (larger species).

EAT Cooked: Pan-fry, grill, bake, stuff.

FLAVOUR PAIRINGS Fennel, Pernod, coriander, lemon, saffron, parsley, garlic.

CLASSIC RECIPES Bream en papillote; *besugo al horno* (a classic festive Spanish dish).

Firm and sweet, gilt-head bream is very popular in many Mediterranean countries.

Yellow fin sea bream ▶
Acanthopagrus latus
Found in the Indo-West Pacific, yellow fin sea bream dwells in fresh, brackish, and marine waters. It is used in Chinese medicine and is popular for recreational fishing.

The sharp points on the dorsal and anal fins should be trimmed before scaling, as they are sharp.

Black sea bream ▼
Spondyliosoma cantharus
Also known as old wife, the black sea bream is common to Northern Europe and the Mediterranean, where it is fished extensively. Like other members of the bream family, it is a shoaling fish. It is silver in colour with black markings across the body. Considered to be one of the finest of the bream family, it can be cooked whole or filleted: roasting, pan-frying, or grilling the fillets. Its firm, white, textured flesh is admired in many Mediterranean countries.

As with the gilt-head bream, the cheeks of the black sea bream are sought after.

Gilt-head bream ▲
Sparus aurata
Gilt-head is the most popular bream in Europe and is farmed extensively throughout the Mediterranean. It has a lightly scaled, silvery skin with a spiny dorsal fin, and a deep body with a distinctive gold band across the brow. Farmed fish has white, firm flakes, with a medium texture.

The lateral line of this species slightly rises over the shoulder of the fish.

Common pandora
Pagellus erythrinus
Also known as Spanish sea bream, this fish is found in the East Atlantic from Norway to the Mediterranean, Madeira, and the Canary Islands. An hermaphrodite, it changes from female to male on reaching a certain size. It grows up to 60cm (24in) in length but the usual landed size is around 30cm (12in). It is a popular game fish and like many of its group, it has an excellent flavour, slightly herbaceous with firm white fillets. It is delicious roasted, grilled, and en papillote.

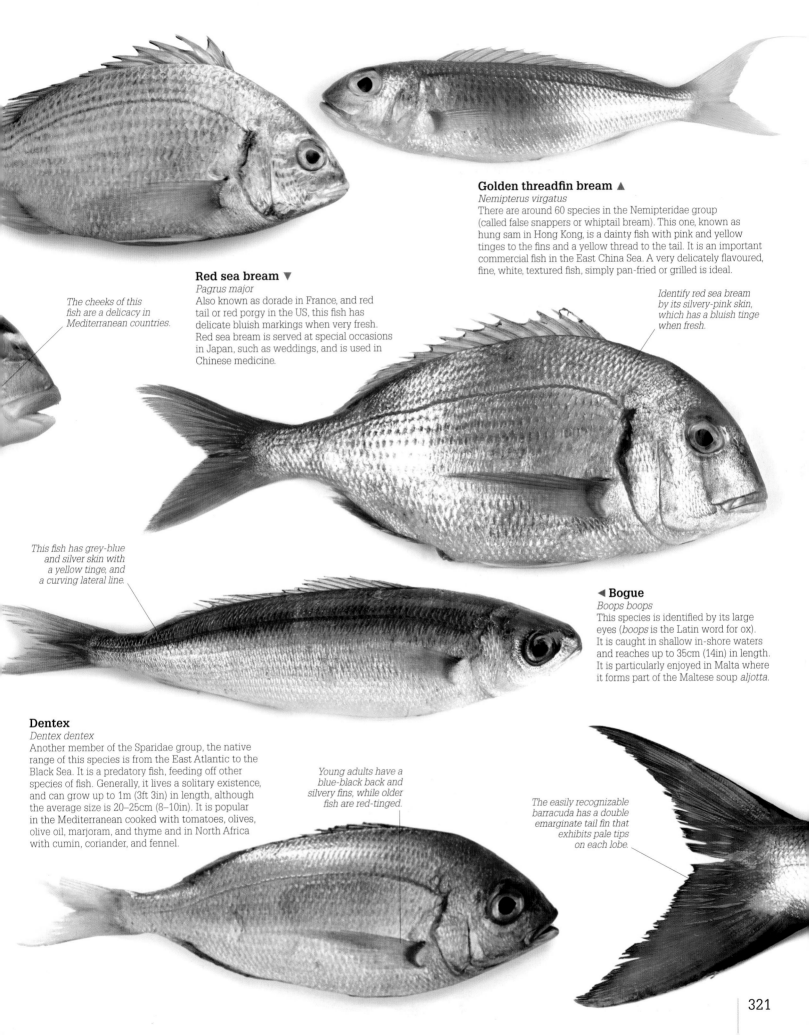

Golden threadfin bream ▲
Nemipterus virgatus
There are around 60 species in the Nemipteridae group (called false snappers or whiptail bream). This one, known as hung sam in Hong Kong, is a dainty fish with pink and yellow tinges to the fins and a yellow thread to the tail. It is an important commercial fish in the East China Sea. A very delicately flavoured, fine, white, textured fish, simply pan-fried or grilled is ideal.

The cheeks of this fish are a delicacy in Mediterranean countries.

Red sea bream ▼
Pagrus major
Also known as dorade in France, and red tail or red porgy in the US, this fish has delicate bluish markings when very fresh. Red sea bream is served at special occasions in Japan, such as weddings, and is used in Chinese medicine.

Identify red sea bream by its silvery-pink skin, which has a bluish tinge when fresh.

This fish has grey-blue and silver skin with a yellow tinge, and a curving lateral line.

◄ Bogue
Boops boops
This species is identified by its large eyes (*boops* is the Latin word for ox). It is caught in shallow in-shore waters and reaches up to 35cm (14in) in length. It is particularly enjoyed in Malta where it forms part of the Maltese soup *aljotta*.

Dentex
Dentex dentex
Another member of the Sparidae group, the native range of this species is from the East Atlantic to the Black Sea. It is a predatory fish, feeding off other species of fish. Generally, it lives a solitary existence, and can grow up to 1m (3ft 3in) in length, although the average size is 20–25cm (8–10in). It is popular in the Mediterranean cooked with tomatoes, olives, olive oil, marjoram, and thyme and in North Africa with cumin, coriander, and fennel.

Young adults have a blue-black back and silvery fins, while older fish are red-tinged.

The easily recognizable barracuda has a double emarginate tail fin that exhibits pale tips on each lobe.

321

Emperor bream *Lethrinidae*

Emperor bream or emperor fish are also called scavengers, rudderfish, and porgies. They are members of the Lethrinidae family, a relatively small group with 39 known species located in tropical reef seas of the Indo-Pacific through to Australia, and also off the west coast of Africa. They are carnivorous, feeding off the bottom of the sea. Most of the species are esteemed food fish and are recognized by their two dorsal fins with 10 spines. Emperor bream has a beige back with brown lines along the flanks and an orange mark around the gill flap. The lateral line curves over along the body to the forked tail or caudal fin. The flesh is white, full flavoured, and firm.
CUTS Usually whole.

EAT Cooked: Pan-fry, bake, roast; it takes robust flavours well.
FLAVOUR PAIRINGS Oriental flavours: chilli, lemongrass, coconut.

Red spot emperor bream
Lethrinus lentjan
This exotic fish has a firm texture and slightly sweet flavour. It works well with Indo-Pacific flavours such as ginger, chilli, and coriander.

The fish is densely scaled and needs trimming and scaling, prior to cleaning or filleting.

Grey mullet *Mugilidae*

The dashing sleek, silver-grey mullets of the Mugilidae family are found near the shore, in brackish and fresh water, and in tropical, subtropical, and temperate seas worldwide (in the Atlantic, Pacific, and Indian oceans). Grey mullet is very common and is a popular food fish, which is highly commercial in many countries. They are also used in Chinese medicine. There are around 75 species, which have silver-grey, elongated bodies with no visible lateral line. They are noted for their small mouths and, sometimes, thick lips. In Southeast Asia, grey mullet is cultivated in ponds. It can have a slightly earthy taste, but soaking it in a little acidulated water before cooking improves the flavour.

CUTS Whole; fillets (scaled, but skin on).
EAT Cooked: Pan-fry, roast, bake. The roe is used fresh and smoked.
Preserved: Dried and salted.
FLAVOUR PAIRINGS Citrus flavours, Moroccan spices, garlic, chilli.
CLASSIC RECIPES Taramasalata; *besugo al horno*.

The flesh is pink in colour, cooking to an off-white, and is firm and meaty.

Common grey mullet
Mugil cephalus
Its numerous names include black true, flathead or striped mullet, harder, and, in Australia, poddies or hardgut mullet. Its olive-green back has silver shading to the sides.

Goatfish and Red mullet *Mugilidae*

Members of the Mugilidae family, include goatfish and red mullet. Many of the 55 species are beautifully coloured. Caught in warm-temperate and tropical seas in the Indo-Pacific, Atlantic, Pacific, and Indian oceans, they are sometimes found in brackish waters. They have thick scales (which should be removed before cooking), forked caudal fins, and a distinct pair of chin barbells, used to detect food and, in the case of males, attract a female. Most are sold at around 15–20cm (6–8in), although many reach around 30cm (12in) in length. The red mullet's liver is considered fine eating and should be left intact.

SUSTAINABILITY There are some sustainability issues in relation to the method of fishing. Responsibly farmed bream or sea bass are alternatives.

CUTS Whole (gutted and scaled, with liver intact), fillets.

EAT Cooked: Pan-fry, grill.

FLAVOUR PAIRINGS Citrus flavours, tarragon, cream, garlic.

CLASSIC RECIPES Provençal fish soup with rouille; *fritura malagueña*.

This highly prized fish is dark pink, becoming white when cooked. It has a delicate flavour.

Red mullet
Mullus surmuletus
This fish is a particularly fine eating fish. It has many bones, so it is best to cook it whole so they can be located easily. Red mullet works well with citrus flavours, and herbs such as chervil and tarragon complement it nicely.

Indian goatfish
Mullus indicus
Indian goatfish is popular in Oman and East and South Africa, where it is landed. Its firm, white flesh is slightly earthier in flavour than its close relative, the red mullet.

This well-flavoured fish has a flaky texture, which is slightly coarser than that of red mullet.

Barracuda *Sphyraenidae*

Also known as sea pike and giant pike, barracuda are aggressive predators with plenty of sharp teeth. They are found in several oceans but are essentially warm-water marine dwellers known to frequent tropical reef areas. Species include the great barracuda of the Western Pacific, and the Eastern Pacific and Atlantic species. They vary in size, but only smaller specimens should be eaten because the toxins that can cause ciguatera poisoning affect larger fish. (This affects a handful of fish that live in some reef areas. Ciguatera poisoning has no effect on the fish, but it can cause extremely unpleasant symptoms in those who consume it, and has been fatal in a small number of cases.) Avoid marinating this fish for too long – particularly in an acidic juice – as the flesh will change texture and can become dry when cooked.

CUTS Fresh or frozen: whole fish or fillets.

EAT Cooked: Pan-fry, grill, deep-fry, roast. **Preserved:** Smoked.

FLAVOUR PAIRINGS Olive oil, garlic, paprika, spices, coconut.

With a firm, meaty texture and excellent taste, this fish takes robust flavours well.

Their large pointed heads contain a jaw lined with two layers of razor sharp teeth.

Barracuda
Sphyraena sphyraena
The elongated fillets are dense, meaty, and succulent. This fish works well with many flavours and is an excellent dish when it is grilled with olive oil and herbs.

Dory

There are several varieties of the dory that come from two fish groups. The six species belonging to the Zeidae family are found worldwide in temperate waters. These solitary fish have a wide, compressed body, a dramatic display of dorsal fins, and retractable jaws (so they are able to vacuum up their prey). The group from the Oreosomatidae (oreo) family include the smooth oreo and black oreo dories. With similarities to the dories of the Zeidae group, they have extremely large eyes set in a big head, a compressed body, and grey and black skin. These fish are found in waters around Australia and New Zealand, where they are fished commercially. They are thought to be slow-growing, living up to 100 years. They reach 70–90cm (28–35in) in length. Silvery John Dory (*Zenopsis conchifer*) is also known as the American John Dory, sailfin dory, or buckler dory in the US and Australia. It is caught in the Western Indian Ocean and the Atlantic, and is popular in Japan. The mirror dory (*Zenopsis nebulosa*) is a similar species found in Indo-Pacific waters.
CUTS Whole (usually gutted), fillets.
EAT: Pan-fry, grill, steam, bake.
FLAVOUR PAIRINGS Red peppers, garlic, olives, capers, tomatoes, mushrooms, robust, creamy sauces.
CLASSIC RECIPE Bouillabaisse.

These extremely sharp barbs make filleting hazardous: trim them off with scissors first.

This species bears a black mark, encircled with a gold band, on each side of the body.

John Dory
Zeus faber
John Dory is highly prized for its excellent eating quality. Sharp barbs around the fish need to be trimmed before filleting. The skin is delicate and can be left on if cooking the fish whole, or it can be skinned, revealing the fillet's three natural sections. The fish's wonderfully sweet and firm texture is often matched with rich, creamy sauces, wild mushrooms, sage, capers, lemon, and crème fraîche.

The best part of this fish is the loins (the thickest part of the fillet and excellent for barbecuing and pan-frying).

Gurnard *Triglidae*

Also known as sea robin in the US, varieties of gurnard (from the Triglidae family) found in the Atlantic, Pacific, and Indian oceans have only recently gained a reputation as being worth cooking. However, gurnard is part of the traditional cuisine of the South of France (where *grondin* is the common name), of which the classic Provençal stew bouillabaisse is a fine example. This fish has a triangular-shaped bony head, a tapering body, and noticeable pectoral fins. Several species are sold in Europe, including yellow, red, and grey gurnard, and tubs. Some species are available in the US and Australia. Usually 25–40cm (10–16in) long, they

can reach 60cm (23½in). Over 40 per cent of their weight is made up of bone. The head (with gills removed), bones, and skin make good fish stock. Gurnard has many pinbones and is tricky to prepare, as it has sharp dorsal spines and spiny barbs at each gill flap. The head can be removed and the fillets lifted off either side of the "tail".

CUTS Usually whole (ungutted).
EAT Cooked: Roast, pan-fry, grill.
FLAVOUR PAIRINGS Bacon/pancetta, thyme, sage, rosemary, olive oil, Moroccan spice, lemon.

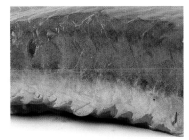

The fish is often best cooked on the bone and the tail is sweet and flaky.

Red gurnard
Aspitrigla cuculus
Also known as cuckoo gurnard and soldier, this is one of the most readily utilized of the species in Europe. It is caught around the coast of Britain and further south to the Mediterranean. Look for brightness of colour (the deep red or orange colour begins to fade as the fish loses condition).

Grey gurnard
Eutrigla gurnardus
This member of the group is also found in the Eastern Atlantic from Norway to Morocco, Madeira, and Iceland. In most parts of the world it is relatively abundant and should be enjoyed in place of overfished species. The sweetly flavoured flesh can be roasted or barbecued; it requires a little olive oil or a pancetta or chorizo jacket to help prevent it from drying during cooking.

Toothfish
Nototheniidae

The group of fish known as toothfish and rock cod are all found in cold water, particularly in the Antarctic, but also in the Southeast Pacific and Southwest Atlantic. They can reach considerable lengths, but most landed fish are around 70cm (28in) long. Toothfish are often marketed under the name of sea bass, but are not related to that group.

SUSTAINABILITY Toothfish are endangered in some parts of the world. As it is a slow-growing fish, there have been concerns, but the MSC (Marine Stewardship Council) has certified the South Georgia Patagonian Toothfish Longline Fishery as sustainable. The white flesh has a dense texture and sweet flavour to rival other white fish, so there are no immediate alternatives, but any firm, white, textured fish, such as cod, sea bass, or pollock, can be used instead.

CUTS Steaks, fillets (usually frozen and occasionally fresh).
EAT Cooked: Pan-fry, grill, barbecue, crust, sauté, roast, bake. **Preserved:** Cold and hot smoked.
FLAVOUR PAIRINGS Smoked bacon, garlic, chilli, soy, sesame oil.

Patagonian toothfish
Dissostichus eleginoides
The popularity of some toothfish species has grown in recent years, as they are considered fine eating. This species (also known as Chilean sea bass, Australian sea bass, and Antarctic ice fish) has become a favourite with Californian chefs.

Fillets are dense with a gentle sweetness that works well with piquant flavours.

Wolf fish *Anarhichadidae*

The wolf fish group is a small number of related species found in both Atlantic and Pacific waters. Aggressive in appearance with a mouth with lots of uneven teeth, wolf fish resemble an eel in shape but have a thick-set body. Also known as seawolf, ocean catfish, and wolf eel (the common name for the Pacific species), they vary in colour from a simple brown to sporting strips or spots. The flesh is firm, white, and meaty with a good flavour.

SUSTAINABILITY Wolf fish are endangered in some parts of the world. They have been subject to over-fishing and there are concerns over rapidly depleting stock. Alternatives include Pacific cod and barracuda.

CUTS Skinned fillets (fresh or frozen).
EAT Cooked: Steam, fry, grill, poach, bake.
FLAVOUR PAIRINGS Butter, garlic, cream, tomatoes.

Rabbit fish and Surgeon fish *Siganus*

Also known as spinefoots or ratfish, there are around 28 species of rabbit fish. Caught in the Indo-Pacific and the Eastern Mediterranean, several species are fished for food. Many species are colourful and some are also very decorative, which makes them popular in aquariums. They grow to around 40cm (16in) long and are easily identified by their small, slightly pouting lips over obvious front teeth, giving the fish a rabbit-like appearance – hence the name. The dorsal fin is spiky and particularly hazardous, and it needs to be trimmed away before cooking. There are around 80 species of surgeon fish found in marine tropical waters worldwide, often around a reef. The Latin name of the surgeon fish means "thorn tail", but it is also known as doctorfish and unicornfish. Each of these fish has a sharp barb, like a scalpel, on either side of the tail, that the fish can flex to protect itself from other predators.

CUTS Whole (ungutted and uncleaned), fillets.
EAT Cooked: Grill, pan-fry, bake, add to curries and stews.
FLAVOUR PAIRINGS Thai and African-Caribbean flavours of coconut, coriander, and spices.

Mild and delicate, the fillets need combining with robust flavours.

The yellow band around the shoulder makes this fish easy to identify.

Rabbit fish
Siganidae
Dark khaki-coloured skin with lines running laterally along the body. The flesh is white with a subtle flavour, but dries easily and becomes quite tasteless. It is a good addition to curries and stews that have robust or oriental flavours.

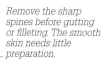

Remove the sharp spines before gutting or filleting. The smooth skin needs little preparation.

The dorsal fin on the wolf fish runs the length of the body and leads into a seal-like tail.

Atlantic wolf fish
Anarhichas lupus
Also known as rock fish, sea leopard, and sea cat, this is the largest of the wolf fish group, measuring up to 1.5m (5ft) long. The fish inhabits very cold water and is able to produce anti-freeze to keep its blood fluid:

A diet of spiny sea urchins and crab may account for wolf fish's sweet, meaty, and succulent flesh.

Easily recognizable by its fierce appearance, the wolf fish has a plain, dark brown, reddish skin with vertical black bands.

The barb is 1cm (½in) from the tail and needs careful removal, as it is as sharp as a surgeon's scalpel.

Surgeon fish
Acanthuridae
This species is particularly popular in African and Caribbean communities, who use it in curries and other spicy dishes. The flesh is delicate, so it can dry out and lack flavour if overcooked.

Redfish *Scorpaenidae*

Redfish are a selection of fish that include rockfish, the spiny scorpion fish (including the rascasse, one of the key ingredients in bouillabaisse), some ocean perch, and also rose fish. Found in temperate waters worldwide, some species are commercially significant. Norway haddock is an important member of this group; it is located in the North Atlantic coasts of both Europe and North America. Younger redfish have brown skin, but as an adult the back develops a deep red colour that fades to a paler red-orange on the flanks. The fish have a large mouth and prominent eyes and can grow up to 1m (3⅓ft) in length; however, the normal market size tends to be around 30–46cm (12–18in). This fish has one long dorsal fin and a spiny,

sharp front section, so it needs to be handled with care.
SUSTAINABILITY Redfish are endangered in some parts of the world. Alternatives include members of the cod group.
CUTS Whole (fresh and frozen), prepared (head off and gutted), fillets.
EAT Cooked: Pan-fry, stir-fry, bake, grill.
FLAVOUR PAIRINGS Cream- and dill-based sauces, tomatoes, peppers, chilli.

Redfish
Sebastes marinus
The names redfish and Norway haddock are interchangeable. The fillets are white, flaky, and delicately flavoured, and are particularly enjoyed in Scandinavia and Eastern Europe. It is harvested, frozen in fillets, and then exported.

Only 50 per cent of this fish produces fillets, as it has a heavy head and plentiful fins.

Grouper and Rock cod *Serranidae*

There are several hundred members of the Serranidae group, including groupers, gropers, rock cod, sea perch, and some fish called sea bass. The grouper family includes Jewfish, and the coral trout that is popular in Australia. They are often labelled by their Creole names, such as croissant and vieille rouge. This diverse family are tropical water dwellers and are found in the Atlantic, Pacific, and Indian oceans. The skin of a grouper is thick and slightly rubbery, and underneath it is a layer of fat that can cause stomach irritation. It is therefore advisable to skin the fish deeply prior to cooking.

SUSTAINABILITY Many of these species are important commercial fish and have been exploited to the point of collapse. Alternatives include cod, mahi mahi (dolphin fish), and barramundi from sustainable sources.

CUTS Fresh and frozen, whole, fillets, steaks.

EAT Cooked: Grill, pan-fry.
Preserved: Salted.

FLAVOUR PAIRINGS Soy sauce, sesame, Parmesan, olive oil, butter, lime, red chilli, coriander, ackee.

CLASSIC RECIPE Jamaican jerk fish.

Coral trout
Plectropomus leopardus
Also known as leopard coral grouper, footballer cod, and lunartail rockcod (Australia), this brightly coloured fish is listed as endangered, but it is carefully managed in Australian waters. It has also been associated with ciguatera poisoning. Firm, white, and sweet-flavoured flesh, it is great for pan-frying, barbecuing, and roasting.

The white flesh has an excellent flavour that is popular with chefs, particularly in Australia.

Red grouper
Epinephelus morio
This marine and subtropical species is often located near a reef in the West Atlantic. It is fished to unsustainable levels in some areas. Generally the fillets of these fish are white and the flavour is not dissimilar to cod, but less sweet.

All members of this group have handsome heads and prominent jaws.

Jewfish
Epinephelus itajara
This important game fish is found in subtropical marine waters and close to reefs of the Western and Eastern Atlantic and in the East Pacific. An aggressive fish, it feeds on crustaceans, which may account for its firm texture and sweet flavour. Confusingly, Jewfish is also the name for a member of the Sciaendidae group – (kob, see page 334). It is good for baking and pan-frying, usually as steaks.

These fish have a thick, rough skin that requires deep-skinning before cooking.

Bass *Moronidae*

Confusingly, sea bass is a name used to identify several species of fish, but the group from the Moronidae family include several bass and perch, found in the temperate waters of the East and West Atlantic. They are mainly marine fish; in the wild they often locate to brackish and sometimes fresh water, specifically the American striped bass, which is a popular fish for recreational fishing.

All members have sharp spines and a thick covering of scales that need to be removed prior to cooking. Bass is often compared to sea bream, and although in Northern Europe sea bass is popular, in the Mediterranean bream is generally the favourite.
SUSTAINABILITY Its flavour and popularity has led to over-fishing that has threatened stocks of these species. In some areas, landed fish

must be of a minimum size, while other areas have a closed season for recreational fishing. Sea bream is an appropriate alternative.
CUTS Whole unprepared fish, trimmed whole fish, fillets. Fish is scaled and rarely skinned.
EAT Grill, bake, pan-fry, en papillote.
FLAVOUR PAIRINGS Oriental flavours such as fermented black beans, sesame, dark soy, and ginger. Mediterranean flavours including

tomatoes, garlic, olive oil, and red peppers. Pernod and other ingredients that have a hint of aniseed.
CLASSIC RECIPE Branzino in salt.

Sea bass
Dicentrarchus labrax
Also known as bass, sea perch, and occasionally sea dace, this fish is found in the Eastern Atlantic from Norway to Senegal, the Black Sea, and the Mediterranean. It is extensively farmed in the Mediterranean, particularly in Greece. Farmed fish have a good flavour and fat deposits as a result of the feeding process. There is a minimum size in place for landed fish. Traditionally cooked in a salt crust, also excellent en papillote with aromatic flavours.

Farmed fish have a good savoury flavour with a slight oiliness; wild fish are leaner and meaty.

This fish is sometimes known as a lunar tail grouper because its curved tail looks like a crescent moon.

Bass have sharp spines and scales over a silver body that fades to a white belly.

The cheeks of bass are sweet and lightly flavoured, and are considered a delicacy.

The fish gets its name from the black stripes on bright silver.

American striped bass
Morone saxatilis
This temperate water dweller, like other members of its group, is found in brackish, marine, and fresh water. It is a popular sport fish found on the West Atlantic Coast from St Lawrence in Canada to the Gulf of Mexico. There is a minimum landing size in many areas and some quantities are responsibly farmed. Good cooked en papillote with black beans, chilli, lemongrass, olive oil, and soy.

Jack, Pompano, and Scad *Carangidae*

The Carangids are a large group of over 150 species of fish that includes some very notable members. Found in the Atlantic, Indian, and Pacific oceans, most members are voracious predators. Their body shape is not dissimilar to the mackerel group, having deeply forked tails, although they have a different fin structure. Many of these species are highly commercial and are used extensively across the world, although in some species there have been reports of ciguatera poisoning in endemic areas. The flesh varies between species, but generally the fillets are a pink that lightens to white on cooking, with firm, white flakes. Exotic species have a delicate sweetness and most take robust flavours well.

CUTS Depending on the fish – but generally whole, fillets, and steaks. Fillets can be large on some species so these will be taken as a shoulder, loin, and tail cut.
EAT Cooked: Grill, barbecue, pan-fry.
FLAVOUR PAIRINGS Red and green chilli, ginger, soy, warm spice mixes, coconut milk, tomatoes.

The flavour and texture of this group varies, but the fillets are usually pale and delicate.

Crevalle jack
Caranx hippos
Crevalle jack, jack, or jackfish is found in subtropical marine and brackish areas of the East and West Atlantic. The flesh dries easily so it needs careful cooking; it is good pan-fried or grilled with flavoured butter or brushed in oil.

Greater amberjack
Seriola dumerili
The largest member of the Carangidae group is found in many subtropical areas of the Mediterranean, Atlantic, Pacific, and Indian oceans. Fast and powerful in the water, this pelagic fish is a voracious predator. It looks similar to the kingfish and has silver-blue skin with a delicate gold lateral line. Meaty steaks make excellent eating.

Laterally compressed, it has a silver body and yellow fins.

Mahi mahi *Coryphaenidae*

Mahi mahi, meaning "strong strong" is the Polynesian name for this fish. Other names include dolphin fish and *lampuga* (in Malta). This warm-water, marine, and brackish dwelling fish is caught in the tropical and subtropical waters of the Atlantic, Indian, and Pacific oceans. It grows rapidly, often to over 2m (6ft 6in), but is more commonly seen just under 1m (3ft). A striking fish, it has a domed head (particularly noticeable on a mature male) and a long, single dorsal fin running from head to tail. Mahi mahi has a dense, meaty texture that takes robust flavours, particularly spices, very well.
CUTS Whole, fillets (fresh and frozen).
EAT Cooked: Pan-fry, barbecue, char-grill.

FLAVOUR PAIRINGS Caribbean: cardamom, allspice, fennel, coriander, curry powder, cayenne, and ginger; Asian: chilli, garlic, nam pla, lime.
CLASSIC RECIPE Lampuga.

Mahi mahi
Coryphaena hippurus
There is some aquaculture of these prized, premium fish, and there have been reports of ciguatera poisoning in endemic areas. It requires careful cooking, as the flesh surprisingly takes a little longer to cook than flaky fish, and it can dry out in the process.

The colour becomes a rich yellow towards the tail.

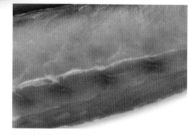

The flesh of this fish is pink and dense.

Trevally has a curved dorsal fin, yellow fins and tail, and golden hues above a greeny-blue and silver belly.

It has a silver-coloured skin with a yellow tail.

Soft fillets with a low oil content; the flesh is a marbled pink that cooks to delicate white.

Trevally
Carangue australienne
Also known as silver trevally, sand trevally, skipjack trevally, and skippy, this fish is found worldwide in waters including the East and West Atlantic, Indo-Pacific, South Africa, Japan, and Australia. The flavour is herbaceous and takes oriental and bold ingredients well, including chilli, ginger, and sesame.

Scad
Trachurus trachurus
A member of the Carangidae family also known as horse mackerel, jack, and chinchard in France. This particular species is found in the Northeast Atlantic, but others are found in global waters. It has a similar texture to mackerel, but many bones. Landed fish must be of a minimum size.

It has sharp spines and a row of bony scutes running along its flank to the tail.

Florida pompano
Trachinotus carolinus
Also known as butterfish, this species is found in the marine subtropical waters of the West Atlantic. A premium fish in the US, it often fetches a high price. It is endangered in some areas, but tilapia is a good alternative. It has a pink, buttery-flavoured flesh that takes spicy and strong flavours well.

Adult males have a vertical head profile with the development of a bony crest.

It has a yellow back with iridescent metallic blue and green along the body and a golden belly.

Snapper *Lutjandae*

This group has over 100 members, some of which are known as jobfish. Found in most tropical waters worldwide, many are key commercial fish. All vary in size, from a plate-sized lane or yellowtail snapper at 25cm (10in) up to the large red snapper mostly marketed at around 46cm (18in). Smaller members of the group, including yellowtail and lane snappers, can be streamlined, but the larger members, specifically the Malabar, cubera, bourgeois, and true red snappers, have a laterally compressed body. As with many fish of this type, they have a generous layer of thick scales and sharp spines on the fins. A fish sold whole should be trimmed, scaled, and gutted before cooking. The flesh of most is slightly off-white, lightening to white on cooking.

SUSTAINABILITY Some members are known to be fished beyond a sustainable level, but a level of aquaculture is developing that will support these important fish. There is a minimum landing size in place to preserve stocks. Alternatives include responsibly sourced sea bass.

CUTS Whole, fillets, steaks.

EAT Cooked: Steam, pan-fry, grill, bake, stir-fry.

FLAVOUR PAIRINGS Sesame oil, soy, ginger, garlic, coriander, palm sugar, nam pla.

CLASSIC RECIPES Blaff (Martinique fish stew); Cajun blackened snapper.

A beautifully flavoured fish with sweet-tasting, white flesh when cooked.

Red snapper
Lutjanus camperchanus
Many of the snapper group are a deep pink colour and are mistakenly labelled as red snapper, but this one is the true red snapper. Also known as pargo, this reef marine fish is found in the Gulf of Mexico and the Southeastern Atlantic coast of the US. It has a dark, red back fading to a lighter red on the flank. It is good cooked with just a squeeze of lemon, and spices. It can be grilled, pan-fried, roasted, and wrapped in banana leaves as en papillote.

Lane snapper
Lutjanus synagris
A smaller member of the group, with fish from 15cm (6in) upwards. It has a delicate pink skin with pink and yellow stripes on its side and a pink tail. Caught in the West Atlantic, it is mostly exported by Brazil. It can be grilled or baked whole with coconut, lime, and lemongrass.

Its sweet, pink meat becomes white when cooked.

Firm pink flesh, excellent for pan-frying, grilling, or baking.

Yellowtail snapper
Ocyurus chrysurus
A striking snapper with a deep pink, scaly skin, a strong yellow stripe along the flank, and a yellow tail. This is commercially caught for the table on the West Atlantic coast of the US, and it is abundant in Florida, the West Indies, and Brazil. Good marinated in warm spices such as cumin and coriander.

The shiny golden stripe on a deep pink makes this a striking member of the snapper group.

Pomfret

Confusingly, the name pomfret is used to describe various fish from several different fish families. Pomfrets come from the Carangidae, Stromateidae, and Bramidae groups, which are found in the East and West Pacific, and some parts of the Atlantic. These fish share several attributes, including their deep and laterally compressed bodies. Their fillets are handled in much the same way as those of flat fish. The firm, white, sweet-flavoured flesh is good for pan-frying and grilling. The Atlantic pomfret (*Brama brama*) is a member of the Bramidae group and is also known as ray's bream, angelfish, aral bream, bowfish, and carp bream. It has a steel-coloured, almost black body, and a large eye, and offers a well-flavoured, meaty, textured, white fillet.

CUTS Whole, fillets, (fresh and frozen).
EAT Cooked: Pan-fry, bake, barbecue, grill. **Preserved:** Some species are dried and salted.
FLAVOUR PAIRINGS Middle Eastern/North African: couscous, orange, lemon, parsley, coriander, *ras el hanout* spice mix, chermoula.

Black pomfret ▼
Formio niger
A member of the Carangidae family, this fish is found in both marine and brackish tropical waters of the Indo-Pacific. It is a shoaling fish, often reaching 30cm (12in) in length. It has a sweet flavour and firm texture and is available fresh, dried, and salted.

The sandy appearance of the fish is off-set by fins that vary in colour from black to sea green.

This laterally compressed fish is filleted in much the same way as a flat fish.

Silver pomfret ▶
Pampus argenteus
A member of the Stromateidae family, this pomfret is found in the subtropical waters of the Indo-Pacific from the Persian Gulf to Indonesia to Japan. The usual market size is around 30cm (12in). It has sweet and dense, white fillets, and is excellent wrapped in foil and barbecued. It also works well with couscous and sweet, dried fruit, including apricots and almonds.

Straight from the sea, this fish is a beautiful silver colour with blue hues that are rubbed off once landed to show darker markings.

The dorsal and anal fins are preceded by 5–10 blade-like spines, and the body has a scattering of black spots.

Cuskeel *Ophidiidae*

Cuskeels are distributed in shallow and deep water worldwide. They have an unusual shape similar to that of an eel, with their elongated bodies tapering to the tail. Both the dorsal and anal fins run along the fish and meet at the tail end. Cuskeels are shy marine-reef dwellers that hide during the day and appear at night to feed. There are over 200 species in the Ophidiidae group, but one particularly notable species is the fabulously flavoured kingclip, whose meaty flesh is reminiscent of lobster. It is found in the Southeast Atlantic off the West African coast from Namibia to South Africa.

CUTS Long, slender fillets.
EAT Cooked: Grill, pan-fry, roast, barbecue.
FLAVOUR PAIRINGS Butter, citrus flavours, chorizo, pancetta, bay, rosemary.

Long and eel-like with a pointed head and pink-marbled skin.

Meagre, Grunt, and Drum *Sciaendidae*

Found extensively in freshwater, brackish, and marine waters around the globe, this large group of fish includes meagres, grunt, and drums. They take their name from the noise that they make by vibrating their swim bladders; it creates a croak or drumming noise that can be heard from some distance. A notable member of the family is the kob or mulloway (Aboriginal for "the greatest one"). This is a popular fish caught around South Africa, Madagascar, and South Australia. Mulloway is considered a great catch by recreational anglers.

CUTS Whole, fillets.
EAT Cooked: Grill, steam, bake.
FLAVOUR PAIRINGS Chilli, lime, orange, white wine vinegar, olive oil, dill.
CLASSIC RECIPES Ceviche; escabeche.

Meagre
Argyrosomus regius
Also known as croaker and corvina, it is distributed around the coasts of some subtropical waters along the East Atlantic and Mediterranean. The off-white fillets cook to a luscious and dense white. It can be grilled, roasted, or wrapped for the barbecue.

This fish has succulent, sweet, and meaty white fillets or steaks.

A firm-textured fish, the striking scales need removing prior to cooking.

The pale pink flesh can be cut into steaks for baking or grilling.

Kob
Argyrosomus hololepidotus
Hugely popular in South Africa, kob is also known as mulloway, butterfish, kingfish, or jewfish in Australia. It is a marine, demersal fish found in coastal and estuarine waters. There is a minimum catch size in place to preserve stocks. It is a sashimi-grade fish that is sold to the European sushi market.

Mulloway has a stunning metallic silver-blue-and-bronze-coloured skin with a spiny dorsal fin.

Kingclip
Genypterus capensis
This species can reach over 180cm (6ft) long. It is rated very highly as an excellent table fish, and is featured particularly in menus across South Africa. Typical South African recipes suit the cooking of kingclip, which, along with other fish, can be added to make the traditional stew, potjie.

This fish produces succulent, sweet, and meaty white fillets or steaks.

The "tail" is the part that is eaten – this runs from the shoulder to the base of the tail fin.

Monkfish *Lophidae*

One of a small group of related species from the Lophidae family, which includes the East Atlantic monkfish caught in European waters and the West Atlantic goosefish caught in North American waters. These demersal fish are extraordinary in appearance, with flattened, long, tapering bodies below wide heads and huge mouths with inwardly pointing teeth. The thick, shiny skin is easily pulled back to reveal a meaty tail. Underneath the skin are several layers of membrane; these need to be removed, as they shrink during cooking and toughen the exterior of the fish. The flesh has no pinbones and a firm texture that holds its shape well in cooking. The cheeks are sweetly flavoured and perfect for stir-frying and barbecuing.

SUSTAINABILITY Some stocks of monkfish are depleting. Alternatives include prawns and scallops, as they have textures similar to monkfish. Responsibly sourced huss is also a good option.

CUTS Whole, head on or off, skinned and unskinned; cheeks; shoulder flaps. The liver is considered a delicacy.
EAT Cooked: Pan-fry, poach, roast, grill, stir-fry. **Raw:** Ceviche/marinated.
FLAVOUR PAIRINGS Chorizo, sage, rosemary, butter, olive oil, lemon.

Monkfish have mild-flavoured, slightly chewy, white flesh.

The cheeks on a monkfish are harvested and sold separately.

The head of a monkfish is most often removed on harvesting, as it weighs a lot.

Monkfish
Lophius piscatorius
Also known as angler fish, this fish is found in Eastern Atlantic waters and has gained popularity over recent years. It has folds of brown and black mottled skin, which are perfect for successful camouflage.

Tuna *Scombridae*

Easily identifiable by their bullet-shaped bodies that taper to a pointed snout and deeply forked tails, these fish can swim fast – speeds of around 70km an hour (43mph) have been recorded. Although they come from temperate and cold waters, many are able to adapt to tropical and subtropical waters. High levels of myoglobin give the flesh a pink to deep red colour,

earning tuna the nickname the "rose of the sea". Although a deep colour, the flesh has a subtle flavour and, once filleted, no bones. It is often likened to a beef fillet steak in texture and flavour. The southern bluefin tuna (*Thunnus maccoyii*) is caught in the temperate and cold seas of the Atlantic, Indian, and Pacific oceans, but it migrates to tropical seas during spawning.

These fish are particularly sought-after in Japan, where they can fetch an extremely high price. Northern bluefin tuna (or giant bluefin tuna) is native to the Western and Eastern Atlantic oceans, the Mediterranean, and the Black Sea, and are also commercially cultivated off the Japanese coast. This species is popular for the sushi trade.

SUSTAINABILITY The extensive desire for this fish has led to severe overexploitation of the species. Some stocks are well-managed globally, but there are many that are not. Choose tuna that comes from a sustainable source that is either pole- or line-caught. Both northern bluefin tuna and southern bluefin tuna are critically endangered and are close to collapse, so avoid

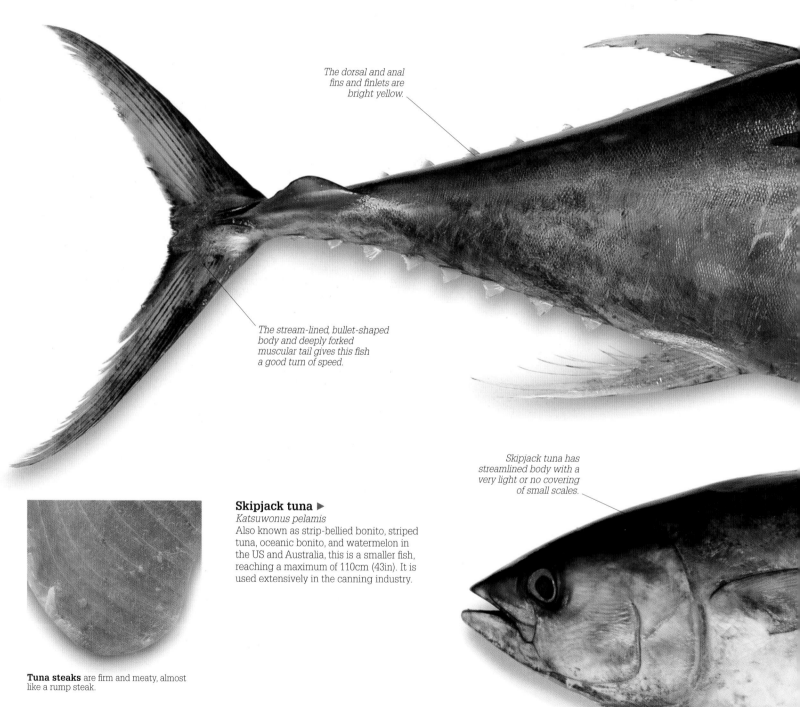

The dorsal and anal fins and finlets are bright yellow.

The stream-lined, bullet-shaped body and deeply forked muscular tail gives this fish a good turn of speed.

Skipjack tuna has streamlined body with a very light or no covering of small scales.

Skipjack tuna ▶
Katsuwonus pelamis
Also known as strip-bellied bonito, striped tuna, oceanic bonito, and watermelon in the US and Australia, this is a smaller fish, reaching a maximum of 110cm (43in). It is used extensively in the canning industry.

Tuna steaks are firm and meaty, almost like a rump steak.

purchase. Responsibly sourced swordfish is a suitable alternative.

CUTS Whole, in sections: loins, steaks, belly.

EAT Cooked: Loins: chargrill, pan-fry.
Preserved: Dried, smoked, salted. Tuna roe is also sold dried.
Raw: Sushi and carpaccio.

FLAVOUR PAIRINGS Japanese: shoyu, sesame, teriyaki, shiso leaf, Japanese rice wine vinegar, wasabi. Mediterranean: tomatoes, garlic, olives.

CLASSIC RECIPES Salade Niçoise; tuna sashimi/sushi; carpaccio of tuna with salsa verde; tuna teriyaki.

Yellowfin tuna
Thunnus albacares

Caught in all tropical and subtropical seas, this species is also known as yellowfin tunny and Allison's tuna. It is overfished in some areas, particularly if it has been net-caught. Pole-caught is the more selective method of capture. It is a big fish that can reach up to 2.5m (8ft) long. The meat taken from the back or loin is lean, meaty, with a slight flavour of rump steak. The belly meat is much higher in fat and is popular in Japanese cuisine.

The back is black metallic turning to dark blue along the flanks.

The yellow to silver belly often has broken, practically vertical lines running along it.

The powerful, shapely tail is a rusty orange colour.

Mackerel and Bonito *Scombridae*

The Scombridae family has around 54 members found in all oceans worldwide. It includes the mackerel, bonito, wahoo, kingfish or king mackerel, and tuna fish groups – all extremely important commercially for many countries. These oil-rich species contain high levels of omega-3 essential fatty acids; the oil is located throughout the body and not just in the liver. All members of this group should be stored at a constant low temperature. High levels of histadine naturally occur in their flesh, and if not stored at a low enough temperature, this converts into histamine, which can cause scombroid poisoning (symptoms of which are upset stomach and diarrhoea). Rather confusingly, the names "mackerel" and "bonito" are used interchangeably. For example, horse mackerel and frigate mackerel are often labelled as bonito.

SUSTAINABILITY Many species from the mackerel and bonito group have a maximum catch quota in place, and landed fish must be of a minimum size. Opt for line-caught fish as they are the more sustainable.
CUTS Whole and ungutted, fillets, steaks of the larger bonito, kingfish, and wahoo.
EAT Cooked: Grill, pan-fry, bake, barbecue, roast. **Preserved:** Canned, smoked, dried, salted.

Raw: Cured and used in sushi and sashimi.
FLAVOUR PAIRINGS Japanese: shoyu, sesame seeds, mirin, rice vinegar, cucumber and daikon, chilli and coriander; Mediterranean: basil, olive oil, garlic.
CLASSIC RECIPES Soused mackerel; mackerel with gooseberry sauce; smoked mackerel pâté; mackerel with rhubarb; gravad mackerel; marmite (Basque fisherman's bonito dish).

The Atlantic mackerel is identified by the bar or scribble markings along its back.

The fins can fold flat against the body to give a streamlined shape that enables it to swim fast.

Damage to the jaw may indicate that it has been line-caught (preferable) rather than netted.

Atlantic mackerel
Scomber scombrus
This commercially important pelagic species is the most northerly member of the family. It is found extensively in the North Atlantic, with smaller pockets in the Mediterranean. It can grow up to 60cm (2ft) long. Look for mackerel that are still stiff with rigor mortis and cook as soon as possible. Grilling, barbecuing, and roasting make the most of the creamy textured flakes.

Wahoo steak has a dense and meaty texture.

Wahoo
Acanthocybium solandri
The wahoo has an iridescent bluish-green back, and silver flanks striped with cobalt blue. It can reach 2.5m (8ft), although is more commonly landed at around 1.7m (5ft 6in). It is found in the Atlantic, Indian, and Pacific oceans, including the Caribbean and Mediterranean seas. An often solitary fish, it sometimes forms small groups rather than shoals. Superb to eat, with a firm, meaty texture and a delicate, sweet taste. In the Caribbean, slices of wahoo are cured in spices.

King mackerel
Scomberomorus cavalla
Also known as kingfish, the king mackerel is found in the Western Atlantic from Canada to Massachusetts, US, to São Paulo, Brazil; also in the Eastern-central Atlantic. It reaches a maximum length of 180cm (6ft), although it is usually found at about 70cm (28in). It lives near reefs, and in some areas may feed on plankton that cause ciguatera poisoning in humans. The meat is full-flavoured, and great for chargrilling or barbecuing.

Deep silvery-grey skin with a long tapering fillet to the tail.

The cheeks of many fish, including the bonito, are considered to be a delicacy.

Dark, rich, and meaty, bonito has a firm texture; the flesh lightens during cooking.

Bonito
Sarda sarda
A selection of fish come under this heading: the belted bonito, horse mackerel, short-finned tunny, pelamid, and strip-backed pelamis. The bonito has an extensive range: it is caught in the Eastern Atlantic from Norway to South Africa; the Mediterranean and Black Sea; in the Western Atlantic, from Nova Scotia to Colombia, Venezuela, and northern Argentina. It can reach up to 90cm (35in), but is most commonly found at around 50cm (20in). Dried flakes of bonito are used in dashi, a Japanese soup stock. Bonito is perfect for grilling or barbecuing with a robust-flavoured baste or marinade.

Chub mackerel is good for sashimi, where the fillets are cured briefly to firm up the texture.

Chub mackerel
Scomber colias
Also known as Spanish mackerel, thimble-eyed mackerel, and southern mackerel, this close relation of the Atlantic mackerel has similar bar markings, but they are not so defined. The chub mackerel grows to about 50cm (20in) long. It prefers warm waters, and is found in the East and West Atlantic. Its related species in the Indo-Pacific, *Scomber japonicus*, grows to 20–35cm (8–14in).

The chub mackerel has a lightly speckled underside.

The king mackerel is an impressive-looking fish with a slim, silver body and dark bars along its back.

Escolar *Gempylidae*

The escolar, or snake mackerel, is a member of the Gempylidae group that also includes gemfish, snoek, and barracouta. It has a fierce appearance, with an elongated body and head, and jaws lined with menacing sharp teeth. It is often associated with the barracuda group and is a voracious predator to smaller species including mackerel, flying fish, and squid. Escolar are located in tropical marine waters worldwide, but some are found in temperate locations. They favour mid-water depth as immature fish, moving to deep water as they mature. Although Gempylidae members are found globally, most are landed as part of a catch of other more valuable species, including tuna. The oil-rich flesh of the escolar is enjoyed in Europe, the US, and Asia, where it may be served as sushi and sashimi. In the US, it is sometimes called "white tuna". In Japan, escolar is often used in fishcakes and sausages; it is also popular in Hawaii and South Africa.

CUTS Whole and frozen fillets.
EAT Cooked: Grill, roast, pan-fry, deep-fry, bake. **Preserved:** Smoked and canned.
FLAVOUR PAIRINGS Chilli, sesame, coconut, and Oriental spices and herbs.
CLASSIC RECIPES Grilled escolar with chilli dressing; teriyaki.

Escolar
Lepidocybium flavobrunneum
This fish has several names: snake mackerel, black oil fish, butterfish, castor oil fish, and rudderfish in Australia. It varies in size but can grow to well over 2m (6ft 6in) long. It has a well-flavoured but very oily flesh (containing a wax ester), and can cause stomach irritation, so eat only small quantities at a time. "Deep-skinning" will remove most of the wax; grilling also helps to release it. Thick, succulent, escolar steaks can be brushed with oil and pan-fried or roasted.

Steaks of escolar are thick and oily.

Once the fish has been cooked, the silver skin can be scraped away because it is so fine.

Scabbard fish *Trichiuridae*

The scabbard fish or cutlass fish is closely related to escolar and shares similar characteristics. There are over 40 members of this group. It is also known as the sabre fish, hairtail, ribbon fish, and frostfish. It gets its name from a very long, thin body, and the colour varies, but most species sport a steely-blue or silver skin. They have fang-like teeth set in a long jaw, which are coated in a powerful anti-coagulant, and so need to be handled with care. Scabbard fish are found in many waters globally, and fished on both sides of the Atlantic. Black scabbard fish is a delicacy in Madeira; it has to be eaten very fresh and does not store well, so is not usually exported fresh. These fish are extremely palatable, with a delicate texture and almost buttery flavour. It may appear difficult to prepare.

CUTS Whole fish, long and thin fillets, usually skinned. Cut into wide steaks.
EAT Cooked: Grill, pan-fry, bake, smoke on a barbecue.
FLAVOUR PAIRINGS Cumin, coriander, orange, cinnamon and North African/Italian flavours.
CLASSIC RECIPES *Filetti di spatola al pane* (Italian breaded recipe); *espada preta vinho e alhos* (Madeiran recipe for cooking in wine).

Silver scabbard ▲
Lepidopus caudatus
This species can grow to over 2m (6ft 6in). The scabbard fish is particularly popular and esteemed in Portugal and Madeira, but underrated in countries such as the US. It is often discarded from a catch. It tastes rich, nutty, and buttery.

Swordfish
Xiphias gladius
The swordfish grows to a maximum of about 4.5m (14ft 9in) long and is found in the Atlantic, Pacific, and Indian oceans and in the Mediterranean Sea. Its flesh colour varies according to its diet and habitat; the meaty-tasting steaks vary from white to a pinkish tinge. It has the longest bill of all the fish in the group, and is aggressive, often attacking before being attacked, and using its sword to slash and tear its prey.

Puffer fish *Tetraodontidae*

This highly poisonous fish must be treated with extreme care, although it is considered a great delicacy. When threatened by a predator, the puffer fish fills its stomach with water or air and enlarges itself to many times greater than its body size. It is found in marine, fresh, and brackish waters globally. The Japanese enjoy fugu, a delicacy, made from puffer fish of the genus *Takifugu, Sphoeroides*, and *Lagocephalus* (they also call the fish fugu). Thousands of tonnes of fugu are consumed in Japan every year. The fugu is notorious, as certain parts of it contain tetrodotoxin and are poisonous. Despite this it is a highly sought-after and very expensive fish. The skin may be used in salad, stewed, or pickled.

CUTS Fillets; must be prepared extremely carefully by a licensed chef.
EAT Cooked: Fry. **Raw:** As fugu.
FLAVOUR PAIRINGS Pickled ginger, soy sauce, wasabi, sake.
CLASSIC RECIPES Sashimi; fugu kara-age (deep-fried); hire-zake (fried; served with sake).

Puffer fish
Takifugu, several species
The toxin in parts of the fish causes paralysis and asphyxiation – there is no antidote; the safe preparation of fugu, by specially trained chefs, is very time-consuming. Fugu sashimi is a very popular fugu dish. Wafer-thin slices are typically arranged in a chrysanthemum pattern, which symbolizes death in Japanese culture.

The puffer fish has a rounded body. When it is prepared for sashimi, fillets are cut so thinly that the slices are almost transparent.

Swordfish and Marlin

The billfish family includes swordfish and marlin. These fish have a long bill or spear. They produce meaty, dense steaks. Billfish are found in most warm and tropical oceans worldwide. Most are slow-growing species that take years to reach maturity. The swordfish, also known as the broadbill, resembles other members of the Istiophoridae family, but belongs to the Xiphiidae group. There are four main species of marlin that belong to the Istiophoridae family. They can grow to over 1 tonne (1 ton) in weight. The Atlantic sailfish (*Istiophorus albicans*) is closely related to the marlin, and is found in the Atlantic and the Caribbean Sea. Some billfish have a high metal content, particularly traces of methylmercury. Pregnant women

and small children should avoid eating it. But, it is argued that, for the general population, the benefits of eating it outweigh the possibility of consuming too much mercury, as it contains omega-3 essential fatty acids, vital for the heart.
SUSTAINABILITY These big, impressive fish are of great commercial importance. They have been hunted mercilessly and are seriously endangered in some countries. Many are harvested from the Pacific every year, but are carefully managed. Systems are in place in the North Atlantic to protect juvenile fish. Alternatives include sustainably and responsibly caught tuna.
CUTS Steaks or whole loins, sometimes whole.
EAT Cooked: Chargrill, barbecue,

pan-fry. **Preserved:** Smoked.
Raw: Sushi, sashimi, marinated raw.
FLAVOUR PAIRINGS Basil, rosemary, coriander. Warm spice mixtures including cumin, paprika, coriander. Citrus flavours, olive and sesame oils, mesquite smoking chips.
CLASSIC RECIPES Smoked marlin with scrambled egg (Latin American); chargrilled swordfish with salsa verde.

Loins are taken from each side of the backbone and cut into thick, succulent steaks, ready for pan-frying or char-grilling.

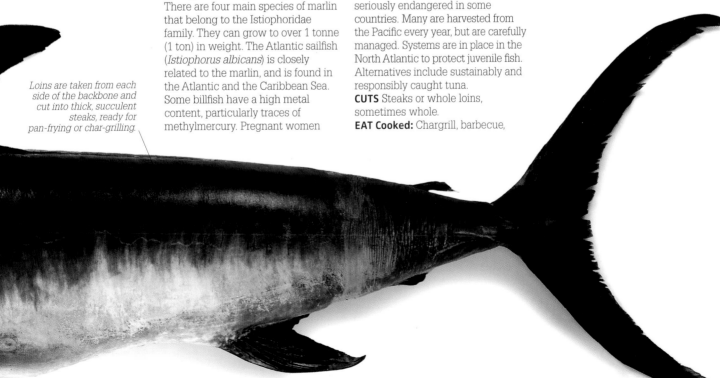

Herring and Sardine *Clupeidae*

With over 50 species, the Clupeidae group of fish includes the herring, shad, sardine/pilchard, sprat, hilsa, and menhaden. Anchovies (see facing page) are closely associated with this group. The species are mostly marine, but some are freshwater. These shoaling, pelagic fish feed on plankton and grow rapidly. They are an important food source for large predatory fish. Herrings are an oil-rich fish, caught extensively worldwide, and form a key low-cost food for many countries. They are one of the most abundant species in the world, although, as with many other fish, some stocks around the world are currently overexploited. Landed in huge quantities, the fish spoil quickly and if eaten fresh, need to be cooked while they are as close to rigor mortis as possible. This fact has led them to be processed into various products, from salted (in times past) to canned (for today's market). A whole herring, split and salted or pickled and then smoked, is called a kipper.

SUSTAINABILITY Some stocks are threatened but others are well managed. Their landing sizes vary and controls are in place in many areas to protect stocks.

HERRING
CUTS Whole, gutted, or filleted, frozen, and canned. Roes, both hard and soft (milt), are available. Female roe is a less expensive alternative to other caviars and is a delicacy in Japan. Small, immature herring members are harvested and marketed as whitebait (but are overexploited).
EAT Cooked: Pan-fry, grill, barbecue, roast, souse. **Preserved:** Smoked, salted, marinated, cured, canned.

See pages 384–389: kippers, bloaters, buckling, and maatjes herring.
FLAVOUR PAIRINGS Soured cream, dill, oatmeal, bacon, horseradish, lemon, capers, parsley.
CLASSIC RECIPES Herrings in oatmeal; herrings with bacon; rollmops; jugged kippers; devilled whitebait.

SARDINE
CUTS Whole, gutted, or filleted.
EAT Cooked: Pan-fry, grill, barbecue.
Preserved: Smoked, marinated, cured, and canned (in olive oil or different kinds of prepared sauces, such as tomato).
FLAVOUR PAIRINGS Mediterranean: olive oil, garlic, lemon, sultanas, pine nuts, parsley, oregano, thyme.
CLASSIC RECIPES Grilled sardines with Greek salad; barbecued sardines with oregano and lemon.

SPRAT
CUTS Whole (you will usually need to gut the fish yourself).
EAT Cooked: Grill, bake, pan-fry.
Preserved: Smoked, canned, salted.
FLAVOUR PAIRINGS Beetroot, white wine and red wine vinegar, flat-leaf parsley, coriander, coriander seeds.
CLASSIC RECIPE Pan-fried sprats with lemon.

The twaite shad has a bright silver body with a covering of scales.

European sprat
Sprattus sprattus
Also known as bristling or brisling, this small member of the herring family is found in European marine waters from the Northeast Atlantic (North Sea and Baltic Sea) down to the Mediterranean, Adriatic, and Black seas. Its flesh appears grey, but changes to off-white when cooked. It has a smooth, oily texture and it can grow up to 16cm (6½in), but 12cm (5in) is more usual.

Sprats are a startlingly bright silver, with a small head and a beady black eye.

Sardine or Pilchard
Sardina pilchardus
Pilchards are known as sardines if they are less than 15cm (6in) in length. This fast-growing fish is immensely important to many countries. It is a rounded, oil-rich fish, high in omega-3 essential fatty acids. It has a greeny-blue back, with bright, silvery sides and belly, and loose scales. The fish can grow to 20–30cm (8–12in) in length. Sardines have a lot of bones, a coarser texture, and are meaty with a robust flavour.

It is best to gut sardines and cook them on the bone, as the fine bones are easier to locate when the fish is cooked. The loose scales also need removing with the back of a knife.

These fish have shiny, loosely scaled skin and swim in shoals.

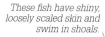

Atlantic herring
Clupea harengus
Also known as sild, yawling, digby, and mattie, Atlantic or sea herring are found on both sides of the Atlantic. This pelagic species forms huge schools of billions of fish. They can grow up to 45cm (18in) long, but 30cm (12in) is more usual. They were overfished during the 1990s, but today there are some well-managed, sustainable stocks. Fresh herring is at its best simply grilled with a slice of lemon. It is high in omega-3 essential fatty acids; if eaten extremely fresh, the flakes are fine and sweet, and not overly oily in texture. Lots of fine bones make this fish a challenge for some to eat.

Atlantic herrings have a bluish-green back, bright silver flanks, and loose scales.

Twaite shad
Alosa fallax
The twaite shad is found along the west coast of Europe, in the Eastern Mediterranean, and in some large rivers along these coasts. It has declined in many parts of Europe over recent years. With a similar appearance to a herring, this fish is generally larger, with a more delicate taste. It produces decent-sized fillets and has a delicate, grassy, and milky taste. If cooked well, it has lovely succulent flakes, but lots of pinbones.

Anchovy *Engraulidae*

Anchovies are from the Engraulidae family group of about 140 species, and resemble herrings in many ways. They are a small, oil-rich, saltwater fish, and are found in the Atlantic, Indian, and Pacific oceans. They are generally concentrated in temperate waters and are rare in very cold or very warm waters. Huge schools of anchovies are usually found in the shallows in estuarine waters and bays. The small, greenish fish have a hint of iridescent blue to their skin. They vary in size dramatically, from 2cm (¾in) to 40cm (16in) long. Body shape varies according to species, but on the whole it is a long, slender fish. Once landed, anchovies need to be cooked quickly – as they do not keep well – or preserved by curing in vinegar or salting. Sometimes they are available fresh from the boat.

SUSTAINABILITY Anchovies are overfished in some areas. Sprats make a good alternative.
CUTS Whole.
EAT Cooked: When available fresh, pan-fry. **Preserved:** In jars as salted, cured, or marinated/brined fish. Also made into anchovy essence.
Raw: Traditionally marinated and enjoyed in a raw state.
FLAVOUR PAIRINGS Sherry vinegar, white wine vinegar, shallots, marjoram, oregano, sage, thyme, parsley, Mediterranean olive oil.
CLASSIC RECIPES *Boquerones en vinagre* (Spanish marinated anchovies); deep-fried anchovies with sage; *alici ripiene; alici al limone;* salsa verde; salade Niçoise. Dried: *Bagna caoda; asparagi in* salsa; *polenta nera; puntarelle in salsa di alici* (Italy); *anchoïade* (France).

European anchovy
Engraulis encrasicolus
This fish is abundant in the Mediterranean and is caught off the coasts of Sicily, Italy, France, and Spain, where it is sold straight from the boat. It is also found along the coast of North Africa, and can extend as far north as the south of the Atlantic. It grows to a maximum of 20cm (8in). Salty anchovies make a classic partner to chargriddled beef steaks. They also make an excellent butter, which is delicious with grilled white fish such as brill and Dover sole.

Nile perch, Barramundi, and Murray cod

Several key species of freshwater fish are found in the warmer waters of Africa, Asia, and Australasia. Nile perch (*Lates niloticus*) is also known as Victoria perch and capitaine. It is a predatory fish living mainly in fresh, but some brackish, waters. It was introduced to Lake Victoria in Africa, where it has caused much damage by virtually wiping out other species of fish. It is an important commercial fish, harvested for export and sold at a good price. It is mostly wild, but some aquaculture has been established. The barramundi (*Lates calcarifer*) is found from the Persian Gulf to China, Asia, and Australia. It inhabits creeks, rivers, and estuarine waters. In Australia, it

is farmed as a highly commercial species, and is a major export. It is very similar in taste and texture to Nile perch. The Maccullochella genus of predatory freshwater fish is native to Australia and known as "cod". A few species are found in the river systems, including the Murray cod (*Maccullochella peelii peelii*) and the trout cod (*M. macquariensis*). Murray cod is renowned for its flavour.

SUSTAINABILITY Many of these species are now listed as critically endangered. Murray cod is seriously threatened, though it is farmed in Victoria. All Murray cod on sale or served in restaurants is from this source. Commercial fishing of Murray cod is banned in Australia.

Responsibly sourced snapper and coral trout are suitable alternatives.
CUTS Whole, fillets, steaks.
EAT Cooked: Pan-fry, grill, barbecue, poach, steam.
FLAVOUR PAIRINGS Nile perch and barramundi: pak choi, lime, chilli, fresh herbs, white wine. Murray cod: butter, white wine, beer, white wine vinegar, orange, mild to medium spices.

Nile perch is usually sold ready prepared: the neat, creamy-white fillets are excellent pan-fried, battered, or cooked in breadcrumbs. The fillets taste like barramundi and can be cooked in similar ways.

Nile perch ▲
Lates niloticus
The Nile perch is native to the River Nile and other major West African freshwater rivers. It has been introduced to lakes in East Africa and North Africa, and in North America. It may grow to over 2m (6ft 6in) long. It is most often cut into fillets, which are firm, white, and succulent. As a freshwater fish, it can have a slightly earthy taste. New-style Asian flavours complement it well, such as steamed pak choi with shiitake mushrooms.

Murray cod
Maccullochella peelii peelii
Murray cod is known to be the largest of Australia's freshwater fish, measured by weight, rather than length. It is a slow-developing species that lives for over 30 years. It weighs in at 20kg (44lb); the largest recorded specimen was 112kg (247lb). The flesh of this fish is considered excellent, producing large, thick, white steaks with a delicate texture. It is a versatile fish that suits many methods of cooking and flavour combinations. It can also be cooked over an open fire; good, too, for escabeche.

Murray cod is farmed to a suitable size for individual portions.

The firm and meaty flesh of the Murray cod works well with Asian flavours and is equally good served battered, with chips.

It is light to dark green in colour. The underside is a creamy white

The scales of the barramundi are notoriously well attached to the flesh; the best way to remove them is with a scaler, running from tail to head.

Barramundi
Lates calcarifer
Juvenile fish are brown and mottled; adult fish grow to 1.2m (4ft) long. They have a pointed head and large jaw, and light-silver skin with a heavy armouring of scales. This fish has a succulent, flaky, white flesh with a low oil content, although there can be a tendency towards an earthiness, depending on where it is caught. Farmed fish are rarely much bigger than plate size; they differ in flavour from wild fish. Barramundi was popular with the native Aboriginal people, who would cook a whole large "barra" by wrapping the fish in wild ginger leaf and cooking it in the embers of a fire. The pearl (or cheek) of a barramundi is a particular treat: this is juicy and sweet flavoured. Barramundi is excellent barbecued, steamed, and grilled. The large fish can be filleted. For small fish, scale, gut, and cook whole.

Catfish and River cobbler

Catfish from various families have been caught in the wild and farmed on most continents for hundreds of years. They live in fresh inland and coastal waters. Many are nocturnal, bottom-feeding, and predatory. Catfish are considered a delicacy in many parts of the world, particularly in Central Europe and Africa. Migrants from these areas took catfish to the US, where it is now a popular part of traditional Southern food. Different species are common to each continent. Channel catfish and blue catfish (from the Ictaluridae family) are native to the US, living in freshwater streams, rivers, and creeks. The "channel cat" is farmed in an industry worth millions of dollars. River cobbler or basa (Pangasiidae) is native to Vietnam and Thailand, and has recently become valuable in the international market.

CUTS Live, whole, fillets (fresh or frozen).

EAT Cooked: Pan-fry, grill, bake, poach, deep-fry. **Preserved:** Smoked, dried, salted.

FLAVOUR PAIRINGS Corn meal, sesame seeds, soured cream, mushrooms, spring onions, parsley, bay leaf, thyme.

CLASSIC RECIPES Southern deep-fried catfish with corn meal; *pecel lele*; *ikan kele*; Tuscaloosa catfish.

Catfish skin is thick and slippery like an eel, and requires some effort to remove it with pliers.

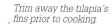

African sharptooth catfish ▲
Clarias gariepinus
This air-breathing freshwater catfish lives in rivers, lakes, and swamps. It is farmed in Africa, Europe, and the US. Farmed and wild catfish grow to a weight of 2kg (4½lb). It is hugely popular in the US and Africa. Catfish is moist and succulent, and as with many other freshwater species, it has a distinct taste of the river. The flesh is white and firm-textured, and suits various methods of cooking; it combines well with oriental flavours, including ginger and chilli.

Tilapia *Cichlidae*

There are around 100 species in the Cichlidae family and tilapia (also known as St Peter's fish) is their common name. These fish are found in warm areas of fresh water, where they can grow to 40cm (16in) long. Tilapia are second only to carp in their production through aquaculture, and some species are extensively farmed in many areas of the world. They are omnivorous, and aquatic vegetation makes up an important part of their diet, which makes them environmentally friendly to produce, as they do not need the extensive quantity of fish meal that other species demand. Many different hybrid species of tilapia are now farmed to produce sweet-flavoured, firm-textured white flesh. Tilapia are invasive and have become problematic in some areas where they have been introduced.

CUTS Fresh: Whole (unprepared and gutted), fillets. **Preserved:** Salted, dried.

EAT Cooked: Pan-fry, deep-fry, steam, bake, barbecue, grill.

FLAVOUR PAIRINGS Thai: bird's eye chilli, palm sugar, nam pla, shrimp paste, coriander, coconut, galangal.

CLASSIC RECIPE *Pla tub tim tod samrod.*

Trim away the tilapia's fins prior to cooking.

Take care to avoid spines when preparing the fish: there are some sharp ones that can cause a nasty wound.

River cobbler or basa is available ready processed into neat, white, frozen fillets.

River cobbler
Pangasius bocourti
The river cobbler is a member of the shark catfish family, and is also known as basa, bocourti, pangasius, and panga. It grows to 25–30cm (10–12in) when farmed and is now one of the most extensively farmed species worldwide (along with carp and tilapia). Its availability takes pressure off the threatened wild stocks of some species of catfish, and it is easy and environmentally friendly to farm. The river cobbler has very little flavour, but cooks to a flaky texture; it is ideal for deep-frying or taking strong flavours to help enliven it.

Tilapia scales are firmly attached to the body and require a scaler to remove them successfully. The skin of the fish is also cured and used for leatherwork.

Red tilapia
Oreochromis niloticus
Tilapia varies in colour from species to species, in much the same way as koi carp. Red tilapia are pinkish in hue; prepare and cook in exactly the same way as grey tilapia.

Fillets of tilapia are white and densely textured. They hold together well, so are suitable for pan-frying and grilling.

The fins are notoriously thick and dense, and require a good pair of scissors to cut through.

The sturgeon fish's tail is distinctive, as it's sickle-shaped and the upper fin is longer than the lower fin.

◀ Tilapia
Oreochromis niloticus
In Thailand, tilapia is known as pomegranate fish and cooked in a variety of ways. This hybrid tilapia, which is grey with a darker grey banding, is underused, but becoming steadily more accepted and important. The fish produces very firm, white fillets with a sweet flavour, which lend themselves to various methods of cooking, and take many flavours well. Farmed species are usually marketed at 20–25cm (8–10in) long.

Carp *Cyprinidae*

There are over 2,500 members of the Cyprinidae family including the carp, minnow, tench, roach, bream, dace, chub, and bitterling, as well as aquarium species, such as the koi and goldfish. As a group, most are native to North America, Africa, and Eurasia. They have no stomach or teeth and feed mainly on vegetation and some invertebrates. The species vary in size from a few millimetres to 1.5–2m (5ft–6ft 6in) long. The carp, as head of this family, was one of the earliest farmed species. It is still the top farmed species in the world today. Although extensively used and farmed in China, carp are not so popular in many cultures. This is because they tend towards an earthy, slightly muddy flavour (dependent on habitat), and have lots of fine bones. Some species are farmed for the Chinese, Eastern European, and kosher markets as well as land-locked countries that have no access to marine fish. Angling for coarse fish is a popular hobby and members of the carp family are particularly sought after. They have acute hearing, making them quite a challenge for fishing.
CUTS Fresh: Usually whole, or live.
EAT Cooked: Steam, roast, pan-fry, pané (cook in breadcrumbs), fry, bake. Use carp frames for stock and soup. **Preserved:** Carp roe, and smoked and salted.
FLAVOUR PAIRINGS Paprika, butter, capers, dill, garlic, parsley, corn meal, ginger, rice wine, sesame.
CLASSIC RECIPES *Carp au bleu*; roast Hungarian carp with paprika sauce; gefilte fish; carp in fennel sauce.

Grass carp
Ctenopharyngodon idella
Farmed extensively in China, this fish is also known as white amur in the US. It has been introduced to the US and New Zealand for sport, and to help maintain aquatic vegetation, although its presence can be destructive to certain plant life and aquatic species. It grows up to 1.2m (4ft) long. It has a herbaceous taste and benefits from the addition of robust flavours. In Eastern Europe it is served at feasts and festivals.

The grass carp is olive, shading to brownish-yellow, with a white underside.

Sturgeon *Acipenseridae*

The sturgeon is probably best known for the exquisite delicacy of its roe, marketed as caviar. Ultrasound is used to check for eggs in females. It also produces dense fillets with an excellent flavour. There are around 25 sturgeons in the Acipenseridae group, found in the northern hemisphere. Some live in brackish and fresh waters, while other species are anadromous (migratory fish that enter fresh water to spawn, then return to the sea). This unusual species looks quite prehistoric. Only some of its bones are calcified and bony; the skull and most of the vertebrae are made of cartilage. It has an elongated body with rows of scutes along the length of its back. Most species have sensitive barbels on the chin, which they use to suck food from the mud and into their mouth. Sturgeons grow slowly, and can live to be 100 years old. Well-known species prized for their roe include beluga (*Huso huso*); osetra (*A. gueldenstaedtii*), sevruga (*A. stellatus*), and sterlet (*A. ruthenus*). The freshwater Siberian sturgeon (*A. baerii*) is farmed, primarily to raise female fish for their roe, but male fish are used for their meat.
SUSTAINABILITY Due to the price that caviar can reach, these fish have been relentlessly overexploited and some are now seriously endangered. For the flesh, alternatives include carp and pike, for the roe, try lumpfish or salmon roe.
CUTS Fresh: Whole fish, steaks, and fillets, female roe.
EAT Cooked: Bake, pan-fry, steam.
Preserved: Smoked.
FLAVOUR PAIRINGS Horseradish, soured cream, beetroot, vinegar, butter, citrus.
CLASSIC RECIPES Caviar.

Take care when preparing a sturgeon whole: the scutes are sharp.

Freshwater bream
Abramis brama
Also known as carp bream, this fish is native to Europe and the Balkans. It is also found in the Caspian, Black, and Aral seas. It is usually landed at around 30cm (12in) long, but is known to grow to nearly three times this size. It produces white fillets that lack the earthiness of carp. Grill or bake with herbs, such as thyme or rosemary.

The freshwater bream has a generous covering of scales and is silver-bronze in colour.

The common carp has scales firmly attached to the body. Wash it to remove the slime, before scaling, otherwise it will be too slippery to handle.

Common carp
Cyprinus carpio
Also known as mirror carp, spiegel, or leather carp, this fish has a brown back fading to a golden belly; sometimes it is a more silvery colour. It has high flanks and, as with other coarse fish, a very thick slime that needs to be washed away prior to handling. This fish was traditionally soaked in acidulated water to help remove the slime and balance its slightly earthy flavour. It grows to 1.2m (4ft).

Siberian sturgeon
Acipenser baerii
Farmed in France for its roe, this species is native to China and Russia. It has a brownish-grey back and a pale belly, and can grow up to 2m (6ft 6in) long. The flesh is firm, meaty, and well-flavoured. It is good for grilling, pan-frying, and barbecuing. (See fish roes on pages 390–391.)

Pike *Esocidae*

A member of the Esocidae family, the pike is a predator that feeds on other pike, smaller fish, birds, snakes, and mammals (including mice and rats). It is a freshwater fish, caught commercially and by recreational fishermen. The pike is also known as the pickerel (usually used to describe smaller species), snoek, and jackfish (US). Pike are found in the rivers of North America, Western Europe, Siberia, and Eurasia. There are several species, including the muskellunge pike (*E. masquinongy*), grass pickerel pike (*E. americanus vermiculatus*), and the northern pike (*E. lucius*). It is famously used in France for *quenelles de brochet*, a mousseline of sieved pike flesh with cream and egg white. Pike has a fine flavour, but contains many small bones. This recipe makes the best of the flesh, as the bones are dealt with prior to serving.

CUTS Whole; fillets.
EAT Cooked: Pan-fry, grill, steam, poach, roast. **Preserved:** Smoked, salted, dried, roe.

FLAVOUR PAIRINGS Unsalted butter, sage, lemon, cream, bay leaf, white wine.
CLASSIC RECIPES *Quenelles de brochet* (pike quenelles); traditional roast pike.

Zander, Walleye, Perch, and American yellow perch *Percidae*

The Percidae family of freshwater fish is found globally. Once eaten by those with no access to the coast, many species are now less frequently used for the table. They remain popular with recreational fishermen; commercial fishing and aquaculture are still viable in some cases. Percids share the same fin pattern: the first dorsal fin is spiny (the number of spines varies), the second is soft. The family includes the zander, perch, ruffe, American yellow perch, silver perch, sauger, and walleye. The largest is the zander, a predatory fish found in fresh water; some are caught in brackish water. Native to Eastern Europe, it has also been introduced to Western Europe and the US. The perch (also known as the European perch or English perch), native to Europe and Asia, has been introduced to South Africa, New Zealand, and Australia. It is deep green with some stripes, scaly, and has red fins. In cool European waters, it rarely reaches more than 40cm (16in); it can reach a greater size in Australia. Another sought-after species, the walleye, is closely related to zander. It is native to Canada and the northern US. The walleye is not farmed, but for decades has been used to replenish stocks in some river systems.

CUTS Usually whole fish.
EAT Cooked: Pan-fry, grill, bake, roast.
FLAVOUR PAIRINGS Butter, herbs including chives, sage, rosemary, thyme, and bay leaf, lemon and white wine vinegar, cream, eggs.
CLASSIC RECIPES Perch: water souchy (fish soup); Zander: matelote (fish stew from the Loire). All these fish could be used for quenelles and gefilte fish.

Walleye
Sander vitreus
Chefs often say that the walleye has the best flavour of any freshwater fish. It grows to about 92cm (3ft) long and its colour depends on its habitat. The meat has few bones and is light and flaky, with a mild taste.

Remove the generous layer of scales prior to gutting and cooking.

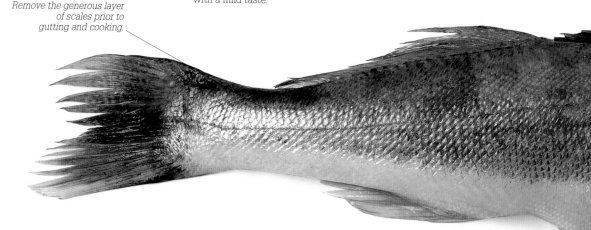

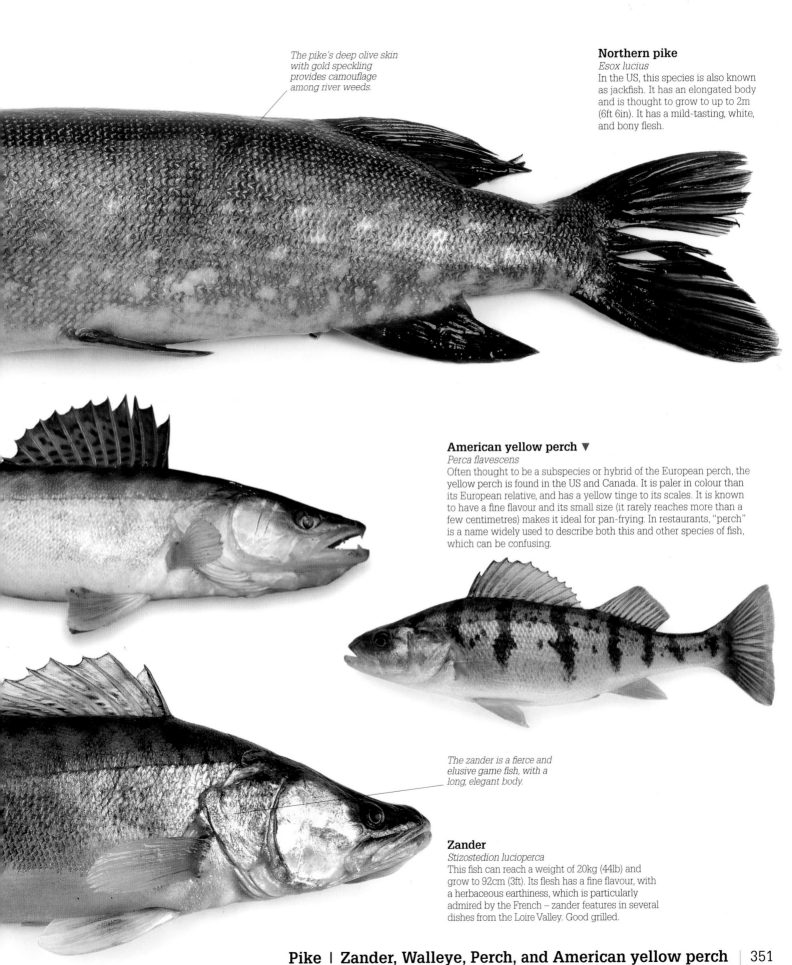

The pike's deep olive skin with gold speckling provides camouflage among river weeds.

Northern pike
Esox lucius
In the US, this species is also known as jackfish. It has an elongated body and is thought to grow to up to 2m (6ft 6in). It has a mild-tasting, white, and bony flesh.

American yellow perch ▼
Perca flavescens
Often thought to be a subspecies or hybrid of the European perch, the yellow perch is found in the US and Canada. It is paler in colour than its European relative, and has a yellow tinge to its scales. It is known to have a fine flavour and its small size (it rarely reaches more than a few centimetres) makes it ideal for pan-frying. In restaurants, "perch" is a name widely used to describe both this and other species of fish, which can be confusing.

The zander is a fierce and elusive game fish, with a long, elegant body.

Zander
Stizostedion lucioperca
This fish can reach a weight of 20kg (44lb) and grow to 92cm (3ft). Its flesh has a fine flavour, with a herbaceous earthiness, which is particularly admired by the French – zander features in several dishes from the Loire Valley. Good grilled.

SUSTAINABILITY CHOICE

Buy farmed mussels

The development of some shellfish farming, particularly mussels, has been very positive. Set a small distance from the shore, the mussels grow like bunches of grapes on ropes or wooden stakes placed in the water. After around three years the mussels are harvested – a process that causes minimal harm to the environment. Fish meal is not used, as the mussels feed on naturally occurring nutrients in the water to develop a wonderful sweet flavour. As a species that are at the bottom of the food chain, they are one of the world's most sustainable seafoods.

Trout, Char, and Grayling *Salmonidae*

This group of fish is extensive and an important food globally. The species are all rich in oil. The pink colour of the flesh is the result of a diet of crustaceans that have a naturally occurring caryatid pigment. Farmed fish are sometimes given a chemical substitute to replicate this. Some species of trout are used for aquaculture or to stock trout lakes. Most trout spend their lives in fresh waters around the world; others are anadromous and migrate to the sea, returning to their natal river to spawn. Trout can have an earthy taste, because they feed over muddy riverbeds. Farmed fish may be reared with a gravel bed and then purged in clean water prior to harvest, in order to prevent this. Indigenous North American trout include the rainbow, Dolly Varden, and brook trout. Other popular species include lake trout (*Salmo trutta lacustris*), golden trout (*S. aguabonita*), and the cut-throat trout (*S. clarki*). The char is similar in size and appearance to trout. Lake char (*Salvelinus namaycush*) reach around 4kg (9lb) in weight; the Arctic char can reach over 6kg (13lb). The grayling (*Thymallus thymallus*) is a popular game fish in Europe and North America. It has a distinct aroma of fresh thyme when landed. It is not harvested commercially.

CUTS Whole, gutted, fillets, roe.
EAT Cooked: Pan-fry, bake, grill, roast. **Preserved:** Hot- and cold-smoked, salted roe.
FLAVOUR PAIRINGS Classical French: white wine vinegar, butter, lemon, chives, almonds, hazelnuts.
CLASSIC RECIPES Trout with Serrano ham; trout in breadcrumbs; trout with almonds; *truite au bleu* (trout poached immediately on capture in an acidulated court bouillon, and turns blue); potted char.

Rainbow trout ▲
Oncorhynchus mykiss
The North American rainbow trout was introduced into Europe at the end of the 19th century. It grows quickly and is farmed extensively. In European waters, wild fish rarely grow bigger than 10kg (22lb); in the US they can be twice this size. It can be cooked whole and then gutted, or as fillets. Its very fine bones can be difficult to locate.

The rainbow trout has a bright, silvery skin with rainbow-hued speckles.

Once cooked, rainbow trout fillet breaks into neat flakes and has a herbaceous flavour.

The brown trout has a pale skin with chocolate-brown and orange speckles across its flanks.

Brown trout ▲
Salmo trutta
Indigenous to the rivers of Europe, the brown trout is not fished from the wild commercially; it is farmed in small quantities, particularly organically, and can grow to up to 15kg (33lb). Wild fish are usually much smaller and are often extremely earthy in flavour. Farmed fish tend to be more delicate and sweet. Make the most of the flavour of this fish by wrapping it with faggots of mixed herbs and barbecuing it.

The Arctic char has light spots on a dark background; its colour varies according to habitat and time of the year.

Arctic char
Salvelinus alpinus

These fish are also known as mountain trout and salmon trout. Some are landlocked in deep glacial lakes, specifically the Lake District in the north of England, where they were trapped at the end of the last ice age. Farmed fish are harvested at about 3kg (6½lb) in weight. The flesh is less earthy than that of trout, with an aroma of thyme and cut grass. Excellent poached and potted with butter, mace, and citrus; serve on Melba toast.

Robust herbs, such as sage, rosemary, and parsley marry well with the sweet, flaky texture of Arctic char.

Brook trout
Salvelinus fontinalis

Also known as brook char, speckled trout, red trout, and squaretail. Its colour is green to brown with a distinctive marbling. It grows up to 65cm (25½in), and its white-to-yellow meat is very tasty.

The shiny silver skin of sea trout is interspersed with black and green dots towards the fish's back.

Sea trout
Salmo trutta

Sea trout, also commonly known as salmon trout, is the migratory form of the brown trout. It has a particularly sweet and fine flavour that is not as intense as that of salmon. Poach it whole or in fillets, and serve with hollandaise sauce and lemon.

Atlantic salmon *Salmonidae*

Salmon are found in both Atlantic and Pacific waters. The salmon is anadromous, spending part of its life cycle in fresh water, and part in the sea. Only one species is found in the Atlantic. Most Atlantic salmon is now farmed in Scotland and Norway. Japan consumes one-third of the world's salmon, but it is also enjoyed in many European countries and worldwide. Wild salmon and farmed species are quite different. Farmed fish can be of excellent quality and flavour, with a good balance of oil.

SUSTAINABILITY The high demand for the "king of fish", the wild Atlantic salmon, has led to overexploitation and many fishing bans are now in place. Once prolific, a wild specimen of Atlantic salmon has become a rare sight and it subsequently fetches a very high price. The aquaculture of the Atlantic salmon became a big commercial enterprise during the 1980s and it caused much controversy at its inception, as there were many environmental issues to overcome.

Alternatives to Atlantic salmon include organically farmed trout and responsibly sourced Pacific salmon species, such as sockeye.
CUTS Whole, fillets, steaks, head, roe.
EAT Cooked: Pan-fry, poach, grill, bake. Head often used as a base for soup. **Raw:** Frozen and sold for sushi and sashimi. **Preserved:** Hot- (kiln-roasted salmon) and cold-smoked. Salted roe used as keta, a caviar substitute.
FLAVOUR PAIRINGS Lemon, butter, dill, samphire, tarragon, ginger, sorrel, kecap manis.
CLASSIC RECIPES Poached salmon with hollandaise sauce; gravadlax; salmon coulibiac (Russia); traditional poached and dressed whole salmon.

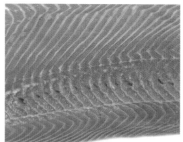

Atlantic salmon fillets are particularly good roasted, barbecued, or pan-fried.

Atlantic salmon ◄ ▲
Salmo salar
Salmon may be described as fry, smelt, parr, grilse, or kelt, depending on the stage of its life cycle and whether it's in fresh water or the sea. Farmed fish are sold at 3.5–4.5kg (8–10lb). The flesh is firm, moist, and oily with a delicate flavour. To cook a whole salmon, measure the thickest part of its girth with a piece of string. For each 2.5cm (1in), calculate 4 minutes cooking time at 230°C (450°F/Gas 8). It will be sweet and succulent.

Pacific salmon *Salmonidae*

There are several species of Pacific salmon, including the chinook (king), sockeye, chum, coho, pink, and Japanese cherry salmon. They are prolific species and although there is some farming, they are caught commercially by many countries of the Pacific Rim, particularly Alaska and Canada. Unlike the Atlantic salmon, which can return to the river after spawning, Pacific species die. The chum salmon (*Oncorhynchus keta*) (MSC certified) is also known as dog salmon, keta salmon, qualla, calico salmon, hum, and fall salmon. It is abundant in the North Pacific, in the waters of Korea and Japan, and the Bering Sea. It is also found in Arctic Alaska and south to San Diego in California. The flesh is canned, dried, and salted; the roe is also used. Pink salmon (*O. gorbuscha*) is also known as humpback salmon and gorbuscha. This is the smallest Pacific salmon (it averages 2.25kg/5lb) and is found in the Arctic and Northwest to Eastern Central Pacific Ocean. Coho (*O. kisutch*) (MSC certified) is also known as silver salmon, blueback, medium red salmon, jack salmon, and silverside. Growing to around 110cm (43in), it is

found in the North Pacific from the Anadyr River in Russia, south towards Hokkaido in Japan; from Alaska to Baja California and Mexico. It has a fine-textured flesh and full flavour. The Japanese cherry salmon (*O. masou*) is also known as masu. It is caught in the northwest Pacific, the Sea of Okhotsk, and the Sea of Japan.
CUTS Whole, fillets, steaks.
EAT Cooked: Poach, pan-fry, microwave, grill, bake, steam.
Preserved: Smoked, roe, dried, salted, frozen, canned.
FLAVOUR PAIRINGS Asian flavours: coriander, soy sauce, sesame, chilli, lime. Excellent for plank cooking.
CLASSIC RECIPES Salmon coulibiac (Russia); salmon sashimi; poached and dressed salmon; squaw candy.

Chinook salmon
Oncorhynchus tshawytscha
Also called the king, Pacific, spring, black, quinnat, and chub salmon. It can grow to 1.5m (5ft); the usual size is 70cm (27in). It is caught in the Arctic, and Northwest to Northeast Pacific from Alaska down to California and Japan. This fish has a similar oil-rich texture and flesh to Atlantic salmon and suits the same methods of cooking.

In the sea, the chinook salmon has a greeny blue back with lots of small, dark spots.

A wild Atlantic salmon has iron-grey skin along the back with black specks and well-developed fins. Farmed fish are likely to be more speckled and often have malformed fins.

Sockeye ▶
Oncorhynchus nerka
Also known as red and blueback salmon. Caught in the North Pacific, this is one of the most commercially important species and can grow up to 84cm (33in). It can take a little longer to cook than an Atlantic fish; the lack of fat also means that it can dry out: baste or use a marinade to keep it moist.

The chinook salmon is a little leaner than the Atlantic salmon. It is succulent and sweet, and good for grilling, pan-frying, and baking.

The sockeye's closely knit, lean, meaty, dense flesh is a deep orange from the crustaceans in its diet.

A chinook resembles the Atlantic salmon more closely than any of the other Pacific species.

Atlantic salmon | Pacific salmon | 357

Needlefish and Flying fish

The billfish family of needlefish (also known as garfish) is related to that of the flying fish. The needlefish (from the Belonidae family) are slender, elongated fish found in fresh water, brackish, and marine environments, with around 45 species in all. It has a long beak containing many sharp teeth for a jaw, and is found in temperate and tropical waters worldwide. It makes small jumps out of the water to escape predators. It is often caught at night, when it is attracted to the surface by lanterns and torches. The flying fish, a member of the Exocoetidae family, is a marine fish with around 64 species. It is found mainly in tropical and subtropical waters of the Atlantic, Pacific, and Indian oceans. It uses its long pectoral fins that are similar to a bird's wing, to escape predators by leaping out of the water for up to 50m (164ft). It can leap much further if there is updraught on a wave and the fish vibrates its tail. An ingenious way of fishing for it is by holding nets in the air. These fish have long, slim fillets that are generally pale grey with a sweet taste and delicate texture.
CUTS Whole, fillets, roe (tobiko).

EAT Cooked: Pan-fry. **Preserved:** Dried. **Raw:** Sushi.
FLAVOUR PAIRINGS Okra, corn meal, chilli, onion, garlic, peppers.
CLASSIC RECIPES Cou cou (national dish of flying fish from Barbados).

Atlantic needlefish
Strongylura marina
Caught in the Western Atlantic from Maine to the Gulf of Mexico and Brazil. It grows to 1.2m (4ft) and has a sweet, succulent, white flesh.

In fresh water, eels are a deep emerald green; in brackish water they revert to dark brown and silver.

European eel
Anguilla anguilla
This species usually grows to about 80cm (31½in). Eels are popular for eating at various stages in their life. Bootlace eels or elvers are usually deep-fried – a delicacy in parts of Europe. Smoked eel is also a delicacy and the eel's very oily flesh is especially suitable for hot-smoking. For cooking fresh, eels are usually skinned as soon as they have been killed, then gutted and cut into steaks or fillets. For smoking, they are often left whole. They have a very distinctive firm, slightly rubbery, and oil-rich texture.

Eel *Anguillidae*

There are 22 known members of the eel group. They have a long, slithering, snake-like body. The eel is a catadromous fish: it is spawned in the sea and moves to fresh water to mature, then returns to the sea to spawn, after which it dies. Eels live in temperate, tropical, and subtropical waters worldwide. They have a distinct spawning ground, depending on the species. Eels have firm and rich-tasting flesh, and an oily texture.

SUSTAINABILITY There has been a massive decline in eels over recent years, which is attributed not only to overfishing but also to pollution. They are listed as critically endangered. Some species are extensively farmed in Northern Europe and Asia, to try to take the pressure off the wild stocks, but this has done little to halt the decline. There is no close alternative, but you could use an oil-rich species such as mackerel.
CUTS Live, whole; smoked whole and in fillets.
EAT Cooked: Grill, pan-fry, bake, poach (for jellied eels).
Preserved: Smoked, dried.
FLAVOUR PAIRINGS Bay leaf, vinegar, apples, red and white wine, allspice berries, cloves, mint, parsley, cream.
CLASSIC RECIPES Jellied eels; *matelote d'anguille* (France); deep-fried elvers; *anguilla allo spiedo* (Italy); eel and bay leaf kebabs; *bisato sull'ara*; fried eel; *capitone marinato* (Italy).

Garfish ▲
Belone belone
The garfish is also known as the garpike, hornpike, or greenbone. It is famous for its luminous green bone structure. It is widely distributed in the Northeast Atlantic and the Mediterranean. (There is another group of fish found in North American waters that are considered to be "true gars" – *Lepisosteidae*.) Garfish grows to about 46cm (18in) long. It is used both fresh and frozen. Try it fried, grilled, and baked. It has a delicate taste and a fine, flaky texture.

The Atlantic needlefish has a silvery skin; its needle-shaped body does not contain an extensive amount of meat.

Japanese flying fish ▲
Cheilopogon agoo
Flying fish are a popular commercial fish for Japan, Vietnam, Indonesia, India, and Barbados (where it is the national fish although it has been overfished in this area). Japanese flying fish grow to 35cm (14in) long and have a subtle flavour; the flesh is quite meaty and firm. Best seasoned and then barbecued or fried. Their golden roe is used to garnish sushi.

Moray eel and Conger eel

There are over 190 known species in the conger group of eels and 200 species of moray eels (from the Muraenidae and Congridae groups respectively), caught in many oceans worldwide. They are not particularly noted for their eating quality: most are caught as a by-catch or for sport. Some conger eels are over 3m (10ft) long and weigh well over 100kg (220lb). They are ferocious predators, with sharp, snappy teeth – so handle live fish with extreme caution. The largest and most prolific conger is the American conger (*Conger oceanicus*). The Japanese serve a delicacy of raw baby conger eels, called *noresore*, often with ponzu sauce. Moray eels are found in tropical and subtropical waters. As adults they are usually vividly marked and have the long, slender body of other eels. They are well known for their sharp teeth, poor eyesight, and excellent sense of smell. As a fierce predator, they are known to attack humans if disturbed. All eels are popular in South American, Japanese, and Chinese cookery; smoked eel is a European delicacy.

SUSTAINABILITY Conger eels have been overfished. There are no close alternatives, but monkfish has a similar firm texture.
CUTS Whole, gutted, or cut into steaks.
EAT Cooked: Pan-fry, bake.
Preserved: Smoked, dried, sometimes jellied.
FLAVOUR PAIRINGS Onions, paprika, smoked paprika, chilli, peppers, olive oil, red wine, parsley.
CLASSIC RECIPES *Caldeirada* (Portugese fish stew); fried eel (Middle East).

Conger eels have a smooth, scaleless skin. The body tapers towards the tail.

The tail end of a conger eel is notoriously bony so it is best used for stock.

Conger eel
Conger conger
Found in the Eastern Atlantic from Norway to Senegal; also in the Mediterranean and Black Sea. It can reach over 3m (9ft 10in) long. This fish has a sweet, almost pork-like flavour and is best simply grilled with a flavoured butter. It has an extremely dense texture and is also perfect for pan-frying or casseroling. It takes strong flavours, such as smoked paprika and spices, well.

Shark, Skate, and Ray

Several thousand species of shark, from many families, are found globally, from the Great White to the dogfish. They often find their way to fish and chip shop menus, where they are sold as rock salmon, flake, and in the EU, huss. They are available whole, skinned, and boned. Skates and rays belong to the Rajidae family and are related to the sharks. They are found in all oceans from the Arctic to the Antarctic. They are flat and their large pectoral fins or "wings" give them a rhomboid shape. The mouth and gills are on the underside of the body and the eggs are laid in a leathery capsule known as a mermaid's purse. Their skin can be challenging to remove without pliers and gloves. Such species expel their urea through the gills and if incorrectly stored, smell strongly of ammonia. If a fish smells of ammonia, do not buy it. The wings of skates and rays take longer to cook than most thin white fillets. They have an unusual fibrous texture and taste herbaceous and woody. A thick piece of cartilage at the shoulder end of the fillet comes loose when the fish is cooked.

SUSTAINABILITY There has been a decline in the stocks of some shark species, which like the Great White, are now protected. They have been overfished for their use in Chinese medicine, and the Chinese classic, shark fin soup. Skates have also been overexploited in many areas. They are subject to a fishing quota and the landing of some species in designated areas is banned. Alternatives include responsibly sourced monkfish.

CUTS Shark: Fresh and frozen, fillets, whole. Skate: Wings, "knobs" (muscles taken from the back of the fish).

EAT Cooked: Shark: Pan-fry, grill, roast, deep-fry. Skate: Pan-fry, deep-fry, poach, roast. **Preserved:** Shark: Smoked and dried.

Thornback ray
Raja clavata
Also known as roker, thorny, and maiden ray, the thornback ray is caught in the Eastern Atlantic, from Iceland, Norway, the North Sea and the Baltic, south to Morocco and Namibia, including the Mediterranean and the Black Sea. Most thornback rays grow to 85cm (33½in). The back of the fish is different shades of brown with variegated dark spots. There are some responsibly sourced rays available. It has a strong taste and is best poached, baked, or dusted with seasoned flour and pan-fried. The dense flesh of a ray wing takes 10–12 minutes to poach.

FLAVOUR PAIRINGS Shark: Beer batter, tartare sauce, soy, sesame oil, ginger, and chilli. Skate: Vinegar, capers, parsley, lemon juice, butter.
CLASSIC RECIPES Skate with beurre noisette; skate with beurre noir and capers.

Smoothhound
Mustelus mustelus
Also known as flake and rock salmon, smoothhound, from the Triakidae family, is very similar to dogfish and huss. This small shark variety usually grows to around 50cm (20in) and lives in coastal waters worldwide. Once the shark is fully mature, it ventures out into deeper water. The variety has been heavily overfished and there is a strict catch quota in place. The flesh is firm and meaty with a very distinctive, almost pork-like taste. It is great deep-fried, pan-fried, or used in stir fries.

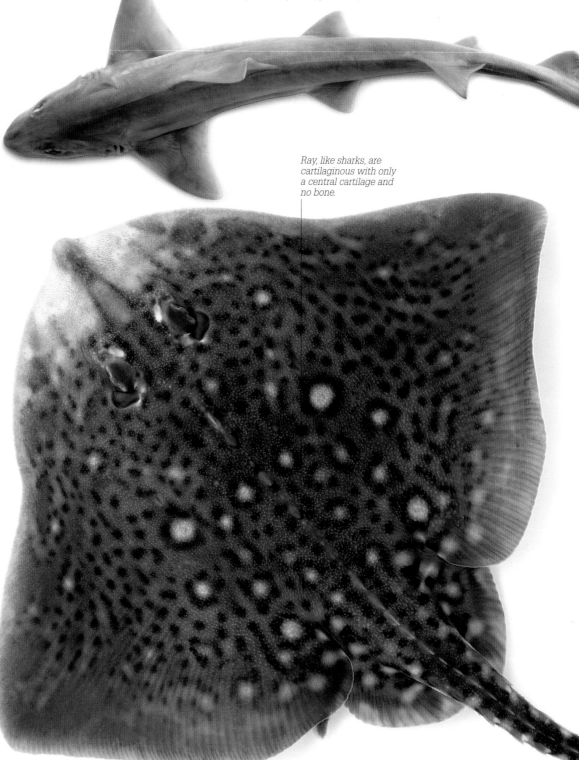

Ray, like sharks, are cartilaginous with only a central cartilage and no bone.

Plaice and Sole *Pleuronectidae*

The Pleuronectidae group (the name means "side swimmers" – these are flat fish) includes plaice, some flounders, halibut, and some types of sole, such as lemon sole (*Microstomus kitt*), petrale sole (*Eopsetta jordani*), rex sole (*Glyptocephalus zachirus*), and North Pacific sole (*Eopsetta grigorjewi*). True sole belong to the *Soleidae* group. All are demersal fish and have white flesh; the main concentration of oil is in the liver. They are fished in Europe, North America, and in the northern Pacific. When a flat fish hatches, it is a tiny, round fish; as it grows, it turns on to its left or right side and the eyes move to one side of the head. Most flat fish are dextral, with eyes on the right side. The fish use the seabed to hide and have highly camouflaged skin on the upper body to enable them to blend into their habitat. The underside of a wild fish is pearlescent white, helping it to blend in with its environment if viewed from underneath. These fish have a delicate taste and texture. They are usually gutted on landing, enabling the fish to retain quality. Most flat fish have a heavy coating of slime that in the main should be clear. As the fish loses condition, the slime becomes sticky and discoloured (known as "custardy") and this indicates that it is past its best.

SUSTAINABILITY All of these species are heavily targeted in many countries and are subject to a legal-minimum landing size. There are some MSC-certified sources.

CUTS Usually gutted on landing. Sold whole (head on or off), cross-cut and quarter-cross fillets, skin on or off.

EAT Cooked: Pan-fry, poach, deep-fry, bake.

FLAVOUR PAIRINGS Seasoned flour, butter, lemon, parsley, breadcrumbs, sage, chestnut mushrooms, cowberry, potato.

CLASSIC RECIPES Plaice/lemon sole meunière; sole Véronique.

Lemon sole
Microstomus kitt

Also known as smear dab and Scottish sole, lemon sole is caught in shallow seas in Northern Europe. Its usual size is 25–30cm (10–12in). A very fresh fish has a heavy coating of creamy slime, unlike other fresh, flat fish, which have a clear slime. It has a sweet, mild taste and delicate texture.

Lemon sole is good simply rolled in flour and pan-fried, grilled, or poached.

Lemon sole can be identified by lemon piping (a strip of yellow flesh) around the gill flap.

Plaice
Pleuronectes platessa

This plaice is common in European waters, and is the most popular flat fish in Europe, with a mild taste and fine texture. It has a distinct "wrist" at the tail and a bony ridge from the head to the gills. The underside is white with chevron markings that indicate the pattern of muscle bands. It can grow to 60cm (23½in), but this is rare. It is best from May to December/January.

Some species have a weak electrical organ in their long, slender tail.

Plaice have a greenish-brown skin and orange or rusty-green spots.

Plaice and Sole *Continued*

Petrale sole ▶
Eopsetta jordani
The petrale sole is also known as Pacific coast sole and regarded as one of the finest sole in that region. It is usually caught at around 30cm (12in). It is found in the Eastern Pacific, from the coast of Alaska to northern Baja California and Mexico. It is usually skinned and filleted for sale. It has a sweet flesh that is best pan-fried.

The upper surface of the petrale sole is a uniform light to dark brown.

Petrale sole's head is deep with large eyes on the right side. The fish is white in colour on the blind side.

White, flaky fillets of petrale sole can be deep-fried, pan-fried, or grilled.

The skin of the Atlantic halibut is a uniform dark brown to black; young fish are often marbled.

The witch produces very slim fillets. It's best to trim the head and fins when cooking whole.

▲ Witch
Glyptocephalus cynoglossus
Also known as grey flounder and occasionally marketed as Torbay sole. The witch is found in the Eastern Atlantic, from Northern Spain to Northern Norway, and in the Western Atlantic from Canada to North Carolina in the US. It grows up to 60cm (2ft) long and has a subtle flavour. Best baked whole; or filleted, rolled in seasoned flour, pan-fried in butter and then finished with a splash of lemon.

Dab ▶
Limanda limanda
Dabs are found in abundance in the Northeast Atlantic. It is one of the smaller flat fish and can grow to around 40cm (16in), but 30cm (12in) is more common. The white flesh of a dab is best eaten fresh, but has very little flavour. It is small, so is usually trimmed and cooked whole on the bone. Also sold dried, salted, and smoked.

Dabs are usually pale brown with darker coloured blotches.

Halibut *Pleuronectidae*

Sometimes called the "Cow of the Sea", this fish is the largest of all the flat fish. A handful of halibut species are caught in Atlantic and Pacific waters, and are highly regarded. As with all flat fish, halibut vary in colour depending on the seabed that they inhabit; the top side provides camouflage. A wild fish can reach mammoth proportions: some specimens have been recorded as weighing over 330kg (700lb). However, most landed today would not exceed 11–13.5kg (24–30lb). This fish has a dense, white, firm-textured flesh and has become so sought after that it is now extensively farmed to meet high demand.

SUSTAINABILITY Halibut mature slowly, making them very susceptible to overfishing. Wild Atlantic halibut has been overexploited and there is a minimum landing size and strict regulations for catch quota in many areas. It is better to choose the farmed or Pacific species as an alternative.

CUTS Large fish: steaks/cutlets; Small fish: whole, fillets, also called fletches.

EAT Cooked: Steam, pan-fry, grill, poach, bake. **Preserved:** Dried, salted, cold-smoked.

FLAVOUR PAIRINGS Butter, seasoned flour, nutmeg, gherkins, capers, lemon.

CLASSIC RECIPES Poached halibut with hollandaise sauce; grilled halibut with beurre blanc.

Atlantic halibut ▼
Hippoglossus hippoglossus
This fish can reach up to 4.5m (14ft 9in) in length. It is found in the Eastern and Western Atlantic, and is extensively farmed. The fish is moist and very lean with a sweet, mild taste; the lack of fat makes it easy to over-cook, as it dries easily.

The wild halibut has an even covering of clear slime and farmed fish may be covered in an inky slime.

A halibut's cheeks can be harvested, as they are sweet and succulent.

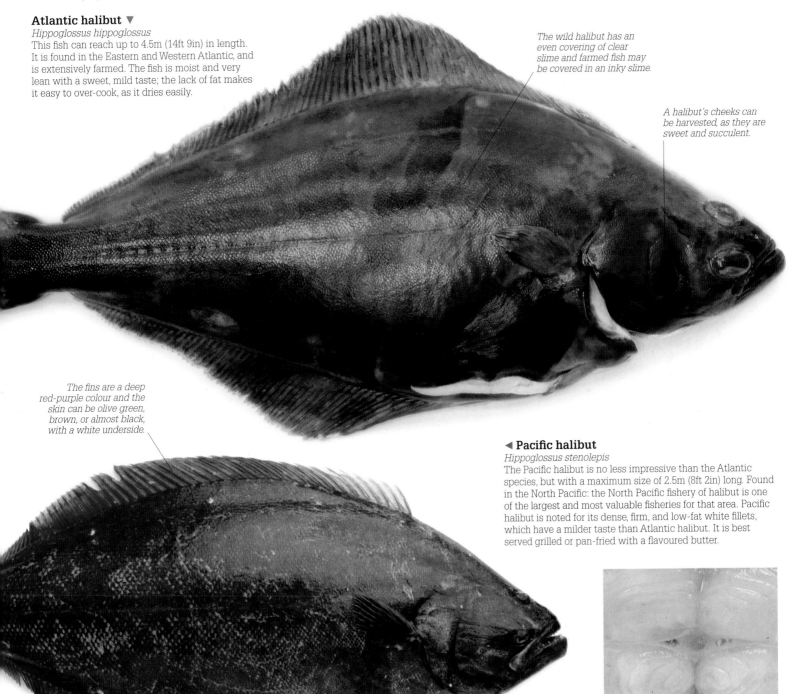

The fins are a deep red-purple colour and the skin can be olive green, brown, or almost black, with a white underside.

◄ Pacific halibut
Hippoglossus stenolepis
The Pacific halibut is no less impressive than the Atlantic species, but with a maximum size of 2.5m (8ft 2in) long. Found in the North Pacific: the North Pacific fishery of halibut is one of the largest and most valuable fisheries for that area. Pacific halibut is noted for its dense, firm, and low-fat white fillets, which have a milder taste than Atlantic halibut. It is best served grilled or pan-fried with a flavoured butter.

Pacific halibut produces thick, white, flaky fillets with a light flavour.

Sole _Soleidae_

Found in waters worldwide, the "true" sole includes around 165 species. They have a long, slipper-shaped body with small eyes, mouth, and tail. Some members have attractive markings and patterns; most have a unique coarse skin texture – similar to a cat's tongue – if stroked from tail to head. The maximum length is around 70cm (27½in). These species of fish are dextral, with eyes on the right side of the head. The white flesh has a subtle and distinctive flavour.

SUSTAINABILITY Dover sole is popular in Europe, in the restaurant trade. This has lead to overfishing. A strict size for landed fish is in place, as is a catch quota. Look for MSC-certified fishery Dover sole or try responsibly sourced turbot, lemon sole, or plaice as alternatives.

CUTS Usually gutted and sold whole, trimmed and skinned, and in fillets.

EAT Cooked: Grill, pan-fry.

FLAVOUR PAIRINGS Lemon, butter, seasoned flour, cucumber, mint, shiitake mushrooms, mushrooms, truffle oil, capers, parsley.

CLASSIC RECIPES Sole colbert; lemon sole Doria; grilled Dover sole with anchovy butter; sole Véronique.

Dover sole
Solea vulgaris
Also known as common sole, tongue, or slip sole (a small specimen), Dover sole can be expensive. It grows up to 70cm (27½in) and is caught in the Eastern Atlantic and farmed on a small scale. It has very firm and slightly rubbery white flesh; full-flavoured. It is best when well past rigor mortis, as flavour and texture develop properly.

Turbot, Brill, and Megrim _Scophthalimidae_

The family includes turbot, brill, megrim, and a species called topknots. They are found in many temperate seas of the Atlantic and Pacific oceans. Turbot and brill are a valuable species and highly commercial. They are sinistral fish, with their eyes on the left side of the head. They can have a similar coloured skin, but there are differences. Turbot is almost circular in shape and the dark eye-side has no scales but large, sharp tubercles. It is farmed extensively. Although the flesh has a flaky texture, it holds its shape well and so is versatile. Brill is oval in shape and has scales, but no tubercles. Like many other species, it adapts its colour to its habitat. The megrim is noted for its large mouth that extends into a tube. It is a popular food in southern Europe, particularly Spain. Megrim is best eaten quite fresh; it needs seasoning, and butter or olive oil to prevent it from drying out.

SUSTAINABILITY Turbot and brill have a maximum catch quota in place, and landed fish must be of a minimum size. Alternatives can be responsibly sourced lemon sole, plaice, and responsibly farmed or sourced halibut.

CUTS Whole and head on; trimmed; fillets (depending on species). Large turbots may be cut into steaks.

EAT Cooked: Steam, pan-fry, crust, bake, roast, grill.

FLAVOUR PAIRINGS Wild mushrooms, champagne, cream, butter, shellfish stock, lemon, Gruyère cheese, Parmesan.

CLASSIC RECIPE Poached turbot with oysters and champagne.

Turbot
Psetta maxima
Also known as britt, butt, breet, it's one of the most expensive of all flat fish and highly sought after. It is found in the northeast Atlantic, throughout the Mediterranean and along the European coasts to the Arctic Circle. It grows up to 1m (3ft) long. The flesh is meaty and, unlike other white fish, holds together well enough for stir-frying. It's also good for poaching, pan-frying, and grilling. It's often sold cut into thick steaks with the backbone running through the steak. It has a rounded and recognizable, very fine and sweet flavour.

Turbot is firm, white, dense and suitable for various cooking methods.

Wild turbot varies from dark mottled brown to grey; farmed fish are light grey-green to dark grey-black.

The megrim has a glassy, light brown skin and a white underside.

Megrim
Lepidorhombus whiffiagonis
Also known as meg, sale fluke, Scarborough sole, or whiff, megrim is a deep-water fish living in the Northeast Atlantic. It is commonly found at 25cm (10in) long. Best trimmed and cooked whole on the bone; it has a similar flavour to plaice and is flaky, delicate, and low in fat. Suits subtle flavours such as butter and mild herbs.

Sand sole
Pegusa lascaris
Also known as snouted sole, lascar, and Atlantic sole, sand sole is found in the North and Southeastern Atlantic, the Mediterranean, and the Black Sea. It lacks the superior flavour of the Dover sole. It is of minor commercial importance, but is available. Skin the fish whole and cook on the bone.

The sand sole has yellow-brown skin with pale blotches and looks similar to the Dover sole.

The fish has an oval body up to 40cm (16in) in length with smoothly curving dorsal and anal fins.

Brill ▼
Scophthalmus rhombus
Also known as kite and pearl. Brill reaches a maximum length of 75cm (29½in). It lives in the Eastern Atlantic, from Iceland to Morocco, throughout the Black Sea and the Mediterranean. At one time it was underrated, now it's well regarded. It has an equally fine, sweet flavour to turbot, but is more flaky.

Brill has a superb fine, white, flaky texture. It is best pan-fried, grilled, or roasted.

A turbot has a lot of sharp nodules on its skin, known as turbercles.

Brill is a sandy, greenish-brown. The young fish are dark brown. It is often flecked with white.

Abalone *Haliotidae*

Abalone is considered a rare delicacy and gourmet food. It is harvested from the wild and from aquaculture in many coastal waters in oceans worldwide. There are about 100 species of this sea snail, which vary greatly in size. The well-flavoured meat is found in an ear-shaped shell. Abalone is also known as ormer, sea-ear, ear-shell, Venus's ears, perlemoen (South Africa), muttonfish (Australia), and paua (New Zealand). Abalone attach to rocky surfaces using a very strong suction action, and live off green algae.

SUSTAINABILITY Some abalone grow slowly; overharvesting has reduced some stocks and increased prices. Although abalone's texture is somewhat unique, whelks and limpets are similarly chewy.

AVAILABILITY Fresh: Sold in the shell. **Preserved:** Frozen meat/steaks (ready tenderized), canned, dried (used for flavouring soups), salted.

EAT Tenderize by pounding before cooking. Sauté or fry very briefly, as it toughens easily. Add dried abalone to soup and simmer for a long period of time to add flavour.

FLAVOUR PAIRINGS Oriental: Chinese ear mushrooms, sesame, soy sauce, ginger, garlic, butter.

CLASSIC RECIPE Abalone with oyster sauce.

Red abalone
Haliotis rufescens
This species is the most readily available, and the largest of the abalone group. Found in the Pacific from Oregon to Baja California, and Mexico; harvested with restrictions. Sear briefly: if overcooked, it becomes tough. It has a sweet, meaty, and strong seafood flavour.

The foot or muscle is the main part eaten. Remove the meat from the shell and pound it before searing briefly.

Conch *Strombidae*

The queen conch (*Strombus gigas*) is one of many species of saltwater gastropods. It is also known as the pink or Caribbean conch (pronounced conk). The main suppliers and consumers are Jamaica, Honduras, and the Dominican Republic. Conch has an intense flavour.

SUSTAINABILITY Although this species was once abundant, commercial harvesting is now banned in the US. Alternatives include responsibly sourced abalone or whelks and limpets, which are much cheaper alternatives.

AVAILABILITY Wild: Frozen, chopped, minced. **Farmed:** Fresh, prepared, frozen. Farmed conch are generally more tender.

EAT Wild conch needs to be sliced thinly, then tenderized with a mallet. **Cooked:** Roast, grill, pan- and stir-fry, sauté, steam. **Raw:** Marinate in lime juice and chilli as ceviche.

FLAVOUR PAIRINGS Onion, garlic, peppers, tomato, jalapeño, hot sauce, coriander, cayenne.

CLASSIC RECIPES Conch fritters; conch chowder.

The meat, which has a dark membrane, is prized from the shell as a whole piece and can be up to 30cm (12in) long. Good-quality conch is creamy white with hints of pink and orange; if it is discoloured, grey, and smells strongly, do not buy it.

Queen conch
Eustrombus gigas
This conch is farmed in the Calicos Islands making it more available all year round. In the Caribbean, dried or minced conch is used in fritters, pan-fried for salads, and as a base for chowder. The taste is sweet with a rubbery, jellied texture.

Once extracted from the decorative shell, conch meat can be marinated and eaten raw, or cooked by various methods.

Periwinkle, Whelk, and Murex

Sea snails in the form of periwinkles, whelks, and murex are found in waters worldwide. They are considered to be a delicacy by a small number of consumers, but the limited sales have led some to decline in availability. Periwinkles, or winkles (from the Littorinidae group), and whelks are enjoyed in northern Europe and form a part of a traditional Sunday tea in London's East End. There are around 180 species, but only a few of these are eaten. In the UK, whelk refers to species from the Buccinidae family. Whelks are also popular in North America, where species from the Melongenidae group are harvested. Whelks have a distinct salty, seafood taste and are often likened to clam meat. They are tough and very meaty. Murex are another family of small sea snails from the Muricidae group. They are only found in the coastal areas and specialist fish markets of Mediterranean countries. Murex taste similar to whelks but the meat is reputedly tougher.
AVAILABILITY In the shell, both raw and cooked. Periwinkles: fresh, frozen, shucked; pickled in vinegar and canned. In the US, they are sold cooked, shucked, and trimmed.
EAT Rinse in salt water before boiling. Cook periwinkles for 3–5 minutes in the shell, whelks for 12–15 minutes, murex for 10–12 minutes. The operculum (horny "foot") is not eaten: trim this off (see page 281). If desired, coat in crumbs and pan-fry.
FLAVOUR PAIRINGS Chilli vinegar, malt vinegar, salt, lemon juice.
CLASSIC RECIPES Periwinkles in the shell with malt vinegar and salt; periwinkle and watercress sandwiches.

To enhance the colour of the greenish-black shell, roll periwinkles in a little oil before serving to give the shell a gloss.

Angulate periwinkle
Littorina angulifera
These tiny snails are popular in Europe and often harvested by hand, ensuring that little damage is done to their habitat. It is traditionally served as part of a seafood platter and its intense flavour combines sweet and salty tastes. It's prone to be gritty, so rinse well.

Murex shells are often collected because of their beauty: they are fat and spiny, tapering to a tail-like point.

Murex ◀▶
Murex brandaris
The Mediterranean murex has been a popular delicacy for many centuries; it was also collected to harvest a rare purple dye. The flavour is similar to that of a whelk; it needs gentle cooking, as it can be tough. In the South of France, murex make a classic addition to a *fruits de mer* platter.

Many gastropods have a horny "foot" that needs to be removed after cooking.

Common northern whelk
Buccinum undatum
The whelk group of shellfish has hundreds of members in waters worldwide. They are carnivores and scavengers. In Europe, the common northern whelk, found in the North Atlantic, is eaten. It is 5–10cm (2–4in) long and caught year-round in baited pots. This species is best during the summer.

Clams and Cockles

There are hundreds of types of clam and cockles found in waters worldwide. They are a well-utilized food source and create an important income for many countries. Clams are particularly popular in parts of Europe, the US, and Asia. The Veneridae group has hard, tough shells, and names for the species include Venus clam, carpetshell clam, hard-shell clam, and quahog. The Myidae group have a soft, thin, and brittle shell structure. Species are found in both the Pacific and Atlantic oceans. The species include steamer clam, soft-shell clam, and Ipswich clam. The geoduck (pronounced gooeyduck) clam is also known as the piss clam (due to its long siphon) or horse clam. It is the largest clam in the world, and is also thought to be the longest-living animal in the world. Surf clams come from the Mactridae group, and there are several related species. The Solenidae group includes razor or jackknife clams that are harvested worldwide. They resemble a cut-throat razor and have a razor-sharp edge. The amande comes from the Glycimeridae group.

AVAILABILITY Fresh: Live in the shell, shucked as prepared meat. **Preserved:** Frozen, brined, canned.

EAT Large clams: Chopped or minced in chowder; Smaller specimens: shucked and enjoyed raw. Hard-shell: Raw or steamed open to add to soups. Soft-shell: Siphon sliced or minced for chowder, or thinly sliced for sushi. Body meat sliced, tenderized, and pan-fried or sautéd. In the shell: Steamed. Removed from shell: Served raw with lemon juice, also for chowder. Razor clams: In the shell, grilled, or steamed. Removed from shell, raw in ceviche, or pan-fried.

FLAVOUR PAIRINGS Cream, onion, herbs, white wine, tomatoes, garlic, parsley, bacon, chillies.

CLASSIC RECIPES Manhattan clam chowder (tomato-based); New England clam chowder (cream-based); linguine alle vongole; stuffed clams.

The shell of a cockle is corrugated. Use them as soon as possible, as they can't be stored for long.

Cockle
Cerastoderma edule
Cockles are usually sold at around 3cm (1¼in). Wash, and then steam open over simmering stock or wine. Extract from the shell to serve. Excellent in salads or as a starter with a simple dressing. They have a sweet taste of the sea and can be a little gritty, but are a real treat when freshly cooked.

Check that the shells are tightly closed, as this indicates that they are still alive.

The glossy brown shell of the razor clam is brittle and needs careful handling, as it has a razor-sharp edge.

Geoduck clam ▼
Panopea abrupta
Also known as Pacific geoduck or king clam, this clam is usually sold at 10–15cm (4–6in) in diameter. The siphon can be up to 70cm (27½in) long, when fully extended. The geoduck can live to over a 100 years old. It can grow much bigger and weigh as much as 7–8kg (15½–17½lb). The meat can be tough, but the flavour is intense. They are particularly popular in Japan.

Razor clam
Ensis ensis
These are usually harvested at 12cm (5in) or larger. Check that the clam is alive immediately prior to cooking: the shell should close tightly if tapped. Best steamed, or grilled (but toughens easily). Extract the sweet and tender muscle from the shell and discard the stomach contents (see page 279). Slice thinly for a marinated dish such as ceviche. The taste is not dissimilar to that of a scallop.

Surf clam ▼
Spisula solidissima
These are also known as trough, bar, or hen clam, and are found on the eastern coast of the US, where they are highly valued and used for clam chowder. Small related species are found in Europe. Surf-clams are good for steamed clam dishes. Check that they are alive prior to cooking, rinse, then steam open over stock and white wine. They have a delicate, sweet flavour with a salty aftertaste.

Hard-shell clam ▶
Mercenaria mercenaria
These are also known as quahog, round, or Venus clam. Small, young clams may be called littleneck clams, while a half-grown clam is called a cherrystone and considered a delicacy (eaten raw or cooked). Small hard-shell clams can be enjoyed raw, but the larger ones are often used in clam chowder. The shells are quite heavy, but open to reveal a sweet, tender, and pleasantly salty clam meat.

Surf clams have a smooth beige shell. They usually grow to 4–5cm (1½–2in) in diameter, but can reach 16cm (6in).

Hard-shell clams are 8–12cm (3–5in) wide.

Amande ▼
Glycymeris glycymeris
Also known as the dog cockle, the amande is caught around European coasts. Its shell can grow up to 7cm (2¾in) across. It has a firmer texture than most clams, so is good for chowders and stuffing although it is enjoyed raw in Europe. Sweet, meaty, and a little chewy.

The amande is round, with a chocolate zigzag pattern on a cream shell. It is harvested at about 4cm (1½in) in diameter.

The siphon of the geoduck clam is edible, but the thick skin needs to be removed first and the meat cooked slowly until tender.

Scallops *Pectinidae*

Escallops are commonly known as scallops and are a popular shellfish. They are harvested in oceans worldwide and found deeper than most shellfish. There are over 500 species, coming from three groups; some are an important commercial food source, harvested from the wild, or farmed. Scallops are harvested by dredging or gathered by hand. (The latter is considered a more responsible method. The scallops are often larger than dredged ones and fetch a high price.) They are hermaphrodites and comprise a powerful adductor muscle (the white section), coral or roe containing the eggs (the orange section), and milt (the cream section). This swells and bursts in the water, mixing with the eggs for fertilization. This is the only bivalve that is sold raw in a prepared state. The main part of the scallop that's eaten is the sweet, succulent adductor muscle. The roe is also eaten in Europe, but is discarded in the US. The roe may be dried in a low oven and pulverized to add to shellfish sauces, to provide a greater depth of flavour. Scallops have a sweet seafood taste and tender, succulent texture. The roe has a richer and more intense flavour.

SUSTAINABILITY There is a minimum landing size for the king scallop caught off the coast of the UK and many other areas. Try to buy responsibly sourced specimens. Razor clams have a similar texture.
AVAILABILITY Fresh: Live in the shell, prepared on the half-shell, prepared and trimmed (processed).
Preserved: Frozen with roe both on and off, canned, smoked, some species are dried.
EAT Cooked: Pan-fry, steam, poach, barbecue, grill; pan-fry smoked meat. **Raw:** Ceviche and sushi (white meat only).
FLAVOUR PAIRINGS Bacon, chorizo, red peppers, red onions, olive oil, sesame oil, black beans, spring onions, ginger, chilli.
CLASSIC RECIPES Scallops in bacon; scallops with black bean sauce or soy and ginger; scallop gratin; Coquilles St Jacques.

King scallop ▶
Pecten maximus
This scallop is caught in the deep waters of northern Europe, and enjoyed in many European countries. The shell is corrugated, which prevents it from closing very tightly, unlike other bivalves. King scallops are at their very best pan-seared, although intense heat makes the roe pop. Care needs to be taken not to overcook them – cook for about a minute on either side in a hot pan.

Bay scallop
Argopecten irradians
This scallop is found in the western North Atlantic, and is harvested along the coast of the US. Sear in hot butter for a few seconds on both sides to make the most of the tender, sweet meat.

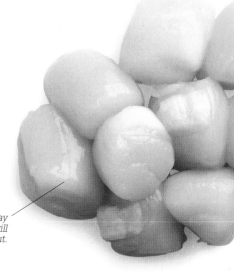

Do not overcook bay scallops, as they will shrink and dry out.

The shell can reach over 20cm (8in) in diameter. It is cream with brown markings; it has a flat bottom shell and a concave top shell.

The mantle and dark stomach sac are removed when a scallop is sold on the shell.

Queen scallops do not usually grow to more than 6cm (2½in) across.

The adductor muscle allows the shell to open and close, giving the scallop mobility.

◀ Queen scallop
Aequipecten opercularis
"Queenies" are rarely sold live in the shell. They are either extracted or trimmed, and sold on the half-shell. They have a sweet, delicate taste. They are best used in a stir-fry or in a fish stew – they overcook very easily and shrink. If served on the shell, they are good with a little flavoured butter and a few seconds under the grill.

Mussels *Mytilidae*

Mussels live in cool waters all over the world. They are abundant and are harvested from the wild by dredging and hand-gathering. They are also farmed in large quantities (see page 300–301). Mussels are one of the most sustainable seafoods available. There are various species.
AVAILABILITY Fresh: Live in the shell, cook fresh. **Preserved:** Frozen meat, canned in brine or vinegar, smoked. Often included in frozen seafood mix. Green-lipped mussel: usually cooked on the half-shell and frozen.

EAT Cooked: Steam, roast, grill. Green-lipped mussel: Topped and réchauffé as baked and grilled. Remove the shell if adding to a sauce or stew.
FLAVOUR PAIRINGS White wine, butter, garlic, cream, ginger, lemongrass, spices, parsley, coriander, dill, rosemary, fennel, Pernod.
CLASSIC RECIPES Moules marinières, moules frites, paella, moules à la crème, moules farcies, mouclade.

The shell of this variety is smooth and glossy and it has uniform angles.

This variety is identified by its distinctive green lip inside its shell.

Green-lipped mussel
Perna canaliculus
Also known as the New Zealand mussel, or green mussel, this may grow to 24cm (9½in) long. It is of economic importance around the New Zealand coastline, where it is harvested abundantly. It has a dark brown shell with a vivid green lip. It is very meaty – almost chewy – and intensely flavoured.

Rope-grown mussels are smooth, blue/black, and glossy in appearance. They require minimal preparation.

You can work out a mussel's age by counting the number of circles on its shell.

Common mussel
Mytilus edulis
Also known as the blue mussel, the common muscle is found in temperate and polar waters worldwide. The shell varies from brown to a bluish-purple. The mussels attach themselves to rocks, or when farmed, to rope, by a strong thread called the byssus thread (or beard), a protein they secrete. They taste slightly salty, with an intense flavour of the sea.

Oyster *Ostreidae*

Eating oysters is a global pastime, and a well-documented gourmet delight. Like other bivalve molluscs, an oyster lives inside its shell, which it opens and closes with a strong muscle. The shell is oval, either cupped or flat, and covered in frilly, rock-like crevices. Fresh oysters are tightly closed, and hard to open without a shucking knife. Mostly found in temperate coastal waters, oysters are harvested from both wild and farmed beds worldwide. Two main genera are gathered: *Ostrea*, native to Europe, and the west coast of the US; *Crassostrea*, native to Asia, Japan, the east coast of the US, and Australia. Once harvested, the fish are purified and graded by size. An all-time favourite is the creamy Pacific oyster *(Crassostrea gigas)*, originally from the coast of Japan, but farmed in northern Europe, the Northeast Pacific, where it is famously cultivated along the coastal waters of British Columbia, and the states of Washington, Oregon, and California in the US. Equally popular is the small, buttery Kumamoto oyster (from Japan), widely regarded as one of the world's finest oysters. A more salty Atlantic choice is the Blue Point oyster (*C. virginica*), native to the East Atlantic coast, and Gulf states, but cultivated in beds all along the east coast of the US. Oysters harvested in different waters differ subtly in flavour and shell colour. Oyster-tasting is an art, much like wine-tasting, with many gourmet terms for the varied flavours, including tangy, metallic, nutty, grassy, ozone, sweet, cucumber, fruity, iodine, earthy, and coppery. One topic still hotly debated is whether to eat oysters cooked or raw, *au naturel*, or dressed. Eat wild oysters during late spring or early summer, when they are not spawning. Farmed oysters can be eaten all year round.

AVAILABILITY In the shell, smoked, canned.
EAT Cooked: Deep-fry, pan-fry, poach, grill, bake. **Raw:** In the half shell.
FLAVOUR PAIRINGS Cooked: Anchovy essence, butter, spinach. **Raw:** Red wine vinegar, Tabasco, lemon juice.
CLASSIC RECIPES Oysters in the half shell with shallot vinegar; oysters Rockefeller; oyster po-boys.

Native oyster
Ostrea edulis
Also called the European flat oyster, it is often served raw on a bed of crushed ice, dressed with lemon juice, Tabasco, and shallot vinegar. Graded by size, from 1 to 4, the largest "royals" can reach 10cm (4 in).

Native oysters have an oval scaly shell, intense taste, and firm texture.

Pacific oyster
Crassostrea gigas
The taste of this widely cultured oyster varies enormously, depending on where it is grown. Flavours range from smoky to grassy and acidic, through to milky and creamy. Usually graded by weight, a fair size would be 115g (4oz), or 11cm (4½in). Store the oysters cup-side down to prevent their natural juices from escaping.

The meat of the Pacific oyster is a delicate beige colour, with a smooth, creamy texture.

The head is wide, but it is the meaty tail that is eaten, either pulled off the cooked fish, or preserved in brine.

The large, robust, smooth claws are orange on the underside.

Once immersed in boiling water, the heat-sensitive pigment in the brownish green shell turns a bright cardinal red.

Freshwater crayfish *Astacidae*

Also called crawfish (in the US), écrevisse (France), and camarón (Spain), the crayfish is a freshwater crustacean related to the lobsterette (see below). Caught mainly in fresh waters, many species are harvested in the US, where they feature in the Cajun cuisine of Louisiana and New Orleans. They also thrive in the lakes and rivers of New Zealand, East Asia, and Europe and are popular in France and Scandinavia. Most crayfish have a segmented body, varying in colour from chocolate-brown to sandy-yellow. Equally variable in size, crayfish range from 7.5–30cm (3–12in), depending on the species. They are quite feisty, but it is impractical to band their claws. Handle carefully to avoid a sharp nip. Many crayfish caught in the wild are hand-gathered by turning over rocks in streams and farm dams.

SUSTAINABILITY Some Australian cousins, including the West Australian marron (*Cherax tenuimanus*) and the yabby (*C. destructor*), have been farmed for an overstretched market. The crayfish found in the UK faced sustainability issues because of a virus. The American signal crayfish was introduced but it's a very invasive species. Alternatives include responsibly sourced langoustine.

AVAILABILITY Whole, most often live; frozen tails; cooked.

EAT Cooked: Boil and sauté.

FLAVOUR PAIRINGS Butter, garlic, lemon, cream, tomatoes, parsley.

CLASSIC RECIPES Crayfish jambalaya; crayfish étouffée.

Signal crayfish
Pacifastacus leniusculus
This crayfish is native to North America, where it thrives in freshwater ponds, lakes, rivers, and streams. It is a robust creature and easy to farm. As the crayfish are not huge, just 10–15cm (4–6in), serve around 12 to 15 per person, with lots of melted butter and bread.

Lobsterette *Nephropidae*

Lobsterettes are mini-lobsters, much like prawns, but with minuscule claws. Many species live on the muddy or sandy sea floor of the world's oceans. Commonly known as Italian scampi, popular varieties include the Dublin Bay prawn (*Nephrops norvegicus*), and Florida lobsterette (*Nephropsis aculeata*). They are caught commonly along the West Atlantic and East Atlantic coasts, from Iceland in the north to Morocco in the south. For the European market, especially France and the Mediterranean, where they are a popular seafood, lobsterettes are harvested around the British Isles, and then exported. Much like prawns in appearance, most live lobsterettes are amber-rose, or coral-coloured. Unusually, they do not change colour much when cooked, which can be confusing. Look instead at the tail, which curls under the body; and at the flesh on the underside, which turns from translucent to opaque.

SUSTAINABILITY There is a minimum landing size in place to prevent overuse.

AVAILABILITY Fresh: Whole live, raw, cooked. **Frozen:** Whole, raw, cooked; also tails, breaded for scampi.

EAT Cooked: Boil, roast, pan-fry or as scampi, deep-fry, poach.

FLAVOUR PAIRINGS Lemon, basil, sage, butter, garlic.

CLASSIC RECIPES Scampi Provençale; deep-fried scampi and chips.

Dublin Bay prawn
Nephrops norvegicus
Also known as nephrop, Norway lobster, and langoustine, this prawn has recently become prized for its sweet, tender meat, and now fetches a high price. Whole langoustine can pose a challenge on the dinner plate. Traditionally, the claws are cracked and opened, then the meat prized out with a lobster pick. As the tail can be sharp, it is best pinched until the underside cracks, exposing the meat.

The sharp, spiny claws contain little meat. Scoop it out with a cocktail stick, and break up the claws for stock.

Rock lobster *Palinuridae*

Unlike "true" clawed lobsters, rock lobsters (also known as spiny lobster) lack claws. Instead they have a rocky carapace (head), and short, sharp spines running the length of their body. Some species also have a distinctive orange-brown shell, flecked with green, yellow, and blue spots, which intensify in colour when cooked. Also known as crawfish or crayfish, especially in Australasia, rock lobsters thrive along rocky coasts below the tidal zone, hiding in crevices and caverns. Typically found in the Western Atlantic, from North Carolina to Brazil, and in the Gulf of Mexico and Caribbean Sea, most are caught in the tropical and subtropical waters of the northern hemisphere and in some cold waters of the southern hemisphere. They are harvested and sold to around 90 countries worldwide, and valued as a delicacy in their own right. Although some taste less sweet than true lobster, many have particularly succulent and dense tail meat. If overcooked, however, they can become tough and fibrous.

AVAILABILITY Fresh and frozen, whole and tails.

EAT Cooked: Whole tails: Boil, steam, deep-fry, grill. Tail meat: Dice and stir-fry, and add to soups and stews.
FLAVOUR PAIRINGS Chilli, garlic, lemon, olive oil, butter.
CLASSIC RECIPES Boiled with lemon and garlic; barbecued rock lobster.

Rock lobster
Palinurus elephas
Although fairly large, about 40cm (16in), these shellfish lack the fleshy claws of true lobsters. Instead, the dense, sweet meat typical of the species is concentrated in the tail shell, although some meat can be extracted from the legs.

The legs of a lobster contain sweet juice that can be sucked from the shell.

The claws do not contain as much white meat as those of clawed lobsters.

A lobster uses its long antennae to navigate its way around the murky ocean floor.

The carapace is slightly compressed in this variety.

American lobster ▶
Homarus americanus
Also known as the Atlantic or Maine lobster, this traditionally large and meaty shellfish can grow to at least 60cm (2ft), and take seven years to reach 450g (1lb). An ideal weight for a main dish is 750g (1lb 10oz) or 1kg (2¼lb), before the shell grows too thick and heavy.

Lobster

Lobster is prized worldwide as a luxury food. Many lobster families populate the oceans of the world. Classified as invertebrates, with a hard, protective shell, lobsters live in burrows, or crevices in rocks, mud, and sand, feeding on molluscs and other crustaceans. A lobster's body is made of several sections: a carapace (head), and tail shell with legs, swimlets and, in some species, claws. Like crabs and other arthropods, lobsters moult their shells in order to grow. For the chef, lobsters come in two main types: clawed (see below) and clawless (see facing page). Among the Nephropidae family several members are clawed, including the European, American, and Canadian lobsters, and the Dublin Bay prawn (or langoustine). Both the European and American varieties are extensively farmed and harvested from the wild to feed the appetites of Europe, the US, and

Canada. Most are caught by one-way baited traps and pots. Many American lobsters are exported to Japan where they are also prized as a delicacy. The European lobster, rather less abundant than its American cousin, is usually more expensive. It is often wondered which of the two provides the best flavour. When served in a classic dish, such as lobster Thermidor, it is hard to tell the difference. Typically, the tail meat of most lobsters is sweet, succulent, dense, and highly valued. On harvesting, lobsters usually have their claws "banded", which makes them easier to handle and curbs their naturally aggressive and cannibalistic

behaviour when captive. However, if banded for too long, the claw meat will start to atrophy.

SUSTAINABILITY Most American lobster from Nova Scotia and Newfoundland has to be a minimum size when landed. The size is measured along the carapace.

AVAILABILITY Whole: Live and cooked. **Frozen:** Cooked whole and frozen, extracted from the shell. Canned.

EAT Live: Freeze briefly or stun before boiling. **Cooked:** Boiled – 10–12 minutes per 500g (1lb 2oz); grilled, baked, both extracted from the shell and in bisque.

FLAVOUR PAIRINGS Cream, butter, Parmesan, tarragon, parsley, chervil, paprika, white wine.

CLASSIC RECIPES Lobster Thermidor; lobster Newburg; lobster bisque; dressed lobster.

The large and heavy crusher claw is filled with dense, sweet meat that can be extracted whole to garnish a dish.

Once caught, strong rubber bands secure the claws so the lobster cannot attack.

Slipper lobster *Scyllaridae*

Colourfully named the shovel-nosed lobster, Spanish lobster, sand lobster, or locust lobster, slipper lobsters lack the meaty claws of "true" lobsters (much like the spiny lobster). Various species thrive on the sea floor in warm waters worldwide, mostly around Thailand, Singapore, and Australia. Close and commercially important cousins include the Moreton Bay bug (found in northern Australian waters), and the Balmain bug (found off the south coasts of Australia). Most slipper lobsters have a sweet, delicate, mellow taste and medium texture, firm to the bite.

AVAILABILITY Whole and tails.

EAT Cooked: Boil, steam, poach, deep-fry, barbecue.

FLAVOUR PAIRINGS Butter, herbs such as tarragon, chives, and dill, garlic, citrus, lemongrass, soy sauce, chilli.

CLASSIC RECIPES Seafood platter; barbecued bug tails with garlic butter.

A fair-sized bug, 25cm (10in) long, should have a hard, rosy shell, and feel heavy for its size.

The eyes of the Moreton Bay bug, unlike the Balmain bug, are located towards the edge of the head.

Balmain bug ▼
Ibacus peronii
Sometimes called a flapjack, or mud bug, this tasty Australian shellfish is especially popular in Sydney. Its meat, found only in the tail, tastes strong and sweet.

Moreton Bay bug ◄
Thenus orientalis
Named after Moreton Bay in Queensland, where it is enjoyed as a local delicacy, it looks like the Balmain bug (above), roughly 25cm (10in), but fatter, with wide-set eyes, and more of an amber hue. It is a versatile fish, with a sweet flavour, ideal for poaching and steaming, deep-frying, pan-frying, and stir-frying.

Slipper lobster
Scyllarus arctus
Nicknamed the flat lobster, langosta, or cigale, various species of this clawless lobster are found worldwide and are popular in the Mediterranean. Smallish, at 15cm (6in), it traditionally forms part of a shellfish platter. Only the tail is eaten.

Once the hard, pebbly, reddish shell is removed, the tail meat is sweet and firm to the bite.

Prawn and Shrimp

Prawns and shrimp thrive in all waters, cold and warm, fresh and marine. Widely popular, especially in Australia, the US, Europe, and Japan, prawns are extensively harvested and farmed. Varied use of the terms "prawn" and "shrimp" can be confusing. In the UK and Australia, "prawn" mostly refers to warm-water species, such as the giant black tiger prawn (*Penaeus monodon*), as well as some fair-sized cold-water species, such as the deepwater prawn (*Pandalus borealis*), while "shrimp" refers to smaller species, such as the brown shrimp (*Crangon crangon*). In the US, "shrimp" often means the same as "prawn". The largest prawns are the warm-water, or tropical, variety, at least 35cm (14in), compared to cold-water shrimps, about 5cm (2in).

SUSTAINABILITY Tropical prawns provide more than three-quarters of the world's supply. Found mainly in the Pacific and Indian oceans, they are harvested or farmed by Latin America, Australia, China, Vietnam, Sri Lanka, and Thailand. Tropical prawn farms can cause environmental damage. Mangrove swamps are flooded to make a site suitable for farming. Toxic chemicals ward off disease and, after a few years, the farm becomes too polluted to sustain more farming. Some farms, however, have adopted responsible practices; check the label. The smaller, slower-growing, cold-water prawns, found mainly in the Atlantic, Arctic, and Pacific oceans, are caught by the UK, US, Canada, Greenland, Denmark, and Iceland. Many fisheries have a minimum mesh size, as trawling for these prawns creates a huge bycatch.

AVAILABILITY Cold-water: Fresh and frozen; cooked as crevettes (poached). **Warm-water:** Cooked and frozen; peeled and soaked.

EAT Cold-water: Serve defrosted as part of a salad; or serve as potted shrimps. Use the shells for stock and flavoured butters.
Warm-water: Pan-fry, stir-fry, deep-fry, barbecue, grill, bake. For a sweet, roasted flavour, pan-fry in oil with vegetables. For a subtler flavour, simmer in water.
FLAVOUR PAIRINGS Mayonnaise, capers, paprika, pepper, lemon juice.
CLASSIC RECIPES Cold-water: Prawn cocktail; avocado pear and prawns.
Warm-water: *Gambas pil pil* (garlic prawns); prawn tempura.

Crevette rose

When poached, the white Pacific white shrimp (right) is often called a *crevette* (French for "shrimp"). It is wonderfully sweet and dense and makes an attractive rosy garnish to paella. Confusingly, crevette rose is also the name of a prawn from the Palaemonidae family.

Giant black tiger prawn ◀
Penaeus monodon
A meaty tropical prawn, which can reach 35cm (14in), it is harvested globally, and farmed extensively. When buying, check how responsibly the fish have been sourced and choose organically farmed. To barbecue, snip off the legs and antennae; then twist and pull out the tail section. The taste is mellow, honeyed, and succulent.

Pacific white shrimp
Litopenaeus vannamei
A popular prawn species farmed in both Latin and South American countries, these white prawns are harvested, graded, and frozen for sale. Often large, up to 25cm (10in), they are meaty and sweet. The shells provide a tasty addition to shellfish stock.

Brown shrimp
Crangon crangon
Although measuring no more than 5cm (2in), this common shrimp is regarded as quite a delicacy, fetching a higher price than larger, warm-water species. Caught in the East Atlantic, it looks transparent when live, but turns amber-brown on cooking. Brown shrimps are traditionally served as potted shrimps. Although fiddly to peel, they are sweet, succulent, and absolutely delicious.

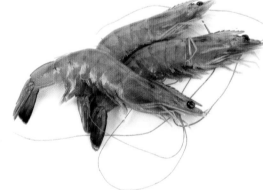

Deep-water prawn
Pandalus borealis
Valued for its sweet, mild taste, and succulent texture, it is also called the northern or Greenland prawn in the UK, and the northern red shrimp or Alaskan pink shrimp in the US. A fair size for a cold-water prawn, at 6cm (2½ in), it is always cooked on landing, and frozen for sale. The shells make a tasty stock, ideal for pilaf, risotto, and soup. They can also be whizzed together with butter, and sieved to make prawn butter.

Crab

Crabs come in all sizes and are a popular crustacean on many continents. The wide availability of crab (they are found in oceans worldwide) and the variety of species makes them a favourite in many countries. Crabs come from a selection of groups including the Cancridae, Grapsidae, Portunidae, Lithodoidae, and Majidae families. A crab has a carapace or cart as a main shell, legs, and in most cases claws, though the size of claws and legs varies from species to species. They periodically moult their shell as they grow – frequently in the first two years of life, and every 1–2 years thereafter. Crab provides two distinct meats: the white meat, found in the claws, legs, and main body, and the brown meat found in the carapace of the crab. As a general rule, the white is often the favoured of the two and is more expensive. Brown meat from the carapace is well flavoured. Some species are renowned for their white claw meat, specifically the Brown edible crab, Jonah, and Dungeness crab of the Cancridae group. Snow crabs and King crabs have valuable sweet succulent meat in their legs. Male crabs have larger claws and are therefore more valuable, hens are considered to have more intensely flavoured brown meat and less white meat and are usually less expensive.

SUSTAINABILITY Many crabs are sustainably sourced, although depending on the species and the area of capture, it can be illegal to land crabs carrying eggs (berries). In some cases, it is illegal to land hen crabs. There is a minimum landing size in place globally for some species, measured width ways across the carapace. For the white meat, alternatives would be responsibly sourced prawns and scallops.

AVAILABILITY Cooked: Whole and claws. **Prepared:** Dressed/hand-picked; processed and pasteurized white and brown meat (usually frozen separately).

EAT Live: Boiling for 15 mins per 500g (1lb 2oz) is usual. **Cooked:** Toss into salads, rechauffé in pasta, rice dishes, and sauté. **Raw:** Sushi.

FLAVOUR PAIRINGS Mayonnaise, chilli, lemon, parsley, dill, potato, chilli, butter, Worcestershire sauce, anchovy essence.

CLASSIC RECIPES Thai crab cakes; chilli crab; dressed crab (usually brown edible crab); potted crab (crab paste); pan-fried soft shell crab; Maryland crab cakes.

Blue crab
Callinectes sapidus
Native to the West Atlantic, this crab is seen in both Japanese and European waters. Known as "busters" or "peelers", blue crabs nearing a moulting stage are held in tanks, so that once the carapace lifts away revealing the soft, delicate body underneath, they are harvested. The gills, mouth, and stomach sac are removed and the crab is frozen or sold fresh ready for the "soft shell crab" season. Alternatively, meat from these crabs is used for crab cakes, soups, and dips. The fresh season is usually late spring to early summer.

It is known as the "swimmer" crab because of the paddles it has in place of its back legs.

The blue crab can be identified by its beautiful blue front and an olive brown body.

Once cooked, the shell becomes a vivid red. The best meat is found in the legs and claws.

Dungeness crab
Metacarcinus magister
A member of the Cancridae group, the Dungeness crab is found in the Pacific Ocean from Alaska to California, and is the most popular crab in the Pacific Northwest and western Canada. It can measure up to 25cm (10in). It's recognized for its delicate and sweet flavour, and is popular for a seafood platter, served simply with melted butter.

The meat in the legs is highly prized while the brown meat is negligible, so the legs are usually removed and sold separately, as "clusters".

Take care when extracting the white meat, as the legs are very prickly.

Red king crab
Paralithodes camtschaticus
King crabs from the Lithodoidae group are also called stone crabs. This is the largest crab group and most popular, with particularly succulent and well-flavoured leg meat. Red king crab is one of the largest of the group and it can have a leg span of 1.8m (6ft).

Its colour ranges from beige to light brown with blue trim and is often light orange on the underside.

The elongated, hard shell is periodically moulted to allow the crab to grow.

Succulent, white meat is found in the claw; make sure you remove the bone.

Brown edible crab
Cancer pagurus
This species is caught in baited pots around the coasts of Northern Europe. Male crabs are famed for their big claws containing sweet, succulent meat. This crab can take around seven years to grow to 500g (1lb 2oz). It is traditionally served dressed and returned to the clean carapace, with mayonnaise, brown bread, and butter.

Squid *Cephalopod*

Although many species of squid have thrived for centuries in the world's oceans, it is only in recent years that this shellfish has become globally popular. Squid is now quite possibly the most widely consumed seafood, partly due to its availability. The common squid (*Loligo vulgaris*), popularly nicknamed "ink fish", is probably the best known. It ranges widely in size from a baby squid, measuring 2cm (¾in), to much larger specimens, some growing as long as 80–90cm (31–35in). The size of a squid is what determines the cooking method – whether fast or slow. The smaller the squid, the quicker the cooking; the larger the squid, the longer it will need in the pot. Squid is made up of a long tubular body (mantle), which, once prepared, is called a "tube". The body is flanked at one end by a pair of wing-like fins, which sometimes look like arrows, most famously on the arrow squid (*Nototodarus gouldi*). The live squid is covered in a reddish, purple, or coffee-brown membrane, sometimes with intricate brown "veins" or markings, providing camouflage. The membrane is thin and easily pulled away, especially after the squid has been packed in ice and jostled around in its box. Attached to the head are 10 tentacles, two long and eight smaller ones. In the centre of the tentacles is the hard beak (mouth-piece). The ink, after which the "ink-fish" is named, is contained in a small, silver ink sac in the tube. Running up the middle of the squid is an internal shell (or "pen"), which resembles plastic, and should be pulled away before cooking (see page 282). The flesh of a good-quality squid is white, turning pink as it decomposes.

AVAILABILITY Whole: Fresh, dried, smoked, and canned. Parts: Frozen tubes or rings; sometimes part of a mixed seafood cocktail.

EAT Cooked: Pan-fry, stir-fry, deep-fry, braise, sauté, casserole. For rings or small pieces, grill or poach. Whole tubes, flattened out into a sheet and scored, taste excellent barbecued. The tube can also be stuffed with a savoury breadcrumb mix, couscous, quinoa, or rice. Choose a fair-sized squid, usually with a tube that is no more than 7.5–10cm (3–4in) long. Prepare it, and cut it into rectangles or rings; or leave whole, if barbecuing.

Raw: In sushi.

FLAVOUR PAIRINGS Chilli, olive oil, breadcrumbs, lemon juice, garlic, spring onion, mayonnaise.

CLASSIC RECIPES Fried calamari; squid cooked in ink; squid stuffed with rice; Sichuan-fried squid.

Common squid
Loligo vulgaris

The "ink fish" has gained a reputation for being tough and chewy, but is only ever so if it is overcooked. In a hot pan, the meat takes no time at all. At its best, it tastes tender and mellow, with a subtle, distinctive flavour.

The tough, wing-like fins are best either finely sliced or stir-fried, or reserved to flavour stock.

The long, fleshy mantle is often cut into rings. It's tasty and succulent if not overcooked.

The mottled skin is best peeled off and reserved for stock, as it toughens and shrinks around the flesh when cooked.

Eight arms are relatively short, while two are longer, and used to catch prey.

Octopus *Cephalopod*

Various species of octopus inhabit tropical, subtropical, and temperate waters worldwide. Commonly regarded as one of the most intelligent invertebrates, the octopus has keen eyesight and an acute sense of touch. Using its sensitive skin camouflage to change colour, or even texture, it has an uncanny capacity to evade capture and confuse its predators. If all else fails, it squirts ink at the enemy, escaping under cover of an "ink-screen". Despite their intelligence, most octopuses live for no more than 12–18 months. Unlike the squid and cuttlefish, the octopus lacks any internal shell, allowing it to hide in and squeeze through slim cracks. The only hard part of an octopus is its beak (mouth-piece). Its soft, tubular body (mantle) is armed with eight long tentacles. Octopus is prepared and cooked in various ways by different cultures. Used extensively in Japanese cuisine, octopus, or *tako*, is often served as sushi and takoyaki (fried or grilled octopus); some smaller species are eaten alive. Octopus is equally popular in Asian cuisine, and forms a major part of the Hawaiian diet. In Europe, Spain is the biggest consumer, followed by Portugal.

SUSTAINABILITY There are some concerns over sustainability, as octopus has been overfished in areas where it's considered a delicacy. Alternatives include responsibly sourced cuttlefish (in season) and squid.

AVAILABILITY Fresh and frozen, whole and prepared; also tumbled. Prepared: In marinade and brine, canned, smoked, and dried.

EAT Cooked: Braise or stew; unlike squid and small cuttlefish, which can be cooked briefly, octopus benefits from a slow, gentle stew. Smaller specimens or baby octopus can be briefly blanched, and marinated to serve. Blanch and refresh prepared octopus by dipping very briefly in boiling, then cold, water.

FLAVOUR PAIRINGS Red wine, onions, balsamic vinegar, parsley, sage, rosemary, paprika, chilli, soy, sesame oil, Japanese rice wine vinegar.

CLASSIC RECIPES *Polvo a modo ze de lino* (octopus stew); pickled octopus; *ceviche de pulpo* (marinated octopus); octopus in red wine.

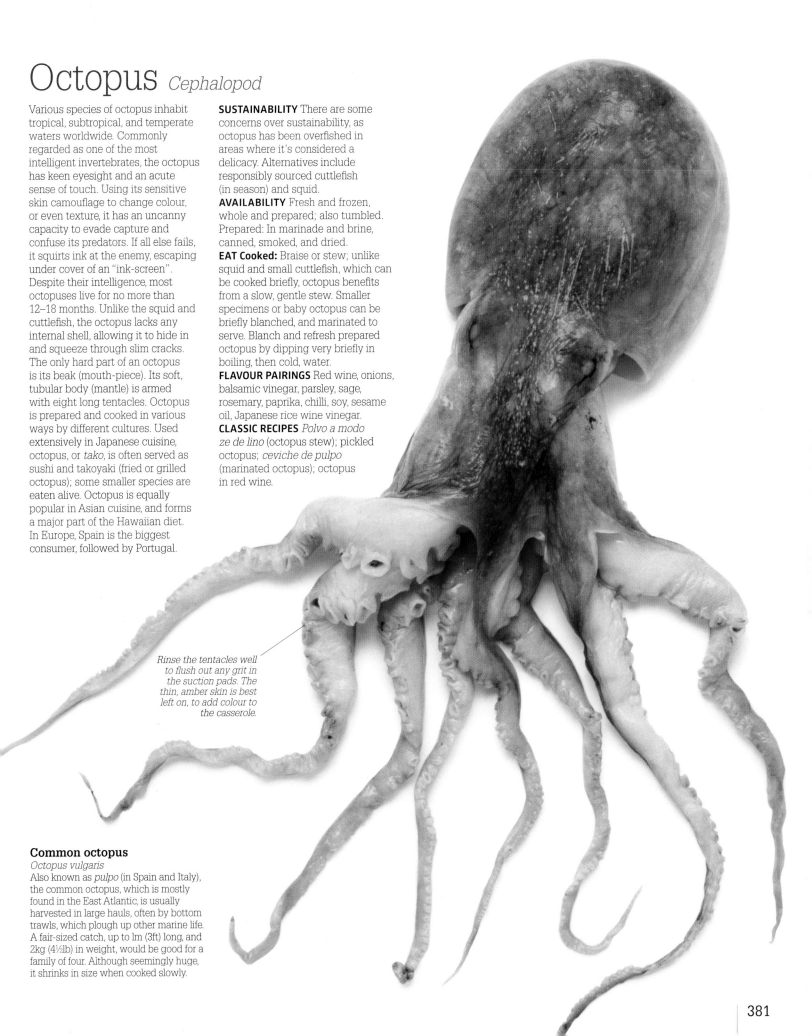

Rinse the tentacles well to flush out any grit in the suction pads. The thin, amber skin is best left on, to add colour to the casserole.

Common octopus
Octopus vulgaris
Also known as *pulpo* (in Spain and Italy), the common octopus, which is mostly found in the East Atlantic, is usually harvested in large hauls, often by bottom trawls, which plough up other marine life. A fair-sized catch, up to 1m (3ft) long, and 2kg (4½lb) in weight, would be good for a family of four. Although seemingly huge, it shrinks in size when cooked slowly.

Cuttlefish *Cephalopod*

Popularly nicknamed "ink fish" for its ability to squirt ink at its enemies, the cuttlefish is often the tastiest but quite possibly the least appreciated member of the cephalopod group. Various species thrive in the depths of the world's oceans, except for North American waters. Cuttlefish are caught for their internal shell (cuttlebone) and the copious ink they produce to confuse their predators. The ink is harvested and pasteurized for commercial use, for dying pasta black, and for cooking: typically, risotto nero. Cuttlefish are mostly caught by trawl, and as bait for recreational fishing. With a wonderfully sweet, seafood taste, and firm, meaty texture, cuttlefish is enjoyed as a delicacy in many countries. If pan-fried for more than a minute, though, it will toughen and lose its translucency. The fish is particularly prized in the cuisines of China, Japan, Korea, Spain, and Italy.
AVAILABILITY Whole: Unprepared. **Frozen:** Ink and shell sold separately. **Preserved:** Dried.
EAT Cooked: Slice the body thinly and pan-fry, deep-fry, or bake. The legs and tentacles are best casseroled slowly and extensively.

CLASSIC RECIPES Risotto nero; chilli cuttlefish; soupies krasates (cuttlefish in wine); Tuscan cuttlefish salad.
FLAVOUR PAIRINGS Red wine, garlic, red onions, balsamic vinegar, chilli, lime.

Common cuttlefish
Sepia officinalis
Native to the East Atlantic and Mediterranean, it is one of the largest cuttlefish, at about 40cm (16in). The tough tentacles need to be tenderized in a slow casserole or braised.

The frilly fins of the cuttlefish peel away with the flesh. They give shellfish stock a wonderful flavour.

Sea urchin *Echinoidae*

Prickly and uninviting, sea urchins thrive on the ocean floor. More than 500 species exist, most are edible. Sea urchins feature in Japanese, Italian, Spanish, and classic French cuisine. The edible part of the urchin is its roe, which needs to be carefully extracted. The entrance into a sea urchin is on its underside, through its mouth, which can be opened with a knife. First the viscera should be removed; then the creamy orange roe (attached to the top of the shell) can be scooped out with a spoon (see page 281). The resultant treat is small and relatively expensive, but offers an intense, creamy taste, much like seaweed. In Japan, the urchins, or uni, are eaten fresh with sushi, and fermented to form sea urchin paste.
SUSTAINABILITY In some cultures, especially Japan and the Mediterranean, sea urchins are popular as a delicacy, which has led to overfishing. There is no real alternative to sea urchin.

AVAILABILITY Whole and, in some countries, extracted from the shell.
EAT Usually raw, although they do add flavour to a creamy fish sauce.
FLAVOUR PAIRINGS Lemon.
CLASSIC RECIPES *Linguine con ricci di mare*; sea urchin omelette.

Sea urchin roe
Prised out of its prickly shell, sea urchin roe is often enjoyed raw, but is equally delicious cooked. Add it to cream, white wine, and fish stock for the perfect addition to pan-fried fish, such as turbot.

Sea urchin
Echinus esculentus
Globular, pink, and spiky, the common sea urchin found in shallow waters off the British Isles can be up to 15cm (6in) wide. Sea urchins are a challenge to prepare, but the seaweed flavour is strong and creamy – never pungent or fishy.

To avoid the spines, either split the urchin in half or cut out the central beak and scoop out the middle with a teaspoon.

Sea urchin roe (or "tongues") have a umami (essence of savouriness in Japanese) that is slightly salty and rich.

Peel away the outer membrane to reveal the tough, pure white body beneath.

These eight pairs of arms and two longer tentacles are used to capture prey and can be retracted completely into the body.

Goose barnacle
Lepadidae

The goose barnacle takes its name from its striking long, goose-like neck. Like other crustaceans, it lives attached to exposed rocks in many coastal waters, except in the Arctic. Barnacle meat comes from the creature's soft protruding body, covered in thick skin. Before cooking, the tough skin needs to be removed with the help of a nail; or it can be peeled away after cooking. The barnacle has a sweet seafood taste much like crab and crayfish. Cooked to perfection, it is succulent and tender; if overcooked, it is tough and rubbery. In Portugal and Spain, goose barnacle is prized as the iconic delicacy _percebes_.
AVAILABILITY Usually whole.
EAT Cooked: Steamed or poached; only 2–3 minutes in boiling salted water with a bay leaf and lemon.
FLAVOUR PAIRINGS Lemon, butter, garlic.

Before cooking, remove the chalky (calcareous) plates and peel the skin away.

Goose barnacle
Lepas anatifera
A sought-after delicacy in several Mediterranean countries, goose barnacles are often enjoyed simply steamed over stock, then served straight from the shell. Measuring about 25cm (10in), two or three provide a good helping.

Sea cucumber
Stichopodidae

Although commonly found in the world's oceans, sea cucumbers are something of an acquired taste, with a rather salty, savoury flavour and chewy, gelatinous texture. Reflecting their nickname "sea-slug", they shuffle slowly across the sea floor, scavenging for food. After being caught, the fish are gutted, boiled, salted, and dried, for long-term storage. To prepare them for eating, they are soaked in water to rehydrate, and then tenderized with extensive simmering. In China, the fish is a delicacy and is often slowly braised in rice wine and ginger. Sea cucumbers are also popular in the Philippines and parts of Europe, especially Barcelona.
SUSTAINABILITY Sea cucumbers have been overfished in the Mediterranean and other seas. Alternatives include whelks, which have a similar texture.
AVAILABILITY Whole, usually dried.
EAT Cooked: Soak and simmer, or braise.
FLAVOUR PAIRINGS Southern European/Spanish flavours: Pil-pil chilli, garlic, parsley.
CLASSIC RECIPES Braised sea cucumber with mushrooms; braised espardenyes.

Sea cucumber
Stichopus regalis
Enjoyed for centuries by fishermen, it is prized as a delicacy, eaten fresh in Japan, and dried in China. Typically slug-like in shape and size, it grows up to 20cm (8in).

Feather-like tentacles sweep up food from the sea floor.

Rows of tubular feet have tiny suction caps that help it move along the sea floor.

Some sea cucumbers discharge sticky threads from their base when they are attacked.

Hot-smoked fish

Hot-smoking is a technique of preservation in which fish or seafood is brined or salted for a short period, allowed to dry briefly, then smoked and cooked in a temperature-controlled kiln. An initial smoking takes place at a low temperature. The duration of this phase is dictated by the producer and the type of fish. Once the fish is impregnated with smoke, it is smoked for a second time at a higher temperature, which cooks the fish. Fish often treated in this way include mackerel, trout, and salmon, and shellfish include mussels and oysters. Hot-smoked fish has a lightly salted, densely smoked flavour, an opaque appearance, and a moist texture. Although products will keep for a number of days, hot-smoked fish generally have a shorter shelf life than cold-smoked fish.

BUY Choose fish that is moist, but not slimy, and has a strong, but pleasant aroma.

STORE Keep refrigerated, but not directly over ice. The salt added during the smoking process automatically gives the fish a slightly extended shelf life.

EAT Hot-smoked products can be eaten straight away or added to other dishes. Because they have already been cooked, care needs to be taken when reheating them or adding them to a hot dish. Serve them piping hot, but do not overheat, as it will toughen and change the texture.

FLAVOUR PAIRINGS Horseradish, cream and crème fraîche, honey, soy sauce and sesame oil, dill, coriander.

CLASSIC RECIPES Beef and smoked oyster pie; smoked mackerel pâté; smoked eel with beetroot and potato salad; smoked mackerel fishcakes.

Remove the sprat's head and peel away its skin to reveal a fillet with an excellent flavour.

Smoked sprats ▲
A popular treat and delicacy in Germany, Sweden, Poland, Estonia, Finland, and Russia, smoked sprats are also known by their Swedish name of brisling. They are smoked whole and, because of their soft bones, usually eaten whole – diehard fans may eat the head, too. The smoking process dries them somewhat and gives them a robust flavour.

Arbroath smokie
This is a speciality from Arbroath in Scotland. Gutted, small haddock, heads removed, are tied into pairs at the tail using locally sourced jute, dry-salted for an hour, and then densely smoked. Served as they are, or used in mousses and smoked haddock pâté, Arbroath smokies have an intense flavour.

The salting process makes the texture of the herring quite dry.

Smoked mussels
The mussels are cooked, brined, and hot-smoked. They are delicious as an addition to a seafood platter, or tossed into a salad. Smoked mussels are firm, sweet, and tasty. They are available freshly smoked or canned in oil.

Smoked oysters ▶
Firm and verging on tough, brined and cooked oysters are kiln-smoked for this speciality, which is popular in oriental cooking. Most are canned in oil; also available freshly smoked or vacuum-packed. The smoking process masks a lot of their natural taste. Use in beef and smoked oyster pie, or blend with cream cheese for a dip.

Smoked eel ▲
Firm and slightly rubbery, smoked eel is considered a delicacy, particularly in The Netherlands, so it is expensive. European and New Zealand eels are cleaned, dry-salted, and hot-smoked. The smoke cuts through the oily texture of the fish.

Kiln-roasted salmon

The advantage of hot-smoking is that the "greasiness" associated with some cold-smoked fish is lost. Kiln-roasted salmon is excellent eaten cold, forked into salads, or substituted for cold-smoked salmon in recipes. It can also be heated and tossed into pasta and rice dishes.

Kiln-roasted salmon is usually smoked in steaks (cold-smoked salmon is smoked as a side).

The skin of smoked mackerel peels away very easily.

Smoked mackerel

Mackerel's oil-rich flesh lends itself to hot-smoking. Whole gutted fish and fillets are used. Smoked mackerel is available dyed and undyed, and as fillets encrusted in pepper or other toppings. Smoked mackerel works well with a spicy relish, or combined with creamed horseradish. Some of the best smoked mackerel comes from the UK, where Scottish-caught mackerel, which tends to have a high oil content, is used.

The oil-rich flesh needs no further cooking and can be eaten straight after smoking.

Hot-smoked trout flesh has a robust flavour and flakes easily.

Smoked trout

Hot-smoking is an effective way of cooking many oil-rich species. It reduces some of the earthiness of the fish, particularly trout. You can buy it whole or as a fillet.

Buckling

This is a herring, sometimes gutted and with the head removed. It is dry-salted for a few hours, then hot-smoked in very dense smoke for a few hours. The result is dry, salty, and smoke-flavoured, with an intensely fishy taste.

The trout's small size makes it ideal to smoke whole.

Cold-smoked fish

This method of smoking fish takes place over a period of days. The fish is brined, and a relatively heavy salt solution is used in order to extract as much moisture from the fish as possible. Temperature is crucial: the product should not reach more than 30°C (84°F), so as not to cook the flesh or encourage bacterial growth. The fish is smoked for between 1 and 5 days, the flavour becoming richer and more intense as time goes on. Some cold-smoked fish may then be cooked (such as smoked haddock, cod, and pollock). As cold-smoked fish is essentially raw, fish that is not going to be cooked is frozen at -18°C (0°F) for around 24 hours to destroy parasites that may be present in the fish (this is a legal requirement in some countries). The flavour of smoked fish depends on how long a fish is left salted, and how long it is in the smokehouse. The taste of many fish – such as oily fish – is enhanced by smoking.
BUY Pick fish that looks dry, glossy, and smells smoked but not too strong.
STORE Smoked products have a slightly longer shelf life than fresh fish. They are never placed directly on ice, as with fresh fish, but must be chilled in the refrigerator.
EAT Smoked salmon and more artisanal products (such as smoked

swordfish, grouper, and tuna) can simply be sliced and served with a squeeze of lemon juice and bread, or added to more complex dishes.
FLAVOUR PAIRINGS Citrus, horseradish, delicate herbs including dill and parsley.
CLASSIC RECIPES Finnan haddock with poached egg; smoked salmon with capers; kedgeree; Cullen skink.

Atlantic smoked salmon
Both Scottish and Irish smoked salmon are considered a delicacy, but the price of wild salmon is prohibitively high, and most smoked Atlantic salmon is now farmed. It may be smoked over peat, apple wood, or oak; whisky is also popular. Oak smoke can give an intense taste, peat smoke produces quite a sweet woodiness.

Traditionally, kipper is split down the back and smoked on the bone, but it is also available as a fillet.

Kipper
A kipper is a cold-smoked herring. It is split down the back and cleaned, brined, sometimes dyed, then smoked over sawdust fires. English herrings are often considered the best species of herring for smoking. Many kippers are particularly fine. Kippers can be grilled or jugged (boiling water poured over the fish and left to stand). They have a dense, intensely salty, sweet, and smoky taste – but it varies according to producer.

Finnan haddock
Named after the fishing village of Finnan, this smoked fish is popularly referred to as Finnan haddie, and was once the most popular type of smoked fish. To make it, the haddock is cleaned, the head is removed, then the fish is opened out flat (left on the bone), brined (sometimes with dye), and smoked – traditionally over peat. The taste is similar to that of smoked, undyed haddock. Finnan haddock with poached egg is a breakfast classic.

Bloater
A bloater is a smoked herring. Whole fish are dry-salted in barrels for several hours, then cold-smoked over smouldering wood to dry the fish, and give it a lightly smoked flavour.

The bloater's skin is easily pulled off to reveal the ready-to-eat flesh under the skin.

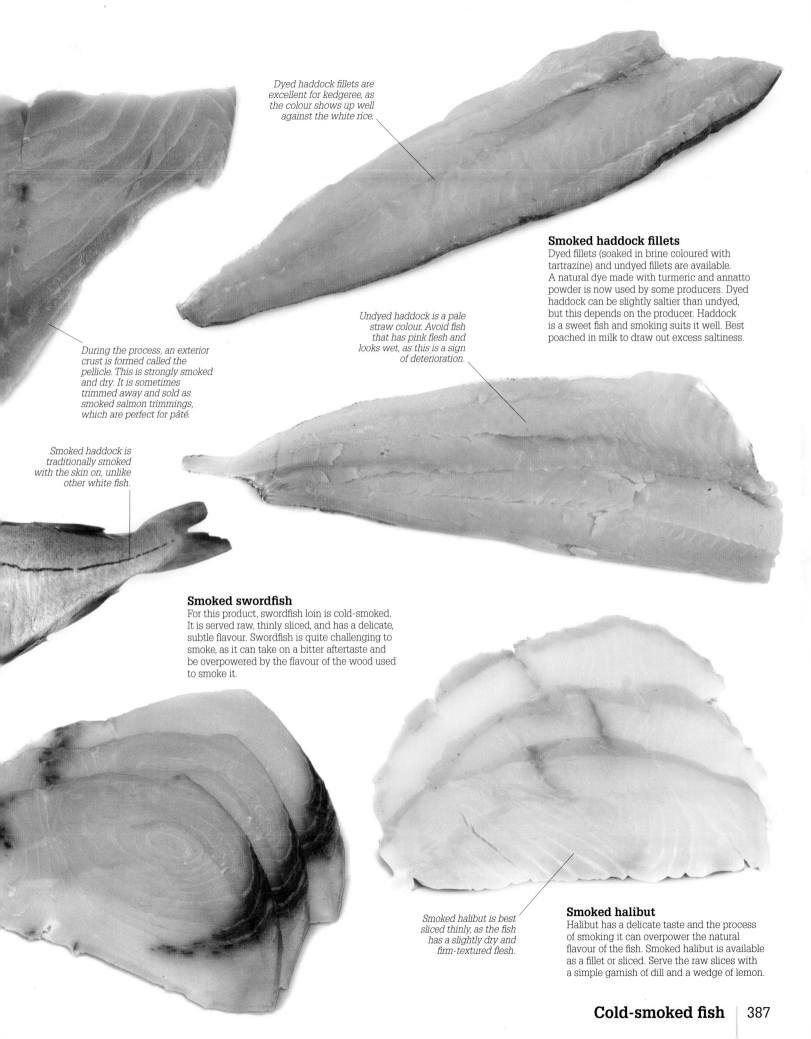

Dyed haddock fillets are excellent for kedgeree, as the colour shows up well against the white rice.

Smoked haddock fillets
Dyed fillets (soaked in brine coloured with tartrazine) and undyed fillets are available. A natural dye made with turmeric and annatto powder is now used by some producers. Dyed haddock can be slightly saltier than undyed, but this depends on the producer. Haddock is a sweet fish and smoking suits it well. Best poached in milk to draw out excess saltiness.

Undyed haddock is a pale straw colour. Avoid fish that has pink flesh and looks wet, as this is a sign of deterioration.

During the process, an exterior crust is formed called the pellicle. This is strongly smoked and dry. It is sometimes trimmed away and sold as smoked salmon trimmings, which are perfect for pâté.

Smoked haddock is traditionally smoked with the skin on, unlike other white fish.

Smoked swordfish
For this product, swordfish loin is cold-smoked. It is served raw, thinly sliced, and has a delicate, subtle flavour. Swordfish is quite challenging to smoke, as it can take on a bitter aftertaste and be overpowered by the flavour of the wood used to smoke it.

Smoked halibut
Halibut has a delicate taste and the process of smoking it can overpower the natural flavour of the fish. Smoked halibut is available as a fillet or sliced. Serve the raw slices with a simple garnish of dill and a wedge of lemon.

Smoked halibut is best sliced thinly, as the fish has a slightly dry and firm-textured flesh.

Salted fish and Dried fish

The earliest form of preservation was to dry fish in the sun and wind. Other fish were preserved in brine or dry-salted. In the Mediterranean, eels, anchovies, sardines, herring, tuna, and roe were commonly salted. One of the earliest dried and salted fish, cod, was caught by boats that travelled long distances to fish it. The cod was cleaned, air-dried, and packed in brine or salt for the voyage home. The process of salting fish is influenced by the weather, the size and species of fish, and the quality of the salt used. The fish must be completely saturated with salt, or "struck through", to ensure that it will be safe to eat. There are two methods of salting – placing the fish directly in a brine or packing it in salt, which in turn creates its own brine as moisture is drawn from the fish. The amount of salt used differs from one fish and product to another. Fish may also be dried to remove moisture content but left unsalted. Stockfish is unsalted fish, usually cod, which is dried by the sun and wind on wooden racks, or in specially adapted drying houses. Other species of white fish, including ling, tusk, grey mullet, bonito, and coley are dried, as are some shellfish, such as cuttlefish, squid, oysters, shrimps, and scallops. Some salted and dried fish are rehydrated, by soaking in several changes of water, to draw out as much of the salt as possible, and then cooked as a fresh fish (the flavour is more intense than that of a fresh fish and a gentle, lingering saltiness is evident). Some fish, such as Bombay duck and cuttlefish, are served dried.

CUTS Whole (gutted), split whole fish on the bone, shredded fish strips.

EAT Poach, pan-fry, or grill.

FLAVOUR PAIRINGS Olive oil, garlic, orange, capers, onion, parsley, milk, coconut.

CLASSIC RECIPES Salt fish and achee; salt fishcakes; bacalao; brandade de morue (salt cod purée).

Salted anchovies
One of the most popular salted fish, anchovies are also brined. Intensely salty, they are often used to top pizzas or to garnish Mediterranean dishes such as salade Niçoise. They can be soaked briefly in milk before use to remove some of the saltiness; this softens and rounds the flavour.

Dried tuna loin is firm and dry, and best shaved or grated. It tastes very strong so only a little is needed to flavour a dish.

Maatjes herrings are usually eaten whole and unadorned, or simply with bread. They have a sweet, intense flavour.

Dried tuna loin
Mosciame del tonno is a delicacy in Italy and Spain (where it is called mojama). Strips of tuna loin are salted and sun-dried, to make a firm slab that resembles a dried meat. It has a rich, meaty flavour and may be grated to add to pasta and salads.

Maatjes herring
Hailing from Amsterdam, maatjes herring is also known as virgin herring, as it is made from young fish that have not produced roe. The fish, caught around Norway and Denmark, are soused (soaked in a mild brine). They are only partly gutted, as the offal is key to the success of the curing process. A similar product from Germany is made using more intense brine.

Bombay duck
The small bummalo fish is native to Southeast Asia. It is eaten fresh in India, where it is usually fried to serve as a side dish. It may also be dried in strips and called Bombay duck. It has a strong, aromatic, fishy flavour.

Bombay duck is served in its dried state as an appetizer. It has a strong, hearty taste.

Dried shrimps

Unshelled shrimps, lightly salted and dried, are used extensively in China, Southeast Asia, and parts of Africa. They are usually added to a dish to give it a depth of flavour.

These have a distinctive smell that is strongly seafood-like and also sweet. Soak prior to use, or use dry as a seasoning.

These scallops have a strong flavour and very dry texture. Use dry or soak in water to rehydrate.

Dried scallops

Dried scallops are used extensively in the cuisine of the Far East. One popular recipe is as part of a spicy chilli salsa. They add a dynamic seafood flavour and a certain sweetness to a dish when used whole or grated.

Salt pollock ▼

Alaskan pollock is abundant. Salted pollock is popular in the Far East and Caribbean. It requires a long soak before use; is excellent poached or used in fishcakes. It has a milder flavour than salt cod. Good with spices and mashed potato.

Salt pollock is usually sold as a fillet or in strips, often ready pinboned.

Salt mackerel is available both as whole gutted and salted fish, and as fillets.

Salt mackerel

This product is popular in the Far East, particularly in Korea. The fish must be soaked in cold water overnight before use. Poach for about 30 minutes and use for pâté or salad; it is also good pan-fried. After soaking, the fish still has a strong salty taste, and the flesh is a little fibrous.

Salt cod is sold as whole split fish, fillets, loins, and in strips. Strips are quickest to use.

Salt cod

Dried unsalted cod is called stockfish and used in several countries in soup and as an additional ingredient. Salt cod is prepared in Scandinavia, and is also a speciality in Portugal, exported globally. It requires 36–48 hours of soaking, in several changes of water, prior to use. A salty taste is present once cooked, and the flavour is strong and almost meaty, with little comparison to fresh cod.

Fish roe

Although the roe of both male and female fish is edible, it is the "hard" roe, or eggs, of the female fish that has gained extraordinary heights as a delicacy, and often fetches a premium price. The milt or "soft" roe is the soft male roe or sperm of some species, particularly herring, and it is also sometimes valued as a delicacy, especially in Europe. Several species of fish produce excellent "hard" and "soft" roe, whether for use as a garnish or stand-alone *hors-d'oeuvre*, and many countries favour specific varieties. In Japan, *kazunoko*, the salted eggs of herring, are most popular. In Southeast Asia, a particular favourite is crab roe, harvested from female mud crabs. In Europe, "*caviare*", originally the name for the eggs of sturgeon, has long been prized. Traditionally the three most celebrated sturgeon caviars – beluga, oscietra, and sevruga – were processed by the Russians and Iranians. Methods of preparation vary. With most "caviar"-type products, the female roe is harvested, rinsed to remove the egg membrane, lightly salted, drained of excess liquid, then packed. Many are also pasteurized to extend their shelf life by a few months. Caviar substitutes treated in a similar way include the roe of Pacific salmon (or keta), Atlantic salmon, salmon trout, trout, lumpfish, capelin, carp (or icre), and flying fish (tobiko). There is even a seaweed caviar now available. Non-caviar roes are sold either fresh or preserved, whether salted and dried, or smoked. Most eggs are soft and translucent, with a salty taste and grainy texture.

SUSTAINABILITY The popularity of sturgeon roe has led to overexploitation, with many species now almost extinct. Sturgeon are now being farmed in France. Other alternatives include icre, herring roe, and keta.

AVAILABILITY Caviars: Fresh and pasteurized. Other roes: Fresh, salted, smoked.

EAT Usually raw, except for fresh cod and haddock roes, and herring milt, which is served cooked.

FLAVOUR PAIRINGS Caviars: Melba toast, chopped egg white, chopped onion, parsley. Soft herring roes: Butter, capers, lemon. Smoked roe: Olive oil, garlic, lemon.

CLASSIC RECIPES Taramasalata; caviar with scrambled eggs; grated bottarga with truffle oil and linguine.

Sevruga caviar
After beluga and oscietra, sevruga ranks third in the line-up of popular sturgeon caviars. Of the three, sevruga eggs are the least expensive and most readily available, as the fish matures relatively early at 7 years old. Although small, the eggs are a rich metallic grey, with an intense flavour, often preferred to that of beluga or oscietra.

Salted herring roe
A popular alternative to caviar, lightly salted herring roe is marketed under various names. It is better than lumpfish roe, as it does not run colour, making it ideal as a canapé topping.

Salted herring roe has a delicate fish taste with a slight lemony tang, and a hint of salt.

◄ Beluga caviar
Illegal in some countries, beluga is considered the grandest of caviars. The beluga sturgeon (*Huso huso*) is the biggest of the family and known to live for up to 20 years. The eggs are large, soft, and smoky grey in colour. It is one of the most expensive caviars and traditionally served with a round-edge, mother-of-pearl spoon, to protect the eggs.

Herring roe ▲▼
Marketed under a variety of names, female herring roe is now readily available and sold as a low-cost alternative to other caviars. It competes on the market with lumpfish roe, but is unlikely to be dyed, making it ideal as a garnish. Kazunoko, a salted variety, is a Japanese delicacy.

Bottarga di muggine
Huevas de mujol or *poutargue*
The amber-coloured eggs of grey mullet, sometimes called the "poor man's caviar", are a Mediterranean delicacy. Traditionally, the eggs are washed, salted, pressed, and sun-dried, then dipped in beeswax to hold their flavour. To serve, the roe can be thinly sliced, or freshly grated and tossed into pasta (but not cooked).

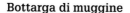

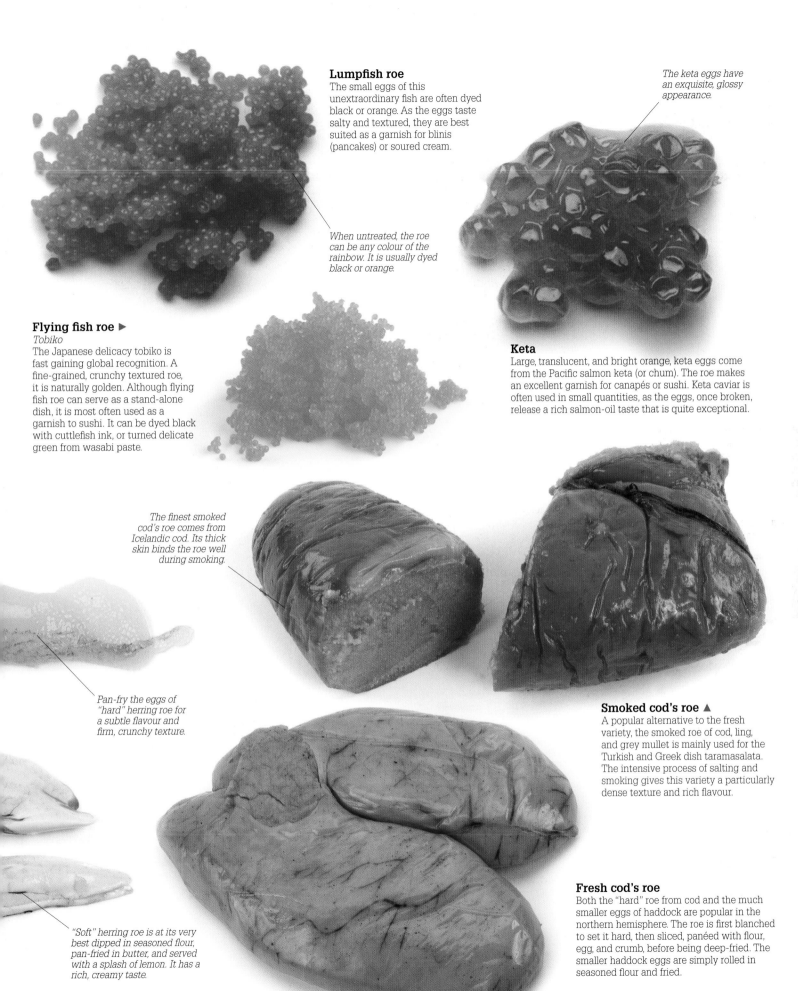

Lumpfish roe
The small eggs of this unextraordinary fish are often dyed black or orange. As the eggs taste salty and textured, they are best suited as a garnish for blinis (pancakes) or soured cream.

When untreated, the roe can be any colour of the rainbow. It is usually dyed black or orange.

The keta eggs have an exquisite, glossy appearance.

Flying fish roe ▶
Tobiko
The Japanese delicacy tobiko is fast gaining global recognition. A fine-grained, crunchy textured roe, it is naturally golden. Although flying fish roe can serve as a stand-alone dish, it is most often used as a garnish to sushi. It can be dyed black with cuttlefish ink, or turned delicate green from wasabi paste.

Keta
Large, translucent, and bright orange, keta eggs come from the Pacific salmon keta (or chum). The roe makes an excellent garnish for canapés or sushi. Keta caviar is often used in small quantities, as the eggs, once broken, release a rich salmon-oil taste that is quite exceptional.

The finest smoked cod's roe comes from Icelandic cod. Its thick skin binds the roe well during smoking.

Pan-fry the eggs of "hard" herring roe for a subtle flavour and firm, crunchy texture.

Smoked cod's roe ▲
A popular alternative to the fresh variety, the smoked roe of cod, ling, and grey mullet is mainly used for the Turkish and Greek dish taramasalata. The intensive process of salting and smoking gives this variety a particularly dense texture and rich flavour.

"Soft" herring roe is at its very best dipped in seasoned flour, pan-fried in butter, and served with a splash of lemon. It has a rich, creamy taste.

Fresh cod's roe
Both the "hard" roe from cod and the much smaller eggs of haddock are popular in the northern hemisphere. The roe is first blanched to set it hard, then sliced, panéed with flour, egg, and crumb, before being deep-fried. The smaller haddock eggs are simply rolled in seasoned flour and fried.

Index

Page numbers in **bold** indicate information on the uses, availability, and sustainability of the fish, and their descriptions in the Fish Gallery.

Page numbers in *italics* indicate techniques and equipment used in choosing, preparing, and cooking the fish, including suggested Flavour Pairings.

The symbol (a) indicates an alternative, i.e. the use of a fish other than the one named in the recipe title.

Acknowledgments

About the Editor-in-chief

C.J. Jackson spent many holidays as a child in Scotland, catching and preparing fish. In the 1980s and 1990s, she worked in Australia, the Far East, the Middle East, North Africa, Switzerland, Spain, Italy, and France where she was exposed to seafood cookery in many of the world's great culinary traditions. In 1989, she enrolled as a student at the prestigious Leith's School of Food and Wine in London and went on to teach there, a post that gave her further opportunities to research into and write about seafood.

Today, C.J. is Director of the Billingsgate Seafood Training School, a charity situated above London's Billingsgate Market, the UK's largest inland fish market. Here she runs courses, teaching people how to select, prepare, and cook sustainable seafood. Working in this historical market, with its many wonderful personalities, the degree of expertise, and, of course, the range of fish, C.J.'s fish fascination is indulged every day.

C.J. is the author of *The Billingsgate Market Cookbook*, the co-author of *Leith's Fish Bible* and *The Cook's Book of Ingredients*, and a regular contributor to the BBC's *Good Food Magazine*.

C.J. Jackson would like to thank the merchants at Billingsgate Market, but also my friends and colleagues, particularly Steve Clements from J. Bennett Exotics and Ron Peacham for their help in sourcing and identifying various exotic species; Mike Eglin from James Nash and Sons for his help in sourcing fish for photography; Chris Leftwich, Barry O'Toole, and Robert Embery of Fishmongers' Company and the fisheries inspectorate at Billingsgate Market; Paul Joy and Yasmin Ornsby from Hastings Fishermen's Protection Society for their help with the photography and an early morning trip to sea; Dr Tom Pickerell for all his expertise not only about responsible sourcing, but also the shellfish industry; Mary-Clare Jerram, Sara Robin, and Andrew Roff at Dorling Kindersley for their focus and drive to complete this book and for Andrew's organizational skills; my team at the Billingsgate Seafood Training School for their patience; and especially, apologies to Colin and Joseph for all the "lost" weekends over the last 6 months – and while we were trying to move house!

Dorling Kindersley would like to thank everyone at Billingsgate Seafood Training School, including Ron Peacham and Adam Whittle; Yasmin Ornsby, Paul Joy, Ken Moss, Michael Adams, and Richard Adams at the Hastings Fishermen's Protection Society; Dr Tom Pickerell from The Shellfish Association of Great Britain, for his advice on sustainability; Jocelyn Barker and Lowri Holness from The Alaska Seafood Marketing Institute; Stuart West, Ian O'Leary, and Myles New for photography; Luis Peral for art directing the photoshoot; Rob Merrett for prop styling; Katie Giovanni and Bridget Sargeson for food styling; Abigail Fawcett, Anna Burges-Lumsden, Jan Stevens, Katy Greenwood, Sal Henley, and Rachel Wood for recipe testing; Jenny Baskaya and Karen Van Ross for picture research; Roxanne Benson-Mackey and Charis Bhagianathan for their editorial assistance; Devika Dwarkadas, Divya PR, Heema Sabharwal, Katherine Raj, Kathryn Wilding, Danaya Bunnag, and Emma and Tom Forge for design assistance; Steve Crozier and Gary Kemp for retouching; Angela Baynham for proof-reading; and Sue Bosanko for the index.

Useful websites

Fish Online
www.fishonline.org
Supported by the MCS, this site uses a traffic light system to list fish that are sustainable: green are good choices; amber are those to buy with caution; and red-listed are those to avoid completely.

The Marine Conservation Society (MCS)
www.mcsuk.org
A UK charity that works to conserve the UK's seas and wildlife.

The Marine Stewardship Council (MSC)
www.msc.org
An international organization that certifies sustainable fisheries. Check their website to find out which fisheries are certified in your area.

Sea Fish Industry Authority
www.seafish.org
A UK organization that works across the seafood industry to promote sustainable fish. The site offers up-to-date information about catch quotas in place in the UK.

Seafood Choice Alliance
www.seafoodchoices.com
An international organization that works with the seafood industry towards a sustainable future. Subscribe to their mailing list for up-to-date information about sustainability.

South West Handline Fishermen Association
http://linecaught.org.uk
A fishery that tags its fish with a unique number so you can see when and where your fish was caught.